D0889999

OUT TAKES

A Series Edited by Michèle Aina Barale,

Jonathan Goldberg, Michael Moon,

and Eve Kosofsky Sedgwick

OUT TAKES

Essays on Queer Theory and Film

Edited by Ellis Hanson

Duke University Press   Durham & London   1999

© 1999 Duke University Press

All rights reserved

Printed in the United States of America on acid-free paper ∞

Typeset in Berkeley Medium by Tseng Information Systems, Inc.

Library of Congress Cataloging-in-Publication Data appear

on the last printed page of this book.

CONTENTS

Ellis Hanson

INTRODUCTION

Out Takes

I love the film *Bound* (1996). As a naughty, violent, ironic, and otherwise amusing bit of wish fulfillment about two smooth-talking dykes who outsmart the Mafia, this film came as a welcome alternative to the spate of clunky and vacuous lesbian romances and curiously interchangeable mob movies that I had seen that year. The publicity for the film was not, I admit, very encouraging, apart from the promise, published in *Entertainment Weekly,* that Gina Gershon is a "fierce hot patootie of Linda Fiorentino proportions," an inspired turn of phrase wholly unthinkable in reviews of other recent films on lesbian themes. I was impressed, however, by the visual and verbal savvy of *Bound.* Far more skillfully than Sheila McLaughlin's 1986 film, *She Must Be Seeing Things,* which has been virtually canonized by feminist film theorists despite its amateurishness, this noirish crowd-pleaser engages many of the central issues of lesbian and gay studies of film, namely, stereotyping and the politics of representation, the gendering of cinematic production, the queering of the look, fetishism and scopophilia, and the queer appropriation of popular visual and narrative styles. *Bound* is preoccupied with the articulation of power and sexuality within the field of vision—how desire is rendered visible, for whom, and to what end. Much of the plot hinges on lesbian invisibility, and yet the film uses the whole gamut of classic scopophilic lures—carefully staged sex scenes, fetishistic costumes, killer cosmetics, shadowy lighting, voyeuristic point-of-view shots, and so on—to help us to recognize the sexual intensity of the relationship between the two female leads, Violet and Corky. Theirs is a desire that the men in the film cannot see, though the women hide it in plain sight. Violet—what else could one call the femme heroine?—is married to a mobster named "Caesar," a fatal name in his case: since he never "sees her" desire, he is never quite able to "seize her," to keep her bound within the narrative of his own pleasure. The film becomes a slick meditation on love, trust, and vision—their interdependence, their tenuousness—within a cinematic tradition where lesbianism has usually been coded as pathology, betrayal, invisibility, or something affirming and crunchy that one does in Northampton. In a key moment in the film's articulation of the visual, Corky rolls over in the sack after a satisfying sexual romp with Violet and triumphantly proclaims, "I can see again!"

I was saying much the same thing as I watched this film. I take that line, with its clever collapsing of sexual and visual pleasures, to be emblematic of a particular moment in the history of queer spectatorship and film theory. "Now you see it," Richard Dyer proclaims with equal enthusiasm in the title of his book on the queer cinematic underground, and with good reason one might applaud the mainstream cinematic movement toward greater visual explicitness in sexual matters. It is now de rigueur, however problematic, to regard classic Hollywood as a regime of censorship and heterocentrism that, at least since the days of the Hays Code and the Legion of Decency, fastened blinders onto the American sexual imagination. Certainly, *Bound* is about as frank and steamy as one could hope. *Bound* is not Doris Day—though neither was Doris Day, as Eric Savoy demonstrates in his essay in this volume. I would further add that, for me, the line "I can see again!" also marks a moment of relief from feminist and gay film criticism itself. For purely ideological reasons, such criticism has sought to alienate spectators from Hollywood's fetishism and voyeurism and from the stereotypes of queer sexuality as inherently perverse or monstrous. In so doing, however, we have come to subordinate every discussion of the aesthetic or the erotic to surprisingly simplistic conceptions of the political, and this practice promotes a certain blindness of its own. The lesbian and gay seal of approval is often stamped on films that are politically impeccable, but visually and sexually illiterate.

Finally, the line "I can see again!" raises the question of its own validity, since the suspenseful twists and turns of fortune in this film, not to mention its campy irony, render the self-confidence of such an exclamation all the more impressive, if not entirely delusory. Can she see again? Does she know what she is looking at or what she is looking for? Will she be betrayed by the woman who has enticed her look? The question also disrupts the self-confidence of the spectator. If Caesar never really sees her, why should we think we can? How have we come to be convinced of our privileged position in seeing, in politicizing, in theorizing? What are the ideological conditions of our seeing? What is the narrative and psychological structure of our look? The very title of the film begs a number of questions. Once the title disappears from the screen, we are unsure what we are looking at. We cannot make sense of the shapes on the screen. Slowly they resolve themselves into a scene in which a woman bound with rope is trapped in a closet. The visual cues slip from bondage as sexual play to bondage as sexual assault—and so we are still unsure what we are looking at. We cannot fix the scene or the fantasy that motivates it. A woman is in the closet, in bondage, and yet her very restraints, not to mention all those shiny shoes, turn the bondage into a fetish and release the very eroticism that closets are supposed to negate. The gangsters, the threat of assault, only fans the flame of the fans, who are also bound (by the narrative, by the genre) and unbound (by their queerness, their indeterminacy). The title suggests at once a stasis and a direction, since we are bound up in the closet and even out of the closet, but where, after all, are we bound to? What destination, what destiny? To whom are we bound, or to what narrative, to what image are we sutured? This enigmatic word *bound* is forever evolving into a question that floats gleefully free through the film, unpossessed and unanswerable—in a word, unbound. We are seduced not merely by the spectacle of lesbian sexuality, inviting and unusual as that might be in a popular film, but also by the very conditions of our looking, by the somewhat paranoid sensation that the gaze of desire, like the gaze of the camera, is never quite our own, that it is a social and aesthetic construction that might not have our best interests at heart—that it is above all a question with a great many possible answers. To proclaim that I can see again is always also to proclaim that I am seen again, that I am found out, that I am implicated in the film to whose questioning glance I respond with pleasure. To trace the implications of that erotic implication has become the role of queer film theory.

Out Takes is an anthology of new essays that seeks to bring queer theory into further dialogue with film criticism. Given the number of important writers in the field of queer theory who are turning their attention now to cinema—who are indeed writing books on the subject—film theory is already becoming a locus of lively academic debate and speculation in the field. The study of film is especially important to questions of desire, identification, fantasy, representation, spectatorship, cultural appropriation, performativity, and mass consumption, all of which have become important issues in queer theory in recent years. Film theory already has a relatively long history and a highly sophisticated critical language, but only a very small handful of writers have sought to bring the specificity of that language into the context of queer theory. For this anthology, I have brought together some of those disparate voices, along with a few new ones.

The study of homosexuality in cinema has been a serious critical enterprise in the popular press since the 1960s, and in the last two decades in particular it has been pursued more substantially by academic scholars. Queer theory, however, is a very new coinage peculiar to the 1990s, though it developed from myriad theorizations of sexuality that preceded it. The term generally presumes an analytical style strongly influenced by deconstruction, feminism, Lacanian psychoanalysis, the work of Michel Foucault, or some mixture thereof, depending on whom one reads on the subject. To define the field as simply as I can—and it is not known for its simplicity!—queer theory submits the various social codes and rhetorics of sexuality to a close reading and rigorous analysis that reveal their incoherence, instability, and artificiality, such that sexual pleasure or desire, popularly conceived as a force of nature that transcends any cultural framework, becomes instead a performative effect of language, politics, and the endless perversity and paradox of symbolic (which is also to say historical and cultural) meaning. The very word *queer* invites an impassioned, even an angry resistance to normalization. It is a rejection of the compulsory heterosexual code of masculine men desiring feminine women, and it declares that the vast range of stigmatized sexualities and gender identifications, far from being marginal, are central to the construction of modern subjectivity; but it is also, as Michael Warner has pointed out, a resistance to normalization as conceived more generally as a sort of divide-and-conquer mentality by which cultural difference—racial, ethnic, sexual, socioeconomic—is pathologized and atomized as disparate forms of deviance. The aims of queer theory are at once philosophical, political, and erotic—an effort, indeed, at blurring any distinction between them—since it seeks not only to analyze but also to resist, dismantle, or circumnavigate hegemonic systems of sexual oppression and normalization by revealing the theoretical presumptions and rhetorical sleights of hand by which they establish, justify, and reinforce their considerable power. By power, I do not mean merely physical and legislative force in the mundane sense but also those discursive forces that assign a name of their own choosing to every creature in the garden, that presume they know what sex is or ought to be, what pleasure is or ought to be, and what role sexuality might play (if any!) in social relations more generally—in identity formation, politics, education, art, and religion, to name just a few of the more vehemently contested sites of sexual definition.

Cinema is certainly one of those contested sites. With its seductive and seemingly inexhaustible apparatus for image-making, film is a privileged form for cultural self-definition, and sexual minorities are by no means immune to its charms. Despite the legendary eroticism of film, the critical language for understanding the questions about sexuality it raises is still impoverished. On the question of homosexuality in particular, the literature tends to shuttle between three influential and equally problematic models: first, a moralistic *politics of representation* that seeks to liberate us from damaging stereotypes; second, a *descriptive style of cultural studies* that takes for granted certain political and historical paradigms, usually Marxist, to define the meanings of a text through a surprisingly uncritical process of "contextualization"; and finally, a *psychoanalysis of the cinematic gaze* that occasionally addresses the phenomenon of same-sex desire, though usually in the rather dated and mechanical theoretical framework established by Freud and his more recent adherents. All of these traditions have influenced my own thinking about film; in fact, even the most casual eye will pick up their traces in my own contribution to this volume. It is difficult to be critical without seeming dismissive, but I initiated this volume in part to rethink the language of feminist and gay studies in film. I do not hope that queer theory will necessarily supersede earlier sexual approaches to cinema—for what would be the point?—rather, I would suggest that queer theory, as a mode of deconstruction and analysis of sexual rhetoric, might help us to clarify and transcend some of their limitations. By gathering together these particular essays, I hope that I am not merely adding to the growing literature that decides which movies are good for the gays or bad for the gays. Nor do I wish to offer a dozen more instances of how queer people became the evil cinematic bugaboo in someone else's Oedipal melodrama—or, in other words, which movies are good for the gaze or bad for the gaze. By way of introduction, however, I do want to discuss these three traditions briefly, not only to clarify their historical importance and their theoretical limitations, but also to speculate on those questions that a queer theory of film might ask.

"How do I look?" is the punning, eponymous question of an earlier collection of reprints and short conference papers on lesbian and gay studies in cinema. The book contains essays from each of the traditions that I have mentioned and ranges from studies on representation and identity politics to more psychoanalytic musings on spectatorship and the cinematic gaze. The question "How do I look?" is seen to be about either cultural representation (as in "what am I supposed to look like?") or spectatorship (as in "is the cinematic look queer?"). On the evidence of the essays, however, the answer must entail either a multicultural complaint or a Freudian search for the phallus. In the first sense, the question indicates a certain confusion when I find I have no role models, no cultural pretext for self-articulation — none, at any rate, that I can live with. How can I possibly look like anything, how can I possibly recognize myself, given the circumstances of my oppression? How can I see myself if I am invisible? The question is further exercised through a number of ethnic and racial permutations in which its essential narrative form remains unchanged: I perform, therefore I am. The subject of marginalized sexual identity makes a political claim for its own "invisibility" and then presents even the most mundane assertions of cultural specificity as a subversive political intervention within the more general cultural tendency to harbor malicious fantasies about "the Other." Such narratives usually have the same hero, the mage of cultural studies who has cracked all the codes of bourgeois mystification and is now willing to liberate us from the snare of cinematic false-consciousness. As in all political fables, the story always ends with an edifying moral.

In lesbian and gay film criticism, this "politics of representation" model is an immensely popular instance of this approach. The respectability of this tradition was established by a number of typological studies on the representation of homosexuality in cinema, especially Vito Russo's *The Celluloid Closet* and Parker Tyler's *Screening the Sexes,* as well as Andrea Weiss's *Vampires and Violets,* which bills itself as "a revelatory survey of lesbian identity in film." For many, there is no other kind of gay criticism. Despite its decline among academic critics in recent years, "the politics of representation" is still the method of choice in the popular gay press, where it has devolved into movie-star interviews that let us know which actors are out of the closet, and brief film reviews that help us to locate "positive" or "liberating" images of gay people. Some criticism in this tradition offers little more than an annotated list of films that contain characters whose behavior might reasonably be construed as queer (for example, the most recent entry in the genre, Wayne Bryant's 1997 survey, *Bisexual Characters in Film: From Anaïs to Zee*). More than a decade and a half after the publication of Russo's book, a documentary film was made of *The Celluloid Closet.* Among gay activists — the Gay and Lesbian Alliance Against Defamation (GLAAD), for example—such studies have excited a mood of political resistance to mainstream cinematic representations that are thought to reinforce homophobia. We are still in the throes of a lesbian and gay campaign for so-called positive images, representations of sexual minorities as normal, happy, intelligent, kind, sexually well-adjusted, professionally adept, politically correct ladies and gentleman who have no doubt earned all those elusive civil rights for which we have all been clamoring. To understand how emotionally and politically volatile cinema can be for those who feel excluded, ridiculed, or vilified by its visual vocabulary, we need only glance at the angry protests with which gay activists have greeted films such as *Cruising* (1980), *Basic Instinct* (1992), and *Braveheart* (1995). The political importance of this effort to make filmmakers say nice things about gay people is obvious: it has had the salutary effect of getting queer people to speak out about their oppression and making Hollywood feel embarrassed on occasion for its history of homophobic weirdness. As Russo points out, even lifting censorship can be scary, and anyone who has suffered through the endless fag jokes and the surprisingly brutal gay-bashing of 1970s Hollywood productions cannot fail to be sympathetic with his argument. Critiques of stereotyping are most valuable in their grassroots appeal to the rage of a community that is offended by what it sees as an insult.

Nevertheless, beyond political agitation, the value of a critical perspective can be judged by the quality of the thinking it produces and the quality of the art it inspires, and in this regard *The Celluloid Closet* is not very impressive. It can ask only one question of a film: Does it offend me? We find in this book no concern for aesthetics or cinematic form, no discussion of the complexities of desire and identification, no appreciation of political nuance, no understanding of homoeroticism beyond the representation of gay characters, and no attention to Hollywood styles or genres that are popular with queer audiences even when there are no ostensibly gay characters (classic melodrama, the buddy film, the musical). In order for his argument to work at all, Russo must first banish the concept of camp from the conversation. Camp is a historically queer aesthetic, and many of its most distinctive gestures are drawn from classic cinema of the sort that Russo pretends to find offensive. His own legendary cinephilia and camp sensibility attest to the fact that Hollywood, despite its history of censorship and its pretense to heterocentrism, is one of the queerest institutions ever invented.

Generally speaking, surveys of lesbian and gay representation assume that queer people are invisible, and then they offer copious evidence to the contrary—they suggest indeed that homosexuality is all too visible, that its meanings and its politics are perfectly obvious to us. Often, the evidence is organized into categorical types, so that the survey reads like a diagnostic manual or one of those quaint nineteenth-century sexological treatises that, with all the moral authority and efficiency of a Christian casuist, devises an official nomenclature for every cinematic sin against gay pride and provides a handy illustration by which we might recognize each individual beast should it ever accost us in a theater. All of these texts concern themselves with the politics of stereotyping, especially in Hollywood and in high-profile European art-house films—we find the chapter on pansies, the chapter on vampires, the chapter on serial killers—and all of it is faulted for being "inaccurate" or "homophobic," though by what standard of judgment, we cannot ascertain. Meanwhile, the question of desire with respect to these various delectable personae is rarely pursued beyond certain threadbare psychoanalytic formulae, and the question of pleasure is generally relegated without question to an affirming identification with so-called realistic images of gay people.

Russo calls for greater accuracy in the representation of homosexuals. But what is the truth of homosexuality? Whose experience is genuine and whose is merely a stereotype? Why valorize verisimilitude over fantasy in works of art? Why suppose that anyone would like homosexuals more if they could see them the way they really are? Does the reality of gay people's lives necessarily make for good cinema? If someone made a movie about *my* life, I doubt I would go see it. Furthermore, the very notion of an image that is inherently homophobic or inherently positive strikes me as naive, since the political effects of an image are contingent upon the context of reception. *Cruising* is only as dangerous as the audience for whom it is screened, which is to say that, in a genuinely homophobic context, there is no such thing as a positive image of gay people. Fortunately, the context of reception is always far more expansive and heterogeneous than we are led to believe by such studies. In decrying Hollywood homophobia, we concern ourselves with only one gaze: the ubiquitous, prefabricated, gullible, voyeuristic gaze of homophobia. It is, of course, a very useful stereotype, the only one we hate to question. Meanwhile, our own pleasure, that elusive gaze of delight, is left curiously undertheorized and at times inadmissible.

Gay protests seem to have made a considerable dent in the conscience of mainstream filmmakers. In the 1980s and 1990s a number of independent and Hollywood films appeared that were marketed to gay audiences and that were eager to challenge earlier bad-gay clichés with a few good-gay clichés of their own. Too many of these films strike me as bland, and they have that prescriptive movie-of-the-week feel about them. There are now a few sentimental romances and melodramas with homosexuals in them, and they are as tiresome as the countless sentimental romances and melodramas that made a point of excluding homosexuals. In relatively popular films about gay men, films such as *Making Love* (1982), *Longtime Companion* (1990), *Philadelphia* (1993), as well as the recent spate of lesbian love-stories such as *Claire of the Moon* (1992), *Bar Girls* (1994), *Everything Relative* (1997), and *The Incredibly True Adventures of Two Girls in Love* (1995), one can hear the ideological machinery grinding as the wooden dialogue strains to undo every "stereotype" that comes to mind. Instead of psychological complexity, we find predictable types and cardboard role-models. Instead of intellectual depth, we find a political slogan disguised as a narrative. Instead of aesthetic ingenuity, we find a stilted form of social realism. Instead of "accurate" or "positive" images of the gay community, we find an anodyne fantasy of the gay community. As Andrew Sullivan remarked about the film *Philadelphia*, these movies are for *them*, for the people whom we characterize vaguely as homophobes living somewhere to the right of civilization and who uncritically absorb everything they are told. These films are supposed to please us, and yet I find myself feeling nostalgia for queer villains. Ironically, some of the films that I have found most stimulating in the past decade or so—*Law of Desire* (1987), *Basic Instinct, Poison* (1991), *Swoon* (1992), *Heavenly Creatures* (1994), *The Addiction* (1995), and *Bound* come readily to my mind—have depicted queer people as stylish and violent criminals.

In this decade there has been a promising backlash against this preoccupation with "positive images." Gay cultural studies has developed from mere self-affirmation into a more critical and politically rigorous mode. Cultural studies itself can be divided into two important tendencies, the "descriptive" and the "critical." The first entails a political call for new representations, preferably by, for, and about minority communities who have been excluded from the mainstream. The difference between aesthetic representation and political representation is, however unwisely, confused. Any characterization is seen as progressive and radical as long as it valorizes a group of people one can designate as oppressed or neglected in some way. The aesthetic and the erotic are collapsed into the vaguely sociological, as if to define a community of consumers were to define a film's significance and pleasures. In the more critical mode, cultural studies seeks to define the significance of filmmaking and other social practices in the broader history of political struggle and capitalist production. In this tradition, cultural studies most overlaps with queer theory in its efforts not merely to valorize or vilify, but to analyze and critique, to theorize the process of production and consumption rather than simply to expose it, and to question the very paradigms through which the cinematic and the political are said to be allied.

I should hasten to emphasize, however, that cultural studies and queer theory are by no means the same thing. Queer theory, at its best, submits even the political premises of much cultural studies to a rigorous examination. One might question a number of presumptions that one finds all too readily deployed in much cultural studies criticism of film: Is there any necessary relation between the aesthetic, the sexual, the psychological, and the political? Is subjectivity purely ideological? Is capital not queer? Is the millennial language of Marxist criticism a more profound engagement with reality or a curiously academic flight from it? In *Epistemology of the Closet,* Eve Kosofsky Sedgwick observes with striking simplicity that "People are different from each other," an axiom that she develops into a habit of resistance to critical dogma, whether it be psychoanalytic, Marxist, feminist, or deconstructive, since dogma inevitably produces insight at the expense of a certain blindness. Our critical vocabulary seems to render palpable only those pleasures it is destined to describe, such that our dogmas result in an impoverishment of language that masquerades as sophistication. There are certainly problems one might consider in the highly politicized language of queer cultural studies, even when it claims to go beyond the preoccupation with identity politics.

For example, in *Queer Looks,* the editors claim that they are bored with the "seventies" campaign for positive images and the "seventies" focus on Hollywood, and yet the essays themselves often resound with that familiar seventies tone. The valorization of independent queer filmmaking is certainly admirable, but the tone remains prescriptive and moralistic. Instead of positive images of lesbians and gay men as bourgeois ladies and gentlemen, many of these writers call for positive images of lesbians and gay men as queer subjects with impeccable multicultural credentials. They complain about the shallowness of Hollywood and valorize the innovative subject matter of queer experimental cinema. As a frequent spectator on the queer festival circuit, however, I have had ample opportunity to meditate on the disturbing connections between the experimental and the unendurable, and I am led to wonder why so many critics on the left seem to presume that preachy radical politics, cheap irony, and low production values must necessarily make for a more exciting night at the movies. Every film with a queer theme, no matter what the sexuality of its director or the origin of its funding, is still embattled in a highly moralistic debate over the correctness of its politics, as though art were to be valued only as sexual propaganda. The filmmakers themselves are often the most confused in this debate. Tom Kalin was quite vocal in his protest against *Basic Instinct,* evidently untroubled by the fact that, by his own logic, his film *Swoon* (a much more troubling biographical study of the notorious queer child-killers Leopold and Loeb) would have been a likelier target for his anger. When I actually saw some of the films that Russo and other queer activists have attacked—when I saw *The Children's Hour* (1961), *The Killing of Sister George* (1968), *Cruising, The Hunger* (1983)—I was often surprised to discover how fascinating they are, how entertaining, daring, intellectually challenging and, in a word, queer. Behind the alcoholic butch and the queer serial-killer of Russo's analysis, I found seductively dangerous figures, vivid characterization, inspired performances, complicated narratives of desire, and an erotic intensity unheard of in the more sanctimonious fare that is favored by much gay criticism and much queer cultural studies. Once I realized that movies are not necessarily good because they reaffirm my politics or flatter my self-esteem, I found a long history of films—Hollywood as well as independent and foreign traditions—that address the question of queerness in ways that challenge my mind, delight my eye, and complicate my understanding of sexuality.

In the question "How do I look?" I do not hear a political call for visibility, honesty, and integrity. I hear, rather, an anxious request for a compliment, or perhaps I should say a narcissistic call for a complement. Do I look all right, am I attractive, do you like me, am I complete, am I behaving correctly? With such questions, I am not asking for the truth. I need a mirror—or another person, community, or theory to act as mirror. Paradoxically, that mirror must preserve every pretense to truthfulness and yet, at the same time, lie. The question is interesting not for the flattery it elicits from the other, but rather in the uncertainty of self-construction and self-recognition it supposes. I cannot locate or recognize myself, nor can I fully locate the other, whose message of love and attention I need desperately to hear repeated. All that is familiar is this inevitable mixture of narcissism and blindness by which, with tenuous self-assurance, I attempt to stay my own disappearance. It is not the truth, nor even realism, that the question begs; rather, it is a disguised plea for idealization and fantasy. We might see this plea as a confrontation with anxiety, a struggle with the very failure of self-definition no matter who we are; and that struggle affords us pleasures, frustrations, and perhaps even insights that can press us beyond the simplistic question of whether what we see is positive, progressive, or true to our experience. If queer theory has anything to offer the identity politics of representation or the descriptive style of cultural studies, it is the rigorous questioning of the very concepts of correctness, identity, stereotyping, visibility, and authenticity—not to render definition or political action impossible but rather to multiply our pleasures and our personalities and to interrogate more radically the critical presumptions we claim as our own.

A more nuanced analysis of queer desire and spectatorship has helped to offset some of the critical dead-ends of the "positive images" tradition in both feminist and gay criticism. The most sophisticated discussions of desire and sexual politics in cinema have taken place in the field of feminist psychoanalytic film theory, which first emerged as a rethinking of the work of Freud and Lacan, Christian Metz, and Stephen Heath and which sought to politicize a set of psychological questions about gender. Theorists such as Laura Mulvey, Teresa de Lauretis, Mary Ann Doane, Jacqueline Rose, D. N. Rodowick, and Kaja Silverman have, after their own fashion, asked the question "How do I look?" with a very different emphasis. They have regarded the "how" of spectatorship as a social and psychological construction. They have sought to develop a theory of subjectivity that would account for the pleasures of the look and the relationship of those pleasures to gender and sexual identity. They enrich political critiques of cinematic pleasure by theorizing the psychic mechanisms of identification and desire, but they also challenge such critiques by deeming impossible any necessary conjunction, any perfect fit, between ideology and desire, narrative and pleasure, the image and the subject. In her groundbreaking essay, "Visual Pleasure and Narrative Cinema," Mulvey sought to expose the position of the feminine in film as *she who is to be looked at*. The masculine subject attempts to appropriate the cinematic gaze for his own voyeuristic pleasure. The masculine look, unconsciously threatened by what it sees as a spectacle of female castration, seeks to fetishize images of women—to reinvest them with the illusion of phallic plenitude—in a manner that accounts for the misogynistic violence and objectification in classic cinema. Within the tradition of criticism Mulvey helped to initiate, the female spectator has emerged as a woman who either identifies masochistically with the fetishized spectacle of femininity or identifies in a "transvestite" fashion with the camera and the masculine position of mastery.

The reader will no doubt notice a number of echoes and revisions of that tradition in this anthology, since most queer theorists working in film have found it to be both enlightening and troubling. A handful of scholars have sought, with considerable success, to redeploy the terminology of feminist film theory within queer theory—among them, de Lauretis, Paul Julian Smith, Earl Jackson Jr., and Patricia White—since it allows for a critique of the sexual politics of representation as well as a compelling account of desire and identity formation. Nevertheless, as Lee Edelman explains in his essay in this volume, this tradition has, in the very intensity of its focus, produced a few blind spots of its own. Queer theorists have already discovered that the heterocentric and exceedingly rigid structure of the look in Mulvey's analysis—patriarchal masculinity leering at objectified femininity—writes homosexuality out of existence. How do women desire women in and through film? How do men desire men? Is a lesbian gaze a male gaze in drag? What about gay male identification with the fetishized diva of classic cinema, all those glamorous gestures of Bette Davis and Judy Garland that virtually constitute the contemporary queer rhetoric of camp? We are led to some difficult questions but also to some improbable generalizations, to theories of cinematic homosexuality as essentially invisible, as cross-dressing, or as a peculiar form of fetishism in disguise. This psychoanalytic approach has also excited a political presumption— we might deem it a paranoid tendency—that views voyeurism, fetishism, sublimation, idealization, masculinity, phallic sexuality, and even identification as not merely suspect but inherently evil. I cannot speak for others, of course, but without those particular pleasures, I would be very, very bored at the movies, though not, I dare say, any more radical in my politics. In her books *Male Subjectivity at the Margins* and *The Threshold of the Visible World*, Silverman comes to the defense of these many, seemingly inevitable pleasures, reassuring us that masochism is okay if it is male, fetishism is okay if it is female, idealization is okay if it glorifies the downtrodden, and identification is okay if it is with someone we are not supposed to be. Instead of being politically correct about what we see, we are asked to be politically correct about how we desire. Her readings of film theory and individual films are among the most rigorous and impressive I have ever read, but I wonder if any film—or for that matter, any spectator—can live up to such a redemptive psychological and political agenda.

The exclusively psychoanalytic framework also poses a problem, not the least since the definition of homosexuality in these theories almost always relies on dubious Freudian conceptions of same-sex desire as a narcissistic crisis in gender identification. Homosexuality becomes the return, or perhaps merely the persistence, of the repressed in an otherwise anxious and heterosexual narrative. This theory does much to explain the paranoid aspect of homoeroticism in classic cinema, queerness as the monster who threatens the heteronormative coherence of the narrative in films such as Hitchcock's *Strangers on a Train* (1951) or the newer film noir such as *Black Widow* (1987) or *Poison Ivy* (1992). Nevertheless, I am struck by how this new Freudian sophistication in the discussion of heterosexuality in film has revived a certain old-fashioned obtuseness in the discussion of queerness. In *The Desire to Desire*, Doane's excellent study of gender dynamics in classic melodrama, the discussion of homosexuality is limited to an analysis of homosexual panic, a momentary crisis of gender identification in the psyche of ostensibly straight women. Silverman's *Male Subjectivity at the Margins* has been criticized by queer theorists, Sedgwick most notable among them, for construing queerness through a series of Freudian clichés about homosexuality as male femininity, maternal identification, masochism, and narcissism. In *The Practice of Love*, de Lauretis (who was instrumental in popularizing the term *queer theory*) arrives at the unlikely conclusion that female homosexuality is a nonphallic form of fetishism, even though Freud deemed fetishism to be inherently phallic and inherently male. Indeed, she seems to be saying that fetishism and sexuality are much the same thing, a point that makes me question the usefulness or coherence of both terms as she defines them. In short, we may not have exhausted the possibilities for psychoanalysis in a discussion of queer desire, but it is certainly not for want of trying. Indeed, film theory is one of the few fields in academia where Freud is still alive and well, where criticism sometimes becomes a mechanical process of exposing the traces of Oedipal conflict in a work of art. I am not saying that these theories are necessarily wrong or unproductive, rather I am simply arguing that their reliance on psychoanalysis as the *only* framework for discussing pleasure and subjectivity has sharpened our understanding and impoverished it at the same time.

Perhaps the profound suspicion with which psychoanalysis is regarded in much queer theory might help to loosen the exclusively Freudian framework through which cinematic pleasure has come to be theorized. Whatever its investments in Lacanian psychoanalysis, queer theory might offer a deconstructive or Foucauldian assessment of psychoanalytic theories of sexuality that have been influential in the study of film. We might ask whether the structures of desire in films presume an Oedipal trauma and a Freudian unconscious. What are the blind spots—historical, political, psychological, aesthetic—in such theories of desire? How does heterocentrism inhere in the very model through which desire is conceptualized? Does psychoanalysis valorize an illusion of interiority and urge us to privatize or individualize phenomena that are more radically social and political? To what extent do theories of subjectivity produce the viewing experiences they claim to demystify? Can psychoanalysis be a critical apparatus for interpreting films when it is already a self-conscious narrative gimmick for making them? How do films self-consciously provide their own visual and narrative rhetoric of spectatorship? How do the narrative and visual patterns of a film resist interpretation and identification, Oedipal or otherwise? Is the erotic—as opposed to, say, the socioeconomic, the ethnic, the racial—always the constitutive or primary site of spectatorial pleasure and subject formation?

These questions are, of course, too numerous and too difficult for any one volume to explore, though they are all questions that queer theorists have attempted to answer. For *Out Takes,* I have chosen essays that in some manner critique, revise, push beyond, or simply stand apart from these traditions in film criticism and identify important issues for the inchoate field of queer film theory. The collection begins with a section called "Cruise Control," where I have assembled new essays by those critics who have already been influential in revising our understanding of masculinity and classic cinema. Steven Cohan on *Picnic* (1955), Alexander Doty on the queerness of television, Lee Edelman on *Laura* (1944), D. A. Miller on *Rope* (1948), are all to my mind excellent examples of the sort of rigorous and nuanced discussion of visual narrative and masculinity that challenges earlier conceptions of homoeroticism in mainstream representations. In their new essays for this volume, all four writers are engaged in an inventive rethinking of classic cinema from the forties and fifties in an effort to explain not only the positioning of femininity within the articulation of male homoeroticism but also the construction of heterosexuality through and against the specter or suggestion of homoeroticism. In much gay and lesbian criticism, mainstream films from this period are generally thought to be naive or repressed, produced as they were during decades notorious for their censorship and their closets. In these essays, however, as in Burns's and Savoy's essays on lesbian looks, we find that the crypto-queer strategies for articulating desire have a sophistication and fascination of their own. In his essay on Bob Hope and Bing Crosby, Cohan reads the peculiar homoeroticism of the "road movies" through the historical shifts in the terms of American masculinity occasioned by World War II and the contemporary culture of military service. Doty explores the queer fetishization of the diva or prima donna and turns to Powell and Pressburger's *The Red Shoes* (1948) as a way of analyzing the relationship of gay men to women and to female creativity. In his deconstructive reading of Hitchcock's *Rear Window* (1954), Edelman explores the visual rhetoric of anality as the structuring blind spot of both the film and feminist film theory. Along similar lines, Miller reads Mankiewicz's *Suddenly, Last Summer* (1959) as a peculiar historical moment in the relationship of gay men to the spectacle of femininity and, in particular, the female backside.

The second section, "Lesbian Looks," is not only about the representation of lesbians in film but also about the vicissitudes of lesbian desire in filmic narratives and the multiple possibilities for lesbian fantasy and identification in cinematic spectators. These essays may at times draw on the psychoanalytic tradition of feminist film theory, but they are certainly not defined by it. The deconstructive essays by Bonnie Burns and Eric Savoy both address the question of lesbian looking in two important mainstream films that have been sadly ignored by feminist and queer film criticism alike: *The Locket* (1946) and *Calamity Jane* (1953). Burns and Savoy, respectively, offer deconstructive critiques of the films' visual languages of looking and identification, in an effort to clarify what a queer theory of spectatorship might entail. In my essay on "lesbians who bite," I question the preoccupation of lesbian and feminist film criticism with negative stereotypes and the patriarchal gaze by offering an appreciation of lesbian vampire films as a genre that foregrounds female visual pleasure. In her essay on *Heavenly Creatures,* Michelle Elleray takes a postcolonial approach to cinematic queerness that analyzes the complicated intersections of sexuality with gender, class, and national identity, thereby raising the question of geopolitical and socioeconomic circumstances that so often disappears from much film theory about desire.

The third section, entitled "Queering the Reel," offers a historical range of essays on independent queer cinema, from H.D. and Kenneth Anger to Derek Jarman and lesbian documentary. The writers in this section discuss artistic and political strategies for subverting conventional images of lesbian and gay people, but they do so with a historical insight and attention to genre that is rare in gay film criticism and in discussions of what is called queer cinema. Jean Walton's essay on *Borderline* (1980) offers the most penetrating discussion I have yet read on the historical interplay between sexual and racial identification in film. Matthew Tinkcom has been engaged in an ongoing materialist rethinking of camp, in which he addresses questions of production and consumption, rather than the usual stylistic considerations; in his essay on Kenneth Anger, he explores the role of fan magazines and gossip in the queering of Hollywood spectatorship. Jim Ellis discusses the politics of the British "period film," and the aesthetic and political strategies of subversion behind Derek Jarman's fascination with the English Renaissance. Finally, Amy Villarejo offers a critique of the authenticating narratives of lesbian and gay "progress" through a reading of pulp fiction as lesbian history in the documentary *Forbidden Love: The True Story of Lesbian Lives* (1992). Through her queering of Marx and Gramsci, she offers a new critical take on the relationship between political agendas, social histories, and aesthetic strategies in the documentary genre.

In choosing the very title *Out Takes,* I hope, through the rhetorical density of a seemingly inevitable pun, to offer this queer examination of film as a general meditation on the play of inside and outside, the binary structure that Diana Fuss has recognized as central to queer theory. One endeavors to be either in or out of the closet, a practice that is never fully in sync with being inside or outside cultural representation. To be in the closet is not necessarily to be sexually out of sight, since discretion and secrecy are curiously readable modes of self-articulation; and to be out of the closet is not necessarily to be sexually in sight, since one is all too often exiled offscreen. The queer subject is always already both inside and out, and queer theory often traces the paradoxical logic of this inside-outness as a textual strategy as well as a political predicament. Film theory and criticism is by no means immune to the uncertain dynamics of inside and out, especially when it comes to the structuring of desire in cinematic experience. In the title of this volume, I have taken the "outtake" as a symbol of the practice of cinema as an aestheticization of sexuality, as an effort to produce sexuality as a social construction that requires scripting, casting, editing, and a vast technology of visualization. The outtake is that part of the film that, for whatever reason, ends up on the floor in the editing room, a scene that is shot but never quite makes it onto the screen. The outtake is the supplement, the remainder, that defines every narrative as a deployment of silences and absences. An outtake has, like the queer subject, a certain reality, a certain place and defining power in the larger narrative of cultural representation, but only as that which should not be looked at. This *should-not-be-looked-at-ness* is the very antithesis of Laura Mulvey's formulation about the spectacle of woman in cinema, but this is not to say that queerness is unspectacular. In its figuration of abjection and popular disidentification in one of the most popular of media, queerness as outtake places in dialectical tension the excluded and the central, the untheorized and the transparent, the unwatchable and the transfixing.

In the history of homophobic censorship, one of the most striking examples of an outtake is the steamy bathtub exchange—or was it merely a Platonic dialogue about seafood?—that occurs between Laurence Olivier and Tony Curtis in Stanley Kubrick's film *Spartacus* (1960). The scene was excised from the film before it opened but was recently restored for its revival thirty years later. As has often been remarked, the explicit representation of homosexuality and other proscribed sexual pleasures was, with varying degrees of success, censored out of mainstream films, such that contemporary queer critics, priding themselves on their outness, are often reduced to indignation at the closeted strategies of silence and indirection that are all too apparent in classic cinema. This outrage is not, however, without its own peculiar and often unacknowledged moments of illicit delectation: being *out* never prevents queer spectators from locating themselves *in* the film, whatever their pretense to critical distance and marginality. They are inducted, perhaps even by their own pose of knowingness and resistance, into the sexual logics and lures of classic films. They are detectives seduced by the traces of their own disappearance, and surely I am not the only spectator who prefers the clues to the crime. The process is no more innocent with films that are, so to speak, out. In the final section of this anthology, the contributors analyze a number of films that one would not describe as closeted, and yet that process of self-determination and self-construction remains difficult. An aesthetic of queer visibility and explicitness has outtakes of its own, selective logics of scripting, editing, and viewing that render the concept of outness rather naive and perhaps even dated. To be out is always already to be in—to be partially obscured or unspeakable and to articulate oneself within and through a rhetoric that can never be fully one's own. The outtake raises the possibility that to be taken out—to be taken out to the movies, to be taken out of the movies— is often to be taken in (perhaps knowingly), to be seduced for better or worse by the spectacle of one's own disappearance—which is to say, one's own constitution—as a subject.

For this reason, I repeat my earlier contention that cinema, especially Hollywood cinema, is one of the queerest things ever invented. To trace the logic of its interpellations of queerness is an exercise in being inside and out at the same time. Indeed, the pleasures that were censored out of *Spartacus* were by no means absent from the original cut, nor are those pleasures necessarily out, in the sense of being frank, in the restored version, so discreetly are sexual tastes presented as a taste for oysters and the like. What counts as out, as queer, or even as pleasure in a film, in a spectator, in a politically engaged critic, is never easy to ascertain, whether one is the closeting editor of classic kitsch or the outing editor of a critical anthology. In this volume, a gathering of out critics offer their out "takes" on various films, but this outness does not in itself solve the various theoretical problems of sexuality and its representation. We may well be committed to a contemporary gay politics of visibility and acceptance, but I think it fair to say that we are also committed to a theoretical analysis of the rhetoric of visibility and acceptance through which gay film criticism has established itself as a field. As queer theorists of film, we are presenting a perspective that has been itself constructed as an "outtake," a particular take or perspective that has been edited out of the history of film criticism, though traces of its voice are as old as cinema itself. The essays here are readings and theorizations that partake of a queer sexual politics, a queer theorization, a particular moment in the articulation of inside and out in the practice of film.

CRUISE CONTROL

Rethinking Masculinity in Classic Cinema

Steven Cohan

QUEERING THE DEAL

On the Road with Hope and Crosby

Lamour: Why didn't you tell me you had a friend in Karameesh—and such a friend?
Crosby: So you didn't tell her about me, huh?
Hope: Well, I didn't want to dicker too much. It might have queered the deal.
—*Road to Morocco* (1942)

Dear Bing and Bob:
All I want is a date with you two fellows when I get back—NO females, just we three. I'm sure the laughs I'd get that one day would make up for all I have missed and will over here. I sure would like to have you send me the "word" even if it is just a "maybe."
—Lt. A. L. G., 3rd Marine Division, "Letters from GIs"[1]

The most popular male stars of the forties—whether together or apart— were Bob Hope and Bing Crosby, whose series of "Road to" films for Paramount helped to make the studio the most profitable one throughout the decade. The success of *Road to Singapore* in 1940 was followed by *Road to Zanzibar* in 1941, *Road to Morocco* in 1942, *Road to Utopia* in 1945, and *Road to Rio* in 1947. All were among the highest grossers of their respective years. Five years later Paramount released a successful revival of the series in Technicolor, *Road to Bali* (1952), and a decade after that, somewhat less successfully, Hope and Crosby reunited for the last time in *Road to Hong Kong* (1962), the only "Road to" movie made independently of Paramount, filmed outside of the United States, and without Dorothy Lamour as the female lead opposite the two male costars.

The popularity of the "Road to" series is particularly notable because it builds its comic value primarily out of a buddy relation. While there were major male comedy teams before and after Hope and Crosby, the buddy relation had unusually strong cultural significance during the 1940s because of the intensity with which men formed close friendships in the all-male military environment of World War II. The Army, in fact, formally organized men into pairs as its primary means of instilling loyalty on a personal level. Giving official sanction to the male couple, the military's buddy system structured masculinity in terms of same-sex bonding, problematizing what we now take for granted as the heterosexual/homosexual binarism that differentiates between "normal" and "deviant" masculinities according to sexual orientation. In his history of gays and lesbians in the armed forces, Allan Bérubé reports: "Veterans of all kinds describe the love they felt for each other with a passion, romance, and sentimentality that often rivaled gay men's expressions of their love for other men and made gay affections seem less out of place." To be sure, "during the war the combat soldiers' acceptance of one another's pairing and physical intimacy was more a recognition of their need for closeness in life-threatening situations than any conscious tolerance of homosexuality."[2] But it was also the case, Bérubé observes, that "[b]uddy relations easily slipped into romantic and even sexual intimacies between men that they themselves often did not perceive to be 'queer.'"[3] Army life, moreover, while never entirely free of homophobic aggression and harassment, allowed for all sorts of transgressions (and digressions) from the norm, such as drag performances. "Military officials," Bérubé comments, "used soldiers' shows and drag routines for their own purposes—to boost soldier morale by allowing soldiers without women to entertain each other and affirm their heterosexuality. Once they had established their masculinity by becoming soldiers, men in these shows could enjoy the benefits of the same wartime relaxation of rigid gender roles that had allowed women to enter both industry and the military."[4]

The team of Hope and Crosby needs to be read in terms of the gender slippages occurring during the forties, when, as institutionalized by the Army buddy relation, the homosociality underlying American masculinity could all too easily "queer the deal," as the bit of dialogue from *Road to Morocco,* which serves as the first epigraph of this essay, suggests. Lamour and Crosby both ask Hope why he has kept his buddy a secret, and the comic's response condenses the logic by which his pairing with Crosby invariably interrupts straight coupling in the "Road to" series by triangulating it, to the point where one has to wonder: does Hope not tell Lamour about Crosby in order to prevent the crooner from stealing her away, or does he refrain from mentioning Crosby in order to keep his buddy all to himself? In evoking the queer subtext of the Hope-Crosby teaming, I do not mean to propose that the "Road to" films openly represent a gay sexual relation between the two male stars; but I am arguing that the comedic framework of the series plays upon intimations of homoeroticism, and that the queer shading of their buddy relation must be taken into account when understanding the immense popularity of Hope and Crosby's teaming in the 1940s. After all, they were enough of a bona fide couple to prompt, in this essay's second epigraph, that marine's request for "a date" on his return home from the war. "NO females," he specified, "just we three."

FIGHTING OVER GIRLS?

The first film in the series, *Road to Singapore*, establishes the buddy relation of the two male stars as a respite from heterosexuality (fig. 1). Crosby and Hope, who is sarcastically called his pal's "boyfriend" at one point in the film, forswear women entirely as their motive for taking off to Asia, vowing, in Hope's words: "No more women. . . . Why if even one of us looks at anything in skirts, the other one can clip his ears off and stuff it down his throat." Crosby observes that "if the world was run right, only women would get married," and he tells his millionaire father that he refuses to follow the family tradition of running their shipping company, preferring instead to tramp the seas with his pal Hope, because "I want to be one of the boys. A regular guy." Of course, once these boys meet Lamour, they change their tune entirely; while the narrative allows Crosby to reject the stuffy values of his upper-class family through his unconventional attraction to Lamour, playing a Eurasian woman whom he and Hope rescue, it also shows that he can only be a "regular guy" through heterosexual coupling. Nevertheless, the initial bonding of the two men over their rejection of women establishes the pattern that the rest of the series more knowingly and comically plays up. The "Road to" films typically open with Hope and Crosby performing as a vaudevillian song-and-dance team or engaged in some confidence game with the local yokels, or doing both. After a musical number (usually on the subject of their friendship) establishes buddy camaraderie—and we see the two men taking more pleasure in performing together than their onscreen audience does—their chicanery is exposed, often at the same time as their womanizing offstage comes to light. Chased out of town and swearing off women, they end up in a remote but exotic

1 Hope and Crosby set up house together in *Road to Singapore* (1940).

colonial outpost, "wide open spaces," as Crosby describes it in *Road to Rio,* "where the men are men." "And the women?" Hope asks him. "No women," Crosby reminds him. "That's how we got into this in the first place."

Once on the road, Crosby tricks Hope into going along with a surefire scheme that invariably subjects the comic to the crooner's selfish manipulations. This comedic setup differentiates the two men in terms of Crosby's active, sadistic, and arrogant personality and Hope's passive, masochistic, and gentler one, or as *Road to Bali* puts it, Crosby carries a blue toothbrush as his "luggage" (because "blue is for boy"), while Hope's is red. When Lamour then enters the plot, tricking the boys into serving a scheme of her own while falling in love with Crosby once he sings his big ballad, she appears in order to gloss over the sexual asymmetry suggested by the men's differences from each other. Lamour's presence sets up a good-natured rivalry between the two buddies that, curiously enough, does not divide them or make them enemies but, on the contrary, intensifies their close relation. "Do you always fight over girls?" Lamour asks Crosby in *Road to*

2 Queering the deal in *Road to Morocco* (1942).

Bali, to which he replies: "What else can we fight over? We've never had any money."

Clearly, the "Road to" films offer a classic instance of Hollywood's narra-tivization of homosocial masculinity. As Eve Kosofsky Sedgwick explains in *Between Men,* the bonding of two men through their rivalry for a woman not only creates a relation between them, "as intense and potent as the bond that links either of the rivals to the beloved," but it also structures "male heterosexual desire, in the form of a desire to consolidate partnership with authoritative males in and through the bodies of females."[5] In the "Road to" films, Lamour provides Hope and Crosby with a common but also socially permissible object of desire. The expectation that she will inevitably turn up on the scene gives these two "friends of Dorothy" more license than usual for transgression, for pushing the buddy relation past its official limits. Once Lamour triangulates their relation, she legitimates their obvi-ous pleasure—and physical intimacy—as a pair of buddies who have sworn off women in order to be together. At one point in *Road to Zanzibar,* Lamour snuggles up to Crosby, who's seated almost as close to Hope. "See what I mean," Hope whispers to his buddy. "She's just using you to get to me."

Through two extended gags about the buddies kissing, *Road to Morocco* shows how the logic of the Hope-Crosby-Lamour triangle actually works the other way around: the buddies use her to get even closer to each other (fig. 2). The first kissing gag occurs very early in the film, after the two men, castaways from an exploded ship, land on an empty beach. Seated alongside Hope in front of a row of bushes, Crosby apologizes for his abusive treatment of his pal while the two were on a raft, confessing, "You know how I feel about you. I guess in my own way I sorta love you." A camel peers over from behind the bushes and nuzzles Hope on the cheek. "All right," Hope replies, assuming that Crosby has just kissed him, "but you don't have to slobber all over me. . . . I guess I kinda love you, too." The camel then nuzzles Crosby on the ear.

> *Crosby:* There now, wait a minute, Junior, stop kissing me.
> *Hope:* What are you talking about? I didn't—
> *Crosby:* You did, too.
> *Hope:* Look, are you crazy? I don't mind being kissed, but this is ridiculous.

The camel "kisses" Hope again, and the two men repeat their accusations, both stating that they felt something: "I thought it was you," each says. They assume what they felt must be the handiwork of the ghost of Hope's Aunt Lucy come back to haunt them and, as the camel raises its head and emits a roaring noise, the two frightened men jump into each other's arms. The gag arises from their misrecognition of the kiss's origin, to be sure, but also, more subtly, from the unmistakable impression that each man does have a strong inclination to kiss the other. After all, Hope says that he doesn't mind being kissed; his protestation, like Crosby's, has more to do with the slobbering than with the kissing itself.

Much later in the film, a similar gag repeats the transgression these two buddies seem to have in mind when seated on the beach. Stranded in a desert and walking a mile without a camel in search of Lamour, who has been kidnapped, Hope and Crosby come upon a desert mirage: Lamour approaches them, singing a reprise of Crosby's ballad, "Moonlight Becomes You." When the two men join her in the song, their voices become disconnected from their bodies, so that Lamour opens her mouth and out comes Crosby's voice, Hope opens his and we hear Lamour, and so on. At the close of the song, the three stars harmonize, restoring voice to body; then Hope and Crosby step back in profile to look at Lamour desirously, but she disappears just as each man leans forward to kiss her. With her fantasized body gone, there is nothing to prevent the two men from kissing each other on the lips, and they do, spitting and wiping their mouths afterward. As the buddies continue their trek through the desert, Hope complains that he is too weak to go any further. Crosby remarks: "I guess that kiss took too much out of you, huh?" Before he spits and wipes his mouth again, Hope mutters, "yeah," and Crosby then carries his buddy on his back. The affectionate gesture on Crosby's part, which reminds us of the physical intimacy of their relation, rhymes this second kissing gag with the earlier one, which began with Crosby carrying Hope out of the water. But whereas in the first gag the camel both motivates and explains each buddy's mistaken if nonetheless desired impression that his pal is kissing him, the second more clearly displays how the cover of Lamour's presence can enable a kiss between Hope and Crosby to take place and, more importantly, to be acknowledged *as* a kiss.

Taken together, the two kissing gags in *Road to Morocco* illustrate quite plainly how the series achieves its particular take on the homosocial bonding of men through an inversion of the pattern Sedgwick analyzes. Instead of serving to cover up the homosexual desire that motivates the heterosexual competition of two men, in the "Road to" films Crosby and Hope's rivalry for Lamour makes their intimacy more visible as a celebration of their bonding and, moreover, shows how it structures the possibility of a queer desire. In the manner of comedian-comedy films generally, as Frank Krutnik has shown about this genre, the "Road to" films invariably close with gags that break the narrative's diegetic illusion, interrupting the heterosexual trajectory of the Crosby-Lamour romance.[6] For instance, in the closing moments of *Road to Utopia,* circumstances separate Hope and Lamour from Crosby, and he does not find them again for thirty-five years. When he finally returns, Crosby discovers that Hope and Lamour married and have a son, Junior—who is the spitting image of Crosby! "We adopted," Hope explains directly to the audience with deadpan expression, and the film then cuts to the Paramount logo. The gag's implication that Crosby has somehow cuckolded Hope has the effect of closing upon the buddy rivals instead of the straight couple, confirming that the homosocial buddies rather than the heterosexual lovers comprise the "true" romantic couple in a "Road to" film.

If there were any doubt that the buddy couple drives the romantic energy of the series, one only has to watch *Road to Bali*. Late in this film, Hope, Crosby, and Lamour are all taken captive by a Balinese tribe that *will* allow the two men to imagine what, beginning with *Road to Singapore* (when the three stars set up house together midway through the film), the series as a whole has always appeared to be proposing as the impossible desire of these two buddies: namely, polygamy, a bride's marriage to two men as the best means of maintaining the homosocial triangle. However, when the villains take over the tribe and decide to keep Lamour for themselves, they want to get rid of Hope and Crosby by arranging for what the series also has always suggested is the unthinkable desire of the two buddies when they fight over Lamour to be near each other—as one of the villains puts it, an unconventional marriage of "two grooms with no bride." At the wedding ceremony each man is masked in a headdress and feathers, and the costuming causes each to assume the other is his intended partner, Lamour. Afterward, the two are asleep with their backs to each other in a large matrimonial bed. They awake; slyly, each moves backward to touch the other's buttocks; with a pleased smile, each leans his arm behind him to clasp hands with his "bride." Crosby moans, "Oh, honey," and a startled Hope cries out, "There's a man in our bed!" As they turn around, both exclaim at the same time, "You!" Given the sexual transgression implied by such a marriage of "two grooms with no bride," it's not surprising that Hope and Crosby escape from this situation without having to consummate it, but, in its gag ending, the film itself does not entirely evade the queer implications of their unconventional wedding. After Lamour finally chooses Crosby over Hope, *Road to Bali* then reconfigures the heterosexual pair in another bisexual triangle with a cameo appearance by Jane Russell (in her costume from Hope's *Son of Paleface*, released the same year [1952]), who goes off with Crosby and Lamour to establish a new *ménage à trois*, much to Hope's chagrin.

WHY WOULD A GUY BUY A GUY?

As the prototype of the series once it hit its stride, *Road to Morocco* is worth looking at even more closely in the light of what I have been arguing so far. This film actually organizes the buddy relation of Hope and Crosby through two homosocial triangles. There is, first of all, the triangle that every "Road to" film arranges for its three stars: two castaways—Jeff Peters

(Crosby) and Orville "Turkey" Jackson (Hope)—compete for the attention of an Arabian princess, Shalamar (Lamour), whom they meet in Morocco. But even before they find her, the buddy relation of the two men has already been triangulated through Orville's deceased Aunt Lucy (who, played by Hope in drag, appears as an angel in several scenes). Before dying, it appears, Aunt Lucy exhorted a promise from Jeff to care for her nephew in her stead. "You're certainly sloughing off your promise to her," Orville complains to his pal early in the film—this after Jeff reveals he has actually contemplated cannibalism as a means of last resort if he and Orville do not get rescued from their raft. "Before I go, Jeff, promise me one thing, she said, promise me you'll always be a friend to little Orville, she said. No matter what happens, you'll never leave the little jerk, she said." In response, Jeff finally confesses that he does have a soft spot for his pal, and his expression of love motivates their mistaken impression, after landing on the beach, that each is kissing the other.

Significantly, in this homosocial triangle, as in the later one involving Lamour, it is the Hope character who is made the object of exchange. Aunt Lucy has in effect bequeathed her nephew to Jeff, who in turn sells him to a slave dealer as a means of paying for their dinner. Jeff intends to keep what's left of the two hundred dollars he receives and then rescue Orville afterward, if he can. "I sold him something," Jeff informs Orville to account for the money, "It was all I had." "You can't sell me, I'm not a horse," Orville protests upon realizing what has transpired. Then Orville asks the more pertinent question: "Why would a guy buy a guy? . . . What does he want me for?" "I don't know," Jeff confesses, "I didn't ask him." Through banter about Orville's being sold into slavery, the film quickly recovers from whatever homosexual content may have been proposed by both Orville's question and Jeff's reluctance to name what this exchange circles around: one man buying another man for sex. However, since Jeff next comes upon his buddy in bed with Shalamar, who is pampering Orville as a kind of sexual slave, his fate once sold to the dealer and repurchased by the princess serves to reinstate the erotic implication of that troubling question even though it is now placed in a safer—that is, more heterosexual—context.

Why would a *woman* buy a man? Well, as it turns out, for the same reason that a guy sells a guy in this film. Shalamar uses Orville for her own purposes much as Jeff does. Informed by the court astrologer that her first husband is fated to die within a week of marriage, Shalamar purchases Orville in order to get the prophecy over and done with so she can then wed her original intended, Mullay Kasim (Anthony Quinn); when she falls for Jeff, she changes her heart's desire but does not revise her plan regarding the luckless Orville. As Shalamar explains to Jeff—with the logic that makes Dorothy Lamour the supreme homosocialist in the "Road to" series—"The more I get to like you, the more reason I will have to marry Orville."

True to convention in the "Road to" films, Crosby's charm as a smooth talker not only gets Hope into trouble but it also invariably means that Hope's competition with Crosby for Lamour is no contest. Consequently, when Jeff berates his buddy for not mentioning him to Shalamar, and Orville replies that he didn't want to queer the deal, the obvious inference is that Orville was simply protecting his own interests with Shalamar: mentioning Jeff to her would have triangulated the arrangement to his own disadvantage, as events prove true. Orville therefore tries to get Jeff to leave Morocco so that the wedding can take place without the latter's interference. Announcing his intention to stick around for the nuptials, though, Jeff promises, "I'll even give you away," to which Orville retorts, "You've already given me away."

A reminder of Orville's place in both homosocial triangles as an object of exchange, this bit of dialogue also suggests the more colloquial sense in which Crosby's presence helps to queer the deal for Hope. Isn't it customary for the *bride* to be given away, not the groom? and by the *father,* not the best man? Crosby's comment actually seems quite appropriate to the circumstances, though, because of the way that Hope appears to enjoy being perfumed, coifed, manicured, and costumed as Lamour's intended by her servants. "What are you made up for?" Crosby asks, "Lady's night in a Turkish bath?" Undaunted, a short while later Hope displays a lacquered toenail, explaining: "We're trying a new shade tonight, nightingale blush." Like his more overt transvestism when he plays Aunt Lucy, this type of fairy joke, which as I shall go on to show is in perfect accord with Hope's forties comic persona, feminizes his character, and this gender transgression visualizes how he also queers the deal for his pal Crosby.

Perhaps because, as in the kissing gags and cross-dressing, it contains so much homosexual horseplay of the sort that typified Army life and camp shows during World War II, *Road to Morocco* turns out to be the most heterosexist of all the "Road to" films, at least in its narrative closure. It is the only one in the series to provide Hope with a girl of his own, Doña Drake, in an effort to balance the coupling of Crosby and Lamour. Drake plays Mihirmah, a young woman in Shalamar's court who, falling in love with Orville, reveals the princess's plan to him. However, the ease with which Orville simply shifts his interest from Shalamar to Mihirmah makes one doubt his desire for *either* woman. "I got her at the harem," Orville boasts to Jeff about Mihirmah, "right off the assembly line." While Mihirmah is always hot and passionate when in Orville's presence, he keeps putting her at arm's length: "Later," he says, "you gotta catch me when I'm in the mood for that kinda thing." Though Hope is not exactly indifferent to her kisses, and Crosby makes a joke about his pal's perpetual horniness, we never do see Orville really change his mood or his mind. Even in the ending, with the two couples symmetrically paired, Orville's heterosexual desire still seems doubtful. After Hope breaks character to boast to the audience that this time he too is getting the girl, Doña Drake asks: "Why are you marrying me?" Hope replies, "I'll think of something." His answer is vague enough to go either way, that is, to suggest he really does know why he's with her (for the sex, presumably, since his recognition that she has no money is what prompts her question) or that he actually has no clue (which is to say that it's to be near Crosby).

Road to Morocco actually ends, though, not with Hope's answering Doña Drake's question but with his going to what he calls the powder room for a smoke. As a result of Hope's misrecognizing his own sissified appropriation of the euphemistic term *powder room,* the ship explodes, and the two couples end up as castaways in New York harbor. On ship, it seems, there is a closet designating neither the gents' room nor the ladies' room, even though its name appears to figure sexual difference, since it contains ammunition; it is a literal powder room. When Hope lights up outside the door, the gag concludes his bending of gender boundaries through his cross-dressing in *Morocco,* and it goes further to literalize the explosive force of Hope's comic persona on the straight romantic couple. Furthermore, this is not the first time in the film that Hope has made this mistake. In the opening he and Crosby became castaways under the same circumstances. Whereas the second explosion disrupts the doubling of the heterosexual couples—not only by blowing up the ship taking all four back to New York but by supplying Hope with the opportunity for the closing gag about his own screen acting and desire for an Oscar that breaks the diegesis as well—the first explosion, by contrast, is what turns the pair of buddies into a queer romantic couple. When the two men reach the beach following the first explosion, Crosby carries Hope out of the water. Hope's eyes are closed, and his smiling face is pressed contentedly against his pal's chest. The sight of this couple clearly mocks the conventional rescue of fair maiden by her hero, but it also conforms to that norm, insofar as this rescue does result in a kiss, although it is disavowed by the camel gag. Hope's persona is tantamount to an explosion, as *Road to Morocco* implies, because he crosses and collapses the binarized gender distinctions that his two costars uphold. In the "Road to" films this disruption takes the form of Hope's revising the homosocial triangulation of the buddy relation so that the third, troubling figure in the triangle is not the woman but the other man, the queer: namely, Hope himself.

"NIGHTINGALE BLUSH": HOPE'S QUEER PERSONA

According to historian George Chauncey in *Gay New York,* American culture during the first half of the century did not follow "the now-conventional division of men into 'homosexuals' and 'heterosexuals,' based on the sex of their sexual partners" but instead categorized men according to their gender behavior. "The abnormality (or 'queerness') of the 'fairy,' that is, was defined as much by his 'woman-like' character or 'effeminacy' as his solicitation of male sexual partners."[7] Chauncey further explains in the conclusion to his study that the systematic "exclusion of homosexuality from the public sphere" in the 1930s worked to repress what had been, particularly in working-class culture, the fairy's tolerated role in urban life as the queer defining the normality of other, more masculinized men, even those who had homosexual liaisons.[8] The visibility of the fairy reached its high point in the so-called pansy craze of vaudeville, nightclub, and live theater during the early thirties; later in that decade, public censorship of this obviously queer sissy figure on stage and then in film (with the renewal of Production Code Administration restrictions on subject matter) resulted in a shift in register from a denotative encoding of queerness (the well-known fairy character) to a more complex, because more covert, one of connotation (sexual innuendo and camp) that, in the postwar era, was crucial in reshaping gay culture in all modes of its representation.

Outwardly, however, the fairy continued to define queerness through effeminacy even after the pansy craze of the early thirties had run its course. For one thing, the fairy celebrated by the pansy craze influenced comedic conventions of the entertainment industry for several decades afterward, as in the sissy personae of stage, screen, radio, and, later, television stars like Eddy Cantor and Jack Benny, as well as Hope.[9] For another, the fairy supplied the characteristics identifying the gender inversion that military induction centers had institutionalized as the Army's means of pinpointing the homosexual personality for exclusion. The official mentality followed a psychiatric profile of gender deviancy that concentrated on "three major traits—effeminacy, a sense of superiority, and fear": "Effeminacy was by far the most common characteristic psychiatrists attributed to the typical homosexual. At a time when national survival depended on aggressive masculinity, military psychiatrists paid special attention to effeminacy as a sign of homosexuality, expressing on the hospital wards the same interest in gender characteristics that their colleagues had shown at induction stations. Researchers described their gay male patients as womanly in their bodies, mannerisms, emotional makeup, and interests."[10]

In his solo films, as in the "Road to" series, Hope's persona is unmistakably readable as queer because of the way his screen personality folds together the fairy of the 1930s pansy craze and the invert of 1940s military diagnostic practice, which identified queerness through the very same signs of gender disorder that his persona exaggerated: effeminacy, superiority, and fear. In *Caught in the Draft* (1941), for instance, made after the first two "Road to" films, Hope plays a movie star of action films who, as he confesses, actually "can't stand the sight of bullets," fainting on the set whenever he hears the sound of phony gunfire. "I'm sort of a Madeleine Carroll with muscles," he explains in his own defense. Though a sissy, he is also a lady's man, which causes him to balk at his agent's suggestion that he get married to avoid the draft. "That's like cutting your throat to avoid laryngitis," he complains. However, after disregarding all of the women he has dated, Hope settles on proposing to Dorothy Lamour, a general's daughter who initially cannot stand him because of his cowardice. His plan backfires, though, as a chain of events leads him right into the Army, where, after he repeatedly displays his incompetence as a soldier, he ultimately gets a chance to redeem his manhood by proving his courage.

Bruce Babington and Peter William Evans point out that Hope's films are, like *Caught in the Draft,* routinely structured in terms of jokes, gags, and comic situations characterizing a screen persona that inverts traditional assumptions about masculinity. Recurring references to Hope's gender ambiguity and sexual ineptitude, his narcissistic self-absorption and undeserved bravado, and his infantilizing cowardliness, passivity, and overall "perversity" all construct what amounts to a fairy persona.[11] Hope's films place him in what is visible as a feminizing position (as when, in

Morocco, he takes so enthusiastically to being costumed as Shalamar's intended or appears in drag as his own Aunt Lucy), just as they verbally link him to effeminacy by making jokes about his manhood. "Remember, you're a man, not a mouse," a grizzled prospector tells Hope in *Son of Paleface.* Hope coyly replies, "You peeked." Later, the prospector repeats this advice when reminding Hope to behave in a more manly style if he wants to win Jane Russell away from Roy Rogers. "Don't forget, this is the West, where men are men." "That's what she likes about me," Hope explains, "I'm a novelty." With the "novelty" of his gender inversion emphasized all the more by the parodic backdrop of established male genres that serve as the premise for most of his comedies—like the war film in *Caught in the Draft,* the swashbuckler in *The Princess and the Pirate* (1944), the Western in *The Paleface* (1948) and *Son of Paleface,* the spy thriller in *They Got Me Covered* (1943) and *My Favorite Brunette* (1947), and the imperial adventure tale in the "Road to" series—Hope's fairy comic persona cannot help queering what, as narrativized by his films, otherwise appear to be decidedly straight male characters lusting after glamorous leading ladies like Virginia Mayo (in *Princess*), Russell (in the two *Palefaces*), and Lamour (in the other comedies named, as well as the "Road to" films).

Thus, while Hope's films usually contextualize his gender inversion in a narrative of progression and disavow its queerness by his (often unsuccessful) hyperactive heterosexuality, his screen persona, which all his comedies reiterate, always has the potential to disturb the straight poles of sexual difference because his roles so routinely refer to the fairy stereotype. His best comedies make full use of that potential, with the gags promoting Hope's persona as a gender invert openly insisting upon the queerness of his masculinity. In *The Princess and the Pirate,* Hope disguises himself as an old crone in order to escape the Hook (Victor McLaglen), a notorious pirate. "Why don't you die like a man?" Virginia Mayo asks the crossdressed Hope, who replies, "Because I'd rather live like a woman." When the wizened and seemingly crazy Walter Brennan then seems attracted to him, Hope tries to resist the homoerotic dimension implied by his transvestic disguise: "Now I'm not so sure." But later, Hope also ends up in the bath with the villain, Walter Slezak, who keeps asking the comic to take off his clothes: "You wash my back and I'll wash yours." The script gives Hope a reason for declining (because he has a treasure map tattooed on his chest), but the scene itself is played as sexual farce, the attempted seduction of one man by another. Indeed, at the end of this film, Hope does not even pair up with his leading lady, since it turns out that Mayo has been using him to return to her true love, a sailor played by Crosby in a gag guest appearance.

The Paleface, produced at the height of the "Road to" series's success, exploits the queerness of Hope's persona even more broadly and explicitly. "Painless" Peter Potter (Hope), an inept dentist wanting to return East, "where men may not be men but they're not corpses either," checks into a hotel with his new wife, Calamity Jane (Jane Russell), and the desk clerk asks, "Would you like a boy?" In response, Potter does not answer but giggles and smiles, looks at Jane, and then the clerk rings the bell, which clarifies his meaning for Potter, who finally mutters, "oh, yes, yes." Babington and Evans claim that the joke in this exchange results from Potter's thinking that the clerk is asking him if "he wants to produce a son," with the gag meant to make fun of Potter's sexual naiveté.[12] Although the two critics parenthetically note "the homoerotic element lurking" in his confusion, the film itself does not exactly conceal the implication that the giggling and smiling Potter may be mulling over in his mind what he takes to be the clerk's offer of a boy for sex. How could a viewer ignore this possibility since The Paleface queers the deal for Potter at almost every opportunity? Welcomed into town as an Indian fighter (though Calamity Jane has in fact done the shooting for him), Potter picks up a cowboy—in order to obtain the latter's clothes so that he can dress appropriately for the West—by asking him: "How would you like a little conversation with a hero? . . . Well, follow me." And the cowboy does, right into the shadows of an alleyway. When Hope emerges following a discreet fade-out, he and the cowboy have exchanged clothes, which means, at the very least, they have also had to take them off.

Even more outrageously, when he marries Calamity Jane, Potter hands the ring to the minister, who gives it back so that the groom can place it on the bride's finger, but Potter pockets the ring instead, as if he does not fully comprehend the heterosexual component of this ceremony—and that's not because of his naiveté, either. "And now the kiss," the minister announces, and Potter kisses him. As in Road to Morocco, kissing in The Paleface results in a gender slippage that aligns Hope's persona with queer desire. Since Jane wants to avoid consummating their relationship, every time they kiss she knocks him out with the butt of her gun, which he misinterprets as evidence of her ability to overwhelm him sexually, as if a kiss were an orgasm. On their wedding night, when Jane sneaks out of the cabin to escape the nuptial bed, Potter does not even notice her absence. A male Indian lurking outside samples Potter's laughing gas and, giggling, takes Mrs. Potter's place. Closing his eyes to respect what he assumes is his new wife's modesty, Potter admires her/his smooth skin, long braided hair, and muscles; they kiss, and the Indian hits him on the back of his head with a tomahawk, the effect of which is indistinguishable from kissing his wife. "Boy, can you kiss!" Potter exclaims as he falls unconscious. Since the next morning he assumes that he has consummated his marriage, it seems perfectly clear that, for Potter, a kiss is still a kiss, regardless of his bed partner's gender.

"TWO GROOMS WITH NO BRIDE"

Hope's solo films refer to his partnership with Crosby because of the frequency with which they include a gag premised on the singer's guest appearance, usually in the role of an unexpected rival for the leading lady. Since the partnership with Crosby homoeroticized the queer dimensions of Hope's persona by linking it to a buddy relation, it is worth noting that the most popular of his solo comedies, such as *The Princess and the Pirate* and *The Paleface,* are also the ones most open in their intimations of his fairy persona's ambiguous sexuality, and that these films followed in the wake of the successes of *Road to Zanzibar* and *Road to Morocco.* By the same token, the "Road to" series itself did not take off until the studio appreciated the full importance of Hope's persona in complementing Crosby's. According to Hope's biographer, Arthur Marx, when the time came to make *Road to Zanzibar,* the sequel to *Singapore,* Paramount "had learned some valuable lessons. . . . First of all, don't let the romance [between Crosby and Lamour] get serious or in the way of the story. And second, Crosby was better when he was the schemer and Hope the victim." [13] Whereas the first film bills Hope after Lamour, he received second billing in *Zanzibar,* in acknowledgment that the buddy team was the primary attraction, and this ranking remained in place for the rest of the series.

Because of Hope's persona, his position in the "Road to" films as the comic playing off of Crosby's straight man also had the crucial residual effect of his playing the fairy to his partner's "trade": a man who, though sexually active with other men as well as with women, was not himself stigmatized "so long as [he] maintained a masculine demeanor and played (or claimed to play) only the 'masculine,' or insertive, role in the sexual encounter—so long, that is, as [he] eschewed the style of the fairy." [14] That an implied fairy-trade relation informs Hope and Crosby's teaming in *Road* to *Zanzibar* is evident in the jokes that arise from their carnival act, which opens and closes the film. Crosby collects money from the crowd while Hope performs a dangerous stunt parodying masculine prowess (posing as "The Human Dynamo," "The Human Bat," "The Living Bullet"); a montage shows how this carnival act keeps resulting in severe physical injury to the comic even though it is rigged. The act sets up the occasion for jokes that differentiate Hope from Crosby by emphasizing the comic's gender inversion (in much the same way that fairy jokes feminize Hope and masculinize Russell in *The Paleface*). As "The Living Bullet," for instance, Hope is seemingly shot out of a cannon, though a dummy is ejected while he remains safely hidden inside the machine. "Everything all right?" Crosby asks after finding Hope in a faint. Upon awakening, Hope reassures him, adding, "But I think we'll have to have a little more room when the baby comes." Another scheme Crosby plans is to have Hope wrestle an octopus: "We'll dress you like a pearl diver, maybe a sarong or something," he tells his pal excitedly. When the team revives their act at the end of the film, Hope refuses to go along with Crosby's latest gimmick, which would require the comic to impersonate a bearded lady. Hope's reply underlines his standing as the fairy to Crosby's trade in this partnership: "You think I want those sailors chasing me?"

In the "Road to" films, Hope's persona instantly evokes comparisons to the fairy because his characters invert the normal behavior and outward manner of Crosby's masculinity: recall that in *Bali*, Crosby carries a blue toothbrush to signify the properly masculine color, while Hope carries a red one, to signify his odd gender standing. Their different masculinities appear to motivate the placing of the comic, not the straight man, in the subordinate position of the effeminate male, Crosby's "victim." Crosby thus routinely refers to Hope by diminutive nicknames like "Junior" or "son," signifying his own superior masculine standing. In much the same vein, whenever the plot requires the team to masquerade, Crosby wears a man's disguise whereas Hope resorts to drag (as when he puts on a Carmen Miranda costume in *Road to Rio* [fig. 3]). Even more significantly, given the official discourse about homosexuality in place at the time, Crosby's occasional wisecracks about the comic's large rear end suggest the homoerotic direction of his gaze while allowing him to maintain a "masculine" position in their partnership. At the start of *Road to Utopia*, Hope thinks he has finally gotten the better of Crosby by refusing to accompany the latter to the Klondike and getting away with their bankroll. "I never thought I'd have

3 Hope in his Carmen Miranda disguise dances with his partner Crosby in *Road to Rio* (1947).

the bigger end," the comic boasts, and Crosby replies, "Oh, you've always had the bigger end." Hope then eyes his friend suspiciously, asking, "Where do you keep *your* butter?" According to Bérubé, in 1942 the Army "listed three possible signs for identifying male homosexuals, all of them based on gender deviance: 'feminine bodily characteristics,' 'effeminacy in dress and manner,' and a 'patulous [expanded] rectum.' All three of these markers linked homosexuality with effeminacy or sexually 'passive' anal intercourse and ignored gay men who were masculine or 'active' in anal intercourse."[15] Hope's fairy persona thus implicates Crosby's seemingly straight masculinity in this queer deal, too, as the kissing gags in *Road to Morocco*—not to say the wedding of "two grooms with no bride" in *Road to Bali*—recognize.

Still another evocation of this couple's queerness as a team arises from the frequency with which the "Road to" series draws on "show business" through asides, gags, and so on as a frame of reference that substantiates their onscreen rapport. In each film Hope and Crosby regularly disrupt the diegesis with their direct address, resorting to show business "shtick" to put forward their star personae over their characters. On one hand, these recurring references to show business follow the conventions of comedian-comedy generally in breaking the diegetic illusion but, on the other hand, they also allude to the way that, in the forties, the queer camaraderie of "show business" had already begun to supply gay men with another, much more covert, lexicon of self-identification. One of the ex-GIs interviewed for the film version of Bérubé's *Coming Out under Fire* remembers: "There was a group of us who met and hung out together. I knew they were homosexual, although I never spoke to another man about it, because they were funny, and they were gay, and they were happy, and they knew show biz."[16] In the "Road to" films, Hope and Crosby are not only "funny . . . gay . . . and . . . happy" every time they stop the story to make a joke about Hope's nose or acting pretenses, Crosby's stable of racehorses or his singing style, Lamour's star persona as a jungle princess, their home studio, other entertainers, and so on, but it is also clear from these extradiegetic gags that these two buddies certainly know their "show biz"!

With their potential for a camp reading, Hope and Crosby's show business jokes register the shift at mid-century from the denotative marking of queerness as a gender inversion (the fairy, defined through his effeminacy and not his sexual practices) to the much more covert encoding of a gay subculture through connotation. As already mentioned, this transformation in the semiotics of queerness, in its turn, manifested what Chauncey describes as "a reorganization of sexual categories and the transition from an early twentieth-century culture divided into 'queers' and 'men' on the basis of gender status to a late-twentieth-century culture divided into 'homosexuals' and 'heterosexuals' on the basis of sexual object choice."[17] As an illustration of how this shift in thinking about homosexuality redefined the relation of queer identity and queer desires, it is revealing that Hope himself once boasted to his writers about doing trade with a fairy, describing for them "a one-night stand he'd had back in his vaudeville days with the premier drag queen of the time." Decades later Hope recounted how he allowed the transvestite to perform oral sex on him, telling his story without embarrassment even though his stunned audience could themselves only understand it from the more contemporary perspective as an admission "that he'd had a homosexual affair." "The only thing he didn't tell us," Marx later recalls, "was whether or not he enjoyed it." [18]

According to Chauncey, until the 1950s the contemporary heterosexual-homosexual binarism, which conflates gender and sexuality, was a middle-class ideology that did not dominate the entire culture. In the first half of the century, the fairy was primarily a gender position in working-class culture. Like Hope himself in his anecdote about his youthful adventure with the drag queen while on the road touring in vaudeville, "many working-men thought they demonstrated their sexual virility by playing the 'man's part' in sexual encounters with either women or men." In this earlier era, middle-class "queers," by contrast, consciously distanced themselves from the fairy's gender inversion in part to distinguish their own social position and in part because, in their own class, "normal middle-class men increasingly believed that their virility depended on their exclusive sexual interest in women," defining "their difference from queers on the basis of their renuciation of any sentiments or behavior that might be marked as homosexual." [19] Generally speaking, whereas the 1950s saw the homogenization of the culture through middle-class hegemony, so that "normal" masculinity became exclusively heterosexual, the 1940s marked a crucial turning point in the reorganization of the culture's understanding of homosexuality, the traces of which continued to permeate postwar representations of gender and sexuality. [20]

To be sure, the war years resulted in the repression of queerness and the pathologizing of the homosexual that characterized the postwar mentality. However, the war also caused, because of its massive disruption of U.S. society and the integration of all classes (but not races) in the military, the momentary collapse of the boundaries between middle-class and working-class masculinities. While an ideology of "home" motivated patriotism by equating a normative masculinity with the national character, setting the terms by which the working class was induced to identify with middle-class hegemony in the decade following, the institutions of wartime also repositioned masculinity in a same-sex environment that challenged the middle-class presumption of heterosexual normality as defined in opposition to homosexual deviance. During the war, the military privileged and encouraged the buddy relation and, in camp drag shows, gave renewed prominence to the fairy as a projection of male desires. Furthermore, while the military officially targeted homosexuality as a specific category of deviation (the sissy), homoerotic desire was nonetheless allowed to diffuse throughout the same-sex culture of the armed forces because of the circumstances of sexual deprivation. As (working-class) novelist Harold Robbins remembers about his wartime bisexuality: "I was on a submarine, and if you're on a submarine for 22 days, you want sex. We were either jacking each other off or sucking each other off. Everybody knew that everybody else was doing it. . . . So we did it, it was fun, and it was over. I don't know whether any of them were really homosexual."[21] Because of its apparent detachment of gender from sexuality, the fairy stereotype did not outwardly threaten the heterosexual basis of normative masculinity but instead defined queerness in such a way that men could engage in homosexual activity without having to acknowledge as "really homosexual" the queer desire that fueled it.

The pairing of Hope and Crosby in the "Road to" series needs to be contextualized in both the war's disruption of middle-class masculinity and the postwar era's reconstitution of gender in sexuality. The series uses its homosocial plot trajectory (can Crosby steal Lamour away from Hope?) simply as the narrative mainstay of the more important, more ambiguous, and more fluid buddy relation, which Hope's comic persona repeatedly queers. As the numerous examples that I have cited from his solo films as well as the "Road to" series illustrate, in his queer persona Hope not only represents a gender inversion, he also incites the possibility of homoerotic desire: hence the number of gags that materialize his fairy persona in a same-sex kiss. The imbrication of his fairy identity in homoerotic desire establishes what is transgressive about Hope's queer persona and helps to historicize the disruption that he personifies as the odd man out—or, more accurately, the "out" odd man—in the homosocial triangle driving the star power of the "Road to" series. It explains, too, why Crosby's "straightness" cannot be so easily extricated from the queer buddy relation of the series— precisely because it *is* a relation, and one formed on the road, away from the heterosexual normality of the home front.

In private life, according to Marx, Hope and Crosby maintained a strict

heterosexual image, having numerous extramarital affairs and even passing women back and forth between them. We might infer, then, that the
two stars themselves did not intend such a queer resonance to be read
off of their buddy relation, which they promoted offscreen in radio and
TV appearances, as well as in their USO shows. However, how else can we
interpret the full weight of the jokes and sight gags that abound in the
"Road to" films to dramatize the intimacy and rapport of their teaming?
The series casts an unmistakable queer shading onto their onscreen partnership, because the 1940s buddy relation, like the era's fairy stereotype,
historically placed the coupling of two men in a larger cultural setting. For
the same reason, after the "Road to" series effectively ran its course with
Bali in 1952, it would be much harder for movie buddies to queer the deal
with either the innocence or audacity that Hope and Crosby, those "two
grooms with no bride," so outrageously put on display when they kissed
onscreen or woke up in bed together.

NOTES

All quotations of dialogue in this essay are my own transcriptions from laser
disc versions of the films or, if unavailable in that format, videocassettes.

1   "Letters from GIs." *Bob Hope: Memories of World War II*. Online. Bobhope.com.
18 August 1996. This home page from Bob Hope Enterprises publicizes the
special aired by NBC on 5 August 1995 and subsequently released on videocassette. This letter is also one read in voice-over on the program (but was
omitted on the videocassette).

2   Alan Bérubé, *Coming Out under Fire: The History of Gay Men and Women in
World War Two* (New York: Plume, 1990), 186.

3   Ibid., 188.

4   Ibid., 68.

5   Eve Kosofsky Sedgwick, *Between Men: English Literature and Male Homosocial
Desire* (New York: Columbia University Press, 1985), 21, 38.

6   Frank Krutnik, "The Clown-Prints of Comedy," *Screen* 25, nos. 4–5 (1984):
50–59.

7   George Chauncey, *Gay New York: Gender, Urban Culture, and the Making of the
Gay Male World, 1890–1940* (New York: Basic, 1994), 13.

8   Ibid., 356.

9   On Cantor, see Hank Sartin, "Eddie Cantor, the Pansy Craze of the 1930s, and
the Intersection of Jewish and Gay Stereotypes" (paper presented at Society
of Cinema Studies Convention, 4 March 1995); and on Benny, see Alexander

Doty, *Making Things Perfectly Queer: Interpreting Mass Culture* (Minneapolis: University of Minnesota Press, 1993), 63–79.

10 Bérubé, *Coming Out under Fire,* 156.

11 Bruce Babington, and Peter William Evans, *Affairs to Remember: The Hollywood Comedy of the Sexes* (Manchester: Manchester University Press, 1989), 103–18.

12 Ibid., 102.

13 Arthur Marx, *The Secret Life of Bob Hope* (New York: Barricade, 1993), 148–49.

14 Chauncey, *Gay New York,* 68.

15 Bérubé, *Coming Out under Fire,* 19; brackets in original.

16 Dialogue from Arthur Dong, dir., *Coming Out Under Fire* (1991).

17 Chauncey, *Gay New York,* 22.

18 Marx, *Secret Life of Bob Hope,* 41–42.

19 Chauncey, *Gay New York,* 41–42.

20 I make this argument in greater detail in my book *Masked Men: Masculinity and the Movies in the Fifties* (Bloomington: Indiana University Press, 1997).

21 Quoted in Gerry Kroll, "Master Harold," *Advocate,* 22 Aug. 1995, 42–43.

Alexander Doty

THE QUEER AESTHETE, THE DIVA, AND *THE RED SHOES*

George Du Maurier's 1894 novel *Trilby* is one of the earliest manifestations of what would become a popular Western cultural paradigm in the late nineteenth and twentieth centuries: the gay (or otherwise queer) high-culture impresario or aficionado who expresses his passions and desires in public through women's bodies and voices.[1] Rooted in the dangerously fascinating Byronic (anti-)hero of the British Romantic period, this figure found his home in the age of Oscar Wilde, which was a time when most popular scientific, medical, and public notions about what was beginning to be called male "homosexuality" centered around the upper-class dandy and gender inversion.

Moving into the twentieth century, newly labeled and legislated against homosexual men of every class found themselves considered—and, as a result, often considered themselves—as being like women, or, more accurately, being connected to the traditionally "feminine." But whereas straight women could be expressive in public—albeit usually within severely limited, compromised, and carefully monitored situations—homosexual men dared not speak their names openly, and resorted to expressing themselves within their own hidden (sub)culture or by using secret codes of language and style to indicate their homosexuality in public spaces. There was another way left for homosexual men to express themselves within dominant culture, however: in some relation to straight women, or rather in relation to notions of the feminine attached to women, the gender to which homosexual men's "inversion" and "perversion" were allied.

It is within just such a cultural context that *Trilby* presents the now archetypal figure of Svengali, a musical genius who mesmerizes both men and women into becoming accomplished performers. Tellingly, Svengali has the men perform duets with him on instruments, while he trains the women to become divas—conducting and hypnotically compelling them during concerts from the orchestra pit or a theater box. In a move to contain Svengali's queer fascination, however, *Trilby*'s narrative is structured

so that the homosocial world of (English) male artists living "la vie bo-
heme" in Paris is established first. Svengali's entrance very early in the
book, however, undermines all attempts by the novel's third-person narrator, the major male protagonist Little Billee, and his two friends to keep
control of the narrative. Indeed, the music Svengali makes when he plays
the piano—sometimes accompanied by his companion Gecko—has an
unmanning effect on the three artist friends (and the narrator): "Then he
fell to playing Chopin's impromptu in A flat, so beautifully that Little Billee's heart went nigh to bursting with suppressed emotion and delight. . . .
Then Svengali and Gecko made music together, divinely . . . till the Laird
and Taffy were almost as wild in their enthusiasm as Little Billee" (10–11).

Almost immediately after Svengali homosexualizes the very tenuously
established homosocial space of the artist friends, Trilby enters. In keeping with this now queered narrative space, the narrator comments that she
has "a portentous voice of great volume, that might almost have belonged
to any sex," that "[s]he would have made a singularly handsome boy,"
and that "one felt instinctively that it was a real pity she wasn't a boy, she
would have made such a jolly one" (11–12). This boyish quality will subsequently attract Little Billee and Svengali to Trilby—the former, initially, to
her androgynous looks, and the latter to her deep voice. As it turns out,
Little Billee will also become interested in Trilby's voice, as we discover "he
had for the singing woman an absolute worship." The narrator continues:
"He was especially thrall to the contralto—the deep low voice" (40). While
Svengali is set up as the gay (or homosexual) impresario in relation to
women like Trilby, Little Billee is placed in the culturally queer space of
diva worshipper. From the beginning, Little Billee is much less convincing
as Trilby's romantic interest than as the sensitive and easily-moved-to-tears
aesthete who complements Svengali's musical performer and impresario in
the culturally feminized and homosexualized world of the arts.

Feminized though it is, the art world in *Trilby* allows little agency for
women. Caught between the artistic vision of a homosexual man and the
domestic vision of a heterosexual man (albeit a nominally heterosexual
one here), Trilby can only respond and react to men's desires. For all her
boyish high spirits, the narrative restricts Trilby's career choices to artist's
model, rich man's wife, or dominated diva. What is more, Trilby becomes
a diva whose brilliant singing voice is not really her own but a product
of Svengali's hypnotic will, which itself is the result of a burning desire
to have the world recognize him as the master of the "lost" art of "il bel

canto," which he says he found "in a dream" (20, 194). Finally, the narrator describes Trilby's performances as being a direct expression of her mentor's artistic passions: "It was as if she said: 'See! what does the composer count for? . . . The "Nussbaum" is neither better nor worse than "Mon ami Pierrot" when I am the singer, for I am *Svengali*; and you shall hear nothing, see nothing, think of nothing, but *Svengali, Svengali, Svengali!*'" (193).

Why doesn't Svengali sing in public himself? First, the lost art of "il bel canto" that he is desperate to express is most famously associated with women singers. Then there are ethnic, class, and sexuality issues to consider, all of which are connected to each other in the narrator's initial description of Svengali: "[He was] a tall, bony individual of any age between thirty and forty-five, of Jewish aspect, well-featured but sinister. He was very shabby and dirty. . . . His thick, heavy, languid, lustreless black hair fell down behind his ears on to his shoulders, in that musician-like way that is so offensive to the the the normal Englishman. . . . [He] spoke fluent French with a German accent . . . and his voice was very thin and mean and harsh, and often broke into a disagreeable falsetto" (9–10). While a few pages earlier, the narrator proclaims that the possibility of a "very remote Jewish ancestor" in Little Billee's background "is of such priceless value in diluted homeopathic doses," he also makes it clear that, in the late-nineteenth-century English culture of the author, Jewishness "is not meant to be taken pure" (6). In the quotation above, Svengali's "pure" Jewishness is "sinister" and associated with the underclass, foreignness, and queerness (as gender inversion/homosexuality)—much like Dickens's Fagin in *Oliver Twist* and any number of characters in Western texts.[2]

After failing to make "a dirty, drabby little dolly-mop of a [French] Jewess" (39) the new queen of bel canto, Svengali turns his attentions to the more culturally attractive (to the novel's target readers) figure of Trilby O'Ferrall, a Scotch-English milk seller living in Paris. That Trilby has no artistic ambitions of her own fuels Svengali's desire to use her as a vehicle for expressing his bel canto passions in order to gain public recognition. His marriage to Trilby is conducted off-page. That he has shown little romantic interest in her (or any woman) before this leads us to understand Svengali's marriage largely as a means for him to offer Trilby to the public as Madame (or La) Svengali—that is, as his feminine extension. It takes Svengali's death from a combination of heart disease and a knife wound from one of his former protégés to release the narrative and the other characters from his queer thrall and allow for their (re)heterosexualization.

After *Trilby,* most fictional gay impresarios and other aesthetes would retain some elements of Svengali's combination of fascinating monstrousness, foreignness, and "gender inversion." But they would rarely be members of the underclass again. The late-nineteenth-century example of Oscar Wilde would forever after link the gay aesthete with the upper-class dandy. Wilde's status as the most (in)famous homosexual in the Western world would also reinforce the connections between male homosexuality and the arts—for both homosexuals and heterosexuals. If they were not already, such upper-class "feminine" areas as fashion and interior decoration, and such high-culture forms as opera, theater, and ballet became bastions of coded, translated, or otherwise indirect homosexual expressiveness in the public sphere. During the first half of the twentieth century, these arenas became more and more widely, and usually pejoratively, understood by dominant culture as homosexual (or somehow queer) as well as feminine—indeed with gender inversion being the most common understanding of homosexuality, the "feminine" *was* "homosexual" where men were concerned.

Almost every man who associated himself with the artistic pursuits mentioned above placed himself within what were considered homosexual or more vaguely queer spaces, whether he identified as homosexual/gay/queer or not. In the twentieth century, one could add the "art film" to the list of cultural forms "queered" for men. Flourishing since the teens in Europe, these films were initially transcriptions of "famous players in famous plays" (and novels) and were usually produced to confer some measure of class and prestige upon what initially appeared to be a commercial mass-culture industry. It is no coincidence that, besides transcribing plays and literary classics, many art films concerned themselves with other high-culture forms: ballet, opera, classical music, and painting (the latter two somehow appearing queerer, most of the time, when they became film subjects). Of course, fashion (as costume, hair, and makeup design) and interior decoration (as art design and set decoration) were very important to almost all of those high-culture forms that made their way into art films.

As may be clear at this point, I am not using the term *art film* in the more recent American and British sense, which labels only certain foreign films—generally by auteur directors—as "art films." Indeed, most of these films would not fall under my use of the term. I employ *art film* in the older sense of prestige productions with some connection to high-culture forms, or with some pretentions to high-culture status through their subject or style. These are generally films produced within studio systems, but ones that fall outside the prevailing standards of popular (that is, working- and middle-class) tastes. These films are calculated risks taken by studios, producers, and directors—bids for critical acclaim, awards, the infrequent "discerning" moviegoer's business, and some crossover business from regular moviegoers who might temporarily be convinced to place themselves in queerer viewing spaces for their (high-)cultural enrichment. By the definition I am using, I would consider as art films such works as *Sunrise, Fantasia, A Song to Remember* (and most 1940s and 1950s biopics about classical composers), *Lust for Life* (and most biopics about the lives of painters), *Specter of the Rose, Invitation to the Dance, Don Giovanni* (and other British and American attempts to transcribe opera), and a number of films by Michael Powell and Emeric Pressburger, including *Black Narcissus, The Tales of Hoffmann, The Red Shoes,* and *Oh . . . Rosalinda!!*.[3]

While films like these are frequently reviled as middlebrow kitsch for what appear to be their failed attempts to combine high-culture subjects with popular cinema forms and styles (or, occasionally, vice versa, as with *Sunrise*), I see the tensions in these films as being also a function of attempts to mask or neutralize the feminine queer (or queerly feminine) charge of high-culture subjects through certain heterosexualizing film and cultural conventions. We should recall, though, that tensions similar to these already exist in such high-culture forms as opera, ballet, and theater. Consider the musical and visual "excesses" of many opera productions in relation to their very conventional gender and sexual narratives. Putting high-culture forms like these on film—particularly into mainstream films —just complicates the discussion of how femininity, masculinity, straightness, and queerness circulate in relation to these studio art films.

One of the films that most strikingly illustrates the frequent queerness of the studio art film—both onscreen and behind the scenes—is *The Red Shoes* (1948). Not only is the narrative centrally concerned with the world of classical ballet but the film appears to have been planned self-consciously as an art film by Britain's most famous writing, producing, and directing partners, Michael Powell and Emeric Pressburger.[4] Once under the sign of the art film, both those making the film and the film narrative itself became associated with queerness—more particularly with male homosexuality. Discussing the concept of "gay sensibility," Seymour Kleinberg remarks, "In our times, two dominant areas of this expression in art and commerce have been in ballet and movies"—and *The Red Shoes* combined them both.[5] Powell recalls how producer Alexander Korda never understood the success of *The Red Shoes,* as he felt that men associated with the ballet "were a lot of poofs,"[6] while the film's director of photography, Jack Cardiff, thought ballet was "sissies prancing about." Even so, he became a self-confessed "balletomane" while working on the film.[7]

Adding to the aura of queerness surrounding the making of *The Red Shoes* are certain production events that strikingly parallel the film's narrative, as Powell and Pressburger became determined to make a film star of ballet dancer Moira Shearer, just as gay impresario Boris Lermontov is consumed by the idea of making Victoria (Vicky) Page a star through his staging of a ballet based upon Hans Christian Andersen's "The Red Shoes," which itself is the story of a young woman who is tempted by a queer shoemaker into wearing shoes that will not let her stop dancing. To carry the "male aesthetes expressing themselves through a diva" parallels surrounding *The Red Shoes* a step further: Andersen, himself homosexual, has been described as a "would-be dancer and actor who channelled many of his own frustrated desires" into stories like the one about a young woman who dances around the world in red shoes.[8]

The Red Shoes takes its place in Powell's two autobiographies and in the Pressburger biography (by his grandson, Kevin Macdonald) as the film that, in retrospect, marked the height of their team collaboration, as it became the film that did the most to keep their names twinned in cinema history.[9] It was a creative partnership of which Powell said in the 1980s, "The press were intrigued and puzzled by the collaboration. . . . Nobody understood it at the time, and nobody understands it now."[10] Wayne Koestenbaum's book, *Double Talk: The Erotics of Male Literary Collaboration,* offers an angle from which we might understand Powell and Pressburger's work as the collaboration of queer, if not exactly gay, artists: "I would say that collaboration between men in the 19th and early 20th centuries was a complicated and anxiously homosocial act, and that all the writers in this study, regardless of their sexual preference, collaborated in order to separate homoeroticism from the sanctioned male bonding that upholds patriarchy."[11]

While he acknowledges that there is the *attempt* to separate the homosocial from the homosexual in these collaborations, Koestenbaum goes on to say that artistic collaborations by heterosexual men always finally work "within a framework dominated by homosexual desire, whether draped in the discrete [sic] charm of the 'homosocial continuum,' or left impolitely naked."[12] Since anxieties about the lines between the homosocial and the homosexual have persisted up until the present, Powell and Pressburger's partnership might still be discussed within Koestenbaum's notions of the erotics of male artistic collaboration.

The autobiographics, biography, and letters of Powell and Pressburger are filled with intriguing tidbits that, added together, make a good case for there being a very blurred homosocial-erotic line between the two men during their friendship and creative partnership. Powell refers to his first meeting with Pressburger, to work on *The Spy in Black* (1939), as something akin to love at first sight.[13] Part of what Pressburger's grandson, Kevin Macdonald, calls the "uncannily close relationship [that] began to develop between the two men"[14] seems to have been initiated over the body of someone Powell describes as "one of the most romantic and magnetic men alive"—the star of *The Spy in Black,* gay actor Conrad Veidt.[15] Recalling their first meeting with Veidt, Powell says: "Conrad Veidt was seated alone at a table by the window drinking coffee. . . . Emeric and I exchanged a glance. This magnificent animal was reserved for us. Then we looked at each other."[16] Queerly creative ménage à trois, anyone? "It's like a marriage without sex," Powell said about his creative relationship with Pressburger. "[L]ucky the collaborator who finds his rightful partner."[17]

If Powell and Pressburger's pairing was a marriage without actual physical sex, it was a union that did express itself erotically and romantically in many other ways, on- and offscreen. Powell's correspondence to Pressburger is filled with touching and funny salutational endearments: "My angel Imre," "Dearest One of Both," "My Dear First Class Male!" "Old Austrian Cock," and two particularly interesting ones in the context of this essay—"Dear Old Fruit" and "Dearest Red Shoemaker."[18] In one note to Pressburger, Powell comments on their late-1970s business affairs and plans: "I think things are shaping [up] better for us. What a romance!"[19] After Powell, Pressburger, and their films had been rediscovered in the 1980s, they were asked how they had managed to remain together for so long: "[T]he two men looked at one another for a moment, each awaiting a reply from the other, before Powell quite unselfconsciously replied: 'The answer is love. You can't have a collaboration without love. We had complete love and confidence in each other.'"[20] "For twenty years we had been as close as a man and wife,"[21] Powell remarked in one autobiography about their partnership. "I knew Emeric better than his wife, better than his daughter, better than all his girlfriends, better than his current mistress, but not, I hope, better than his two Scottish grandsons."[22]

This last women-excluding "between men" remark should remind us that, since we are speaking of studio filmmaking here, discussions of the production contexts of the Powell-Pressburger films as queerly charged might be extended beyond the writing-producing-directing team to include their other regular Archers Production collaborators: Alfred Junge, Brian Easdale, Jack Cardiff, Hein Heckroth, Anton Walbrook, Christopher Challis, F. A. Young, Reginald Mills, Arthur Lawson, Sydney Streeter, and others. Indeed, far from invoking classic patriarchal auteurist or studio mogul rhetoric, Powell and Pressburger usually spoke of their filmmaking as a close collaboration among a team of men. In his autobiography, Powell recalls a scene cut out of *The Red Shoes* that "illustrat[ed] the way Emeric and I [and, one might add, the Archers team] worked together." During this scene Lermontov and his collaborators toss around ideas for "The Red Shoes Ballet," something Powell and Pressburger found themselves doing off-camera with their collaborators. According to Powell, when the time came to film the scene, "[t]here was no longer anything to talk about or explain, because we were going to show the film audience what we had created." By Powell's final "we," the Archers film team has overlapped and even replaced the "we" of the Lermontov Ballet company as the group of creative male artists producing what Powell calls "the fruit of all this collaboration and love."[23] Elsewhere in his autobiographies, Powell does recall a sequence involving male artistic collaboration that did remain in the film: "[T]he scene when Marius [Goring, who plays Julian Craster] comes to the villa and plays the new Red Shoes music to Lermontov, Ljubov, Ratov and Livy. . . . There are lots of clever scenes in *The Red Shoes,* but this is the heart of the picture."[24] As Kevin Macdonald puts it, "*The Red Shoes* was probably the pinnacle of the collaborative principle of movie-making. . . . It is ridiculous to speak of *The Red Shoes* as a Powell-Pressburger film. It is a production of the Archers."[25]

However much the Lermontov Ballet and the Archers Production company liked to see themselves as a men's club of collaborative artists, the truth is they vitally depend upon women—or at least one woman per project. Indeed, these teams often focused their collective creative energies upon a straight female character and the performer playing her. Where Lermontov trusts the talents of neophyte ballerina Victoria Page to preserve the reputation of his company, Powell and Pressburger (and the rest of the Archers) counted upon film neophyte Moira Shearer to carry their most ambitious and expensive art film to date. Where Lermontov (and his creative team) become fixated upon red shoes (there is even a shot of Lermontov selecting just the right pair for Page from a row of ballet slippers), Powell, Pressburger, and most of the Archers became transfixed by Shearer's red hair—not surprising, considering the film's investment in Technicolor. Powell's autobiography, *A Life in Movies,* in particular, is almost embarrassing in its rhapsodizing: the "most glorious hair of Titian red that I have ever seen on a woman," "red-headed beauty," "red-headed mackerel," "that glorious, tall, red-headed dancer," her "cloud of red hair as natural and beautiful as any animals, flamed and glittered like an autumn bonfire."[26] "The main thing that all publicity, exploitation, advertising and selling should concentrate on is The Girl. The Red-Head who wears the Red Shoes," Powell wrote in a letter to Pressburger discussing promotional ideas for the film's American release.[27]

From all accounts, once a number of the Archers had seen red-haired Shearer no one else would do for the *The Red Shoes.* But they were hard-pressed to convince her to take time off from the Sadler's Wells Ballet, where she was just beginning to make a name for herself, to star in a Powell-Pressburger-Archers film. Her artistic sights were set upon being a prima ballerina; the Archers were fixed upon making another success-ful art film after *Black Narcissus.* In short, they needed her more than she needed them—and they all seemed to recognize this situation, although not without some resentment on Powell's part. In his autobiographies, Powell praises Shearer as a great talent, and even includes her in his usually all-male list of collaborators when he discusses the film, but his frustra-tions at her resistance to making *The Red Shoes,* and his feeling that she saw the Archers team as being far less sensitive and artistic than her ballet company, finds its outlet in some rather crude straight, patriarchal rheto-ric: "I never let love interfere with business, or I would have made love to her. It would have improved her performance. . . . We were very much alike. . . . It was a curious relationship. I sometimes wonder whether she had a heart to break."[28]

Shearer's involvement with *The Red Shoes* appears to have made Powell feel somewhat threatened as one of the major (queerly positioned) au-teurs of a ballet art film. Indeed, at one point in the quotation above, he casts Shearer as Lermontov and himself as the diva by reworking one of the lines in the film with a gender switch: "He has no heart to break, that man." By her resistence to filmmaking—even to being in a classy Powell-Pressburger-Archers production—Shearer made the importance of her contribution to the otherwise "boys only" collaboration stand out. Perhaps recognizing that the Archers might be producing *The Red Shoes,* but that Shearer was actually wearing them, Powell was left to reassert himself, where and when he could, by shifting the terms of the discussion from artistic creation (the red shoes/*The Red Shoes*) to personal matters (the red hair). By doing this, Powell the heterosexual man might have felt he could put Shearer in her gender place for Powell the queerly positioned artist. The director's complicated relationship with ballet diva Shearer in connection with *The Red Shoes* is classic: in his queer position as ballet film director-producer, Powell identifies with ballet dancer Shearer ("[w]e were very much alike"), but he also seems somewhat resentful and threatened by the ways in which Shearer's attitude about the production emphasizes his (and the Archers team's) artistic dependence upon her and her red shoes/red hair.

Given this creative situation between diva and "impresario," it comes as no surprise to discover that a number of Archers productions include an onscreen male character who attempts to control or regulate the central female character(s) and the development of their heterosexual relationships. Often this character is not only coded as homosexual or otherwise queer but is played by an actor who is homosexual. Think of Theo Kretschmar-Schuldorff (as played by Anton Walbrook) in *The Life and Death of Colonel Blimp;* Thomas Colpepper, JP (Eric Portman) in *A Canterbury Tale;* Mr. Dean (David Farrar) in *Black Narcissus;* Boris Lermontov (Anton Walbrook) in *The Red Shoes;* Edward Marston (Cyril Cusack) in *Gone to Earth;* Hoffmann's rivals (Robert Helpmann) in *The Tales of Hoffmann;* and Dr. Falke (Anton Walbrook) in *Oh . . . Rosalinda!!.*[29] Quite a few critics have understood characters like these as Powell's alter egos—even though one might point out that they were largely written by Pressburger, and, therefore, could also be considered Pressburger's screen representatives in some way.[30] Indeed, Powell and Pressburger were not averse to pointing out connections between themselves and many of these characters, as well as the actors who played them.

To be more specific, the queer aura of many Archers collaborative productions—and of the Powell-Pressburger partnership—is often linked to gay actor Anton Walbrook, the performer most closely and frequently associated with their films—just as gay actor Conrad Veidt had been for pre-Archers Pressburger and/or Powell films: *The Spy in Black, Contraband,* and *The Thief of Bagdad.*[31] Walbrook's homosexuality, the queerness of many of the characters he played, and the elements of foreignness and an aristocratic bearing associated with his image, came together at least twice to create a figure who seemed to represent the Powell-Pressburger team in their queer position at the head of a multinational group of men collaborating to produce art films under the Archers banner. In *Oh . . . Rosalinda!!* Walbrook plays an upper-class doctor who, as part of a revenge plot, seeks to manipulate the heterosexual lives and loves of a number of people in postwar Vienna. An updating of the operetta *Die Fledermaus,* the action revolves around an elaborate masquerade party stage-managed by the Walbrook character ("the Bat") in order to entrap and embarrass many of his guests. Crucial to his direction of events is the Bat's ability to encourage two women to come to the party disguised, so that they can fool the men who know them. This scheme enables the Bat to wreak havoc on their straight relationships, at least temporarily. While their characters are not singers, the two women here, for all intents and purposes, register upon audiences as operetta divas—and the Bat becomes another gay man who uses their various talents to express his desires (here for control and revenge) indirectly. In discussing Walbrook's Bat, Powell conflates the character with the actor playing him:

> As the champagne flowed on the screen, I thought of Anton and the strange art of acting. Larry [Olivier] said that real acting, the big stuff, is walking a tightrope between the two sexes: sooner or later you fall off one side, or the other. . . . No actor that I have known had such control as Anton had—until he played the Bat. Then, the Bat controlled him. . . . The Bat was different. In order to play Dr. Falke, Adolf Wohlbruck had to return to his sources. . . . I knew that this was Anton's only failure, because he had to play himself.[32]

If Powell hints at the gayness of Walbrook and his director-impresario-type character in *Oh . . . Rosalinda!!* by resorting to suggestive references to gender inversion, he lays all the cards on the table in discussing the actor and his role as Boris Lermontov in *The Red Shoes:* "When it came to *The Red Shoes* and that devil, Boris Lermontov, there was no question in our minds as to who should play him, and give a performance filled with passion, integrity, and, yes, with homosexuality."[33] Written with Walbrook in mind, Pressburger contended that in Lermontov there is "something of [homosexual ballet impresario Serge] Diaghilev, something of Alex Korda, something of Michael, and quite a bit of me."[34] In considering the connections between Lermontov, Powell, and Pressburger, it might be wise to reemphasize here that the queerness I am discussing in relation to Powell-Pressburger and their (male) Archers collaborators has more to do with the circumstances surrounding their creative work than with their "real life" gender and sexuality identifications. As John Russell Taylor puts it, more generally, in terms of Powell:

> [There] is ample evidence of Powell's identification with his artist-supermen. He has, for instance, compared the film-maker's role so often to that of the Diaghilev type of impresario, channelling and coordinating the headstrong talents of many other artists to one unified end, that it is barely conceivable there could be no sort of identification in his own mind between himself and the impresario Lermontov in *The Red Shoes*. It seems, too, that some of the more abrasive and highly-coloured of his favourite actors, Eric Portman and Anton Walbrook in particular, regularly stand in for the director as *meneur du jeu* and therefore represent Powell the artist, if not necessarily Powell the man, within his work.[35]

All evidence onscreen and behind the scenes to the contrary, however, many people insist upon heterosexualizing the Diaghilev-like Lermontov and his relationship with Page. Besides general cultural heterocentrism, this might be traced, in part, to frequent discussions of the film as a "heterosexual reworking of the Diaghilev/Nijinski/Romola triangle," with Lermontov, Craster, and Page, respectively, taking on these roles.[36] But far from setting up Lermontov and Page as lovers, the critical tendency to make Page the Nijinski figure emphasizes the theme of the gay impresario's vital investment in the diva as his erotically expressive stand-in. Karen Backstein suggests that "at a point in which Powell [and, one might add, Pressburger] could not openly explore a gay relationship, [he] collapses female physicality and homosexual identity."[37] The narrative of *The Red Shoes* works itself out to force Page/Nijinski to choose between Lermontov–high art–queerness and Julian Craster–domesticity-straightness—although you would never know this from most of the contemporary reviews of *The Red Shoes*, or from almost all of the subsequent popular and academic pieces on the film. For most viewers and commentators, Page's choice between a ballet career and a domestic life is also a choice between two straight men. In other words, many people understand Lermontov as romantically desiring Page for himself, and because of this supposedly suppressed passion, he is jealous of Craster's romantic relationship with her. Comments like "Intertwined with Lermontov's stern supervision of Victoria's career is an underlying love and sexual attraction" are representative of this kind of heterocentric reading.[38]

To be fair, even Page initially misreads Lermontov's intentions when he invites her to his villa for what she thinks is a date. Dressing in a lavish ballgown, Page ascends the stairs to the villa only to find Lermontov (sporting a red neckerchief) surrounded by his male collaborators—and they are all discussing her suitability for their new production. Besides moments like this, which indicate Lermontov's lack of romantic interest in Page, the film suggests the queer difference in Lermontov's jealousy over Page when, during the climactic argument in Page's dressing room, Craster accuses Lermontov of "waiting day after day for a chance to get her back." When Lermontov asks Craster if he knows why he has waited, Craster replies, "Because you're jealous of her." "Yes I am," Lermontov shouts back, "but in a way that you will never understand."

So Lermontov is not jealous of Page in the heterosexual way Craster and many viewers think he is. Then how is he jealous of her? Lermontov does not elaborate, but from the evidence of the rest of the film we are left with two interrelated propositions: (1) he is jealous of her artistic abilities because he needs to use them for his own creative expression, and (2) he is jealous of her career because he wants to see her fulfill her promise as a great dancer—so that (1) can occur, it should be pointed out. To these counts of "red shoes envy" might be added Lermontov's jealousy of Page's red shoes as fetishistic reminders of her easy sexual access to men— particularly to Lermontov's most important "Red Shoes Ballet" collaborator, composer Julian Craster. Like Svengali before him, Lermontov "makes music" with this male collaborator, while using the bodies of his divas for the "artistic" expression of his sublimated sexual desires. Recall, along these lines, that the story of "The Red Shoes Ballet" has the protagonist, in her red shoes, promiscuously move between many men.

In *The Red Shoes* this situation sets up a relationship between the gay impresario and the woman artist that is, to say the least, fraught. From very early on, the film wants us to understand Lermontov and Page as being alike and connected in their intense devotion to ballet. Lermontov asks Page, "Why do you dance?" To which she replies, "Why do you live?" But even this exchange hints at the difficult positions culture has them take in relation to each other and to artistic expression, for, as it turns out, Lermontov lives to have dancers like Page perform ballets he develops and stages with his collaborators. Page lives to dance, but feels she must put herself under the disciplinary tutelage of Lermontov and company to push her art to its highest level. As one critic puts it, Lermontov is "[a]n artist without talent of his own, he seeks personal satisfaction by finding others with budding talent and nurturing them to greatness: 'I want to create something big out of something little,' he confides to Vicky. 'To make a great dancer out of you.'"[39] Later, Lermontov adds, "You shall dance, and the world will follow. Shhh! Not a word. I will do the talking, you will do the dancing." Just as Powell, Pressburger, and company were not particularly interested in Shearer's aesthetic opinions (she was "infuriated by the Archers' lack of ballet knowledge"),[40] Lermontov reveals time and again in the film that he is artistically interested only in Page's body as an instrument or a vehicle and not in her mind. Page wants to be "a great dancer," but the cost will be her subjugation to Lermontov's will and his artistic vision, and, secondarily, to those of the men who make up the creative staff of the Lermontov Ballet.

Part of what Page is asked to give up in order to enter Lermontov's charmed circle is being a "practicing heterosexual." While she is still in the corps de ballet, she hears Lermontov's railing against the company's diva, who has announced her engagement: "I am not interested in Boronskaja's form anymore, nor in the form of any other prima ballerina who is imbicile enough to get married. . . . She's out, finished. You cannot have it both ways. The dancer who relies upon the doubtful comforts of human love will never be a great dancer—never!" When Grischa Ljubov, the choreographer, comments, "That's all very fine, Boris, very pure and fine, but you can't alter human nature," Lermontov responds, "No, I think you can do better than that—you can ignore it." The terms in which Lermontov discusses love/sex are interesting. "Human love" seems to be equated here with heterosexual relationships/marriage, the implication being that women dancers should turn to the "inhuman" or "non-human" love of Lermontov and his ballet company in order to become great.

This suggestion that what Lermontov offers Page is, somehow, the antithesis of "human love," connects with some common cultural notions: the spaces of high art are homosexual or queer and, therefore, perverse and suspect (both Page and Powell refer to Lermontov as being monstrous, as do a number of critics);[41] the spaces of high art are somehow "beyond" or "above" such messy things as sexuality. Both ideas are attempts to place high art, and those who create it, in non-straight territory, with the second notion really being just a way for people to avoid dealing with the first, as it allows homophobic and heterocentrist viewers to take comfort in the idea that someone like Lermontov (or Powell, or Pressburger) is asexually consumed with desexualized notions of high art and aesthetics. And so, understanding high art and artists as being beyond sexuality is, finally, just another case of the "I know it's/he's gay, or somehow queer, but would rather not think about it" position that homophobia encourages in people whether they are responding to characters or to real personalities.

But cultural pressures being what they were—and are—many gay, lesbian, bisexual, and queer artists also have come to understand their creative work as being beyond or above issues of sexuality. It appears Lermontov is one of these people from the evidence of his comment about ignoring "human nature"—in this context meaning any type of sexuality, as opposed to "human love," which is contextualized to refer to heterosexuality and marriage. For Lermontov, "ignoring human nature" seems to mean suppressing the direct expression of his (homo)sexuality while also attempting to control the expression of the (hetero)sexuality of his prima ballerinas. What is more, Lermontov's desire to have Page (and before her, Irena Boronskaja) forgo heterosexual love is linked in the film to his artistic aspirations. So by a tortuous route of suppression and substitution he is able to have his divas stand in for him. Supposedly purged of their heterosexual desires, they can become the vehicles for expressing the gay impresario's disavowed desires, through codes of the "feminine," within the queer spaces of ballet.

We might pause here to wonder about the homosexual men onstage in ballets, including the Lermontov Ballet's lead male dancer, Ivan Boleslawsky. Why can't they be the vehicles of gay, or otherwise queer, expressiveness? The most obvious response, of course, is that open gay/queer expression was not possible in high-art venues—and still is not, to a great extent. Thus, while almost all male ballet dancers are considered queer by most of the public, they perform within heterosexualizing narrative contexts.[42] Granted, even given these contexts, queerness enters into many people's understanding of the ballet as they see the male dancers as (to quote Jack Cardiff again) "sissies prancing about," or, more benignly, as gay men being artistically expressive. There is some space for gayness to be expressed in public by ballet performers, then, but this kind of expressiveness seems to be less about direct and open expression, and more about homosexuality being signaled or read in spite of the heterosexual narrative and cultural frames of reference within which both the male dancers and the audience are asked to work.

For someone like Lermontov, who has decided to "ignore human nature" in relation to his art, and therefore place himself within the acceptable dominant cultural category of "asexual artist," using gay dancers to express himself would most likely open up a troublesome Pandora's box. As suggested earlier, men like Lermontov could not be seen—and often did not want to see themselves—as creating "obvious" homosexual art. Although they work behind the scenes with homosexual and otherwise queerly positioned men, and might even find certain ways to express their gay desires through gay performers, high-art producers like Lermontov choose—or feel forced to choose—to be expressive in less direct ways by using feminine codes connected to women performers—with the Diaghilev-Nijinski team as perhaps the most notable real-life exception in the ballet world.

An earlier draft of the film's script contained a short exchange that encapsulates the very different relationships gay impresarios-aesthetes like Lermontov have with divas and with gay performers. Prima ballerina Boronskaja is late again, and Boleslawsky confronts Lermontov:

> *Boleslawsky:* Well, if I dared to be as late as that . . .
>
> *Lermontov:* You would, of course, be discharged immediately. But you, my dear boy, are *not* Boronskaja. Furthermore, you've got too much make-up on. Go to your room and do something about it.[43]

Lermontov is willing to make concessions for the diva, but he feels compelled to put some distance between himself and his company's leading male dancer. However, Lermontov's admonitions to the dancer are symptomatic of his confused, self-oppressive position. For while Lermontov takes pains to point out that the gay performer will always fall short for the impresario because he is not the diva, he also warns the dancer that his appearance is too effeminate for him to go onstage. It seems that for Lermontov, having a gay diva performing in one of his ballets would be like coming out himself, as he has sublimated his homosexuality into the creating and staging of ballets.

So where does this leave the straight woman diva? In earlier versions of the script, Page was given a close woman friend, who was also a member of Lermontov's troupe. With this friend came opportunities for Page to be more expressive about her artistic ambitions, as well as to be more vocal about her frustrations with Lermontov's treatment of her. By the final script, however, the friend-colleague is gone.[44] In the finished film, we find Page, caught between the all-male creative collaborators of Lermontov's ballet company and the conventional domestic demands of her husband Craster, is left with only her moments onstage to call her own, at least partially. The film emphasizes Page's artistic dilemma through some startling subjective camera work during the two extended ballet sequences. In the first of these sequences Page dances *Swan Lake* for a small ballet company run by a woman. Soon after her entrance, the sequence is presented to mirror Page's experience while dancing. A series of zip pans over the audience alternate with shots of her ecstatic face to convey how intensely she feels these moments of artistic creation. When she sees Lermontov in the audience, however, her face registers panic, and there is a rough change-over between the records Page is dancing to. Her brief moment of laying sole claim to her art is over.

The second sequence of Page dancing onstage is more extended, and it is more disturbing in representing the precarious and compromised position of women performing artists. Page is dancing "The Red Shoes Ballet," which, as noted earlier, is the story of a young woman who wants to dance, and the queer shoemaker who gives her a pair of red shoes that allow her to dance—but, ultimately, to their/his (or Lermontov's and composer Julian Craster's) tune. Most of the ballet is shot "objectively," that is, from the position of the theater or film audience watching it. As the ballet's narrative reaches the point where the protagonist realizes the red shoes are controlling her, the filming style becomes more subjective, inviting the viewer to understand and to empathize with both the protagonist's and Page's conflicting feelings about putting on those red shoes. At one point, the queer shoemaker changes into Lermontov, and then into Craster, before Page's horrified eyes. Page then dances with a newspaper man before the shoemaker returns to lead her on. Soon afterward, Page hallucinates that Craster leaves the orchestra pit (where he is conducting) and walks out over the footlights to be her partner. When he lifts her, she changes into a flower, a cloud, then a bird. After these shots, the style of filming the ballet returns to the "objective."

During what should be the moment of her greatest artistic expression and satisfaction, Page is haunted and hemmed in by the two key men in "The Red Shoes Ballet" creative team. Her connecting Lermontov and Craster to the shoemaker, and Craster to her dancing partner, trouble her creative pleasure and suggest that she is becoming aware of how she is being monitored onstage and off: by Lermontov and Craster as the queer collaborators of "her vehicle" (she is really their vehicle), and by Craster as a creative and, potentially, as a personal partner (later, she will be "lifted" by him out of her place as prima ballerina and into a position as ethereal love object and artistic muse). However, within the subjective portion of "The Red Shoes Ballet," we are presented with those shots of Page in a newsprint dress as she elegantly and skillfully dances with that newspaper man. Here we are made aware that Page's art can stand on its own, apart from her male dance partners and those behind-the-scenes male collaborators, who become mere paper men when the diva dances. However, her newsprint dress also suggests she is the three-dimensional, flesh-and-blood doppelgänger of the newspaper man, who is associatively linked to Lermontov, Craster, and Boleslawsky, her gay dance partner. Between them, the two onstage dance sequences present Page as both "little more than the projection of . . . [gay and queerly positioned] men's desires" and as someone who feels, even if momentarily, the "power and pleasure" of putting on her red ballet slippers (which also allow her to see these men as projections of *her* fears and desires).[45]

Koestenbaum notes that within much of male artistic collaboration "[h]omoeroticism and misogyny palpably intersect," as "collaborators [make] use of the 'feminine' in appropriative ways . . . improperly diffusing homoerotic desire in female go-betweens."[46] In light of Koestenbaum's ideas, it is interesting to recall that at the same time Lermontov forms his important new collaboration with Craster, he is also beginning his gay impresario-diva relationship with Page. Initially, Page does act as the "go-between," being passed among Lermontov, Craster, Ljubov, and Boleslawsky, in an attempt to get her ready to dance "The Red Shoes Ballet." The role of the diva as a (not fully successful) heterosexualizing counter in what otherwise might seem too intensely and clearly queer male collaborations is most strikingly presented in *The Red Shoes* during the scene in which Lermontov tells Craster the story of the ballet. As he summarizes the tale, Lermontov moves away from Craster to stand next to, and then to fondle, a marble statue of the "dismembered" foot of a ballerina on pointe. Considering Lermontov by himself, it is possible to understand the statue as representing his intense identification with the diva. In the artistic collaboration between men, however, the diva becomes a fetishized artistic object. Even more outrageously telling, the diva, in this particular scene, becomes an aestheticized "feminine" phallus in the possession of the gay impresario, to be displayed by and for himself and his collaborators as they discuss their productions.

Given these circumstances, it is fitting that the protagonist of the ballet, danced by Page, should be given the red shoes by a queer shoemaker (read: Lermontov, Craster, and the other members of the creative team).[47] While the red shoes initially allow the nameless woman character to dance gracefully, winning the romantic attentions of a young man (read: Craster away from Lermontov), she soon finds that she cannot take the shoes off (read: Lermontov's pressures upon her to stay in the queer world of ballet at the expense of heterosexual relationships). Compelled to dance wherever the shoes take her, she is prevented from continuing her heterosexual romance — as well as from returning home — because the slippers constantly dance her away from her lover and her mother (that is, away from heterosexuality and homosocial bonding). What the shoes do is dance her into sexual adventures, including promiscuous "back alley" encounters with "rough trade" men and lesbian-suggestive situations with prostitutes: that is, the red shoes dance her into gender and sexual "excesses," which initially she seems to enjoy. In this way the queerly created red shoes/"Red Shoes Ballet" offers straight women the opportunity to express their sexual and artistic desires: to be exhibitionistic rather than to be fully objectified. In the end, however, these shoes are presented as seemingly queerly controlled ones that dance the character — and Page as it turns out — to her death.

Once again, in high art — the ballet, the art film narrative — queerly positioned men appropriate a woman's body. However, as mentioned earlier, this practice is encouraged by certain interconnected misogynistic and homophobic patriarchal attitudes, which require gay men to give over the direct expression of their sexuality in order to achieve career success, while also demanding that women in the public sphere somehow be monitored or controlled by men (whether gay or straight). On the one hand, *The Red Shoes*'s narrative seems to suggest that male queerness in one form or another is to blame for Page's death: first the Lermontov-Craster–et al. collaboration on "The Red Shoes Ballet," and later Lermontov's possessive desire to have Page do his artistic bidding at the expense of her heterosexual relationship.

Since it was created under the queer sponsorship of the Lermontov Ballet company, it makes sense that Craster's split from Lermontov leaves "The Red Shoes Ballet" in the maestro's possession and marks the beginning of Craster's solo "straight" career as a composer, which, unsurprisingly, coincides with the beginning of his domestic life with Page as his wife and artistic muse. Because of conventional cultural prejudices about these things, most viewers and critics feel that Page's death is largely Lermontov's fault, as the film finally emphasizes how he, rather than Craster, has forced her to choose between the queerly coded spaces of high art and a straight domestic life. Recall how in the final sequence the film cross-cuts between the poignant moment when Craster takes the red shoes off of a dying Page—at her request—and Lermontov's unsettling, guilt-ridden curtain speech announcing that Page will not dance "The Red Shoes Ballet." The death of the gay impresario's artistic stand-in forces him onto the stage and into the public eye, where he is exposed for many viewers as a pathetic (queer) monster.

On the other hand, Lermontov may be understood, and even be empathized with, as a tormented figure who, culturally encouraged to suppress, displace, and camouflage his gay desires, tries to find some means to express them within one of the few public spaces straight culture has left open for him, the high art of ballet. Besides, if Lermontov tries to control Page on- and offstage in an attempt to express himself queerly through her "feminine" artistry, he is also concerned that Page fulfill her potential as a great dancer, which is more than can be said for Craster, who is more concerned that Page stay close to him while he becomes a great composer, taking whatever second-rate dance engagements she can find in the vicinity of their apartment. To some extent, Lermontov and his male collaborators provide a space within which women's creative talents can be expressed—and their career goals achieved. One critic summarizes the complex and contradictory responses *The Red Shoes* elicits in connection to its gay impresario and his relationship to the diva as follows: "Boris comes across as the bad guy because he insists Vicky sacrifice Julian for dance. . . . But what Boris wants for Vicky is what is best for her, what she truly wants for herself. . . . The selfish Julian is the piece's villain—Boris would never have removed the shoes from Vicky's feet at the end." [48]

No, Lermontov would not have removed the red shoes, but let us not forget that it is Page who asks Craster to "take off the red shoes" as she lies dying, just as in the ballet the protagonist asks a clergyman to take off the shoes, and, in the original story, the young woman begs a woodsman to chop off her feet (he then makes her artificial feet and teaches her how to walk again). All these versions suggest that the straight women protagonists finally recognize their queerly influenced transgressive ways as bad. The key moment in this recognition is the women asking a straight man to relieve them of the symbol of their transgression. That is, to "castrate" them by taking the powerful queerly feminine phallus from them.

In the film narrative and in the ballet, the red shoes are reclaimed by the homosexual men who really own them, and both the ballet and the narrative go on with a spotlight where Page as the ballet's protagonist should be dancing. In one way, then, it all seems horribly clear now: the "feminine" power of the red shoes were just on loan to the women artists, and Page and the ballet's protagonist are stand-ins to express something else—after all, the show can go on without them. But publicly exposing the mechanisms behind the production of queer aesthete–and-diva art also forces Lermontov to "come out" in a way, which leads him to a near nervous breakdown onstage—while actor Walbrook was himself accused of being too "over the top" in his performance of this moment by certain critics and some of the Archers production team.⁴⁹ Martin Scorsese finds that Lermontov's "hysteria" during his final speech before a red curtain makes him like a "puppet": "Barking out a eulogy for his creation, he has become a character in one of his ballets—Dr. Coppelius."⁵⁰ The ballet and the film end simultaneously with the queer shoemaker offering the red slippers to the camera/audience.

In more than one context, Powell has said that *The Red Shoes* encouraged audiences to "die for art," after a period of being told to die for patriotic ideological reasons (in World War II, most recently).⁵¹ While Powell may have thought the film was being celebratory about this idea of defending and sacrificing oneself for the queer spaces of art, rather than dying for the patriarchy, *The Red Shoes* seems to end on a note of warning for certain audience members. Most immediately, the finale seems to reinforce the suggestion that straight women like Page are the ones being asked to sacrifice themselves, in one way or another, on the altar of queer high art—and Lermontov does refer to the ballet as his "religion," while seeing himself as one of this religion's celibate high priests. However, men like Lermontov, Powell, and Pressburger who are offstage, out in the theater, or behind the camera are also being proffered the red shoes by the ambiguously sad-sinister shoemaker. As their mirror image, the shoemaker appears to be asking gay and queerly positioned aesthetes who have some expressive investment in straight women to reconsider their position. Lermontov and company will most likely discover and build up another prima ballerina in another original ballet. From the spectacle of Lermontov's near breakdown in public, however, it is difficult to believe that he has not been chastened somehow.

All of *The Red Shoes*'s (melo)dramatic warnings to straight women and queer men about their relationships with each other, particularly where artistic creation and collaboration is concerned, should not keep us from remembering that these relationships usually are carried out within straight patriarchal cultural contexts. Consider this thought: Craster is the only major character whom the film suggests does not have a problem or a dilemma as an artist or in his personal life. It is only people like Page and Lermontov who have problems. Once Craster has broken away from Lermontov—and left him with the now tainted "The Red Shoes Ballet" score—he successfully moves on to both a solo composing career and a marriage. Craster is able to express grand heterosexual passions in his opera, "Dido and Aeneas," and to expect that Page will remain by his side during its composition. Within this privileged position, he feels he can pass judgment on the ambitions of his talented wife, on her "jealous" former impresario, and on their artistic relationship.

Craster—and most of the film audience—conveniently forget that the culture that allows straight, white, middle-class, heterosexual men so much expressive freedom, as well as the luxury of not having to choose between a personal or a professional life, is the very culture that encourages or forces Page and Lermontov to carry out their love-hate relationship with each other. While he might not mean for us to take "love" as "homosexuality" here, David Thomson, with reference to *The Red Shoes*, concisely sets down what living and working within homophobic and misogynistic cultures means for many gay artists and straight divas: "[T]he impresario urges her to perform at the cost of her life and the love he cannot even admit."[52] For me, the final lesson of *The Red Shoes* is that, for the gay aesthete–and-diva team, artistic creation within dominant culture can exact two interrelated costs. Since it often costs the aesthete the open expression of "the love that he cannot even admit," he frequently turns to the diva to speak for him through codes of the "feminine." Using the diva to express the homosexually feminine, however, often leads the gay aesthete to forget there is a straight woman artist there with desires of her own. If it doesn't often cost the diva her physical life, this situation can cost her something in terms of her creative life. Yes, she is the one who is actually performing, but with a largely queer male creative context frequently surrounding her, and with straight patriarchy surrounding that, she must often wonder "whose art is it anyway?" Page's final, desperate, beautifully executed ballet leap to her death might be her way of asking Lermontov, Craster, the Archers, and the rest of us divas and aesthetes in the audience, to carefully consider this loaded question.

NOTES

Thanks to grand diva Ben Gove and to the British Film Institute Library staff for all their help. Thanks also to Kevin Macdonald for permission to use and to quote from materials in the Emeric Pressburger Collection at the British Film Institute Library.

1   George Du Maurier, *Trilby* (London: Penguin, 1994). All subsequent quotations in the text are from this edition.

2   Edgar Rosenberg's *From Shylock to Svengali: Jewish Stereotypes in English Fiction* (Stanford: Stanford University Press, 1960) discusses how a number of Jewish characters in English literature from 1600 to the late nineteenth century were linked to sorcery and sexual "degeneracy." In his chapter on Svengali, Rosenberg reads the sexual threat Svengali poses as being connected to miscegenation: the "mating of the inferior racial type with the higher" (256). While I agree that Du Maurier encourages some miscegenation anxieties in relation to Trilby and Svengali, the novel also suggests that Svengali's sexual "degeneracy" is not limited to heterosexual forms.

3   Film cited in this section: *Sunrise* (1927, dir. F. W. Murnau); *Fantasia* (1940, dir. Ben Sharpstein); *A Song to Remember* (1945, dir. Charles Vidor); *Lust for Life* (1956, dir. Vincente Minnelli); *Specter of the Rose* (1946, dir. Ben Hecht); *Invitation to the Dance* (1954, dir. Gene Kelly); *Don Giovanni* (1979, dir. Joseph Losey); *Black Narcissus* (1946, dir. Michael Powell and Emeric Pressburger); *The Tales of Hoffmann* (1951, dir. Michael Powell and Emeric Pressburger); *The Red Shoes* (1948, dir. Michael Powell and Emeric Pressburger); *Oh . . . Rosalinda!!* (1955, dir. Michael Powell and Emeric Pressburger).

4   See, for example, Pressburger's comments in relation to *The Red Shoes* in Kevin Macdonald's *Emeric Pressburger: The Life and Death of a Screenwriter* (London: Faber and Faber, 1994): "I was always fascinated by the idea of actually creating and showing a genuine piece of art on the screen" (279).

5   Seymour Kleinberg, *Alienated Affections: Being Gay in America* (New York: St. Martin's Press, 1980), 39.

6   Michael Powell, *Million-Dollar Movie* (London: Walter Heinemann, 1992), 83.

7   Jack Cardiff, commentary track, *The Red Shoes* laserdisc, Criterion Collection, Voyager Company, 1995.

8   Ian Christie, *Arrows of Desire: The Films of Michael Powell and Emeric Pressburger* (London and Boston: Faber and Faber, 1994), 64. For an interesting take on the opera diva and her gay fans ("opera queens"), see Wayne Koestenbaum's *The Queen's Throat: Opera, Homosexuality and the Mystery of Desire* (New York: Vintage, 1993).

9   Besides Macdonald's *Emeric Pressburger* and Powell's *Million-Dollar Movie*, there is Powell's first volume of autobiography: Michael Powell, *A Life in Movies: An Autobiography* (New York: Alfred A. Knopf, 1987).

10   Powell, *A Life in Movies,* 649.

11   Wayne Koestenbaum, *Double Talk: The Erotics of Male Literary Collaboration* (New York: Routledge, 1989), 3.

12   Ibid., 5.

13   Powell, *A Life in Movies,* 304–6; Powell, *Million-Dollar Movie,* 153–54.

14   Macdonald, *Emeric Pressburger,* 155.

15   Powell, *A Life in Movies,* 306.

16   Ibid., 304.

17   Powell, *Million-Dollar Movie,* 153.

18   These salutations are taken from various letters and notes in the Emeric Pressburger Collection, British Film Institute Library, special collections.

19   Note from Powell to Pressburger, March 30, 1979, Emeric Pressburger Collection.

20   Mark Brennan, "Powell and Pressburger at the NFT," *Films and Filming* 373 (October 1985): 27.

21   From certain remarks and letters, it seems clear that Powell saw himself as the often difficult and ill-tempered "husband," and Pressburger as the long-suffering "wife." For example, writing to Pressburger to apologize for his delays while working on the novelization of *The Red Shoes*, Powell says, "I was very inconsiderate, you poor housewife! I'm sorry." "Housewife" is also a reference to Pressburger's penchant for cooking, something Powell enjoyed the results of many times. Later, in reference to the same novelization, Powell remarks, "Dearest Imre—I have discovered rather belatedly that I love you: your faults as well as your virtues. In any case your virtues outweigh your faults. Unlike mine, alas!" (Letters from Powell to Pressburger, July 1977 and January 21, 1978, Emeric Pressburger Collection).

22   Powell, *Million-Dollar Movie,* 420–21.

23   Powell, *A Life in Movies,* 616–17.

24   Ibid., 657.

25   Macdonald, *Emeric Pressburger,* 284.

26   Powell, *A Life in Movies,* 619, 625, 634–35, 659.

27 Letter from Powell to Pressburger, n.d. [1948?], Emeric Pressburger Collection.

28 Powell, *A Life in Movies,* 656.

29 Films in this section not previously cited: *The Life and Death of Colonel Blimp* (1943, dir. Michael Powell and Emeric Pressburger); *A Canterbury Tale* (1944, dir. Michael Powell and Emeric Pressburger); *Gone to Earth* (1950, dir. Michael Powell and Emeric Pressburger).

30 See, for example, John Russell Taylor, "Michael Powell: Myths and Superman," *Sight and Sound* 47, no. 4 (autumn 1978): 226–29, and David Thomson, "The Films of Michael Powell: A Romantic Sensibility," *American Film* 6, no. 2 (November 1980): 48–52.

31 Films mentioned: *The Spy in Black* (1939, dir. Michael Powell); *Contraband* (1940, dir. Michael Powell); *The Thief of Bagdad* (1940, dir. Michael Powell, Ludwig Berger, Tim Whelan).

32 Powell, *Million-Dollar Movie,* 280–81.

33 Ibid., 279.

34 Macdonald, *Emeric Pressburger,* 286.

35 Taylor, "Michael Powell," 228.

36 Andrew Newman, "Film Choice: *The Red Shoes,*" *Observer Magazine,* June 14, 1981: n.p. (in the cuttings files of the British Film Institute Film Library). See also Christie, *Arrows of Desire,* 67; Beth Genne, "The Red Shoes: Choices Between Life and Art," *The Thousand Eyes Magazine* 7 (February 1976): 8–9; and Karen Backstein, "A Second Look: *The Red Shoes,*" *Cineaste* 2, no. 4 (1994): 42–43.

37 Backstein, "A Second Look," 42.

38 Patricia Erens, "A Childhood at the Cinema: Latency Fantasies, the Family Romance, and Juvenile Spectatorship," *Wide Angle* 16, no. 4 (October 1994): 33.

39 Danny Peary, *Alternate Oscars* (New York: Delta, 1993), 97.

40 Macdonald, *Emeric Pressburger,* 293.

41 See, for example, Powell, *Million-Dollar Movie,* 280; Danny Peary, *Cult Movies* (New York: Dell, 1981), 287.

42 According to Richard Dyer, "heterosexuality in classical ballet is so . . . ethereally idealized that it becomes rather unreal. . . . In a camp appreciation, this means enjoying the spectacle of heterosexuality parading as glittering illusion" (qtd. in Backstein, "A Second Look," 42). For a similar discussion of gay men and ballet's heterosexual aspects see Kleinberg, *Alienated Affections,* 59–64, where he says things like, "The ballet then, represented an idealized image of a romantic relationship that gay men did not find alienating because it had no correspondence in reality. . . . [It was] a celebration of feminine grace that ignored conventional masculine posing and could be interpreted as a justification for accepting one's own effeminate yearnings" (63).

43 Emeric Pressburger and Keith Winter, "The Red Shoes," draft script, n.d., #S946, British Film Institute Library.

44 Emeric Pressburger and Keith Winter, "The Red Shoes," draft scripts, n.d., #S946 and #S4204, British Film Institute Library. For an example of Page's lashing back at Lermontov and company to her girlfriend: "Oh, it's so damned unfair! Haven't I behaved like an early Christian martyr ever since I got here? . . . Have I ever complained when they have been marching me up and down that stage like an old race-horse? Or made a single protest about any one of the idiotic things they make me do?" (n.p., script #S946).

45 Ian Christie, commentary track, *The Red Shoes* laserdisc.

46 Koestenbaum, *Double Talk,* 6–7.

47 Danny Peary, in *Cult Movies,* objects to the staging of "The Red Shoes Ballet" because he sees it as being more in the style of Powell-Pressburger-Archers than in the style of "ballet purist" Lermontov and his company (288). This is a very astute point, and it might be taken as more evidence of how Lermontov and his ballet company can be read as the onscreen representatives of Powell, Pressburger, and the Archers in this art film.

48 Peary, *Alternate Oscars,* 97.

49 Powell, *A Life in Movies,* 640.

50 Martin Scorsese, commentary track, *The Red Shoes* laserdisc.

51 See, for example, Powell, *A Life in Movies,* 653.

52 David Thomson, "The Pilgrim's Progress," *The Movie* 27 (1980): 532.

Lee Edelman

REAR WINDOW'S GLASSHOLE

"What one looks at is what cannot be seen."
—Jacques Lacan, *Four Fundamental Concepts of Psycho-Analysis* [1]

We have learned, and learned perhaps all too well, as a result of the feminist, psychoanalytically oriented theorization of narrative cinema, to observe the dynamics of power that inflect the masculinist desire to see. Learned perhaps all too well, I suggest, insofar as that lesson, despite itself, can bind still more tightly the ideological blindfold, which it enabled us first to perceive, around eyes so fully adapted to vision as a piercing of the dark that greater light could only thrust them into darkness more profound. It can work, that is, complicitously with the seductions of dominant cinema to keep us from seeing a no less significant—and no less significantly male-associated—desire to *escape* the phallic regime that casts its shadows both as and across the visual field it thus frames, the regime in which presence and absence define male and female antithetically. Indispensable, then, as that lesson has been, and crucial as its focus on the determining relation of sexual and visual logics remains, especially in the quasi-canonical form of Laura Mulvey's remarks about such narrative films as Hitchcock's *Vertigo* (1958), *Marnie* (1964), and *Rear Window* (1954) ("The power to subject another person to the will sadistically or to the gaze voyeuristically is turned on to the woman as the object of both"),[2] it can nonetheless conceal the intrinsic ambivalence—analogous to that by which Homi Bhabha identifies colonial discourse[3]—shaping a Symbolic order founded, however blindly, on the clear-cut distinctions that carve out the landscape of meaningful forms from the umbrage of the Imaginary by cutting back the Imaginary's ambiguating overgrowth through the power, always already seen, of the castratory saw. Seeing so very clearly the difference that sexual difference can make, the feminist insight can risk reproducing the razor-sharp optic of a Symbolic vision positioned on

the side of the social "reality" it offers as "naturally" self-evident, as unambiguously clear, so that anyone but the silliest goose knows how, with
a single gander, to distinguish—before they are carved and served up in a
blood-colored sauce of bing cherries deemed, axiomatically, good for them
both—the gander from the goose.

Suppose, however, one came at the question of vision from what a binary system construes as the "other" side; suppose the redoubtable cut
of castration that seems to star in each high-concept remake of cinematic
theory—while pocketing, like its own wily agent, a cut of the profits for
itself—were cut from the picture for a moment, became the face on the
cutting room floor, so that theory could do an about-face in order to focus
instead on what cannot be faced: the agency of a fundamental disturbance,
a fundamental disorientation of vision, that must seem to vanish, to be
foreclosed, for the visual field to open, through the transformation of asshole into glasshole, thus offering a window on the world by keeping the
behind behind the scenes, its aperture aptly concealed, as if, behind the
various fabrics with which it is carefully draped, a rear window threatened
to open—and open not onto an alternate view but onto an alternative to
the clear-cut logic of Symbolic viewing as such, and thus, onto an alternative to the Symbolic view of itself. The behind, in this, may be imagined,
like woman to man in the hackneyed expression, as behind, and thus as
other than, *whatever* may be seen, but it also may, as I hope we will see,
be seen *within* the scene, like and as the woman who, herself the fashionable mannequin wearing castration to best advantage, does a turn on
the stage that turns toward her and her costume of castration—no Chanel
more compellingly cut—an attention thereby channeled toward the cyno-
sure of difference (which is to say toward the Symbolic's kind of, if not its
kindest, cut) by cutting away from what cuts it only with those of another
kind: the anus as site of a cut, as D. A. Miller has taught us to see it, and,
equally important, of a rhythm of cutting as compelling as the music to
which the runway model with studied insouciance turns.[4]

It was Hitchcock himself, in discussing *Rear Window*, who drew attention to "the rhythm of the cutting," and he did so in the context of explaining his sense that this film was "purely visual," representing for him
"the purest form of cinema which is called montage."[5] Returning to this
theme while discussing *Rear Window* in his interview with François Truffaut, Hitchcock, donning, according to his habit on the various occasions
when he spoke of this film, the costume, too narrowly tapered perhaps, of

theoretician or historian of the cinema, evoked what appealed to him in mounting this project by alluding to V. I. Pudovkin's analyses of montage as the defining attribute of film's visually oriented language:

> It was the possibility of doing a purely cinematic film. You have an immobilized man looking out. That's one part of the film. The second part shows what he sees and the third part shows how he reacts. This is actually the purest expression of a cinematic idea. Pudovkin dealt with this, as you know. In one of his books on the art of montage, he describes an experiment by his teacher, Kuleshov. You see a close-up of the Russian actor Ivan Mosjoukine. This is immediately followed by a shot of a dead baby. Back to Mosjoukine again and you read compassion on his face. Then you take away the dead baby and you show a plate of soup, and now, when you go back to Mosjoukine, he looks hungry. Yet, in both cases, they used the same shot of the actor; his face was exactly the same.[6]

As this illustration of the art of the cut, adduced often by Hitchcock, suggests, montage as the face of the filmic aesthetic discovers its representative instance in the ability to fashion facial "meaning"—or even to fashion the face *as* "meaning"—as if its own privileged meaning as foundational act of cinematic creation gained ironic prestige through its metonymic link to the individuating front of the face even while subjecting the face itself (as window onto a spiritualized or metaphysical subjectivity) to a critique that reduces the subject's "meaning" to a wholly mechanical effect of a larger cultural apparatus.

Though montage may animate cinema, then, it does so, as Hitchcock's example implies, only by recognizing the will to meaning by which spectators animate faces that montage would implicitly frame as mortified, and thus as the properly specular counterparts to the luridly adduced "dead baby." The figure that embodies montage here may draw on the meaningfulness of the face, but insofar as it reduces the face to the figural, insofar as it performs what Paul de Man would call an act of "disfiguration" whereby the humanizing face becomes the mannequin on which various meanings à la mode can be draped, montage perversely confronts the front with a violent, though carefully veiled, affront that induces the blush of vitality at the moment of cutting it to the quick.[7] It gives birth, thereby, to the pathos that the face as front (and front not least for the machinery of Symbolic meaning-production) must be made to (re)produce when faced

with a failed transcendence of mortality through heterosexual reproduction: when faced, that is, with its implication in the wasted meaning—
the wasting of meaning—portended by the "dead baby." To the extent that
Hitchcock's commentary decks out *Rear Window* in the Russian equivalent
of Parisian haute couture, de-emphasizing its narrative focus on situations
of human distress to stress instead the distinctively cinematic material of
the film itself, flaunting the tailored cut of montage that flatters the face
in the very process of cutting it behind its back, this account of the film
skirts the issue of what gets cut from the discursive fabric by insisting on
configuring montage with the face (understood as a cut above the rest)
and thus as being cut out to serve as the template for filmic art in general
and for the art of *Rear Window* in particular.

Let us cut from this view of *Rear Window* as the very model of cinematic
cutting, to the moment in the film where Grace Kelly, modeling castration and its fetish at once, introduces herself to the audience as the model
Hitchcock blonde by turning on various lights in the apartment of her boyfriend, L. B. Jefferies (played by James Stewart and referred to throughout
the film as "Jeff"), and defining herself, while displaying the latest in expensive Parisian gowns, as, "Reading from top to bottom, Lisa . . . Carol . . .
Fremont." Fremont here may be the name that designates the bottom, but
that bottom can only be freely mounted—in the heterosexual fashion that,
like one of Grace Kelly's classic suits, seems always to be in style—insofar as it first gets turned around, becoming, in the term that the Wolf Man
bestowed on the female genitals, the "front bottom."[8] And if, as the advertisement used to say, it's what's up front that counts, then what's left
behind, what doesn't count, though it registers somatically the rhythm of
counting and psychically the earliest economy of accounts, is demeaned,
which is to say, emptied of meaning except for its residual meaning as
waste and its consequent association with that very emptying or wasting
of meaning as such. The asshole, in other words, means nothing more than
the nothingness it materializes. Valued at less than zero, it, like the zero's
bounded hole, is consigned to signifying nothing and thus to framing the
system of values that refuses to grant it a substantive place. "Fremont," at
bottom, and even *as* bottom, invokes, by displacing, this cut: the cut that
rhythmically articulates the shape of our cinematic viewing, as if her name
were always, properly, Lisa Fre/montage. For just as montage can favor
the face while undercutting the prospect of a "meaning" that might inhere
in the face itself, Lisa, wearing the cut of montage like a dress so tight it

conforms to her skin as the site of another frontal cut, the cut of sexual difference that makes her a summa of all the film's women—as if her (w)hole were the sum of the female parts that get sandwiched, like soup or dead babies, between shots of her boyfriend's attentive glance—Lisa, precisely by displaying it up front, effectively takes the sting out of the otherwise mortifying cut of the end. Doing a turn that exhibits herself no less than her costly and eye-catching gown, Lisa simultaneously turns or inverts the mountable bottom as well, refiguring the anal opening as the promise of the genital cut that may put her under the label of castration's enduring designs but only to the extent that castration's signature, its unmistakable embroidery of the front, covers over, by turning or troping upon, the bottom Miss Fremont's name names (fig. 1).

The mode of montage Lisa models reinterprets the cut, in this way, as suture—as the defining instance of filmic as also of visual productivity more generally—insofar as its castratory slice gets refigured as cinematic splice, thus offering, like a pornographic loop, an endless return to the primal scene of cinema itself. And if the infantile theory of anal birth, which informs the primal scene's primal scene in Freud's account of the Wolf Man's case history, suggests that the signifying capacity of the female genitalia—their capacity to figure, as Courbet would have it, *L'Origine du monde*—derives in part from a substitutive relation to the anus they double and displace, then this vital substitution of suture for cut, of reproduction for meaningless waste, invariably repeats the imperative through which the Symbolic reproduces itself, cutting itself off from the mess and obscurity from out of which it emerges by taking as its defining characteristic the clear-cut definition of sexed human characters invested with sexual identities through the logic, redemptive because also reproductive, of the castratory cut.[9] Evoking just such a logic in his comments on *Rear Window,* Hitchcock defines, through apposition, the moment when "film was originally invented" as the moment "when cutting was invented." But the cinematic cut attains to this foundational status in Hitchcock's account only insofar as it undergoes and occasions a seminal transformation, becoming *l'origine du monde du cinéma* through the coupling or joining of frame to frame it allows to take place around it—through the labor, that is, in which Hitchcock insists the true art of the cinema resides: the "piecing together of the montage which makes what I call a pure film."[10]

"Pure film," "the purely visual," the "purest form of cinema": these phrases proliferate to such an extent as Hitchcock describes *Rear Window* that one is hardly inclined to demur when the director boasts—or is it confesses?—in explaining his particular fondness for this film, "I'm a purist as far as cinema is concerned."[11] With so much insistence on purity we might be tempted, like L. B. Jefferies watching the salesman across the way, to speculate, somewhat suspiciously, about just what is being cleaned up: what threat of impurity, in other words, is Hitchcock hoping to conceal by imagining a film made "pure"—and thus purged of difference or division—by virtue of the cut of division itself that would return us, in Hitchcock's representation, to the cinematic *status nascendi,* the moment, as he tellingly puts it, when "film was originally invented." In order to answer these questions let us note that *Rear Window* situates in Lars Thorwald's bathroom its own diegetic cleanup (fig. 2), and while this, on the level of narrative, permits us to catch him in the act of washing away the telltale signs by which others might see toward what end he made use of his saw, what is seen as his concealment of the scene of a crime (the cutting up of a woman's body) is incorporated into the filmic text, like the postcard that Thorwald has had sent to his apartment to look as if it came from his wife, expressly to *be* seen and thereby to screen another cut, the structural impropriety (or even, indeed, the *crime*) of which finds its proper site only out of sight in the behind that stands behind the narrative logic—or more precisely, the narrative alibi—used to justify Hitchcock's inclusion of the bathroom scene in the film.

Or, rather than standing behind that scene, which might give us its proper site, should I say that in the bathroom alone it might find its proper seat, or, at any rate, might do so were its seat not taken already, and not, need I add, by Miss Fremont, however much that last of her three names bears the refigured mark of the bottom and however much she may bear a resemblance to Goldilocks on top? No, watching the cleaning of the bathroom through the rear window from which, near the end of the film, he is destined to be thrown, it is Jefferies himself who is seated on the seat not seen in Thorwald's bathroom—the toilet seat that is often, as Freud's disciple, Karl Abraham, reminds us, "denoted as the 'throne.'"[12] Though made to testify diegetically to his temporary disability, the wheelchair in which Jefferies is seated, after all, for virtually the whole of the film, affords him the ability, precisely by virtue of his remaining seated in it, to cover up *his* hole—but to cover it up in a mode that alludes to the single position in which it is proper for that hole to be *uncovered,* the single position in which, therefore, its link to an erotic economy of pleasure and power can be *recovered* by him for whom, as subject of the Symbolic, the world as social organization appears through the slash of the wand-like Lacanian bar at the moment he learns to see through the eyes of the either/or dispensation that conjures heterosexualized genitality (fig. 3).

But the world thus born through the institution of an optic of clearcut distinctions, the world of Symbolic vision that originates, like film according to Hitchcock, with the invention of a cut, cannot see—since it cannot *afford* to see—that its own economy is propped up on the repudiated pulsions of the anus, from out of which the governing logic of economy itself emerges to the syncopated rhythms of withholding and producing, rhythms that make the anus not only, as Miller has memorably put it, "what remains and reminds of a cut,"[13] but also the common denominator of such libidinal cuts or divisions as those between auto- and allo-erotism, or between preserving and destroying the object. The eros distinctive of the anus holds these forces in a violent tension that cuts, as it were, both ways: that marks, on the one hand, what will later emerge as the consequential opposition between them, and that preserves, on the other, the final occasion of their non-differentiation. Confounding, in this, the difference whereby sameness and difference are distinguished, while founding the sadistic order of identity as segmentation and division, the anus may only in fantasy be seen as the hole from which we are born, but it designates, in a larger sense, the hole from which—around which, against which—Symbolic reality takes shape, establishing the empire of genital difference precisely in order to fill it.

Thus if Freud identified the question of origins with the riddle of the sphinx, then perhaps we should note that *sphinx* itself is etymologically cognate with *sphincter*. Derived from the Greek *sphingein,* "to hold tight," the sphinx, like the sphincter, gets read, after Oedipus, as holding men's lives in a fatal grip unless and until they succeed in solving, by becoming the solution themselves, the developmental riddle whose answer, *mirabile dictu,* is "man." Although Oedipus, then, like L. B. Jefferies, may have suffered a wound to the leg, the cultural order for which his name stands can only displace by means of that figure what it otherwise disavows: the narcissistic wound that it locates, and secretly cherishes, in its seat. It is *that* wound, and not his rather more ostentatiously wounded limb, that keeps Jeff—for all his vaunted eagerness to regain his lost mobility—so firmly in his chair, even as it was, I want to insist, what put him there in the first place.

4

Consider the picture of the auto race taken by Jefferies just seconds
before the sheared-off wheel of an overturned vehicle felled him (fig. 4).
Miran Božovič construes its depiction of the car's wheel suspended so omi-
nously mid-air as a visual blot analogous to that of the distorted skull float-
ing obliquely in the foreground of Holbein's painting, *The Ambassadors,* an
anamorphotic image famously characterized by Lacan as visualizing "the
subject as annihilated," insofar as it tauntingly confronts us with "the im-
aged embodiment of . . . castration."[14] Provocative as such a reading may
be, it propels us once more to enter the race that the phallus wins even by
losing, a race that is never close enough to call for the scrutiny of a photo
finish. Were we, however, to scrutinize this photo more closely before we
were finished, we might observe, in the first place, that the wheel, by which
Jefferies, behind the camera's shutter, is shown as about to be struck, returns in the machinery and the signifier both of the wheelchair to which his
bottom will be, thereafter, all but stuck. What deprives him of a leg to stand
on, effectively sweeping him off his feet, reappears substitutively in the
visual plane as the figure of his seat. Or, to put this somewhat differently,
if the photograph captures the image of what knocked Jefferies on his ass,

then the wheel, which the picture renders as nothing so much as a sort of hole, is the sort of hole to be located precisely in Jefferies's ass itself.[15] And once he has been laid flat by the force, here literally shattering, of that hole, Jeff, as a heterosexually identified male, might seem to have good reason to want to sit tight and keep it covered, especially since on the few occasions when we see him leave his chair, he quickly ends up face down on the day-bed with someone either manipulating or assaulting his body from behind.

The chair he sits on like a burnished throne thus gives him a sense, how-ever illusory, of being on top of things, of holding an absolute sovereignty over himself and his desires, even as it offers a persistent reminder of the posture through which the desire on which he most emphatically wants to sit tends to find itself no longer suppressed but rather, in privy-like privacy, enthroned. Nor is the visual pun of the wheelchair limited to the latitude of the latrine; even before introducing herself, so memorably, from top to bottom, from the moment she first appears in the form of a shadow falling across Jeff's body, to register, like the photographic negative of the blonde whose image anticipates hers, the Symbolic order's self-constituting decree of sexual differentiation, Lisa Fremont, as she looms above Jefferies, dem-onstrates one other all-important social truth: that if it is as the bottom suc-cessfully turned round, as the "front bottom," that she manages to top him, then it is also as a bottom himself that he requires so emphatically to be topped. Jeff, as a straight male subject, stands—or sits—in need of what the film, one might almost say "cheekily," labels "Fremont": the Symbolic pro-duction of woman as bottom who will top him in the name of love so that she can embody the bottom he no more dares to have than to be. Hence the salacious import of her comment, read as if its double entendre bespoke a wholly *genital* bravado, when she surprises Jeff by displaying her compact but capacious Mark Cross overnight case: "I'll bet *yours* isn't this small" (fig. 5). Tania Modleski can rightly construe this as "echoing the Freudian notion of male and female sexuality, but reversing their values since it takes the latter as the standard,"[16] but the witticism thus condensed in the case as a figure for sexual difference unpacks that difference as a figure itself—a figure for the anxious, aggressive, resistance of the hetero-genitalized male to the baggage of an older desire he can posit as always already behind him precisely insofar as he deposits it in, and as, the woman's front.

But the hole that is glimpsed in the photograph marks the return, the inescapability, of this anal libidinal cathexis through the repudiation of which the subject of genital law comes into being: a return, traumatic and

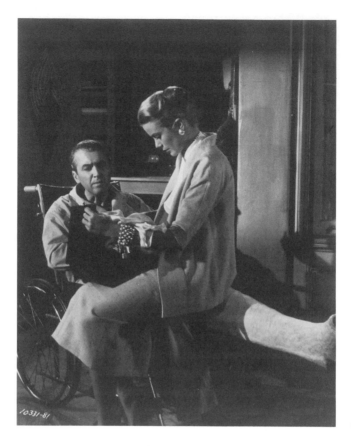

5

desired at once—traumatic *because* desired—articulating a deep-seated ambivalence toward the logic of clear-cut distinctions, of genital presence or absence, established only by appropriating, though necessarily for other ends, the articulating cut first felt, in its complex rhythms, at the "other" end. Shattering his camera and his leg at once, denying him proper standing as a subject by challenging his access to the either/or of visual understanding, the wheel as hole, as asshole, that Jefferies manages to capture on film, functions less as the blinding obverse of his camera's shuttered hole, less as the negative image of the Symbolic's privileged ocular orifice, than as that which compels a seeing and an unseeing in the eye, that which strives to locate, within the space of the visual field, an image of the pulsions, the fluctuations, of the scopic drive: those rhythms in the grip of which vision brusquely wheels round on itself, turning inside out as if to apprehend its

ruptures, and thus to come upon what we might see as the visual unconscious, both structuring and inhabiting the frame of vision itself.

And what film, however celebrated for its consciousness of the visual,
for its self-reflexive focus on spectatorial perception, seems more intent on
lapsing into the logic of the unconscious? Each of the protracted fade-outs
that rhythmically punctuate the film has the effect, at times disorienting,
of seeming to puncture it as well, thus piercing it and us with the force of
the punctum that Roland Barthes defined as "this wound, this prick, this
mark made by a pointed instrument" and also as a "sting, speck, cut, little
hole."[17] These holes of blackness, these black holes in the image-flow of
cinema, are more than conventional indices by which to register lapses of
time; they signify, and anticipate, lapses of another sort altogether insofar
as they represent moments where vision withdraws into itself, refusing the
distance, the separation, that allows it to take in objects so as to take in,
instead, the articulating cut from which seeing as such proceeds. Like the
visual image of the suspended wheel, *Rear Window*'s fade-outs, so often
linked to occasions when Jefferies, having fallen asleep, has given himself over to the unconscious, articulate cinema's primal cut—the enabling
fissure that holds us tight with the strength of a sphincteral grip—before
its redemption through marriage to the order of visual productivity in the
form of continuity editing and the hetero-genetic castration fetish: that is
to say, in the form of what I call Lisa Fre/montage.

And indeed, to return to the photo that offers a glimpse of the film's
primal scene, can we fail to note that the wheel as hole—as asshole, as rupture, as fade-out, as cut—also appears in the form, diegetically central to
the film, of a ring? If on the one hand—Lisa Fremont's perhaps, or possibly
Mrs. Thorwald's—the ring portends the Symbolic marriage of cut to the
filmic montage, the regenerative piecing together of parts that gives birth
to the cinema as a whole, then on the other hand, or even, to dispense with
false binarisms, on the same, the ring, to the contrary, must be understood
as nothing of the sort. Indeed, it might be said to be, instead, a sort of
nothing: the image, as such, of the anal hole, and therefore of de-meaning,
from out of the rhythmic pulsions of which cinematic meaning is born only
so as to preserve and return to the originary moment, the limit point of
visual meaning and also its punctum: the cut. After all, as Hitchcock himself observed, "the MacGuffin in this story is . . . the wedding ring" and the
definition of a MacGuffin, as he put it elsewhere, "is . . . nothing at all."[18]

Ernest Jones, the student of Freud's well known for his efforts to redress what he saw as the phallocentric tendency of psychoanalysis, declared in his study of symbolism—the same study in which he observed with surprise that "there are probably more symbols of the male organ itself than all other symbols put together"—that a wedding ring, though "an emblem of marriage, . . . is not a symbol of it"; instead, he argued, such rings "unconsciously are symbols of the female organ."[19] And so once more into the breach, as it were, of the genital either/or that urges us, like L. B. Jefferies, toward a narrative end that would let us see Lisa as bearing on her body, if not wearing on her hand, the ring that holds open the promised bliss of night after night of . . . montage. And see her he does in one of the film's most celebrated moments as Lisa, having stolen into Thorwald's apartment to find and steal the ring that his wife would be wearing were she still alive, tries concocting, for Thorwald and the police at once, a story to explain what she's doing there, while gesturing across the courtyard to Jeff, who watches through his telephoto lens, to show him that she has found the ring and has slipped it onto her finger. Everything here conspires to direct our attention to the ring—including most noticeably, Lisa's finger pointing toward it insistently—in this passage that seems intent on teaching us how and what to see (fig. 6). And so, of course, we see the ring as the band that binds the resolution of our doubts about Mrs. Thorwald's fate—we have at last a sort of proof that her husband has done away with her—to the romantic plot that construes the ring as the token of Lisa's desire; and in each case the ring as symbol leads us conveniently back, with Ernest Jones, to woman as site of castration, to woman as bearer of the cut.

But in leading us back, the ring as sexual symbol takes us up front and, coyly lowering a pink and blue shift that softens, like gauze on a camera's lens, the hard-core conjugal rights it confers, leaves the back behind: leaving behind, in the process, the fact that Lisa's finger, as it points to the ring, points also to *her* behind, allowing us to recall what Lacan points out in his refutation of Ernest Jones: "If something in nature is designed to suggest certain properties of a ring to us, it is restricted to what language has dedicated the term *anus* to, . . . and which in their modesty ancient dictionaries designated as the ring that can be found behind."[20] It is just such a ring that Hitchcock shows us in this moment that vividly renders what putting your ass on the line really means; significantly, however, the ass on the line in this shot is less Lisa's than Jeff's. For this image aligns the theatricalized, because genitalized, insistence on the visibility of the ring,

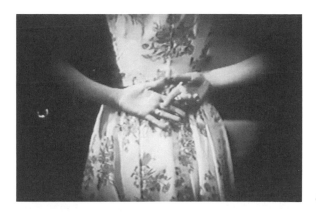

6

7

8

which both figures and screens Lisa's ass, with the secondary visibility of her ass itself, which both figures and displaces his. Hence the movement of the camera—Hitchcock's and, within the cinematic narrative, Jeff's—from Lisa, gesturing toward the ring behind, to Thorwald, catching sight of this gesture and discovering, in the process, precisely what, if not who, must ultimately be behind it (fig. 7). The glance of recognition with which Thorwald then turns his own gaze from Lisa, continuing to point so theatrically behind her back, to the camera, at which, with an icy gaze, he finally stares full-front, puts Jefferies himself in the place of what Lisa, unwittingly, has pointed out (fig. 8). And if, in the process, her ass substitutively doubles for his eye, then it is also fair to note that his eye, at least as evoked metonymically by the diegetic mark of his camera's lens, participates in the visual logic that would return us to the ass. Hitchcock, after all, in offering this rebus of the ring that is found behind, frames the image of that ring in *another* ring, one meant to signify the lens through which Jefferies views this entire scene, as if, with this framing, Hitchcock gives us to see, in the glasshole of every window, of every photographic lens, the articulating mark of the asshole made visible not as the other of vision but as the determining otherness within it—an otherness that, once made visible, threatens to make us thereafter see double, and thus, by disturbing the either/or logic of a castratory clarity, has the additional effect, as Hitchcock suggests, of making us also see red.

I refer with this to the climactic sequence where Jefferies, trapped in his wheelchair as Thorwald approaches to attack, desperately tries to blind him with his photographic flash. In a series of subjective shots meant to simulate Thorwald's dazzled vision as the bursts of light from the strobe-like bulbs disorient him temporarily, Hitchcock again presents the viewer with a graphic inscription of a hole: a red hole that thoroughly saturates and eclipses the image of Jefferies himself, radiating outward from his body until it bleeds across the whole screen (fig. 9). As in *Marnie,* where Hitchcock strategically deploys a similar effect, this overdetermination of the visual field announces a return of the repressed, which is always, as we have to bear in mind, the return of a repressed *desire:* the desire, so intensely rendered here, both of and for a hole. Condensing the anal erotism that structures the rhythm of the film, this sequence both thematizes and performs a disruption of narrative momentum to offer instead a glimpse of a purely rhythmic repetition: the flash of light, the blinding hole—or is

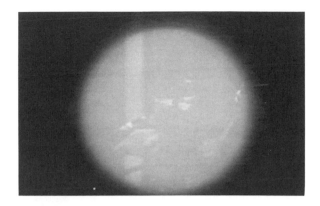

9

10

it the hole revealing a blindness intrinsic to sight itself?—and then again the flash, the hole, and then again the same.

"What do you want of me?" Thorwald had asked when he first confronted Jefferies, and the flash of these bulbs, perverse at best as an instrument of defense, strikingly articulates the ambivalence of a desire that wants both to destroy and preserve—to dazzle Thorwald in order to stop him, to arrest his imminent threat, but also and at once to prolong that threat, to dilate and retain it through a gesture that repeatedly enacts, symptomatically, the process of trying to capture it on film. Retarding, but also protracting, the forward thrust of Thorwald's advance, Jeff uses his camera's attachment as if to mimic the way Hitchcock's camera slowed down, in order luxuriously to extend, the kiss Lisa pressed on Jeff's lips when she, like Thorwald near the end of *Rear Window*, first came into

Jeff's apartment. Discussing that kiss with Hitchcock, Truffaut elicited, as he often did, one of the director's misleading, and for that reason telling, representations of his work:

> F.T.: Both in *Rear Window* and *To Catch a Thief* the kiss is a process shot. Not the kiss itself, but the approach to the faces is jerky, as if you had double-printed that frame in the cutting room.
> A.H.: Not at all. These are pulsations that I get by shaking the camera by hand or dollying backward and forward, or sometimes by doing both.[21]

Though the kiss, despite the director's denial, is depicted, as Anthony Mazella puts it, "in a sequence of repeated frames that just misses being slow motion,"[22] though it is deliberately drawn out, in other words, by means of repetition, Hitchcock's misrepresentation of this effect as a result of the camera's own movement, which he refers to as its "pulsations," speaks to the way it anticipates the rhythmic pulsations of the flashing red hole that serve to delay the moment at which Thorwald gets his hands on Jeff at last.

Caught, like Jefferies, between experiencing this moment as a desired end in itself and the equally pressing—if contradictory—desire to put an end to it once and for all; caught, that is, between the pleasure principle, as embodied in the repetition of the visual pattern whereby Hitchcock finds still another way to show his—or at least cinema's—hole, and the reality principle, which constrains him to translate repetition into narrative development and the resolution of the plot, this sequence performs the anal compulsion at the bottom of Hitchcockian suspense. At the same time, moreover, it allegorizes the cultural imperative responsible for opening our eyes to the whole world of Symbolic signification by closing them—like Jefferies, who covers his eyes before setting off each flash of light—to the other hole that returns in this scene as the image of a stunning illumination, one capable of blinding us to social "reality" by radically severing vision from objects in the world outside the self. To the extent that Hitchcock can end this sequence only by adducing—here, as elsewhere—an image that literalizes the figure of suspense, a dangling body trying to resist the gravitational pull of the void, he also literalizes the ambivalent tensions inherent in an anal erotism defined by its intermittent cadences of holding on and letting go. And *Rear Window* explicitly frames this tension in excremental terms when Stella, the insurance company nurse so bracingly played by Thelma

Ritter, recalls how she predicted the stock market crash of 1929 while working for "a director of General Motors" whose putative "kidney ailment" she correctly diagnosed as a case of "nerves"; as she summarizes her analytic reasoning for a blatantly skeptical Jeff: "When General Motors has to go to the bathroom ten times a day, the whole country's ready to let go."

The relief that comes from letting go, however, for the cinematic no less than for the corporate "director," retains its defining association with anxiety or "nerves." For the satisfaction that puts an end to tension occasions a tension of its own insofar as it offers the prospect of an end to the cycles of tension and release. To let go, to give in to the hole's desire, to come face-to-face with the pleasure of expulsion connected with the hole in the end is also to confront that hole *as* end: to experience, as a social subject, what Freud—and Leo Bersani following Freud—would define as "primary masochism," an energy directed toward the destruction or fall of the ego as internalized object, as an organization or structure erected in obedience to the law.[23] It is thus to experience, again *as a subject,* the same sort of fall and blinding crash that the stock market suffered in 1929 and that Jefferies suffers on the two occasions that leave him with broken legs: the fall that betokens the fate of all those unable to evade the sphincteral grip, like the Sphinx's iron clutch, by planting themselves firmly on their own two legs and defining themselves as men. Like the wheel in Jefferies's photograph, or the ring as which it later appears, the blinding image of this blood-red hole gives visible form to the formlessness of the anal cut or opening from out of which the Symbolic order of visual relations emerges as the law of form as such—the law informing the phallus that, paradoxically, effects that law's formation by releasing the hold of the anus, thereby releasing *us* from its hold, through the gesture by means of which the phallus casts castration as its double (displacing, and also refiguring, the prior displacement of the anus), and formalizes, in consequence, our standing as cultural subjects through the dictate that locates the seat of what only now becomes human identity in a genital determination of sex that depends on a logic both binary and clear-cut.

As a representative instance of dominant cinema's narrative development, *Rear Window*'s self-reflexive meditation on questions of spectatorship and cinema reflects the insatiable necessity of allegorizing this constitution of the social self. Hitchcock, after all, having linked *Rear Window,* as the "purest form of cinema," to the moment when "film was originally invented, when cutting was invented," noted that, "for *Rear Window* each cut was written ahead of time." "It's like scoring music," he added, and then, after making this comparison, went on to express his dissatisfaction with the music scored by the film's composer for the composer within the film whose efforts to complete a song are entwined with the development of the plot: "I was a little disappointed at the lack of a structure in the title song. I had a motion-picture songwriter when I should have chosen a popular songwriter. I was rather hoping to use the genesis, just the idea of a song which would then gradually grow and grow until it was used by a full orchestra. But I don't think that came out as fully as I would have liked it to have done."[24] Gesturing toward the self-conscious metaphorization of the director's own rhythm of cutting while advertising *Rear Window*'s structural fascination with questions of development and birth, this account of an unsatisfactorily realized figure for the "genesis" of a cultural artifact (one that failed to "c[o]me out" as "fully" as Hitchcock "would have liked") specifies "lack of structure" as the threat to its fully achieved identity. That lack, that trace of formlessness, marks a rupture in its organization, an impurity bespeaking its failure to emerge completely from the hole or void against which cinema, like the Symbolic order, or the voice of God in Genesis, decrees that there be light.[25]

However insistently his discourse of purity denies his film's implication in the de-forming impurity of such a hole, Hitchcock's vision of visual relations is framed throughout *Rear Window* by his haunting awareness of the anal hole as the lining of vision itself, as the cut that, inverted and turned inside out, takes form as the phallic fiat whereby the whole of Symbolic reality unimpeachably appears. If the pulsating image of the blood-red hole, combined with the shot/reverse shot montage that sutures it into the narrative of Jeff confronting Thorwald face-to-face, would make it the figure, flamboyant and flaming, of the cinematic glasshole, the cut or canal through which the medium is born with the splicing of pieces of celluloid, then we should note as well that the stain of that hole as it spreads across the screen alludes to the holes that machines of projection can burn through those celluloid strips, dissolving the image as scopic object and reinstating the primal cut in a way that interimplicates production and aggression, glasshole and asshole, beginning and end. As if refuting Hitchcock's fantasy of cinematic purity, this return of the hole to consume the visual images it invariably frames testifies anew to the doubleness of vision, to the contradictions of desire, by which an anal libido compulsively burns its way through the Symbolic screen.

The hole as burn alludes as well to an earlier moment in the film when Jefferies discerns the presence of Thorwald, in the shadowy depths of his apartment, through nothing more than the glowing embers of his burning cigarette, reducing *him* thereby to the status of a pulsing red hole in the dark (fig. 10); and the flickering glow of those embers took point from the prior reference to the punishment historically imposed on peeping toms: "They used to put out their eyes," Stella bluntly warned Jefferies, "with a red hot poker." Searing its way through *Rear Window*, the hole envisioned by the film as the necessary condition of articulated vision pointedly refuses to differentiate between the punctum and the poker, between the cut or mark of a pointed instrument and that instrument itself. For the film understands that the phallic poker, construed by Stella as the *cause* of blindness, can appear in our field of vision only as the *effect* of a prior blindness—can only be seen, that is, insofar as the viewer has been blinded already by the Symbolic's naturalized visual regime, which impels us not to notice the hole by which vision must always be framed.

Rear Window opens onto this question of what stands behind the Symbolic order by taking us back to the anal compulsion that gives birth, paradoxically, to Symbolic meaning through the narrative of sexual difference. Just as Thorwald, having murdered his wife, is compelled to get rid of the waste, the material surplus, to which, through his labor in the bathroom, he manages to reduce her, so Jefferies would seem, contrarily, compelled to *find* the woman's body, and hence, in terms of the ideological imperative dominating the film, to find the body of woman as such in obedience to the Symbolic contract that demands an account of his relation to it. Though seemingly antithetical, these enterprises share a determination to articulate woman together with the cut that demonstrates the primacy of phallic law, construing it as the requisite basis for any meaningful articulation. Both aim to find the cut in the woman, or to find the woman cut, in order to cast out, project, or excrete the cut that threatens to rupture the Symbolic's signifying structure from within, the cut that marks the place of drives resistant to signification. Thorwald's anal problematic, his concern with eliminating the residue of his activity in the bathroom, recapitulates that of the Symbolic in its foundational surrender of being for meaning. For a trace of the Real excluded from meaning, a surplus produced as the difference from meaning precisely by virtue of the Symbolic's organization as the order of meaning as such, remains holed up within the Symbolic in the figural form of the hole it attempts to expel through a gesture that reverses—and, in the process of reversing, unwittingly exposes—the anxiogenic imagining of the Symbolic's own emergence from out of that very hole. Like Thorwald dealing with the remains of his wife, the Symbolic would eliminate that hole in meaning by scattering or distributing it everywhere, transvaluing its threat of rupture into the promise of reproduction and making it thereby the ground from out of which meaning, like the flowers in Thorwald's garden, can seem, as if naturally, to bloom. Not a symbol then, but the Symbolic locus of what simultaneously enables and eludes the cultural work of symbolization, that hole, configured on the body of woman to assure, albeit dialectically, the phallic order of form, both refers to and refigures the anus as the site from which, at least fantasmatically, the Symbolic regime is born; and therefore, *pace* Ernest Jones, one could plausibly argue that it is less the phallus than the anus to which the vast preponderance of human symbols allude, since the phallus itself, as symbol for Jones and as foundational signifier of the Symbolic as signifying system for Lacan, remains determined by the continuous pressure, if only retroactively posited, of an anal formlessness from which, by means of inverting it, of turning it inside out so as to erect it as phallic form, the phallus, in the endless performativity of the various occasions to which it rises, labors—and why resist the temptation to add the adverb *manfully?*—once and for all to escape.

Seated before his rear window, then, on the perch of his mobile throne, attending to the goings-on in the buildings that ring, so to speak, his courtyard, Jefferies, emblematic in this of Hitchcockian cinema as a whole, compulsively courts being pricked by the hole that gives birth to the prick itself as the privileged signifier destined to cut the ambivalent tensions of anality, to resolve them into the Symbolic's genital, and heterosexualizing, either/or. To close one's eyes to the object-refusing insistence of that hole, to focus, instead, with some versions of feminism, on a visual logic imagined as wholly and unproblematically phallic, or to search, like Ernest Jones, for a feminist alternative to the phallus in a genital game for which the phallus continues to function, however invisibly, as referee, must leave a gaping hole in the discourses of cinema, sexuality, and vision: the hole of an originary cut that the cut of castration, despite its repeated efforts to cut it from the picture, must, perversely, by means of that very cutting, always—if blindly—preserve. As the mise-en-scène of this most famous filmic anatomy of the visual suggests, all vision takes place *through* the rear window it proposes to take the place *of*—a window across which, as at the film's conclusion, a blind, like those of matchstick favored by Jefferies, may be lowered, but only to make more visible the subject's fundamental double b(l)ind: to see *is* not to see, and even to catch a glimpse of the glass-hole by means of which seeing transpires is to risk igniting, as if through use of another sort of matchstick, the flame that prepares the red hot poker to blind the too-eager eye[26] and thus to transform the organ of vision into the gaping hole made to figure at once the before and beyond of desire, the hole ordained by Symbolic law to remain behind the seen precisely because, like the gaze of the Other, it will never see us in turn. Exposing the ambivalence to which the Symbolic's regime of the clear-cut would put an end, *Rear Window* frames its vision of desire as a desire for an end of vision, which is also, in the hetero-genitalizing logic *Rear Window* both deploys and displays, to be understood as the phallic order's endless, and endlessly disavowed, desire for what it can only ever see as the end *tout court*.

NOTES

1   Jacques Lacan, "The Partial Drive and Its Circuit," in *The Four Fundamental Concepts of Psycho-Analysis,* ed. Jacques-Alain Miller, trans. Alan Sheridan (New York: Norton, 1981), 182.

2   Laura Mulvey, "Visual Pleasure and Narrative Cinema," in *The Sexual Subject: A Screen Reader in Sexuality,* ed. *Screen* (New York: Routledge, 1992), 30–31.

3   "Although the 'authority' of colonial discourse depends crucially on its location in narcissism and the Imaginary, my concept of stereotype-as-suture is a recognition of the *ambivalence* of that authority and those orders of identification. The role of fetishistic identification, in the construction of discriminatory knowledges that depend on the 'presence of difference,' is to provide a process of splitting and multiple/contradictory belief at the point of enunciation and subjectification" (Homi Bhabha, "The Other Question: The Stereotype and Colonial Discourse," in *The Sexual Subject: A Screen Reader in Sexuality,* ed. *Screen* [New York: Routledge, 1992], 326).

4   See D. A. Miller, "Anal *Rope,*" in *Inside/Out: Lesbian Theories, Gay Theories,* ed. Diana Fuss (New York: Routledge, 1991), 119–41. I wish to acknowledge with gratitude the importance of Miller's enabling work to my thinking throughout this essay.

5   Alfred Hitchcock, *Rear Window,* reprinted in Albert LaValley, *Focus on Hitchcock* (Englewood Cliffs, N.J.: Prentice-Hall, 1972), 42; 40; 40.

6   François Truffaut, *Hitchcock,* rev. ed. (New York: Simon and Schuster, 1985), 214–16.

7   For a fuller discussion of de Manian disfiguration in the context of narrative

cinema's implicit sexual politics, see "Imagining the Homosexual: *Laura* and the Other Face of Gender," in my volume *Homographesis: Essays in Gay Literary and Cultural Theory* (New York: Routledge, 1994), 192–241.

8   Sigmund Freud, *From the History of an Infantile Neurosis* (1918), in *The Standard Edition of the Complete Psychological Works of Sigmund Freud,* ed. James Strachey (London: Hogarth Press, 1955), 17:25. I offer a fuller reading of the Wolf Man's case history, and the fantasy of the "front bottom," in "Seeing Things: Representation, the Scene of Surveillance, and the Spectacle of Gay Male Sex," included in *Homographesis,* 173–91.

9   For a close analysis of the relations between anal and genital logics in Hitchcock's films, see my essay, "Piss Elegant: Freud, Hitchcock, and the Micturating Penis," *GLQ: A Journal of Lesbian and Gay Studies* 2, nos. 1–2 (1995): 149–77.

10   Hitchcock, *"Rear Window,"* 40; 40; 41.

11   Ibid., 40.

12   Karl Abraham, "The Anal Character," in *Selected Papers on Psycho-Analysis,* trans. Douglas Bryan and Alix Strachey (New York: Brunner/Mazel, 1927), 375.

13   Miller, "Anal *Rope,"* 134.

14   Miran Božovič, "The Man Behind His Own Retina," in *Everything You Always Wanted to Know About Lacan (But Were Afraid to Ask Hitchcock),* ed. Slavoj Žižek (New York: Verso, 1992), 170–71; Lacan, *The Four Fundamental Concepts of Psycho-Analysis,* 88, 89.

15   In a film entitled *Rear Window* it can hardly be insignificant that, as the following quotation from the screenplay makes clear, the wheel that lands Jefferies on his ass is identified specifically as a "rear wheel": ". . . the CAMERA PANS to an eight by ten glossy photo print. It shows a dirt track auto racing speedway, taken from a point dangerously near the center of the track. A racing car is skidding toward the camera, out of control, spewing a cloud of dust behind it. A rear wheel has come off the car, and the wheel is bounding at top speed directly into the camera lens" (*Rear Window,* Screenplay by John Michael Hayes, Final White Script, December 1, 1953, Paramount Pictures Corporation).

16   Tania Modleski, *The Women Who Knew Too Much* (New York: Methuen, 1988), 78.

17   Roland Barthes, *Camera Lucida,* trans. Richard Howard (New York: Noonday Press, 1981), 26–27.

18   Hitchcock, *Rear Window,* 43; Truffaut, *Hitchcock,* 138.

19   Ernest Jones, "The Theory of Symbolism," *Papers on Psycho-Analysis* (Boston: Beacon Press, 1967), 103, 128.

20   Jacques Lacan, *The Seminar of Jacques Lacan; Book III: The Psychoses, 1955–56,* ed. Jacques Alain-Miller, trans. Russell Grigg (New York: Norton, 1993), 317.

21   Truffaut, *Hitchcock,* 222.

22   Anthony Mazella, "Author, Auteur: Reading *Rear Window* from Woolrich to

Hitchcock," in *Hitchcock's Rereleased Films: From Rope to Vertigo,* ed. Walter Raubicheck and Walter Srebnick (Detroit: Wayne State University Press, 1991), 67.

23   See Sigmund Freud, *Beyond the Pleasure Principle* (1920), *The Standard Edition of the Complete Psychological Works of Sigmund Freud,* 18:55; Leo Bersani, *The Freudian Body: Psychoanalysis and Art* (New York: Columbia University Press, 1986).

24   Hitchcock, *Rear Window,* 41–42.

25   The threatened return of that unspeakable "formlessness" shapes the Western vision of the territories and the peoples it has colonized, as if they were the archaic remnants of repudiated libidinal systems that must, on the one hand, give way to the triumphant law of the Symbolic, and must remain, on the other hand, forever incompatible with it. This ambivalence, as Bhabha importantly reminds us in his essay, "The Other Question" (see note 2), overdetermines the meaning of "the white man's burden," implying, at least in part, that white men in general, like L. B. Jefferies in particular, may construe Symbolic law itself, with its "civilizing" logic, as a burden that resonates not only with the castration as which Lacan would read it but also with the loss of access to, the cutting off or disavowal of, pregenital pleasures and libidinal pathways that must culturally evoke associations like those assigned to the repudiated racial and ethnic other: associations with dirt and uncleanliness, with foul smells and inappropriate desires. Hence the racist destruction of the other can coincide unproblematically with a romanticization of that very otherness, enacting thereby the self-pity of the dominant for the cost at which they like to think their dominance acquired.

This ambivalence finds a thematic home in *Rear Window's* anatomy of Jeff's regressive investment in postcolonial adventure. The film, after all, immobilizes Jeff the better to mobilize a narrative in which his nominal susceptibility to the hetero-genitalizing charms of Miss Fremont must struggle against the much greater appeal of "hot spots" far from Western eyes, places distinguished, in the lurid descriptions he offers to explain why Lisa could never hope to accompany him there, primarily by their capacity to compel an immersive experience of filth and disgust ("You don't sleep much, you bathe less, and sometimes the food that you eat is made from things that you couldn't even look at when they were alive"). His immobility thus tropes on the ideological imperative to hold in check, by organizing or containing, the insistent pulsions of the drive—mapped as they are for this film and for the cultural regime whose contours it images, onto the anus as the fantasmatic site of the unassimilable Real—that the Symbolic, unable to articulate or escape, figures always as before or beyond it, figures, as at the end of *Rear Window,* as *Beyond the Himalayas,* or even, as we might retitle the volume Lisa skims with so little enthusiasm, *Beyond the Pleasure Principle*. Whether we choose, within the context of the narrative, to read her decision to exchange that volume, speaking as it does to Jeff's desire, for the fashion magazine represented as speaking more "authentically" to her own, as a gesture that reinforces Jeff's constraining views of woman's proper place or as one that suggests a feminist subversion of her apparent submission to masculine demands, the structural logic of her final act invariably affirms the institutionalization, despite the stylized male drag that she wears, of the binary sexual difference on which the Symbolic order depends. And so, by immersing herself in *Bazaar*, she reassuringly essentializes her necessary difference from Jeff and interprets his desire for the dangerous "hot spots" beyond the Himalayas, his desire to follow a path that would lead, like the vision afforded by his capacious rear window, to places other than her own front door, as utterly unaccountable, which is also to say, "bizarre."

26   If the lacerating violence of that poker, piercing *Rear Window* through the various cuts and holes that perversely structure the film, evokes the end to which—and by which—Marlowe's Edward II came, then we might consider placing *Rear Window*, with its figures of the wheel and the poker (not to mention its climactic scene of Jeff's fall), in the orbit of Mortimer's double-edged—or should one say open-ended?—remark as he confronts the prospect of his imminent end for the part he played in that crime:

> Base Fortune, now I see that in thy wheel
> There is a point, to which when men aspire,
> They tumble headlong down. (*Edward II* V.vi.59–61)

D. A. Miller

VISUAL PLEASURE IN 1959

"Got a match?"
"Your face and my ass"
—1950s schoolboy joke

FRONT OFFICE

Peculiarly unlucky in love, Miss Catherine: when her lustful male admirers are not bent on molesting her, they seem no less compulsively determined to make her a front for enacting, or otherwise entertaining, their desire to manhandle each other. This homosexual front may wear its crudest aspect on the beach of Cabeza de Lobo, where her cousin Sebastian Venable first launches her to fish into his clutch the local youths who eventually murder and devour him, but it also informs, *mutatis mutandis,* the very construction of Tennessee Williams's one-act play *Suddenly, Last Summer* (1957), which features Cathy as little more than a device for giving utterance to the story of Sebastian, the homosexual who, though barred from anywhere appearing in the would-be mainstream drama, by means of her recollection becomes its true protagonist.

At least, though, these first exploitations of Cathy retain enough semblance of decency to restrict their operational field both to foreign parts (New York City being for most Americans quite as exotic as made-up Cabeza de Lobo) and to minorities (whether the marginals of a resort in Spain, or the play-going cosmopolites who pay for the distinction of being in on such secrets with a discretion incapable of broadcasting them on any beam stronger than a wink). All remnant of propriety is gone for good, however, when, on the occasion of Joseph L. Mankiewicz's 1959 film version, the front advances to Hollywood, which is to say, a point from which it covers the entire United States. Now a publicity machine makes Cathy over, and puts into universal circulation a voluptuous image of her crouching on the beach at Cabeza de Lobo, attired once more in the revealing white bathing suit Sebastian bought for her there, the one said to reveal still more when wet. (Her new mass appeal reaches us all the more profoundly for being built on a foundation well beneath, and even antithetical to, the usual Hollywood glamour treatment of blanching foundation creams and binding foundation garments: that odd, unobviable fleshliness which unites soft fluency to near-squat compactness; which for all its evident shapeliness suggests something vaguely misshapen, or even excrescent, out of shape altogether; which—just as if we had to do with some hybridized creature of ancient mythology—does not rightly seem to fit with its given face, or to be accommodated by the idea of the person or the ideal of beauty established from within that face's strong, lovely outlines; which is, in short, the almost intolerably *troublant* body, circa 1959, of Elizabeth Taylor.) Even so, Cathy goes on being queer bait: "Suddenly, last summer," this image is captioned, "Cathy knew she was being used for evil." For a public already well notified that the film had received unprecedented permission from the Motion Picture Association of America to make what its own Production Code would otherwise have censored as an "inference" to "sex perversion," the hint suffices.[1] Cathy's image at once becomes an irresistible spur to homosexual fantasy, even as it remains an immovable alibi for it, this highly marketable product still needing to be sold under the counter. Nor does the ad campaign evince any more scruples about thus picking up where Sebastian left off, than the film itself does in reinforcing Williams's dramaturgy with a cinematography that images Cathy literally as her cousin's figurehead—for though the film, more teasing than the play, holds out the possibility of actually seeing Sebastian and witnessing what happened to him "suddenly, last summer," it recurs to a close-up of Cathy, looming large like some enormous classical bust, whenever such possibility would be on the verge of realization.

Yet if it seems odd that this homosexual front should become a thoroughly popular one, it is part of the same seeming oddness that, thus massified, the front should lose all expressly gay agency or aim. Whatever befalls Cathy on the beach of Cabeza de Lobo is obviously to be laid at the door of her gay cousin, who finds in her the means to facilitate his own homosexual activity; and for her subordinate dramatic function on the Broadway stage, no one appears responsible but the gay playwright, whom she affords the acceptable, already classic mediation of a female persona through which he may achieve a modicum of what—if by no measure but that of thoroughly alienated identity—we must still call "self-expression." But the film's homosexual front has no homosexual author equivalently behind it. Nor is this principally because, if one grants Mankiewicz the status of *auteur* (his signature: an obsessive talkiness, of which the typical narrative expression is *the gathering* and the notable formal predilection is for *the voice-over*), then, as all accounts agree, including that of his inter-action with his leading ladies, this "author" is manifestly heterosexual. For even if he were not, or if his title were handed over to Gore Vidal and Tennessee Williams, the gay men credited with the screenplay of *Suddenly, Last Summer,* no gay authorship could adequately govern, where Holly-wood cinema is concerned, the fundamental processes of signification. The reason is less that production is dispersed across too many persons, functions, and technical means ever to be unified in the master plan of one individual creator (however sexually oriented) than that, whether this demiurge defaults or no, another authority advenes to command and co-ordinate the manifold hands at work, so as to succeed in stamping even the most mediocre mass product with that self-evident coherence (that co-herence, in fact, *of* self-evidence) which is the indispensable condition of its consumption. This other authority, anonymous and impersonal, is the force of social prescription, what Roland Barthes called *doxa,* and which he invites us to think of as a kind of dictionary of received ideas, ideations, images, representations, narrative operations, from which nothing comes more mindlessly to everybody's mind than one more citation. Such an author-function—in its right-thinking generality, necessarily heterosexual and antigay—could never share Sebastian's particular interest in augment-ing the number of practicing homosexuals, or that of Williams in finding ways for this silenced minority to be allowed to speak. Accordingly, neither a maneuver of homosexual recruitment nor a mask worn by the gay art-ist, the film's fronting of Cathy presents a paradox as bizarre as the one and perhaps even more conventional than the other: that of a *homosexual closet constructed for general heterosexual use,* for the indulgence, in other words, of a homosexual fantasy that we must mainly understand as not the peculiar coinage of the gay male brain, but the common, even central daydream of the normal world, which, like the cannibal boys of Cabeza de Lobo greedily swallowing their disgust of Sebastian Venable, stands ambivalently fascinated before this privileged tableau of all that its own proudly mutilated desire has consented to sacrifice.

WET DREAM

"Suddenly, he switched from the evenings to the beach." On her way to uttering these words, Cathy has had to suffer as many of misfortune's arrows as her cousin's patron saint; but at long last, having been spared lobotomy, cured of amnesia, intercepted in suicide, and rescued from the assault of a whole wardful of psychiatric patients, she may begin to recount the story whose narration, promised from the start, the film has contrived such frankly feuilletonesque adventures (far more of them than did the play) only to keep in tantalizing suspense: the story of what happened to Sebastian last summer at Cabeza de Lobo. In other words, to anyone following the film's innuendo, or forewarned by its advance billing, she will finally designate the thing that in 1959 was variously called *the queer, the pervert, the homosexual,* if not directly, with any of these terms, still unspeakable under the Code, at all events in a manner that, unlike that of the connotations that have been whispering Sebastian's secret since the very mention of his name, or the first suggestion of possessiveness in his mother, would no longer be deniable.[2] And as if this prospect weren't exciting or obscene enough, the film breaks radically with the play here to install Cathy's narration in Mankiewicz's favorite mode: the flashback. No sooner does she start to talk than, suddenly, a lap dissolve renders her flesh more gauzelike than the chiffon of her blouse, and there where through that blouse we had only seen her firm white brassiere, we catch a glimpse of what must be the beach at Cabeza de Lobo (figs. 1–3). Her body quickly resolidifies, but the extraordinary promise has been given: not only will the narrative at last tell of Sebastian and those to-die-for boys who eat his meat, but it apparently means to show them as well: no longer through a glass darkly, with vague connotations and obscure symbolisms, but face-to-face, perhaps as Sebastian saw God in the Encantadas, or as God—at least according to the surveillance at St. Mary's asylum that takes Him for its model (fig. 4)—might see one of the patients there. Homosexuality will not only appear to pass from connotation to denotation, as in Williams's play, but also from this verbal order of *signification* to a visual one of *perception.* It will, in short, be the object of a demonstration. Thanks to this promise, however, Cathy's soft flesh has been rendered too solid: if her voice could once successfully channel what the play's enigmatic narrative structure made us want to know, her body is now in the way of what the film's cinematographic accompaniment to this structure has made us want

4

to see. No longer satisfied with her epistemology of the closet, we demand the plein-air gay pornography of which she is blocking our view! "Isn't that what everybody wants," Cathy remarked earlier in explaining her suicide attempt, "me out of the way?": and everybody suddenly includes the audience in whom, for this almost statutorily desirable body, the sequence excites no desire, but only a desire to see through it, to watch it once again turn transparent, and so further disclose the fantasmatic scene of gay male sex, "the beach at Cabeza de Lobo," that lies behind it.

It is the desire for *this* transparency that the film proceeds to address—and adjust—in the famous opening episode of Cathy's narration: "He—bought me a bathing suit I didn't want to wear. I laughed. I said, 'I can't wear that, why it's a scandal to the jay-birds!' It was a one-piece bathing suit made of white something. The water made it transparent. I—I told him I didn't want to swim in it. But he just grabbed my hand and dragged me into the water—all the way in, and I—I came out looking naked."[3] Whereas the lap dissolve let us think that we might see the homosexual scene through Cathy's body, her voice-over promises instead that we shall see through her bathing suit *to* that body. Why, in the place of a gay pornography that we do no more than glimpse, the film should put a heterosexual one on which we may feast our eyes (the extensive sequence of Cathy in the white "keyhole" bathing suit, being pulled into the water, emerging in shame, dropping on her knees at a man's feet), the obvious reason is that nothing less than the sight of Taylor's half-naked body and the prospect of its full denudation is required to affirm the compelling force of that "compulsory heterosexuality" that, as regularly as a reflex, must come to discipline this dubious moment. (Would not a "liberal" aversion therapy—one that had renounced the brutality of electric shocks—be exactly this: a practice of merely visual reinforcements in which, whenever the patient were to see the "right" image, he would see it *well*, long and clearly enough to sustain any interest his eye might take in it; while the "wrong" image would always also be, in the same terms, a *bad* image, brief, blurry, unrewarding?)

Yet so energetic a repudiation does nothing to drive back the genie of homosexual desire into the tiny lamp in which he lay confined; on the contrary, he now expands to such vaporously protean dimensions as enable him to envelop and saturate the very body that is, visually speaking, his appointed censor. So be it if he lacks the social substance to expel Cathy's body from in front of the homosexual tableau; his psychic wiliness is more than enough to incorporate her body *into* this tableau, so that it becomes not just a sign but even a symbol of what is thus no longer the altogether invisible spectacle of gay male sex. No doubt, were his satisfactions pinned only on the wish for Cathy's disappearance, he would find them in none but the fast and fugitive, "furtive" mode of its first technified formulation; such transient thrills are hardly to be scorned, in 1959 or any later year, but inasmuch as he succeeds in insinuating himself among the very folds of her body, which unbudgingly sustains the entire flashback as both its frame and chief figure, he may also steal his still flitty but now far less fleeting pleasures all over the place.

Watch what complex mischief he wrecks on the bathing-suit episode from its very start, when the image of Cathy Narratrix, once again vacillating, lets the flashback resume by slipping to the edge of the screen. Her words say, "he bought me a bathing suit I didn't want to wear," but the accompanying image is as odd an illustration of them as if the film's image-bank had just gone haywire, or even were diabolically possessed, spewing out obscenities in place of orthodoxies. For if any bathing suit is in view when these words are pronounced, it is the one worn by an anonymous young man whose beefcake pose suddenly, massively occupies the screen. His suit is tight-fitting, and its intense, isolated whiteness makes the plenum of his crotch the undisputed focus of vision (fig. 5). To straighten out this absurdity, or to exorcise this demon, the expected (not to say: the desired) figure of Cathy, clad in her keyhole bathing suit, follows on-screen only seconds later—"Ah yes," the spectator seeing her image thinks,

5

"this is what I was to have seen"—but in a crucial respect, she has arrived too late. For when she does come, she finds herself already entered in a swimsuit competition, a battle of bulges in which, from the first, she is second. Heralded thus, her figure can't help appearing an equivalence for the gay male object-choice whose image has in any case already been captioned, however nonsensically, with her own self-identification. No doubt she goes on to receive far more of our attention than does the anonymous man in *his* immodest bathing suit (who and which, in 1959, are not to be looked at long or closely), but such attention may never be wholly disentangled from the logic of succession that has introduced her or from its thrilling implication that she is carrying somewhere about her person the baton that, in passing under a cloud himself, he has passed on to her. (The peculiar provocation of Taylor's breasts, here looking "larger than life and twice as unnatural," like Maxine in *The Night of the Iguana*, only reinforces their figural fungibility. Much as a very tall man, especially if he is also very thin, never ceases to represent the rapid process of "shooting up," however long ago it was completed, or at whatever rate it actually occurred, by which we imagine he came to obtain his present stature, so these extraordinary breasts, which seem to be still budding in full flower, suggest the surge of protuberance itself. Cathy's shamed way of bearing them does even more to turn the otherwise familiar, somewhat kitschy insignia of a sexpot into the astonishing new acquisitions of what custom calls, notwithstanding that they seem to be gained overnight, a "developing" young girl; and to return us in the process to that period of our own sexual incipience when suddenly, one season in adolescence, just such harbingers assumed the office of announcing not only their own erotic possibility, but also that of other body parts that did not enjoy—or was it suffer?—this unique public visibility.)

Not only, then, is this "strong" heterosexual pornography no longer the *opposite* of the homosexual one that it averts, but the fullness of its strength comes to depend on the strange fact that, as I shall be explaining in more detail later on, Cathy's body is implicated in male homosexuality not merely as its sign, or even its analogy, but as its very evidence. As everyone knows, when Cathy emerges from the water, her bathing suit, while certainly more adhesive, remains as opaque as ever: this may be disappointing, but our frustration hardly makes the suit any less sexy. Announce an emperor in new clothes, and though he may be wearing nothing at all, everyone but the dullest child is capable of imagining their splendor; allege a bathing suit to turn transparent in the water, then for good measure actually wet it, and it will excite a vivid dream of denudation without ever having to disappear. Likewise, Cathy's own nontransparent body gets all the hotter for having fused—having set, we'll see shortly, *as* a fuse—to its ordained sexiness the forbidden allure of the male homosexual spectacle of which it stands, or more often sits, in the place. Just as the phrase "the water made it transparent" magically sews a phantom nudity into Cathy's bathing suit, the film's strange-seeming collocation of a verbal bathing suit *she* "didn't want to wear" with a visual bathing suit some *he* is wearing performs a phantom transubstantiation over her body: so that, like a believer worshipping Christ's body and blood in the species of bread and wine, the spectator of *Suddenly, Last Summer* thrills to the motions of the male homosexual who is mysteriously present under the perfectly unaltered luscious appearances of a woman's body. It is thanks to the double valence of this transubstantiation, for instance, that when Cathy kneels at Sebastian's feet—their bodies placed in relation to one another according to a well-known scenography of the blow job—we can never quite know whether the fantasy fellation generating our excitement is of the heterosexual type, that rare treat for which a man feels such gratitude that he hardly cares how well or ill a woman bestows it (to realize the scenography being pleasure enough), or of the homosexual, a considerably more routine fare that earns as much envy as contempt for the man who (one way or the other, one way *and* the other) can't seem to stop bingeing on it. And as we watch Sebastian walk past Cathy's abjectly offered body to the boys at the end of the beach, we would be equally hard put to decide in which role, as the woman spurned or the faggot cocksucker, she has provoked our sorry-grateful embarrassment for her.

(*Vingt ans après:* when, the fictive beach of Cabeza de Lobo having evolved into the poolside of a real, if no less fabulous house at Fire Island with, by Andy Warhol's reckoning, "8,000 boys around it," the owner of this house, Calvin Klein, designs for himself "a flesh-colored charmeuse swimsuit that turned translucent when it got wet,"[4] it is still impossible to say whether he is copying Cathy's famous bathing suit, or finally explicating it: trying to be this woman or revealing her to have always already been a gay man.)

SHOT REVERSE

The bathing-suit sequence does not, of course, simply abandon the anonymous man in his white bathing suit for Cathy in hers: the two figures keep succeeding one another in an extended twelve-take alternation. Now, during the half-dozen shots that fall to her share of this alternation, Cathy achieves a downright feral intensity of embodiment. Her spirit may be mortified by the bathing suit she didn't want to wear, but not her flesh, whose affluence spills over the neckline and even (or so the keyhole is suggesting) threatens to dissolve it altogether. Nor does this embodiment merely go to verify the malapropism of the schoolboy who thinks that titillation has all to do with tits. She whom Violet, idealizing as always, has earlier called a "lovely girl" is acknowledged here as a material one through and through: of mass and density enough to need to be dragged, and so given over to the rhythms of her elasticity that she rebounds from submersion, at a purportedly humiliating moment, glistening in almost phocine exultation. When she stalks slowly to shore, she is instinct with physical dignity and grace, and when, with no physical dignity or grace whatsoever, and every likelihood that she is contributing to a disgusting rebus, she breaks into a panicky run just before squatting down on the beach, she remains instinctual in the whole-heartedness of her body's absorption in its functioning.

As for the anonymous young man in the six alternating shots, however, his embodiment undergoes the opposite process, waning in size, amount, and intensity alike. Our first view of him (fig. 5) proves to be our last of his package. By the next shot, his body is already farther away and turned to the side; in the couple after that, it becomes still more remote, with a shadow from a fence-pole censoring the crotch. Then, if it were not enough that, as he shares the screen with more and more boys, his body should disappear in the multitude of theirs, theirs must disappear too, as the camera successively lops full figures to upper torsos, and these to no more than faces (figs. 6–8). Nor is this enough either, for if the point of the series is to correct the exciting, but anxious-making image of the male sex-object with which it began, this correction does not consist solely of obscuring the object from our view but also, in the process, of transforming it into the subject who orients our vision. Like the former, the latter task requires manifest labor, for the opening image has done little to show the anonymous young man as looking at anything; on the contrary, it frames him in ways that actively seclude this possibility. And even when Cathy's image succeeds his, the "field" relation between him and her remains unspecified: both figures might yet be established as being "on the same side" of the camera lens, objects of a third party's (say Sebastian's) gaze. But all ambiguity disappears as, in contrast to the ocular embarrassment evinced by Cathy (who, as Jane Austen might describe her in this sequence, "hardly knows how to look"), the anonymous young man is progressively abstracted into so many pairs of eyes, whose eager, appreciative gaze passes straight through the resulting "shot/reverse-shot" construction to the only object remaining: Cathy's ever more fraught, freighted body.

Regarding this shot/reverse-shot construction, whose reverse fields confer on what literally become opposite sexes the further complementarity of opposing relations to vision, we might first remark on its utter familiarity. Few will need to be reminded that what the film adduces here, with textbook emphasis, is the well-known paradigm of "visual pleasure" in which, according to Laura Mulvey, who first called attention to its pervasiveness in Hollywood classicism, woman is "image," man is "bearer of the Look."[5] And if we were to let ourselves be guided (like half of film theory) by Mulvey's account of what this paradigm signifies for the mascu-

6

7

8

line psyche, we should not be long discovering—say, in Cathy's keyhole, through which there is lacking anything to see, except the vacancy that has succeeded to the place of an ostentatious male fullness—the sign of that "castration" whereby the female body comes to represent for man the inevitable figure of what at once essentially threatens and essentially confirms the validity of his sex; that castration, in other words, which, through the very ambivalence it endlessly generates in man for woman, makes her—for better or for worse, as we like to say—the indispensable partner with which the drama of his desire is to be played, if it goes up at all; that castration, therefore, which is only another name—and, in the rarefied intellectual atmosphere where it usually circulates, not the least bracing one—for the hot-and-bothered affair of heterosexuality itself, an affair that is not so natural, evidently, that it doesn't need to promote itself, for man and woman both, as a heroically dangerous liaison.

Yet though one can hardly miss this hetero-structuration of the visual field, neither can one take it at face value in a context where, like Cathy's body, or her bathing suit, it is not least obvious in the root sense of "being in the way." Here, at any rate, its dynamic seems chiefly evolved in re-action to a primordial *male* image, which must be censored—reduced and replaced—on the superego's behalf.[6] And if this censorship is imperfect, never quite allaying our fears, or destroying our hopes, that the anonymous young man might once again appear to engross the screen, the reason is twofold. For one thing, it comes after the fact, the retrofitting of an image whose irrevocable prior effects reside, tracelike, even in their successful modification. For another, this male image never in fact lies outside the Mulveyan paradigm that would censor it; indeed, that it does not affords precisely the basis of continuity on which the paradigm may do the work of morphing it in the first place. To be necessarily blunt about it, the male bearer-of-the-look is never himself invisible, or visible only as his look: the ontology of his being on film means that he is never *not* given "to be looked at," with all the potential implied in that offer to capture the screen or cap-tivate our own look, with his bodily presence or its sexual objectification. And of anyone who hasn't seen that potential abundantly realized in the screen appearances of Clark Gable, Cary Grant, Marlon Brando, William Holden, or Montgomery Clift, to go no further forward than 1959, it is safe to say that, instead of going to the movies, this person must have stayed home reading Laura Mulvey, for whom the recessiveness of Hollywood's male images is as decided a datum as the neo-Popean maxim in which she dismisses it from further consideration: "Man is reluctant to gaze at his exhibitionist like."[7] No less than it brings out the obstructive character of the obvious, *Suddenly, Last Summer* restores this reluctance to its old, active meaning of *struggle* (L. *reluctari*, to fight back, resist), whether against the sheer being-there of the male image or against the homosexual desire that is seldom a very distant ancestor of even the bluffest identification with it.

But take for granted, with the complete rout of this image, the successful suture of the spectator's look to the boys' ogling of Cathy, and we still haven't done with the strangeness of the shot/reverse-shot construction, whose self-evidence is finally shown to be screening a far more profound homosexualizing prospect than mere male "to-be-looked-at-ness." Internally, of course, the six images of Cathy are all marked as representing the point of view of Sebastian, whose hand we see dragging her forward into the water, or at whose knees we see her drop on the sand; but the shot/reverse construction implies that, from the other side of the alternation, the boys too are looking at these images, which seem to be the very substance of the "bait" Sebastian sets for them. His cool appraisal and their torrid appreciation would both culminate with the famous final shot of Cathy cowering on the beach, equally ashamed of being rejected by Sebastian and exposing her "naked-looking" breasts to everyone else. Observe, however, the continuation of the shot as the camera, as though enacting Sebastian's movements, passes beyond Cathy on the beach to the boys who inspect her through a wire-link fence in the water. *Grosso modo,* such a transition has structured the entire sequence, but now it is made, not as an alternation but from within a single shot, where for the first time the spatial relation between her and them may be clearly established (figs. 9–11). Suddenly, as soon as it is, we know that these boys *cannot* have seen the memorable image of Cathy that has just crossed our supposedly isomorphic vision; they can only have seen the obverse of this famous image, this image *from behind.* What commands their literal retrospect is not her heaving breasts, but, if anything, her crouching buttocks. And though the former may have enticed *us,* we must now be led to wonder—with an insane Darwinism that is, however, wholly at home in the world of *Suddenly, Last Summer*—whether perhaps they have only done so by virtue of adaptively "mimicking" the original, but outlawed offering of the latter.[8] Certainly, at any rate, we have resolved what would otherwise remain (as it does in the play) an abiding puzzlement; we have grasped how Sebastian's bait actually works.

9

10

11

Consider, after all, the striking paradox, contradicting common sense and practical experience alike, that we are here being asked to accept: through their sexual attraction to a woman who looks exactly like Elizabeth Taylor, a town's whole population of toughs turns queer. With good reason is the doctor slow, positively resistant to comprehend what Cathy is telling him. "I assumed that the youngest child in the audience would get the point before he did," Pauline Kael has written, but "getting the point" is no different from missing it altogether if one is not more than a little amazed by it.[9] Something surely requires explaining in the swift metamorphosis of boys who only have eyes for Cathy into the raging man-eaters from whom Cathy escapes with her life because, as she puts it, "they didn't even see me." But what kind, what level of explanation would suffice? Is the switch point where heterosexuality goes homo to be found (as it often was when *Suddenly, Last Summer* came out) in a myth of boys "so hungry that they would do anything for food"?[10] Even so strikingly tangential an account can hardly be excluded from the connotative dimension of a film that would afford its spectators, along with opportunities for gratifying their homosexual desire, rationales for not recognizing it. Yet insofar as the film unriddles the bait paradox with any concreteness, it does so at the level that, in every film, counts most: that of the visual image. Essentially tacit, this image is all the apter to be telling us of what may not—or must not—otherwise be spoken; and here, as we'll continue to see, it articulates a fantasmatics of "the behind," which it specifies not only as the homosexual scene that is behind Cathy, but also, now, as the homosexual scene that is Cathy's behind.

s/c

The same body, then, that only seconds ago seemed to constitute the very icon of normal male desire, and whose bright, broad-beaming self-evidence as such appeared more than adequate to subdue the queer incandescence that was serving for backlighting—this same body now stands in some need of shade itself. Too plainly has Cathy's flesh come to bait men with the anal erotics that, by dropping the usual requirement for an "opposite" sex, must fail to guarantee their desire as having a *female* object, and so leaves it (with every other desire that lacks this assurance) to manifest a thrilling, terrifying potential to direct them to a *male* one. Accordingly, such flesh will be henceforth treated to all the visual discretion that had earlier been reserved for the homosexual scene behind it. More eager on this score than Sebastian himself, who does no more than permit such discretion ("so now he let me wear a decent, dark suit"), the flashback positively cultivates it, restricting Cathy's formerly flaunted body to brief, distant, and altogether more cursory sightings. And in any case, whatever attention we may pay to these must be powerfully distracted by the fact that, at the same time as Cathy submits to her new corporal decency, Sebastian, hitherto represented as no more than a hand or a pair of legs,[11] finally achieves the visibility of a full figure, whose white silk suit dominates the landscape of Cabeza de Lobo almost as conspicuously as did Cathy's bathing suit of "white something." Once again, by what has come to be a habit, the flashback resorts to an "obviousness" meant to obviate the genie of homosexual desire whenever his devilment is beginning to show, but such obviousness now takes a different, even a reverse tack to the one previously followed. As Cathy's body can evidently no longer repress this genie, Sebastian's is requisitioned for the purpose instead. For whenever the genie attracted notice vis-à-vis the former body, he invariably proved himself to be a free-ranging spirit whose subtlety could penetrate the most resistant subjects, objects, images, and scenarios; but if he should only become visible in the vicinity of the latter, perhaps he will appear to be where he belongs, in his bottle after all. To the obviousness of the Woman, there now succeeds the obviousness of the Homosexual, who may be supposed to reabsorb the desires she has just failed to make unthinkable in—or as—himself.

Or rather, it is the obviousness of the opposition between the Woman and the Homosexual that the flashback, as if bent on reheterosexualizing Cathy by such means, now labors to establish. Little wonder that the split screen, behaving almost like a pedagogue's blackboard, proceeds to make far more pointed demands on our attention than it did on its first desultory introduction as a framing device: in that impossibly tight couple which Cathy and Sebastian have become, it now has something to split up. Likewise, if what has been, visually speaking, a pretty familiar Hollywood product suddenly resorts to enough strange angles, cuts, and overlays to pass for a foreign art film, these do more than merely aestheticize the skittishness demanded by censorship as we approach so thoroughly homosexual a climax as Sebastian's "murder."[12] They also less bashfully enforce the formal abstraction required to develop this same opposition, of which the key terms are, obviously enough, those of Front and Behind.

Cathy continues representing the Front, but in order that she do so, it has to retreat upward from her breasts, with the all too ambiguous keyhole between them, to the safer ground of her bust. She is nothing now but an enormous detached head—a front in the true, one might say the least deviated sense of the word (L. *frons,* face, countenance)—that "appears" on the screen much as saintly apparitions are said to do, without substance. As her body is required to fade from the narrative, only this head may remain to preside, more prominent than ever, over the narration. Conversely, for Sebastian's body to take pride of place at the expense of Cathy's, it must be turned around: the famous fact that it is shown only from the back stems not from exigencies of censorship—several homosexual characters had shown their faces before 1959 [13]—but from those of the polarity that must align him, against the Front, with the Behind. Between these two poles, moreover, the film maintains a critical stylistic difference: in contrast to the naturalism of Cathy's Front, on which a wealth of visual nuance confers beauty, expression, identity, and all the value inherent in such qualities, Sebastian's Behind is treated to a minimalism so spare of detail that it must seem equally empty of anything else. The white silk suit that makes him one long backside also makes that backside blank. It emits none of the sensuous suggestiveness of, for instance, the suit worn by Saint-Loup in Proust, of which the material, also white, but soft and thin as well, a much-moved Marcel "could never have believed any man would have the audacity to wear." This one hangs too straight, falls too stiffly—can the stuff really be silk?—to limn so much as the general shape of Sebastian's buns; instead, with the back vent of its skirt, it schematically indicates the vacuum between them. If Sebastian is all Behind, that Behind is in turn all Anus, whose implied penetration in sexual intercourse is all that is needed, at this symbolic level, to define him as homosexual.

Yet as *Suddenly, Last Summer* has already shown more than once, no obviousness ever seems obvious enough. Just as perverse as any other desire—or what means the same thing, just as persevering—paranoia may seek its own relief, but what it always comes to find in place of relief is fresh provision for its indulgence. So now, in continued obedience to this logic, the flashback that has labored to establish an antithesis between homo- and heterosexual object-choices, devising signs of quasi-algebraic purity to do so, proceeds to manifest what is, after all, the latent ambiguity of every antithesis, namely, that its two poles constitute a single figure. Once again electing the mode most friendly to panic—in a word, *suddenly*—it brings the Homosexual Behind into alignment with the Female Front, so that, like interlocking pieces of a puzzle, matched across the split screen whose fissure thus turns into the seam of a juncture, they form the picture of a crossbreed weirder than anything dreamt of in Mendel: half woman, half gay man (figs. 12–14).

Now this queer bird, were we to regard it as a gay man with a female front, would hardly be a rare one; on the contrary, it is common among the avifauna of certain well-attended *cages-aux-folles,* where we recognize it at once, twittering in a nest of froufrou, by its brilliant lamé plumage and tiara crest. But we don't so regard it here; we regard it in its other, far less familiar aspect, as a woman with a homosexual behind. And unlike the spectacle of the Female Gay Man, which offers observers in need of it the assurance that what separates them from the airy thing inside the birdcage is as obvious, as ontological as gender itself, that of the Gay Male Woman, here rendered with an eerily surreal literalism, is neither comic nor comforting. For in it the Woman altogether loses her ability to assume what has long been, in narratives of "homosexual panic," her *rôle à faire:* that of embodying for Man, simply by virtue of his wanting or being willing to engage her in erotic practice, the possibility of a peremptory refusal of homosexual desire. Recall, for instance, how *Tea and Sympathy* (the film version of which Vincente Minnelli directed only a year before 1959) resolves the sexual identity crisis of Tom Lee's schooldays. Though every sign but one suggests Tom is gay, this one entirely suffices to nullify all the others: a woman, his headmaster's wife Laura, proves able to arouse him! As Laura herself pronounces, "Only a woman really knows," or as the playwright pulling her apron strings must mean: only a woman lets a man really know.[14] Between them, they reaffirm that highly durable common sense which certifies male heterosexuality—that is to say, certifies it as a non-homosexuality—by means of a female partner. But *Suddenly, Last Summer* is too committed to the social advancement of paranoia, or too hardly driven by the homosexual desire underlying that paranoia, to ignore thus the fantasy structures that require any partner we hold captive in them to become some person or thing other than, for instance, herself. In the Gay Male Woman, it fashions just such a structure, joining a sodomitical scenario to the object of what, if it can still pass for heterosexual desire, can perhaps no longer escape the thought of itself as doing so. Far from dispelling the nightmare of homosexuality, this Woman makes it uncannily intimate with heterosexual dreaming.

She may now appear with all the grotesque factitiousness of a charade,

12

13

14

but that charade does not exactly help us forget that, as it happens, we have seen her before wearing a more lifelike aspect. In that guise, she has been superimposed on enough images and introduced into enough incidents to adumbrate a story of her own, one that, elaborated wholly from within the shadows of connotation, is nonetheless so substantial that without taking it into account we should never begin to understand how Williams's original one-act play, lasting only forty minutes in performance, has been amplified into a two-hour film. All along, in short, she has inhabited the body, and induced the adventures, of Cathy herself. No viewer of *Suddenly, Last Summer* can have failed to notice, for instance, this peculiarity of Cathy's bearing: that, whether backing up against walls and bookshelves, cowering in corners, or performing with exaggerated emphasis the simple act of sitting down, her carriage seems to have no goal but that of covering her behind, to which, of course, it thus ends up only calling more attention. One can't but think (as soon as, by refusing the ineffable naturalness of connotations, one allows thought to occur) that this attitude means to repulse, through fear or coquetry, that anal penetration which in contrast will not have met with the slightest resistance from her aunt Violet, as whom a queenlike Katharine Hepburn walks no less stiffly, and sits no less gingerly, than if, in a hysterical consummation of incest, she had Sebastian's own stick up her ass. Cathy is fighting—and by fighting, dramatizing—the grip of a similar hysteria, a hysteria that, though variously arising from a wish to have her indifferent cousin at last, an effort to keep him alive despite his death, and an inability, after the outrage she has witnessed, not to identify with its victim, always conforms to a premise that she *is* Sebastian and hence, as the film allows him no other reality, the bearer of the Homosexual Anus. In this hysteria, the seat of "somatic conversion" can only be the seat itself, which, in surrendering it to the prospect of sodomy, Cathy simultaneously tries to rescue from the brutal martyrdom that the practice, as she has seen with her own eyes, ensures for it.

Moreover, far from having the manifest unreality of an illusion, Cathy's hysteria finds an objective correlative in men's actual behavior to her. No different in this respect from the excited, enraged mental patients who frankly want to *have* her ass (figs. 15–16), the calm, kindly doctors who only want to *save* it (figs. 17–18) find themselves consistently taking up quasi-sodomitical positions behind her. As the carrier of what thus ramifies into a truly social disease, Cathy requires to be cured, just as much as, in the eyes of the psychiatrist who treated him during the writing of *Sud-

15

16

denly, Last Summer, Williams himself did, and of the same condition: male homosexuality. In an obvious sense, such a cure would be successfully broached with Cathy's narration itself, as the sign that she has at last fully recalled the cause of her identification with Sebastian and so may begin to win free of its pathogenic effects. ("Remember, Marnie!" Mark urges Hitchcock's heroine at the end of this long-standing Hollywood tradition, which no doubt began when Constance Petersen similarly enjoined John Ballantine in *Spellbound;* all through it, we have the rare comfort of knowing that the psyche will be made whole along with the story of how it came to be sick.)[15] But, as befits a disorder whose main danger inheres in its corporal manifestations, the film is not too proud of its depth psychology to

17

18

be above "treating the symptom"; on the contrary, memory-retrieval has finally a lower priority in Cathy's treatment than a certain physical therapy that Doctor Cukrowicz, as much qua man as doctor, is licensed to practice on her body. Albeit perhaps less brutal than that recommended by Violet, this operation has its own claim to be called a "prefrontal lobotomy."

I refer to the curious scene in which, alone with Cathy in the Venable home, Cukrowicz prepares her to perform the public truth-telling that will follow in the garden. For his labors in this scene remain unfinished even after his serum-injection has given her access to the truth, and his hypnotism has persuaded her of the necessity to tell it. Though nothing should follow on such psychomancy but that she go outside to where the

19

others may hear the story she is now able to relate, yet she finds herself
unable to accomplish, so as to do so, the simple act of rising from the
divan on which she has been sitting. For all the doctor's powers, the illness
that they have driven from her mind has evidently not given up, deep in
her body, more tenaciously occupied positions from which it now makes
a fresh show of force in holding her—as though with glue, or with her
own unconscious cathexis—to her seat (fig. 19). Cathy herself recognizes
that, to counteract this relapse, this literal backsliding, a last intervention
is required. "Tell me to [get up]," she entreats Cukrowicz, "Then I think I
could." And indeed, no sooner does he oblige, having risen himself, than
she finds the strength to lift herself into a standing position opposite his
own. If the musical track salutes her achievement with sonorities befitting
the most wondrous miracle, or the most heroic triumph, this is implicitly
because, in managing to get upright, Cathy has simultaneously become
straight as well. She is hardly on her feet for a second before, throwing her
arms about her doctor's shoulders, she begins to cover his face with passionate kisses. All that keeps the allegory from being obvious is that, like
everything else associated with the anus, it is embarrassingly so. On that

score too, no doubt, Cathy is as desperate to relinquish her "seat" as she is eager to embrace that more civilized or advanced sexuality whose partners, face-to-face, will have put their behinds behind them.

Her misfortunes, however, though already sufficient for a Sadean heroine, may not be over yet. So noticeably uncooperative is the doctor in receiving her advances that, in continuing to make them, Cathy is reduced to pleading, "Let me! let me!" And still at the end, when her narration has yielded its expected catharsis, he refuses to clinch things, merely consenting to take the hand she offers him as, without having so much as tasted its fruit, they leave the garden for good. Only wishful thinking could attribute this inhibition to the force of medical ethics, since in Hollywood narrative (whose organization we should understand no better than the polity of Lerner and Lowe's Camelot if we assumed it were governed by the conditions, customs, and legalities of ordinary life) a law has decreed that doctors shall be as free to fall in love with their patients as teachers with their pets. The propriety of this law is entirely obvious here, where, given the total absence of other eligible men, Cukrowicz alone can administer the heterosexual purging of which—we have seen how precisely—Cathy stands in need to complete her cure. (Even if the cure narrative hadn't required it, moreover, the very alignment of the stars would bring this couple under the sway of romance: for who in 1959 could behold Elizabeth Taylor and Montgomery Clift together onscreen and not wish to see reprised— no matter what modifications time had brought to her girlish waist, or circumstance had worked on his handsome features—the feverish kissing scene with which, not a decade before, they had so memorably raised the temperature of *A Place in the Sun*?) Let us call, then, the doctor's libidinal depression by its name, and recognize that, in the process of ceasing to represent the figment of the Gay Male Woman, Cathy has also forfeited her sex appeal. After all, nothing but a paranoid homosexual desire has determined this appeal in the first place, as consisting in her ability to cut an ambiguous fantasy figure in which the front that meant "no" to such desire might always be mistaken—whether with delight or horror, at all events thrillingly—for the behind that meant "yes." Accordingly, insofar as Cathy is cured, she offers men not so much a purified erotic object as an impoverished one, since, in being evacuated of this double relation to male homosexuality, she will have lost the very foundation of her heterosexual value. Precisely because her cure is already far advanced, the doctor can't take it further: all he can give Miss Catherine now, in the polite form of solicitude, is indifference, a last and not the least cruel reason to consider herself peculiarly unlucky in love.

NOTES

My readers will hardly need to be told that in 1959 *Suddenly, Last Summer* furnished me an object of considerable pubescent obsession, but it may not go without saying that the generation of this essay has at least as much to do with two texts that, when I happened to read them shortly before re-seeing the film a few years ago, helped break the ground for my present understanding of it. In "Rock Hudson's Body" (*Inside/Out: Lesbian Theories, Gay Theories,* ed. Diana Fuss [New York: Routledge, 1991], 259–88), Richard Meyer exemplifies how thoroughly the representations of mass culture are saturated with a male homosexual fantasy that, just because it doesn't know its name, perhaps all the more because it doesn't, is not prevented from circulating in our collective imaginary among men and women alike; and in "Seeing Things: Representation, the Scene of Surveillance, and the Spectacle of Gay Male Sex" (*Inside/Out,* 93–116), Lee Edelman theorizes the regularity of certain confusions between front and rear effected on the visual field by the prospect of sodomy. (Compare his "*Rear Window*'s Glasshole" in this volume, 72–96.) Both authors were also kind enough to give me personal help on various points, as were Anne Anlin Cheng, Suzanne Daly, Naifei Ding, Michael Gallant, Margo Jefferson, Mary Ann O'Farrell, and Elaine Scarry. All the more because it treats a film he knew as well as he loved, I regret that this essay had to be finished without the helping hand of William Nestrick, who died suddenly last winter.

1   The maneuvering by which *Suddenly, Last Summer* obtained a Seal from the Production Code, and a Special Classification from the Legion of Decency, is recounted in Frank Miller, *Censored Hollywood* (Atlanta: Turner, 1994), 187–88.

2   For a discussion of homosexuality and connotation, see D. A. Miller, "Anal Rope," in *Inside/Out,* 123–25.

3   In Williams's play, where almost the identical words are spoken, there is of course no previous dissolve to which they can refer; but neither can Williams's play help us take the measure of the immense semiotic enrichment it receives from being brought, in precisely cinematic ways, to the screen.

4   Steven Gaines and Sharon Churcher, *Obsession: The Lives and Times of Calvin Klein* (New York: Birch Lane Press, 1994), 290.

5   Laura Mulvey, "Visual Pleasure and Narrative Cinema," *Screen* 16, no. 3 (autumn 1975): 11. During the more than twenty years that Mulvey's manifesto has entranced film criticism by the intensity of its strongly concentrated vision,

some of us have had time to understand that we enter that trance, the better to turn them per the mesmerist's instructions, with our eyes half closed. In the ensuing dimness, though we quite clearly distinguish two sexes, we only manage to make out a single sexuality, the approved and enforced one of their conjunction. Not only do we become blind to gay themes and images, but we must also settle for an impaired view of the straight ones that, insofar as the latter, like the former, have been determined by their place in a homo/hetero antithesis, cannot justly be regarded in isolation. We can never even notice, for instance, the famous fact, which this essay has undertaken to annotate, that the most explicit and erotic image of male homosexual desire contained in the entire corpus of 1950s mass culture is one of Elizabeth Taylor wearing a plunging swimsuit in *Suddenly, Last Summer*. See, however, the following note.

6   Most obviously, the spectator to whom this superego belongs, and indeed to whom *Suddenly, Last Summer* addresses its paranoid homosexual vision, is a masculine one. But the representation of male homosexuality always broaches a truly mass fantasy in which the imagined sexual scene between men, saturated in the desire and dread of undermining our whole socio-sexual polity, does not limit its thrilling appeal, any more than it restricts its violent threat, to those whose gender seems to give them the possibility of acting it out. Such literalism is, in any case, beside the point in *Suddenly, Last Summer,* which makes particularly clear that, just as any man might imagine himself in this scene, so might any woman, who would therefore be equally likely to have a paranoid relation to it. (Consider, from this standpoint, the one place in "Visual Pleasure and Narrative Cinema" where Laura Mulvey mentions homosexual desire: a parenthesis on the "buddy movie," in which, so she remarks, "the active homosexual eroticism of the central male figures can carry the story without distraction" [11]. The claim is doubly astonishing. For one thing, as Mulvey must know as well as anyone else, there is no such thing in Hollywood cinema as an active homosexual eroticism that is *not* without distraction, without, that is, a complex narrative and psychic management system that prevents it from having to be seen or experienced as such. But for another, the statement must imply that, in what Mulvey calls "normal narrative cinema," it is the female star who provides just such distraction, that even as the latter is being decked out in all the finery of her castration, she is being fitted to carry out a certain *displacement of homosexual desire.* I am, of course, far from objecting to the point, but nothing in Mulvey's argument has prepared for it or will go on to develop it. It is as though the mere words *male homoeroticism* exerted sufficient power over the author to produce—momentarily and quite automatically—this paranoid homosexualization of her own thesis.)

7   Mulvey, "Visual Pleasure," 12.

8   Readers of a certain age might recall this thesis from one of the first pop biolo-

gists: "Supposing we had reached the stage where the female signaled sexually
to the male from behind with a pair of fleshly, hemispherical buttocks . . .
and a pair of bright red genital lips, or labia. Supposing the male had evolved
a powerful sexual responsiveness to these specific signals. Supposing that, at
this point in evolution, the species became increasingly vertical and frontally
orientated in its social contacts. Given this situation, one might very well expect to find some sort of frontal self-mimicry of the type seen in the gelada
baboon. Can we, if we look at the frontal regions of the female of our species,
see any structures that might possibly be mimics of the ancient genital display
of hemispherical buttocks and red labia? The answer stands out as clearly as
the female bosom itself. The protruberant [sic], hemispherical breasts of the
female must surely be copies of the fleshly buttocks, and the sharply defined
red lips around the mouth must be copies of the red labia" (Desmond Morris,
The Naked Ape [New York: McGraw-Hill, 1967], 75). This extravagantly anal-
obsessed fantasy has nothing over *Suddenly, Last Summer*.

9   Pauline Kael, *I Lost It at the Movies* (Boston: Little Brown, 1965), 140.

10   *Time* magazine, January 11, 1960.

11   Apropos of Sebastian's fragmentation, Vito Russo has written: "he comes at us
in sections, scaring us a little at a time, like a movie monster too horrible to
be shown all at once" (*The Celluloid Closet* [New York: Harper and Row, 1981],
117). One must add, however, that any such movie monster also tends (quite
in keeping with Williams's allegory of Sebastian as a sacrificial hero whose
slaughtered flesh sustains the community that partakes of it) to be a bit of a
monstre sacré, since Hollywood resorted to a similar convention for representing Christ himself, whom until *King of Kings* in 1961 it was considered profane
to lend an all too human actor's face.

12   I hardly wish to minimize, however, the practice of passing off censorship
as avant-garde artistic expression, either in *Suddenly, Last Summer* or in foreign art films where what functions as "the Code" may be merely implicit. On
the U.S. art-house circuit during the 1950s, as William Nestrick recalled for
me, there played a Swedish film by Arne Mattson, *One Summer of Happiness,*
in which the central disappointment of *Suddenly, Last Summer* finds a rather
close precedent. With that delectably open "Swedishness" which so fascinated
Americans during the years before their own sexual revolution, Mattson's idyll
sent its emancipated lovers into the water for a nude swim; thanks to the
sunlight reflecting prettily off the waves, though, the swimmers' naked bodies
were visible only in silhouette.

13   Among them, those of Joel Cairo and Wilmer ("the gunsel") in *The Maltese
Falcon* (1941), Waldo Lydecker in *Laura* (1944), Brandon and Philip in *Rope*
(1948), and Bruno Anthony in *Strangers on a Train* (1951).

14   Robert Anderson, *Tea and Sympathy,* in *Famous American Plays of the 1950s,*

ed. Lee Strasberg (New York: Dell, 1988), 307. About this still painfully familiar 1953 drama, some of us gay men would argue, perhaps because our own
lives eventually proved the point, that such and so many gay signs as Tom exhibits, instead of being invalidated by his heterosexual experience, are more
likely to negate it instead, to the extent, at the very least, of casting over its
implicit closure a long shadow of dubiety. Accordingly, despite Laura's last request, we have shown so little inclination to "be kind" in our assessment of an
episode whose only genuine reality in our eyes is the unacknowledged one of
sexual abuse, that better known than the request itself now is the mockery to
which we routinely treat it in bidding farewell to our tricks. But in making this
argument, I think, we may be greatly underestimating the excitement of submitting to that *social* embrace, all the more desirable to anyone from whom it
has ever been painfully withheld, which is always greeting heterosexual identity: is it beyond belief that on just enough occasions, even without Laura's
reformist zeal in support, so constant a caress might get a boy hard?

15   So tightly knit is the tradition that the obligatory scenes in one film seem to
plagiarize those in another, as in some cases they actually must have done.
Consider, for instance, this sarcasm of Marnie's to Mark: "Okay, I'm a big
movie fan, I know the games. Come on, let's play. Shall I start with dreams or
shall we free-associate?" Marnie must be a big fan of *Suddenly, Last Summer* in
particular, for she has just offered a pretty close imitation of Catherine's own
taunting invitation to Dr. Cukrowicz: "And now you want to play a game?
Look at pictures? Tell you the first thing that comes into my poor deranged
mind?" She follows Catherine too in getting quickly caught up in the game
she thought she could manipulate, but instead terminates in patently symptomatic confusion, begging her therapist for help.

LESBIAN LOOKS

Desire, Identification, Fantasy

Bonnie Burns

CASSANDRA'S EYES

"Before doubt ever becomes a system, *skepsis* has to do with the eyes."
—Jacques Derrida, *Memoirs of the Blind* [1]

Cassandra's talent for prophecy, a gift of an infatuated god, was, as we know, famously and catastrophically ignored. To punish her for eluding him after he had granted her the power of divination, Apollo, so the story goes, spat in Cassandra's mouth, thereby obliterating her tongue's capacity to persuade. For stealing visions instead of stealing kisses Cassandra is punished by a kiss, a perversely fatal one that weds her forever to a spectacular inevitability: the fall of Troy. Musing on the persistence of this narrative, Stevie Smith, ventriloquizing Helen of Troy, wryly adduces Cassandra's predicament: "It's odd, I said (to Cassandra of course) how / Everything one has ever read about Troy . . . / Naturally gets into one's conversation." [2] What gets into one's conversation, Smith suggests, cannily elucidating the ways in which ideologies reproduce themselves, is inevitably someone *else's* conversation. Indeed, the spit of a god fills Cassandra's mouth with the insistent stupidity of a narrative that, in issuing from elsewhere, secures its fatal ends with a mindless, inescapable force. Cassandra finally can elude nothing—neither the fall of Troy, nor her enslavement to Agamemnon as a spoil of war, nor even her death at the hands of Clytemnestra. Prompted by visions, Cassandra's spoiled articulations function with the force of a compulsion, bringing into relation the ocular seduction of the image with an oracular speech emptied of credibility. Cassandra's eyes, in the end, can only ever witness the ruination of the tongue, each irremediably split from the other through a traumatic encounter with a god.

Though the relations between the eye and the tongue as I've just described them suggest their radical disjunction, I would like nonetheless to look at John Brahm's 1946 film *The Locket* in order to speak about the

ways in which lesbianism will be produced in modern culture as an endlessly transferable doubt, a vision that, like Cassandra's, will be ceaselessly
represented, yet destined always to be disbelieved. A ruined oracle unable
to command belief, but doomed to suffer calamitous dreams, Cassandra
serves as an appropriate figure for the film noir, a genre marked by skepticism and paranoia, in which an often complex and cataclysmic narrative
fails to illuminate a frequently hysterical visual excess.

In *The Locket,* this visual excess will be located at the level of the image
when a flashback sequence meant to establish and explain the "hopelessly
twisted personality" of Nancy (Laraine Day) introduces a disturbing portrait of a blinded Cassandra into the film. The sequence suggests that an
overdetermined and fatal blindness circulates between Nancy, the model
for the portrait, and its artist, Norman Clyde (Robert Mitchum), whose
passion for Nancy prompts him to announce prophetically, "I was determined to have [her] if it killed me." When Nancy arrives at his studio one
day with her employer, Mr. Bonner (Ricardo Cortez), a rich and somewhat
guileless patron of the arts, Clyde agrees to show him his latest work:

> *Bonner:* Nancy, which painting did you say I should look at?
> *Nancy:* "Cassandra." [To Clyde] I think it's a masterpiece; I told Mr.
>   Bonner.
> *Bonner:* I always listen to Nancy; she has such excellent taste.
> *Clyde:* I congratulate you Mr. Bonner. Most rich people make the mis-
>   take of relying on their own.
> *Bonner:* I know the ones you mean.

Clyde places the portrait of "Cassandra" on an easel in the center of the
room. Bonner and Clyde stand at the left of the screen separated by the
portrait from Nancy, who stands to the right.

> *Clyde:* Nancy sat for this; you'll notice I used her hair.
> *Bonner:* Really?

Bonner scrutinizes the painting and the camera cuts to a close-up of the
portrait, a stylized painting of a woman with blanked-out eyes (fig. 1).

> *Nancy:* Do you like it?
> *Bonner:* I don't know; I would have to study it more carefully. When
>   I think of Cassandra I see a madwoman; a woman with prophetic
>   eyes . . . wonderful eyes. [Turning to Nancy]. Yes, *you* have them.

The camera frames Nancy and the portrait in a two-shot for a moment (fig. 2) and then cuts back to Bonner and Clyde.

> *Bonner:* Tell me Mr. Clyde, how did you manage to miss the eyes . . . or are you partial to hair?
>
> *Clyde:* I paint pictures, not anatomy.

Mary Ann Doane has suggested that the blinded Cassandra confirms the film's seamless equation of woman and image: "this Cassandra herself is blind, lacking in subjectivity," writes Doane. "Because she *is* the image of doom," Doane argues, "she cannot see it."[3] John Fletcher, in an important critical reading of this film, underscores Doane's point when he claims that the painting "hints at the presence of something [Nancy] cannot see or tell, the striking out of knowledge by repression."[4] While the film insistently produces Nancy as the sightless image of doom, the blank eyes of the portrait with which she is identified suggest as well that there is something about Nancy that fails to be fully represented by Clyde's painting, as if the empty eyes of the portrait signal not the striking out of *Nancy's* knowledge by repression but signal rather, the *artist's* refusal to see.[5] Derrida, in *Memoirs of the Blind,* reminds us that "the drawing," like this painting, "is blind." In consequence, he argues, "the operation of drawing would have something to do with blindness, would in some way regard blindness."[6] In drawing his Cassandra, Clyde paradoxically regards his own blindness after painting his refusal-to-see into the portrait, a projection that the film recognizes fleetingly at the level of narrative in his exchange with Mr. Bonner. Bonner's arch question, "Tell me Mr. Clyde, how did you manage to miss the eyes . . . or are you partial to hair?" attributes the work of repression to *Clyde* and so elicits his sullen and defensive response: "I paint pictures, not anatomy."

As we will see, Clyde's willful blindness stains the canvas with a radical doubt that not only divests the image of its capacity to reassure but invests it with a shocking fatality: after failing to convince Nancy's current husband, Harry Blair (Brian Aherne), of Nancy's devious criminality, Clyde leaves the painting wrapped in paper in Blair's office in payment for his time. As Blair unwraps the package, the camera zooms in for a close up of a blankly staring "Cassandra." Offscreen we hear glass shattering and a woman's scream. A cut reveals the gaping hole of a shattered window through which Clyde has thrown himself to his death. In disavowing anatomy through the wiles of representation, Clyde all the more insistently circulates the dictum "anatomy is destiny." Nancy, however, dramatically determines the destiny of *others,* as one after another of her former lovers falls from an exalted position of authority and knowledge to a debased state in which their attempt to utter anything that anyone might possibly believe *about* Nancy will miserably fail. When he is unable to convince anyone of the credibility of a story that he must compulsively repeat until his death, Clyde exhibits the mark of Cassandra's doom, a mark that will continue to circulate throughout the film in uncontrollable ways.

Clyde's fall from the window rather spectacularly suggests that the painting of Cassandra registers the familiar trauma of castration in which a vision of lack prompts a defensively produced (and always tenuous) narrative of sexual difference. Indeed, Fletcher has convincingly argued that "[t]he portrait of Nancy as Cassandra, a prophetess who can't see, an uncanny image of a woman marked by lack, signifies castration."[7] But the portrait of an eyeless Cassandra speaks as well to something *in excess of* castration, a something that I would like to insist, Cassandra-like, can be read, despite the *skepsis* of the eye that could only ever produce incredulity, as the articulation of lesbian desire.

As Doane cannily points out, the film's narrative attempts to recuperate the doubt that threatens to fracture the tongue from the eye by finally attributing madness to the figure of Nancy. Bonner suggests as much when he identifies the "something missing" in the portrait of Cassandra, with Nancy's "wild," "prophetic" eyes, thereby bringing the two into relation for the first time. But this image of Nancy/Cassandra—the momentary two-shot that frames Nancy with open eyes standing next to a "Cassandra" with empty eyes—registers a visual excess that disturbs the film's capacity to unveil "Woman" as the sign of castration. Indeed, the figure of Nancy wedded to the image of Cassandra produces woman as *lack* only by virtue of a different sort of blindness.

I want to suggest that this doubled image of a blind Cassandra and a wild-eyed Nancy serves as an overdetermined vision that puts into doubt the usual story of female lack, a story that, in the end, can only be recuperated through the relentless imposition of a heterosexual narrative. The visual suture of Nancy and Cassandra brings "Woman" as the image of cinematic fascination into relation with an unspeakable and traumatic lesbian excess, an excess that we must close our eyes to in order for the visual regime to perform its ideological work. What is excessive about Nancy, after all, is her fascination with another woman; Nancy *tells* Bonner that she thinks "Cassandra" is a "masterpiece." Though Bonner claims to "always listen to Nancy; she has such excellent taste," he fails to take her literally and eventually meets *his* doom when he is shot and killed (presumably by Nancy) for witnessing the attempted theft of his wife's jewels.

The visual excess that signals Nancy's desire will be uncannily repeated by the film during a flashback sequence we are meant to believe explains Nancy's uncontrollable urge to steal, a kleptomania that Clyde, and later Blair, believe compels her to commit unspeakable acts. During this flashback sequence—Nancy's memory of a traumatic childhood event—we learn that her father, an unsuccessful artist, has unexpectedly died, forcing Nancy's mother to work as a housekeeper for the Willises, a wealthy and class-conscious family with a son at boarding school and a daughter

Nancy's age living at home. Karen Willis, a diminutive Cassandra, be-
friends Nancy and entertains her with visions that Nancy believes without
hestitation.[8] Early on in this sequence an odd cinematic framing accompanies one of Karen's more delightful prophecies when she retreats to a
storage closet in the back of the house with ten-year-old Nancy (Sharyn
Moffet) after Mrs. Willis (Katherine Emery) refuses to allow Nancy to attend Karen's impending birthday party. In a sumptuous fantasy in which
the tongue promises to indulge the desires of the eye, Karen constructs an
intensely provocative vision of oral pleasure:

> *Karen:* I think it's mean; I won't have any fun now.
> *Nancy:* Don't tell anyone you asked Karen. If mother finds out . . .
> *Karen:* I won't tell, but you're going to have everything the others get;
>   I'm going to see to it. Vanilla cake with candies on it and walnut
>   ice cream. And you'll get a present too; the girls are getting pins.
>   Would you like a real platinum pin Nancy? To wear on your dress?
> *Nancy:* Do you suppose I could?
> *Karen:* Wait, you'll see tomorrow.

During this exchange, a kind of visual bracketing seems literally to fuse
Nancy and Karen in an embrace, repeating the camera's earlier framing
of Nancy alongside the portrait of Cassandra (fig. 3). The shot suggests
that we are witnessing this moment through a door only slightly ajar;
bars of solid black impinge on Nancy and Karen from either side of the
screen while a column of light at its center illuminates their faces, pressed
together cheek-to-cheek. Michael Renov somewhat nervously notices the
force of excess that attaches to this visual display: "The composition is *too*
symmetrical, the faces too closely joined. The image is dominated by hard-
edged shadows, suggestive of the unknowable regions of the mind, which
force an unnatural union."[9] Renov cautions us to resist understanding this
moment as something that could be construed as a "split personality" and
instead calls for a reading that would take into account "the effects of the
uncanny." He describes the moment as an exemplary instance of "topos
noir," in which an overt visual stylization threatens to overwhelm the competing verisimilitude of the framing narrative: "Consistent with the notion
of 'topos noir,' no spatial context is given nor is one possible; one essential
signified of the image is 'disembodiment.' Here as in much of *film noir*, the
integrity of a stabilizing space that situates diegesis and spectator within
a predictable framework is jettisoned."[10] This reading strikes me as both

3

brilliantly acute and oddly mimetic of the defensive strategies staged by the film. Renov identifies the uncanniness of this scene with the vertiginous effect of a striking moment of excess in which "symmetry" ceases to produce the illusory stability of classical form. However, in a disavowal eerily suggestive of Norman Clyde's refusal-to-see, the symmetry of this moment of promise between Nancy and Karen careens suddenly into an instance of "disembodiedness," as if Renov, like Clyde, could only project his perception of an uncanny excess as a radical lack that nonetheless bodies forth, almost inevitably it would seem, "an unnatural union." But Renov can hardly be faulted for articulating an illogic that the film has already produced in its attempt to "explain" Nancy. Rather, Renov's sense of this scene's unreadability emphasizes the film's insistence that we momentarily apprehend our own *inability to apprehend* lesbian desire as anything but an incoherent "disembodiedness" that remains just beyond the margin of a visual symbolic.

That this moment occurs in what must be read as the space of the closet suggests that the film—or more precisely, the visual field—displays, in its ability to penetrate and expose the "meaning" of the closet with an illuminating shaft of light, a knowingness about Nancy that eludes the blindness that afflicts the characters in the film. But Renov's sense that the black edges bordering either side of the screen are "suggestive of the unknowable regions of the mind" points to the unsettling possibility that what appears to be *external* to the illuminating capacity of cinema can be understood as having been precipitated by an event *internal* to the visual system. While a certain divining power seems to accrue to the visible in this moment, the film also bears witness to a simultaneous *narrowing* of the visual field as the bars of darkness continue to press upon the figures of desire. As if unconsciously exhibiting a hysterical symptom, the film seems compelled to seal its eyes to the spectacle of excess embodied in this embracing couple.

But of course the flight into illness of which the hysterical symptom is one sign finds no easy analog in the cinematic apparatus. For film to succumb to hysteria and close its eyes to the spectacle of lesbian excess would mean the *end* of visions, and the end of the cinematic imagination. If the spectacle of lesbian desire exceeds the cinema's capacity to look, producing a blindness that inhabits the visual system like a foreign agent, this blindness might occasionally function as an agent provocateur, revealing the limits of a visual system founded upon the "truth" of sexual difference. More often, of course, the refusal-to-see functions as the visual system's *aide-de-camp,* assisting with the endless work of converting the symptoms of a hysterical blindness into the signs of a knowing illumination. Eve Sedgwick has demonstrated the seemingly inexhaustible capacity of ideology to mobilize the complex relations between knowledge and ignorance that inform the meaning of the closet.[11] If the film at this moment beholds the stain of its own blindness, it does so with a certain canniness absent from Clyde's contemplation of the blank eyes in his portrait of Cassandra. In order to mobilize its blindness in defense of a *cinematic* integrity, *The Locket* will memorialize this erotic vision as the empty token of a benign and vanquished memory.

The film, after all, insists that we read the desiring excess apparent in this scene as an always already lost moment of plenitude, to read it, that is, as "an archaic moment of narcissistic and homosexual jouissance." *The Locket* locates this "uncanny blissfulness" in a temporal past and immediately reveals its rupture and loss as Nancy's voice-over announces during the opening moments of the flashback that Karen is no longer living.[12] Effectively securing lesbian sexuality by locating it in a narrative of development that obliterates the very possibility of a "persistent desire," the film memorializes lesbian desire as a rapturous moment whose traumatic loss founds the machinery of Oedipal normativity.[13]

This process of memorialization, I want to argue, functions almost paradigmatically in modern culture's construction of the *lesbian* closet, insofar as it occludes the disturbing excess that troubles the easy equation that reads "Woman" as lack while simultaneously providing a "meaning" to attach to the blind spot in the visual realm that such an excess invariably reveals. "Memory," after all, as Freud conceptualizes its function in *Beyond the Pleasure Principle,* serves a therapeutic purpose for the patient suffering from traumatic symptoms who "is obliged to *repeat* the repressed material as a contemporary experience instead of, as the physician would prefer to see, *remembering* it as something belonging to the past."[14] Distinguishing remembrance from repetition, Freud, in a rare passage that addresses the therapeutic imperative of psychoanalysis as "cure," identifies and valorizes the memorializing work of memory by setting it against the compulsive repetition of "the repressed material *as a contemporary experience.*" The "memory" of lesbian desire in this film is evoked only in order for it to halt the traumatic repetitions that mark the failure of the visual system to produce Nancy as the sign of lack. Attempting to disassociate repetition — the mark of neurosis — from the cinematic apparatus, the film almost literally follows Freud's prescription for therapeutic success as it narrows the wild desire of Nancy and Karen into a sliver of light, attempting "to force as much as possible into the channel of memory and to allow as little as possible to emerge as repetition." To establish the "memory" that enables us, like a patient cured of hysteria, "to recognize that what appears to be reality is in fact only a reflection of a forgotten past," *The Locket* opens itself as if it *were* a locket to reveal the memorialized desire at its heart.[15]

While the overdetermined image of Nancy and Karen embracing in the closet remains exemplary of the film's memorializing project, the repetition of scenes from the past saturate the whole of *The Locket.* Structured by a series of flashbacks, the film exhibits a compulsion to repeat that exceeds the diegetic representation of Nancy's kleptomania. Indeed, the urgency of the flashbacks, which begin within minutes of the film's opening sequence, quickly subsumes the diegetic "present," a wedding party that has gathered to celebrate Nancy's marriage to the son of a socially prominent family. The ceremony will be delayed by the arrival of Blair, who interrupts the festivities to recount to an incredulous bridegroom the story of his own disastrous marriage to Nancy. When Blair's narrative reaches his encounter with Clyde, who had sought out Blair to ask for his help in preventing the execution of the man accused of killing Bonner, Blair's story is overwhelmed by a second flashback as Clyde begins to narrate the story of *his* fateful encounter with Nancy. A third flashback is embedded in this sequence when Nancy tells Clyde the story of her childhood trauma in an attempt to justify her impulse to steal Mrs. Bonner's jewels.

Meant to reveal Nancy's kleptomania by providing the "memory" that would explain—and distance—the past, these flashbacks seem instead to disturb the film's capacity to tell a story at all by reversing the sequential logic of narrative. If Nancy's fascination for the past signals a regression that heteronormative narratives of development can only interpret as a perversion, the constant removal from one flashback to the next furthers the film's regressive—and potentially perverse—tendencies. The flashbacks question the ability of a narrative to establish even an individual "history" as the dissolves that signal a shift from one temporal moment to the next are preceded by the visual obliteration of each speaker's face. Blair's face disappears in a cloud of cigarette smoke moments before the screen dissolves to the scene of his first meeting with Nancy in Florida. Later, Clyde's face will be engulfed in shadow before a dissolve to the image of *Nancy's* face smiling up at him in his studio. Finally, when Nancy tells the story of her childhood to Clyde, she raises a white handkerchief to cover her face moments before a dissolve to an image of an empty hallway in the Willis home. At the very moment when Blair, then Clyde, and finally Nancy attempt to construct an identity in telling their stories, the apparatus overwhelms the very figure for identity—the face—dissolving and obliterating their narrative efforts. Rather than establishing the ability of narrative to perform the memorializing work of memory then, the compulsive return to a moment from the past, signaled by the dissolve, uncovers the persistently unsettling force of a traumatic repetition central to the cinematic experience itself.

To clarify this point, I want to turn to recent work on trauma and memory by Cathy Caruth, who usefully claims that "[t]o be traumatized is precisely to be possessed by an image or event."[16] The erasure of identity upon which each of these flashbacks turns indicates the degree to which the cinematic image does indeed *possess* its subjects, overwhelming the narratives upon which identity depends. Troubling the film's capacity to unfold conclusively the etiology of Nancy's hysteria, and offering instead an endless catalog of its effects, the film's flashbacks can never quite tell the story, suggesting that cinema's repetitions can never adequately accomplish the social act that Pierre Janet, an early theorist of trauma, identified with "narrative memory." Unlike "traumatic memory," which, in its single-minded automatism, "has no social component," narrative memory, the ability to recount the past *as story,* according to Janet, serves an adaptive function, allowing the patient to integrate and assimilate past traumatic events.[17] The recent recuperation of Janet's work on trauma by theorists such as Bessel A. van der Kolk and Onno van der Hart "for the sake of testimony and for the sake of cure" reveals the ethical imperative that informs contemporary theoretical and practical interventions in the history of trauma.[18] But, as I have been arguing, the reconstruction of historical memory, while crucial to the process of witnessing the traumas that have marked the twentieth century as well as the lives of those caught in the violence that has come more and more to define modernity, might function precisely to foreclose the possibilities of a desire that lies beyond the constitutive acts of the social.[19]

Though the film locates each of Nancy's traumatic episodes in a flashback, her compulsive need to steal remains persistently a "contemporary experience," rather than a scene from the past. After Nancy tells Clyde her story, he decides to return the jewels he had discovered in her purse and asks for her assurance that she "wouldn't ever do it again." Even as Nancy agrees to police her desires, she continues to resist the memorializing efforts imposed on them. Her kleptomania—her compulsion to repeat— remains stubbornly opposed to the normalizing requirements of "narrative memory" and obstinately devoted to the literal reiteration of a traumatic symptom.[20]

In order to theorize what Caruth identifies as the "impossibility" within the traumatic event, an event that, by definition, *exceeds* our capacity to narrate it intelligibly, we might do well to "witness" these events differently in order to account for the exclusions required by the forms of the social as such. Rather than recurring to a reading that understands the repetition of the traumatic symptom as the failure of memory to produce a meaningful narrative, then, I would like to consider how the reiterations that mark *The Locket* might signal instead, in Joseph Litvak's words, "the *temporal* 'promiscuity,' the chronological 'mistakes,' whereby fantasies, pleasures, and loved objects from earlier, supposedly transcended phases in both individual and cultural history turn up, strange bedfellows themselves, within fantasies, pleasures, and loved objects from later phases, and vice versa . . . anachronistically intertwined in a single libidinal intelligence."[21] In *The Locket* the process of memorialization that would locate lesbian desire in the distant remove of the past will be troubled by the perverse repetitions of an initiating trauma that disrupts the very fiction of progress upon which narrative depends. When lesbianism returns in *The Locket*—which it does repeatedly—it returns precisely *as* the trauma that signals the failure of *cinema's* repetitions to produce a narrative unmarked by "chronological mistakes"; that is, insofar as the cinematic apparatus compulsively reproduces the images that constitute it "as a contemporary experience," endlessly reviving images from the past in a literally exact present, film too remains devoted to a libidinal economy that challenges the normalizing narratives of heterosexuality. It is little wonder then that precisely at the site of *The Locket's* most deeply embedded "memory"—the flashback to Nancy's childhood—the film deflects its traumatic encounter with the strange bedfellow of lesbian desire by spitting in its mouth. As we will see, if Apollo exacts his revenge by infecting Cassandra's visions with a narrative of doubt, the film, in a godlike gesture of disavowal, will transfer to the figure of the lesbian its own failure to persuade us that its visions serve the memorializing work of remembrance.[22]

When Karen gives Nancy a heart-shaped locket "with a real diamond" in lieu of the promised platinum pin, Nancy looks heavenward, clasps the locket in her hands, and murmurs ecstatically, "Thank you god. I'll never ask for anything again." By now we should be acquainted with the erratic will of the gods; when Karen's mother learns that her daughter has given Nancy a precious jewel, she demands its return, and Nancy tearfully yields Karen's gift. Soon after, when the locket cannot be found, Mrs. Willis compels Nancy to admit falsely that she stole it, even after Nancy's mother discovers it caught in a seam of Karen's dress. In an excessively melodramatic moment, Mrs. Willis looms over Nancy, seizes her by the shoulders, and shakes her fiercely while demanding a confession from her. Finally succumbing to Mrs. Willis's repeated demands to "say it," Nancy finally moans, "Yes, I took it; let me go." In her attempt to escape from Mrs. Willis's grip, she accidently knocks a music box off of the table next to her. When it falls to the floor, its contents spill out onto the carpet while a mindless tune overwhelms the soundtrack.[23] In an abrupt and highly stylized shot, Nancy's face is framed from below as she stares down into the camera (fig. 4). The camera cuts to a close-up of the open music box with its mechanism revealed (fig. 5) and cuts back again to Nancy staring down into the camera in blank perplexity as the music continues to play.[24] This deliberate cut to the empty music box provides an image for the cinematic apparatus itself, identifying it with a mechanism driven by the motor of repetition.[25]

4

5

Paul de Man reminds us that music "can never rest for a moment in the stability of its own existence: it steadily has to repeat itself in a movement that is bound to remain endless."[26] He makes this point in order to claim that "[l]ike music, language is a diachronic system of relationships, the successive sequence of a *narrative*," or, more precisely, "a succession of discontinuous moments that create the *fiction* of a repetitive temporality."[27] Music functions, that is, especially in *The Locket,* as an allegory of signification's capacity to create fictions of chronology, to "mislead one into believing in a stability of meaning that does not exist."[28] The film's narrative suggests that the loss of the locket and the disturbingly violent confession exacted by Mrs. Willis combine to turn Nancy into a thief and a compulsive liar. Cinematically, however, through the montage that links

Nancy's shocked expression to a representation of the cinematic apparatus, the film suggests that the trauma initiated by Mrs. Willis is inevitably linked to the mindless repetition of a mechanism that, like the spit of the god, inhabits and possesses its oracles.

The fictional claims to coherence upon which narrative depends make it no less terroristic in its capacity to sustain the normalizing ideology of oedipality. While the identification of the cinematic apparatus with the empty music box reveals cinema's participation in a logic of repetition whose claims to coherence can only ever be imaginary, the film simultaneously disavows that identification through the figure of Nancy, who literally stands in the place of the apparatus and in doing so bears the burden of repetition that would otherwise accrue to the film. By confessing to a theft for which she holds no responsibility, she absorbs the doubt aroused by this momentary revelation and absolves the apparatus from recognizing its debt to her.

But the film's own refusal-to-see, cannot, after all, finally closet lesbian desire, nor bury it in the rubble of a psychological history. Nancy's announcement that she will never ask for anything again continues to register with an oracular force since, of course, from this time on, she will *take* what she wants. The locket, then, rather than memorializing desire, serves in its loss to *mobilize* desire. Circulating beyond the scenes of childhood, and indeed, outside the frame of the visual field, the locket, and the desire that it excites, produces cataclysmic consequences that seem only to find their thematization in a different mobilization, a filmic representation of the Allied response to the blitzkrieg that ravaged London during World War II.

A series of reversals haunts the film in its final frames, as the reiterative tendency of desire disrupts the straitening narratives of heterosexuality. In a trajectory exactly opposed to Freud's consideration of war trauma in *Beyond the Pleasure Principle,* which leads to a discussion of a child's game of fort/da, the film moves instead from the trauma of repetition to the scenes of war. But, where Freud remained silent about the connections between oedipality and the mysteriously numbing effect of war trauma, the film establishes a striking connection between the trauma experienced by Nancy, induced by the imposition of a narrative that promises to cure the ills of repetition, and the trauma experienced by her analyst-husband, Harry Blair, a trauma provoked by the return of Nancy's desires *to the* visual field. The return of this desire as, once again, "a contemporary experience," will have a numbing effect on Blair precisely because it fails to be recuperated by the normalizing narratives of heterosexuality.

During this almost surreal sequence in the film, in which the burning of London eerily echoes the ruin of Troy, the portrait of Cassandra returns with an appalling insistence. Soon after Blair and Nancy move to London in order to escape the trauma of Clyde's suicide, the war reaches the city and an air raid destroys the couple's flat. When Blair finally arrives at the scene, he begins to sort through the debris looking for a sign that Nancy, who stayed at home while Blair went on duty, has survived the blitz. Blair reaches what was once the couple's bedroom and, throwing aside the frame of the bed, notices something in the rubble. The camera, cutting to a dark screen illuminated by the gleam of a single jewel, finds what Blair has been looking for—a "sign" of Nancy, who, by this point in the film, is insepa- rable from the circulating jewels that mark her desire. The camera cuts back to a medium shot of Blair kneeling and cuts again to a close-up of the diamond pendant as he lifts it from the rubble. As Blair begins to dig in earnest, pulling another piece of precious jewelry out of the darkness, he is interrupted by Nancy who arrives in her (quite butch) ambulance driver's uniform explaining that she had been called away earlier that eve- ning. Blair, overcome by shock and already suspicious of her, holds out the diamond pendant as "evidence" of Nancy's guilt. She stares at him incredu- lously and asks, "What's that you've got?" Raising the pendant higher, he asks, in almost a whisper, "Can't you see?" Nancy, wide-eyed, responds: "Harry, did you . . . just find it?"

As Harry stands, we see the jewels spilling from a broken and battered box. He continues showing them to Nancy as the camera cuts to her and she asks, "Don't tell me there's more of them?" Blair stares at her dumbly and his look, framed in close-up (fig. 6), is strikingly reminiscent of the child Nancy's dazed expression when she is confronted by the insistent and repetitive tune of the music box. What spills out of *this* box, however, does not precipitate a traumatic subjection to the symbolic but registers instead the return of lesbian desire to the field of vision, a return that transfers the infection of doubt to Blair himself, who, even with the evi- dence in his hands, is unable to speak convincingly of what he sees.

As the camera cuts from Blair's incredulous look and pans in for a tight close-up of Nancy (fig. 7), strobe lights (presumably meant to be explo- sions or shell fire) alternately illuminate her face and cast it into shadow.

6

7

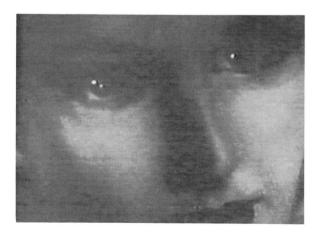

8

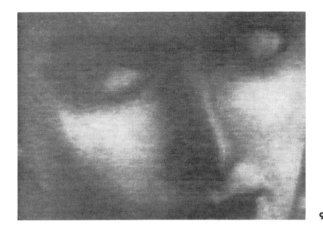

9

10

After a brief moment, during which Nancy's eyes flash like faceted jewels, the close-up of her face dissolves into the portrait of Cassandra, but with a singular difference. For a brief moment we see a portrait of a *sighted* Cassandra, her eyes open and staring into the camera (fig. 8). The dissolves continue as the portrait transforms once again into a painting of the sightless Cassandra (fig. 9). A final dissolve to Nancy behind a veil (fig. 10) ends the sequence as we realize the scene has shifted to a military hospital where Blair lies in bed disheveled and sickly. Offscreen we hear a voice explaining, "You know she didn't steal any diamonds. Can't you understand that you're imagining all this? Now, look at your wife . . . Keep looking." Blair turns his face away and groans.

When the well-meaning psychiatrist patiently tells Blair to "keep looking," in effect he urges Blair to seek the solace of the image in the veiled face of Nancy. But, as this sequence demonstrates, the image that confronts Blair is not a fetishized female beauty that serves to veil over the anxieties prompted by the sight of nothing-to-see but literally something we haven't seen before, signaled by the painting of a sighted Cassandra that appears at no other time in the film. The remarkable appearance of this painting at this moment of crisis stunningly registers the inability of the visual system finally to close its eyes forever to the image of excess that has attached to lesbian desire throughout *The Locket*. What Cassandra's eyes *see* is precisely what the cinema remains unable to *say*, that lesbian desire circulates, like an irresistible jewel, not only beyond the field of vision but, more crucially, within it.[29] Appearing in the impossible space *between* Nancy as the image of doom (a cinematic representation of "Woman") and the painting of a blind Cassandra (the sign of cinema's refusal-to-see), the image of a *sighted* Cassandra inhabits the visual field while remaining inassimilable to its logic. Illuminated by the brilliance of an annihilating shell fire, Cassandra's eyes momentarily reveal the traumatic excess that inhabits a visual system founded upon the logic of castration and unveils a vision of another destiny, one in which the inevitable *failure* of the visual symbolic produces the very conditions through which lesbianism can be divined. Exceeding the film's capacity to recuperate it to the compensatory narratives of female lack, this image remains precisely what Blair must *not* look at if he is ever to recover from the Cassandra-like madness to which he has succumbed. The frantic shot/reverse-shot sequence between Blair and Nancy, rather than locking together the heterosexual couple in a mirroring embrace, figures instead the endless transference of doubt and incredulity that the uncanny excess of lesbian desire produces in the visual field.

However, if Clyde paints his refusal-to-see into his portrait of Cassandra, creating an image for the blind spot in the visual system, Blair's traumatic encounter with this image's obverse does not necessarily register his capacity to see what is staring him in the face. When Blair lifts the diamond pendant and offers it up to the camera's gaze, asking brokenly, "Can't you see?" the film answers in the only way it can, by producing a series of images to suggest that the visual system's only *legitimate* response to Cassandra's eyes is blindness. In an evocative digression on oracular etiquette, Jacques Lacan offers an explanation for the consistent attribution of blindness to the figure of the seer: "The game is already played, the die already cast. . . . That is why the Augurs can't look each other in the face without laughing. It isn't because they tell each other—*You're having them on.* If Tiresias encounters another Tiresias, he laughs. But in fact he can't encounter another, because he is blind, and not without reason. Don't you feel there's something derisory and funny about the fact that the die has already been cast?" [30]

By the end of *The Locket*, fate, another name for the mindless authority of the symbolic, does indeed continue to play out a game already played, when, on her wedding day, Nancy is overwhelmed once again by the tune from the music box moments after receiving a gift—the locket itself—from the mother of her fiancé, who, as it turns out, is the brother of the dead, but not forgotten, Karen. Who can blame her when, moments before reaching the altar, Nancy succumbs to madness and is escorted out by another woman in uniform, a nurse from a nearby sanitorium?

But if Nancy traumatically experiences the imposition of ideology as the mindless repetition of a narrative issuing from elsewhere, Blair traumatically witnesses the breach in the visual field produced by that ideology's failure to negotiate the persistent return of lesbian desire to it. The vision that confronts Blair in the end is not the enabling refusal-to-see that sustains the authority of a compulsively repetitious cultural symbolic. As Lacan's telling fable suggests, the operations of our cultural machinery, when submitted to a heretical critical gaze, can suddenly appear absurd and ridiculous. What stares back at Blair is the blindness of an ideological impasse that can only register as a blank stupidity. The skepticism practiced by a cultural symbolic that reproduces lesbianism as a figure of doubt eventually turns to an incredulity that will momentarily be directed toward the claims of the visible. The persistent return of lesbian desire to the visual field mobilizes that doubt in ways that cannot, finally, enable a lawful symbolic. Like a blinding jewel, lesbianism ruins the capacity of the visual system itself to speak compellingly about the visions it produces, leaving it, like Harry Blair, able to do little more than stare. Such a moment, of course, is painfully brief, but in this pause, as Helen of Troy discovers in Stevie Smith's illuminating poem, in this "ominous eternal moment I am captive in," we can look each other in the face, and, not without reason perhaps, finally hear Cassandra laugh. [31]

NOTES

I would like to thank Matt Bell, Judith Brown, Carol Flynn, Elliott McEl-downey, and Charles Trocano for their help with this project at various moments of crisis. I owe a special debt of gratitude to Lee Edelman, whose skepticism continues to instruct me and whose vision continues to sustain me.

1   Jacques Derrida, *Memoirs of the Blind: The Self-Portrait and Other Ruins* (Chicago: University of Chicago Press, 1993), 1.

2   Stevie Smith, "I had a dream . . ." *Collected Poems,* ed. James MacGibbon (New York: New Directions, 1983), 421.

3   Mary Ann Doane, *The Desire to Desire: The Woman's Film of the 1940s* (Bloomington: Indiana University Press, 1987), 59.

4   John Fletcher, "Versions of Masquerade," *Screen* 29, no. 3 (summer 1988): 64.

5   Maureen Turim suggests that "Clyde is a witness who has in his portrait of Nancy as Cassandra unwittingly provided the film with his self-portrait, for as this cypher shifts to become the portrait of the artist its references suddenly make more sense. It is Clyde whose vision will not be believed, as Nancy can dismiss it through verbal deflection." See her essay "Fictive Psyches: The Psychological Melodrama in 40s Film," *boundary* 2 12, no. 3 and 13, no. 1 (spring/fall 1984): 328.

6   Derrida, *Memoirs of the Blind,* 2.

7   Fletcher, "Versions of Masquerade," 64.

8   Though the young actress playing the child Nancy received a credit for this film, "Karen" remains anonymous, as if confirming the mythological significance of her role in this drama.

9   Michael Renov, "Topos Noir: The Spacialization and Recuperation of Disorder," *Afterimage* 15, no. 3 (October 1987): 15.

10   Ibid.

11   Eve Kosofsky Sedgwick, *The Epistemology of the Closet* (Berkeley: University of California Press, 1990).

12   Fletcher, "Versions of Masquerade," 69.

13   I borrow the phrase from Joan Nestle's edited collection, *The Persistent Desire: A Femme-Butch Reader* (Boston: Alyson Publications, 1992).

14   Sigmund Freud, *Beyond the Pleasure Principle* (New York: Norton, 1961), 19.

15   Ibid.

16   Cathy Caruth, ed., *Trauma: Explorations in Memory* (Baltimore: The Johns Hopkins University Press, 1995), 4–5.

17   Bessel A. van der Kolk and Onno van der Hart, "The Intrusive Past: The Flexibility of Memory and the Engraving of Trauma," in Caruth, *Trauma,* 163.

18   Cathy Caruth, "Recapturing the Past: Introduction," in *Trauma,* 153.

19   For a discussion of theories of trauma in relation to lesbianism and incest

narratives, see Ann Cvetkovich, "Sexual Trauma/Queer Memory: Incest, Lesbianism, and Therapeutic Culture," *GLQ: A Journal of Lesbian and Gay Studies* 2, no. 4 (1995): 351–77.

20   Caruth notices "the surprising *literality* and nonsymbolic nature of traumatic dreams and flashbacks, which resist cure to the extent that they remain, precisely, literal" (*Trauma*, 5).

21   Joseph Litvak, "Proustian Anachronisms: Sophistication, Naïveté, and Gay Narrativity" (paper presented at the annual convention of the Modern Language Association, San Diego, Calif., December 1994).

22   For a discussion of the ways in which the logic of temporality mobilizes credulity and doubt in Freud's articulation of the primal scene in his case study of the Wolf Man, see Lee Edelman's "Seeing Things: Representation, the Scene of Surveillance, and the Spectacle of Gay Male Sex," in *Homographesis: Essays in Gay Literary and Cultural Theory* (New York: Routledge, 1994), especially 176–79.

23   The music box plays "Au Clair de la Lune," a repetitive song whose verses, though well-known, actually make little narrative sense.

24   Turim identifies the music issuing from the box with "Nancy's subjective state," noting that the final scenes of the film present "an image of a Pandora's Box" that Nancy cannot close. Her desires, Turim argues, and her inability to lock them up "are her undoing" (Turim, "Fictive Psyches," 326). I want to suggest that the music box does not simply represent "female" sexuality, whatever that might mean, but, more compellingly, indicates the degree to which Nancy's sexuality serves to absorb the mechanistic repetitions that define the cinema itself.

25   John Fletcher notices that a bawdy music-hall song which begins, "In the naughty nineties, when ladies were so gay," and features the refrain "what is a bump between friends?" is repeated twice in the course of the film, "combin[ing] an infantile playfulness with an arch and knowing—'naughty'—suggestiveness" (Fletcher, "Versions of Masquerade," 69). If the film slyly suggests through this song that it "knows" all about desire between women, it does so only by closing its eyes to the cinematic consequences that this desire provokes.

26   Paul de Man, *Blindness and Insight: Essays in the Rhetoric of Contemporary Criticism* (Minneapolis: University of Minnesota Press, 1983), 129.

27   Ibid., 131–32; emphasis added.

28   Ibid., 133.

29   For a discussion of the relations between jewels, lesbianism, and the cinematic apparatus see my essay, "*Dracula's Daughter*: Cinema, Hypnosis, and the Erotics of Lesbianism," in *Lesbian Erotics*, ed. Karla Jay (New York: New York University Press, 1995), 196–211.

30   Jacques Lacan, *The Seminar of Jacques Lacan, Book II: The Ego in Freud's Theory*

and in the Technique of Psychoanalysis, 1954–1955, ed. Jacques-Alain Miller, trans. Sylvana Tomaselli, with notes by John Forrester (New York: Norton, 1991), 220.

31   Smith, "I had a dream . . . ," 422.

Eric Savoy

"THAT AIN'T *ALL* SHE AIN'T"

Doris Day and Queer Performativity

A tomboy is just a phase on the way to becoming a butterfly; tomboy is not a vocation—
only a temporary, endearing, transcendable affliction.
—Wayne Koestenbaum, *The Queen's Throat* [1]

Sometimes I think I've found my hero,
But it's a queer romance.
—"Ten Cents a Dance" (Rodgers and Hart) [2]

Not infrequently, the deconstructive play with gender identification and sexual identity in popular culture seems, on the one hand, to be entirely resonant with current academic theory, yet on the other hand, to be so complex and incoherent in its representations that even the furthest conceptual reaches of "theory" strain toward an illumination, a knowingness, that remains somewhat remote. This is the case, I suggest, with David Butler's 1953 film, *Calamity Jane,* in which a certain generic tension between the competing demands of the musical and the western reflects an indecisiveness about the possibility, or even the desirability, of coherent gender role. There exists an odd congruence between current theory's promise of analytical mastery and the ways in which *Calamity Jane* positions its spectator: viewership of this comedy of mistaken identity is constructed, in the film's contractual terms, as knowing something about the characters that they do not yet know; academic viewing materializes as knowing something that the actors themselves, and indeed the entire cultural production of *Calamity Jane,* does not and cannot ever know. However, I would argue that such epistemological certainty is at best ephemeral, and at worst illusory, in the reception dynamics required by this film. I begin, then, by marking a critical position that is not exactly an impasse, but rather a predicament; I want to propose an analytical strategy that seeks to work within the constraints of this predicament—and is oddly enabled by it—rather than to resolve it.

Calamity Jane is generally about the possibility of transforming a "tomboy"—a young woman whose gender aspirations are firmly masculine, predicated upon both her male homosocial profession as stagecoach guard and her rather ambivalent, but decidedly immature, sexuality—into what the film understands as "a proper woman," by recalling her to the feminine. Jane Canary's hesitation between resistance of and subordination to dominant ideals of womanhood, in what is possibly the most energetic and engaging performance of Doris Day's entire career, evolves in sharp contrast to supporting characters who, like Jane, pretend to be something they are not, and whose role is to reconstruct their identities clearly and coherently. Such pretense is invariably a matter of gender *performance*, intended to deceive, which the film situates in relation to cross-dressing: this oddly indoor western takes place primarily in the Golden Garter, Deadwood City's music hall, where the actors play performers playing "false" roles. Thus, Dick Wesson's Francis Fryer cross-dresses as "Frances Fryer" before finding acceptance as an effeminate man; Allyn McLerie's Katie Brown attempts to pass as Adelaid Adams, a "real New York actress," but is forgiven and allowed to find her own, more genuine and less mannered, style of performance. Presumably, the lessons about the futility of imposture that are staged on the Deadwood stage are directed at Doris Day's Jane. This regulatory matrix is further consolidated by Howard Keel's Bill Hickock and Gale Robbins's Adelaid Adams, the only characters whose gender identification is represented as fully achieved: and it is from one to the other of these touchstones of gender—Hickock as the embodiment of a masculine authenticity unrealizable for women, and Adelaid as a hyperfeminine spectacle that fulfills male fantasy—that "Calam'" is expected to cross. Is *Calamity Jane's* narrative premise fulfilled by the work of acting? Is Jane Canary successfully reeducated into 1950s constructions of womanhood? Or is there some residual effect of Doris Day's performance that undermines the conclusiveness of the film's narrative trajectory? Such questions are usefully complicated by remarking that the object of "performance" in this film is what Judith Butler has conceptualized as gender "performativity," the cultural matrix in which subjects may be said to materialize through the reiterated stylization of the body. How, then, might the relation of performance to performativity be precisely articulated?

I want to suggest that whatever else we might understand by "performance," it is constrained at the outset in *Calamity Jane* by the requirements of a heteronormative script: it is governed by a fairly rigorous intentionality that must believe it knows what it wants, and it must "want" to bring Jane Canary to a coherent identity in which "femininity" and "heterosexuality" coincide. This is to conceptualize "performance" as volitional, both mastered *by* and in mastery *of* the film's narrative goals. However, if this is the case, then how can one account for what Mandy Merck describes as the persistent "lesbian overtones" in Calamity Jane's relationship with Katie Brown, which somehow are "allowed to survive?"[3] It seems, then, that "performance" is a complicated affair: it may be that the residual matter of Jane's lesbian insubordination is scripted and that the actors know exactly what they are doing, or it may be that a certain queer effect, a certain style of performance, invokes and interpellates a lesbian spectatorial position, possibly inadvertently. Superimposed upon this queer effect—this reception practice that responds to connotative cues to provide an unsettling supplement to Hollywood's dominant practice—is an even queerer hermeneutic field: we can't know with any certainty. It is precisely at this juncture that the opacities of performance—its seeming excesses—can be situated in relation to Butlerian performativity. If "performativity" is understood as the semiotic upon which the subject is predicated, the culturally recognizable matrix in which (in the case of Doris Day's relation to Calamity Jane) the possibility of a lesbian subject, tentative and evanescent, might be said to emerge into visibility, then the *call* of performativity is not referable to volitional performance. Rather, it might be understood as interlining, and pulling against, the narrative requirement of performance that wants to reconstruct Doris Day and Calamity Jane as unproblematically "feminine."

While I do not want to refer "performance" entirely to the (presumed) heteronormative intentionalities of filmic narrative, or to equate "performativity" fully with a lesbian countercurrent, this approach might accomplish two important goals: it might account for lesbian visibility and reception practices—seeing the "lesbian" as a kind of filmic excess that warrants it as a refusal of cultural law—while reconciling the not fully controllable tendencies of the performative with the mysteries of performance's intentionality. As such, this approach builds on Eve Kosofsky Sedgwick's work, following that of Paul de Man, which understands "queer performativity" as resistantly unaccountable, as "a torsion, a mutual perversion," of what the text imagines as "reference" and what it invokes beyond its strictures.[4] It is not an easy business to locate "the lesbian" in *Calamity Jane* with any certainty or conclusiveness. As Molly Haskell observes, in terms of homosexuality "the 1950s were a time of too much and too little."[5] I would conceptualize Haskell's "too much" as the excessive burden of connotation, the very relation of queer performativity to narrative performance, and her "too little" as the impossibility of homosexual presence that generated so much of what constitutes the obliquities of "queerness" in relation to mainstream cinema. What kind of access to 1950s cinematic culture might queer theory provide, taking into account my caveat about theory's problematic goal of epistemological mastery and a film culture that both invites and refuses spectatorial knowingness? Does queer theory privilege such epistemological limits, or does it have recourse to what it imagines as more powerful circuits of knowing? And what, finally, might such a project offer to lesbian and gay fans of classic cinema?

It may be that the recent flurry of activity around the term *queer*—the claims and contestations that have shaped the brief history of its recuperation—yields a critical enterprise that is depleted, or at least endangered, by the comparative ease with which the term is currently invoked. It is precisely this ease of appropriation, combined with the queer project's destabilizations of "coherence" and the refusal of the term itself to settle definitively, that has occasioned so much uneasiness for lesbian- and gay-centered scholarship and the consequent dialogics of reproach.[6] Alternatively, and perhaps more accurately, it seems that the skirmishes of mutual incomprehension between gay identity politics and queer theory—which have tended, strangely and unpredictably, toward binarized and exclusive discourses of re-entrenchment—arise from both a temporal and fashionable academic "currency" in which conceptual work has reached further, and faster, than its analytical deployment. If this is the case, then the extraordinary usefulness of queer *incoherence* for consolidating, paradoxically, lesbian and gay specificity will emerge most clearly in analytical situations in which such "specificity" can be articulated as historically *emergent*, on the threshold of tentative definition. It is within this frame of negotiation that I wish to explore, generally, the uncanny resonances between tumultuous historical moments that mark the "pre" and the "post" of clarified gay and lesbian identities: it may be a convenient historical fiction of circularity that "endings" are immanent in "beginnings," but I am struck nevertheless by the overlapping cultural work—the preoccupation with gender and sexuality as unstable categories—of academic theory in the 1990s and mainstream American cinema of the 1950s.

Is it not the case that contemporary queer critique enables both a startling recognition of 1950s popular culture as *a field of gay and lesbian incipience,* and a sharper grasp of the matrix of possibility and constraint that "queer" has come to signify, in both eras, precisely *as* incipience? In posing this question, I hope to intervene in the misconception that queer paradigms are advanced at the expense of gay and lesbian specificity. Following Foucault, I would suggest that one of the current uses of 1950s cinema is to demonstrate that an incipient specificity of "homosexual" identification and desire was a historical effect of circumlocution, preterition, and oblique referentiality—modes that cannot fully regulate the insubordinate ghosts that they raise into some neutral territory between the visible and the invisible. This attempt to track the ironic coincidence of 1950s and 1990s queernesses has a personal, an autobiographical dimension, one that has everything to do with what constitutes my "specificity" as a gay man at the end of this century. I cannot entirely account for the fascination that 1950s cinema holds for me: it is a period that I cannot claim experientially to "know"—certainly not in the same way that I "know" the academic queer project of the contemporary moment, and even more certainly, these objects of epistemological desire do not share the same aspiration of mastery —yet it is the culture that may be said to have produced a gay man born in 1957. I might say that this epoch produced me, instilled whatever gay specificity I may legitimately claim to an arguably greater extent than the more liberated time in which I came to consciousness. Clearly, then, my interest in a kind of liminal or inchoate gay incipience would not seem to prevent me from smuggling "identity" into my project. But it is an identity that cannot coalesce into what that word customarily signifies: like all genealogical tracings, it materializes in fits and starts, in glimpses of a world that is only oddly my own. As every Americanist knows, it comes under what Hawthorne called "the Romantic definition" in its tentative attempt "to connect a by-gone time with the very Present that is flitting away from us."[7]

A compelling irony of the 1950s is that the most acutely homophobic phase of the American twentieth century generated such a wealth of representation around lesbian and gay potentiality. Queer theory knows how to account for this irony through recourse to the familiar model of the "Foucault effect": anxieties about efficacious regulation in the domain of sexuality yield not a repression but rather a proliferation of discourses that enable both hegemonic control and opportunities for subcultural resistance and resignification. Such logics inevitably conclude that such regulatory instruments as homophobic Freudianism and sensational scandals arose from the same matrix that produced the fiction of James Baldwin and Ann Bannon. But while moments of crystallization are comparatively easy to recognize, it is analytically difficult to comprehend the dialectics of regulation and its refusal[8] — if "dialectics" may denote the odd simultaneity of conformity and transgression — within such hegemonic cultural sites as classic cinema. So, nested within the overarching irony of the homophobic/homosexual 1950s is another, more intricate irony that may be interrogated through a kind of synecdochal logic that is constituted by careers in performance, by "stars" — which brings me to Doris Day.

In this culture, which, according to Eve Kosofsky Sedgwick, "might be said to vibrate to the tense cord of knowingness"[9] — an epistemological mode that empowers, and arises from, ignorance — a rather different synecdochal operation, insidious and impercipient, has long constructed Doris Day as the embodiment of every negative aspect of the "repressive" 1950s. Jane Clarke and Diana Simmonds, who compiled a dossier on Doris Day for the British Film Institute (BFI) in 1980 — one of the very few works that pays serious attention to her career — observe that she is either "the subject of amused contempt" or regarded with "nostalgic affection as the Girl Next Door who exemplified a reassuring and uncomplicated sexuality." In somehow coming to "epitomize the unacceptable face" of the 1950s "to the post-68-generation," Day is seen to "stand for," to be "a sign of," a cultural moment that "America" wishes to forget. The BFI writers pose *the* major revisionist question, one that anticipates the queer project of the 1990s: "Are Doris Day films as reassuring, as comfortable as we remember, or do they too contain instances of resistance or ideological incoherence?"[10]

Doris Day's "incoherent" performances and performatives are my focus: their provision of *a provisional,* an improvisational and emergent "lesbian" possibility — one that is never *quite* overwritten by a heteronormative story or erased by the demands of narrative closure — is their source of beguiling interest for the queer moment at the end of our century. I intend not a "lesbian" recuperation of some biographical version of "Doris Day" but rather an account of what it might mean to be pleasured by a historically specific performance of gender and sexuality that is ambiguous, tentative, multivalent. I concede that it is a pleasure I can afford, since I have no direct stake in presenting a lesbian case for Doris Day's career. My preference for the shadowy realm of connotation, a lesbian specificity that interlines and pulls against, without dismantling, a heterosexual narrative trajectory in her films, is markedly different from the startlingly bald assertion of Margaret Reynolds about the ironies of the 1950s propaganda of gender stereotyping: "Hence cake baking and the New Look for mummy; hence an expanse of desk and a clean jaw for daddy; hence Doris Day and Rock Hudson . . . Only gays could play a straight so very convincingly."[11] My view of Day in the middle distance of film history differs too from the readily identifiable, but unnamed, Doris Day who appears at The Black Cat, a San Francisco lesbian bar, in Mabel Maney's parodic Nancy Clue Mystery, *The Case of the Not-So-Nice Nurse*: she drinks endless pink squirrels, insists that her encounters at the bar be "our little secret." In departing, "'*Que sera sera*,' the woman cried gaily."[12] There is a world of difference between Reynolds's tactics of outing and Maney's campy reconstruction, but it may be that both are guided by a knowingness about what remains, in the signifying play of Day's films, finally unknowable. As Sedgwick observes—specifically in relation to Henry James, but more generally about all figures whose legibility is mired in the historically contingent and "multiple valences of sexuality"—our critical choices should not be "limited to crudities of disruption or silences of orthodox enforcement."[13]

Between 1949 and 1959, Doris Day found herself in a series of diverse cinematic moments in which the signifying gestures of performance tend to pull away from the heteronormative requirements of the script, to gravitate toward or hesitate in the vicinity of an affiliation that the films tacitly understand as an impossibility. This "orientation" rarely materializes in exactly the same manner from film to film. The decade is framed at the outset by *Young Man with a Horn* (1950, dir. Michael Curtiz), which explores a triangulated relationship among characters played by Kirk Douglas, Doris Day, and Lauren Bacall (fig. 1): this female version of a classic Girardian erotic triangle transfers energy away from Douglas, with Day's femme juxtaposed against Bacall's butch.[14] If this kind of complexity is typical of Doris Day's work, then it is highly ironic to see her at the end of this decade in *Pillow Talk* (1959, dir. Michael Gordon), where she attempts to regulate the hypersexuality of Rock Hudson, a sexuality that relocates in a heterosexual register the kinds of uncontrolled appetite that mark the man, always, as pathologically compulsive and therefore tending toward

1   Doris Day, Lauren Bacall, and Kirk Douglas in *Young Man with a Horn* (1950).

"queer." Between these temporal boundaries is *Calamity Jane* (1953), which attempts to regulate Jane Canary's insubordinate gender identifications through the unconvincing relocation of Howard Keel's Bill Hickock from an object of homosocial identification to one of Jane's heterosexual desire. Against this narrative course of repositioning gender in the field of compulsory heterosexuality, gender trouble evolves into sexual trouble as Doris Day's butch *performance* tends increasingly toward a lesbian *performative*, one that interlines and complicates the promise of heterosexual resolution.

The critical appeal of these 1950s explorations of calamitous desire—their potential to complicate what theory "knows" about gay and lesbian specificity—lies in their unstable, shifting propositional logic about what might constitute the *relationality* of both gay and straight normatives to their others. Fifties movies are often predicated upon complex subjectivities—male-homosocialized butch women within heterosexuality, femmes who cross between heterosexual and lesbian matrices, feminized yet heterosexually promiscuous—which cohere only to dissolve, and whose temporal course is motivated in ways that narrative trajectory cannot fully contain or explain. Even the most sophisticated deconstructive maneuvers of queer theory encounter difficulty in exploring the kinds of subjective instabilities realized in, and required by, the narrative patterns of classic cinema. In 1991, Diana Fuss lucidly articulated what would come to be the prevailing deconstructive approach: "the binary structure of sexual orientation, fundamentally a structure of exclusion and exteriorization, nonetheless constructs that exclusion by prominently including the contaminated other in its oppositional logic," thus generating "an outside which is inside interiority making the articulation of the latter possible."[15] As enabling as this conceptualization has been, its structuration seems to rely unconsciously upon fairly static epistemologies and ontologies of what inheres in "the contaminated other." It requires, that is, consistently situated points of view that know where they stand in relation to a semiotic of abjected otherness. The challenge posed by certain historical moments in mainstream cinema, I suggest, is that they consistently undermine the certainties about "what lies where" that seem necessary to oppositional identifications within an exclusionary matrix. The best work of Doris Day, for example, poses the questions of "what is?" and "how do we *know* what is?" but rarely finds conclusive answers in a fluid temporality of the subject. The irreducible irony of queer performativity is that the very possibilities of specifying "otherness" are generated by the preteritions of narrative constraint. Moreover, the simultaneity of diverse spectactorial engagements—responses to highly nuanced registers—effectively and repeatedly decenters the grounds of knowing or the precise *locatability* of transgression. This necessary suspension between intelligibility and unintelligibility constitutes both the queer effect of 1950s cinema and its fin-de-siècle counterpart, queer critique.

Calamity Jane represents "trouble" in a temporal frame of simultaneous, rather than consecutive and strictly dialogic, performatives; lesbian specificity emerges and dissolves instantaneously. In a film that is very much about gender improvisation and its failures—a film in which nearly every character pretends to be something that she or he is not—"calamity" as an object of representation is facilitated by the queer generic hybridity of the script: *Calamity Jane* is a western that is not a western, a musical that parodies the western, or, at times, a western that parodies the musical. Within this tortuous parodic matrix, gender aspiration—pulling performance always toward "impersonation" marked explicitly as such—is the cultural field in which "the parodic" is situated in relation to "the authentic." In this way, gender trouble reflects genre trouble: such "trouble" accrues from the film's uncertainty about—or possibly, its inability to locate convincingly—the site of the authentic. Is the musical a fluffy copy of the western, a sort of western for sissies? Or does it discern the western's illusions about the reality of gender? Is the femme version of Calamity Jane at the end of the film a discovery of "true identity?" Or does the "real" Calamity Jane emerge elsewhere?

The relation of Doris Day's work to queer theory's mapping of gender is illuminated by what Butler imagines as "the refusal of the law in the form of the parodic inhabiting of conformity." In direct proportion to her hyperbolic, butch gender identification, she deploys a lesbian performative—often against the "performance" required by the film's course toward normative resolution—that "produces a set of consequences that exceed and confound the disciplining intention motivating the law."[16] Cumulatively in this film, Doris Day's work "confounds" both the narrative's intent to restrict and regulate and the cultural expectations of feminine subordination to coherent "type," both "heterosexual" and "lesbian." This western attempts a taming of the *shrewd,* an attempt that fails, but cannot be said to fail conclusively. Such irresolution is a function of generic incoherence or unaccountability: the queer intersection of the western's investment in masculinity with the musical's campy excess and dream of infinite possibility.

The promise of the Hollywood western, according to Jane Tompkins, has always been "a translation of the self into something purer and more authentic, more intense, more real."[17] In this, arguably the most conservative of filmic genres, *authentic* selfhood is construed inevitably as masculine "integrity," which signifies not merely the prescriptive ethic of national gender, but more importantly—and more anxiously—an ontological wholeness, an unproblematic sufficiency, a monolithic austerity. Frankly and virulently misogynistic, the traditional western is in constant flight from the perils of "female thinkin'"—which is to say, *"thinkin'"*—because the complexity of the feminine can bring nothing but trouble, gender trouble, the fissuring and unraveling of masculine integrity. Thus, the Hollywood western's promotion of masculine "grit" must always be overdetermined, marked ontologically, as *"True Grit,"* in order to sustain its ideological imperatives and to bring its hero west, west of complication, west of identity crises, west of the feminine, *West*—to borrow the title of Tompkins's book—*of Everything.*

Because the classic western achieved formulaic maturity in the 1930s and 1940s, it was inevitable that, in postwar Hollywood, the genre would provide a rich field for revision, for ironic allusion, and for the reversals and inversions of parodic play. Such experimental opportunity meant that, sooner or later, "Everything" would saddle its own horses and ride off in pursuit, to wreak havoc by crossing over the frontiers of rigid gender role, by interrogating the possibilities for women in the western imaginary, and by problematizing, at least provisionally, the illusion of phallic mastery. Warners' *Calamity Jane*, released in 1953, queers the pitch of the western in several ways, and is perhaps mainstream cinema's most thorough disruption of the western's ontology of gender, though its performative effects are greatly in excess of its intentions.

Calamity Jane was intended by the studio to revitalize the western by inflecting its narrative through the medium of musical comedy, itself in need of resuscitation in the early 1950s.[18] Warner Brothers hoped to capitalize on the popularity of MGM's *Annie Get Your Gun*, and to create a star vehicle for the ineffably androgynous Doris Day by pairing her with *Annie*'s male lead, Howard Keel. (It is the fate of swaggering male musical stars to be generally forgotten; but Keel plays to perfection a type that he brought forward from *Annie* not just to *Calamity Jane* but also to another "taming of the shrew" musical of 1953, *Kiss Me Kate.*) *Calamity Jane*'s queernesses of gender and genre accrue at the parodic intersection of epic western and musical comedy. First of all, the film is governed by a pervasive tension between the western's commitment to authenticity of selfhood and the musical comedy's investment in the problematics of desire and its undoing or remapping of identity. Keel's masterful Bill Hickock incarnates a kind of rock of authentic gender, a touchstone of "the genuine" against which the action unfolds to measure the failures of Jane Canary's imposture. Butler's argument that gender performativity is "a repetition and imitative structure that marks from the start a *failure of adequation*" and is motivated by an "effort *to be* what is always lost and only fantasized,"[19] provides a strikingly useful frame in which to locate "impersonation" on the frontier between the musical and the western. In order for this film to work, Hickock's masculine authenticity must be beyond question; more particularly, he must be entirely free from the potential embarrassment incurred by a legendary western hero appearing in a silly, "feminine" musical. Consequently, "embarrassment" is the very substance of Day's performance as required by the film's narrative: the comedy that arises from her failed investment in the masculine homosocial is interlined with abjection, a continual shaming that can be alleviated only by the promise of "true identity"—of recovery of a lost original—as she turns toward the feminine. Yet, the film's allegorization of failed impersonation cannot fully contain its implications, for this "turn" toward heterosexual femininity never appears as anything other than precarious at best, "wrong" at worst: Jane's *implication* in butch homosociality, and its lesbian correlative, is not subject to erasure. If the exposure of "failure" may be said to fail itself, then Doris Day's calamity may be understood as a queer suspension of coherent gender. In both her masculine beginning and her feminine ending, Jane "enacts the gestus" of different genders, both of which "hold forth the promise of a plentitude that never arrives."[20] It is precisely this queer suspension that I shall conceptualize, in the course of my argument, as a tension between the *performance* required by narrative intentionality, by "story," and the *performatives* of a sometimes butch, sometimes lesbian specificity that resists such compulsion.

While the queerness of generic dissonance invariably refers to competing models of gender possibility, it comes to visibility through the film's incongruous production values. For instance, much of *Calamity Jane's* narrative burden is carried by song, which sabotages the western's faith in silence and repression, its interdiction of lyrical outburst. The parodic "wrong turn" is foregrounded as the very point of the film's opening number: against the rolling prairie landscape of the Dakotas—a scene in which we might conventionally expect the stagecoach to be pursued by "injuns" and to make a desperate run for the haven of Deadwood City—is juxtaposed the soundtrack of a chorus of boys whistling the jaunty theme as the credits are rolled, and then Doris Day appears on "the Deadwood stage" singing "Whip-Crack, Away!" flailing her horsewhip and looking not merely "out of place" but rather like Pat Califia riding into the MLA (fig. 2).[21] If this opening scene—in which the performance of the song carries Jane from the stagecoach to the town and its saloon, where she introduces the other characters—is a high camp parody of such western classics as *Stagecoach* (1939), its role is to situate Jane's masculine identification in relation to the town's ironic mixture of reliance upon and contempt for her competence. As Jane climbs up and down the coach, a chorus of men stick their heads out of the window to sing about the cargo, "care of Wells and Fargo," that rides along with them and that is protected by Jane's expert marksmanship. Yet in the saloon she is the subject of affectionate condescension, and is seen as a teller of tall tales, a girl trying to be a man; even the most cowardly man feels entitled to participate in this infantilization of "Calam'." This ambivalent position of Jane in relation to "the real" is marked in the lyrics at a figurative level: before entering the saloon, she distributes the treasures that Deadwood's citizens have ordered from the East, and among such things as "calico and gingham for the gals" and "a hat from Cincinatti / Same as Adelina Patti / Wore in every famous concert hall" is "a genuine string of artificial pearls!" (fig. 3). The conjunction of the "the genuine" with "the artificial" might profitably be seen as the trope under which this film organizes itself. The "Deadwood stage," then, not only anchors the western in its musical inflection but also establishes *Calamity Jane's* organization around stage spectacles, a structure that links gender aspiration, impersonation, and failure both in and out of specifically theatrical moments. Whereas westerns emphasize the imperative of *doing, Calamity Jane* represents the pleasures of *looking:* much of the film takes place in Deadwood City's saloon and music hall, The Golden Garter, and the camera alternates between spectacle and its reception.

Indeed, it is the desire for feminine spectacle that instigates the complexities of the plot. The saloon-keeper, Henry Miller (or "Milly") attempts to bring "a real New York actress" to Deadwood's stage, but "Frances Fryer" turns out to be "Francis" and, after his drag act fails to pass (due to an unfortunate encounter between his wig and a trombone slide), Jane boasts that she will be able to persuade Adelaid Adams—a music-hall star appearing in Chicago—to take her act west. Adams (Gale Robbins) is *the* icon of femininity in Deadwood's gaze: the cowboys compete to acquire her photograph in cigarette packages and, generally, she represents a legendary, iconic embodiment of the gendered fantasmatic comparable to Hickock's; nobody else, in this film's logic, approaches "authenticity." Ironically, Jane, who immediately sees through Francis Fryer's (Dick Wesson's) drag, mistakes Katie Brown (Allyn McLerie), Adelaid's dresser, for the star herself—demonstrating that she can read cross-dressing but not all modes of female impersonation—and takes her back to the foothills. Katie's attempt to pass as Adelaid fails—onstage, of course—but her charming ways earn her the status of "the most real person in Deadwood"; in the comedy of errors that ensues, Jane's role alternates among a misguided attempt to become "a woman" by identifying with Katie, competing with her for male attention, and reasserting her butch identification as the women's relationship

2 "Whip-Crack, Away!" Doris Day on the Deadwood stage.

3 "Here's a hat from Cincinnati / Same as Adelina Patti / Wore in every famous concert hall!" Doris Day on the Deadwood stage.

acquires lesbian overtones. Ultimately, *Calamity Jane* asks us to believe that sexual calamity is averted when Jane's and Bill's mutual "recognition" transforms their homosocial affiliation into heterosexual desire.

What does this film *think* it is doing? Rebecca Bell-Metereau argues that "*Calamity Jane* attempts to explain away the masculine woman by showing that all she really wants is to get married and settle down," that "in keeping with the tradition of musical comedy, the film takes a discordant note in society and makes it harmonize."[22] This is a plausible reading of the intentionality that shapes the film's narrative trajectory. The queer attraction of *Calamity Jane,* however, lies in the persistent incorrigibility of the tomboy,[23] particularly as she evolves into an embodiment of lesbian desire, conflicted and ambiguous, but at times clearly legible as such. To read against the grain of narrative intentionality is to discern a queer performativity—a recurring signification of lesbian subjectivity as counter-spectacle—that ironizes and destabilizes, without entirely dismantling, the surface of Doris Day's performance of gradual conformity to heterosexual expectations of the feminine.

My point is that the stubborn insistence of Doris Day's queerness remains far in excess of the narrative's heterosexist attempts at containment and "feminization." Moreover, her queerness has a career of its own, one that interlines and pulls against the conventional romantic script. Early in the film, she is queered in terms of gender: the tomboy shoots, rides, and performs feats of courage that surpass those of the men, and no amount of shaming erases or undermines her competence. At this point, the anxiety aroused by her gender transgressions is contained by her evident, though nascent and immature, heterosexual tendencies. Ironically, it is the very attempt to reconstruct Jane as "feminine" that extends her insubordination to heterosexual norms, for gender trouble opens into the possibility of calamitous sexuality. It is true that, as the narrative moves toward its heterosexual closure and the seeming feminization of Calamity Jane, she *performs* a more subdued, chastened femininity. But there is a startling gap between Day's *performance* of heterosexual femininity and a queerly resonant *performativity* of lesbian possibility. For Calamity begins as a tomboy, anxiously marked as heterosexual, and extends her queerness from gender to sexuality through her accessibility to lesbian desire when she watches, ostensibly for "instruction," the embodiment of what her culture regards as the "real woman." Although identification with Katie Brown is impossible—for Jane is resiliently butch—these scenes are charged with Jane's fascinated lesbian look at the woman's body, which deploys a sequence of butch-femme relations that cuts across, and works against, the narrative of Jane's discovery of her love for Bill Hickock.

Doris Day won an Academy Award in 1953 for her song, "Secret Love," which supposedly articulates the emergence into consciousness of her desire for the western hero; yet, when situated in the lesbian context of the film, the song—full of images of love as open book, as open door— seems rather to announce the epistemology of the lesbian closet and its provisional rupture.[24] Throughout the film, the tension within and between the positionalities of heterosexual butch and the lesbian femme is not a matter of contrasting scenes or consecutive performances: indeed, its queerness inheres in the *simultaneity* of straight and lesbian performative registers within single moments, frames, lines, songs, looks. Cumulatively, *Calamity Jane* dismantles the western's rigid categories of gender and sexuality as well as its episteme of seamless identity, fissuring these ideological constructs and replacing them with incoherence, radical undecidability.

My interest in the disruptive effects of a lesbian incipience locatable in *Calamity Jane*—a "specificity" that continually coalesces but is never quite achieved—responds to Butler's mapping of incoherent subjectivity: gender, she insists, is not "a unilateral process initiated by a prior subject"[25] but rather, "there is no 'I' that precedes the gender that it is said to perform"; moreover, gender can be theorized as "a string of performances that constitute and contest the coherence of that 'I.'"[26] Butler's major contribution to queer theory is her distinction between volitional performance— for her, a suspect if not impossible category—and *performativity,* which she understands not as "a singular or deliberate 'act,'" but rather a "reiterative and citational practice." What most engages Butler in the "corporeal theatrics" of gender performativity is the manner in which gendered "identity" is both produced and destabilized in the temporal course of performative reiteration: for it is precisely through repetition "that gaps and fissures are opened up as the constitutive instabilities in such constructions, as that which escapes or exceeds the norm."[27] In other words, if every performance repeats itself "to institute the effect of *identity,* then every repetition requires an interval between the acts, as it were, in which risk and excess threaten to disrupt the identity being constituted."[28]

Although Butler consolidates anti-essentialist arguments into an ecumenical theory of quotidian gender and the temporality of the subject, it seems to me that political and analytical applications of Butlerian performativity require a return to spectacle, that is, to the body in *performance*. I am particularly intrigued by the broadly deconstructive possibilities for queer reading that accrue when performativity is conceptualized as precisely the "gaps and fissures," the risky excesses, that disrupt the coherence of performance itself. I do not want to set up an artificial binary between volitional, intentional theatrics and the excessive citationality of performativity, but rather to emphasize the ways in which "queerness" might be conceptualized as the interlinearity of the two: what is of interest, in short, is the cinematic moment in which performative excesses undermine and destabilize the rigid, normative intentions of narrative trajectory. It is exactly this kind of cinematic moment that makes mainstream, conservative Hollywood film a rich field of queer investigation, for such moments constitute a cultural register in which—and I agree with Butler's assertion—"it is always finally unclear what is meant by invoking the lesbian-signifier, since its signification is always to some degree out of one's control."[29] Butler herself is somewhat dismissive of cross-dressing play in mainstream cinema, arguing that gender trouble in such film is a form of drag that heterosexual culture produces for itself, in which "anxiety over a possible homosexual consequence is both produced and deflected." As "high het entertainment," such cinema provides "a ritualistic release for a heterosexual economy that must constantly police its own boundaries against the invasion of queerness."[30] I would argue that, on the contrary, queer performativity within mainstream cinema is almost always far in excess of the heterosexualizing strategies of containment and remains in suspension, as ideologically fissuring and problematic. I am guided in this position by a number of recent critics: Terry Castle, who caustically accuses Butler of participating in the cultural project of "derealizing" lesbian presence, of obscuring the "specificity . . . of lesbian desire—its incorrigibly lascivious surge toward the body of another woman";[31] Alexander Doty, who sees filmic queerness as occuring "simultaneously beside and within . . . straight positions," working to confuse and challenge "the articulation of the film's straight ideological points";[32] and Eve Kosofsky Sedgwick, who succeeds better than anybody else in *particularizing* a spectrum of performative affects.

Like Butler, Sedgwick provisionally retains homosexuality as queerness's definitional center, but understands the analytical purchase of queerness as requiring a spinning-outward of the term to collapse all categories of identity. What *queer* refers to, for Sedgwick, is "the open mesh of possibilities, gaps, overlaps, dissonances and resonances, lapses and excesses of meaning when the constitutent elements of anyone's gender, of anyone's sexuality, aren't made (or *can't* be made) to signify monolithically."[33] The wonderful applicability of Sedgwick's theory, for me at least, is a function of her swerve away from abstraction to a specifically literary precision. For Sedgwick's model of queerness is derived mainly, I would argue, from de Manian deconstruction. "Following on de Man's demonstration of 'a radical estrangement between the meaning and the performance of a text,'" she argues, "one might, in the context of figures that so urgently intend meaning, want to ponder not so much the non-reference of the performative, but rather (what de Man calls) its necessarily 'aberrant' relation to its own reference—its queer referentiality."[34] Sedgwick's understanding of queerness hovers uneasily between meaning "unaccountable" and meaning "homosexual," and the aberrant relation, the "torsion," between narrative intentionality and queer performativity is entirely resonant with my understanding of the interlinearity between theatrical performance and the slippery excesses of the lesbian performative in classic cinema. Finally, to simplify, and to mark my return to *Calamity Jane:* queer performativity resides in the "unaccountable" lesbian moment—that which can never quite be accounted *for*—the moment that cannot be subsumed within the heterosexist strategies of containment, but remains in excess precisely *as* excess.

Doris Day's work has received surprisingly little commentary, yet the few critics who have written about her are frequently motivated by a discerning feminism that explores the contradiction between Day's conventional image and her resistance to what Molly Haskell calls "the creeping paralysis of adult womanhood as it was coming to be defined in the fifties."[35] T. E. Perkins argues that all of her major films "have as an explicit and important element in the plot a conflict between a man and a woman which is about . . . what constitutes femininity, . . . what a 'woman' should be." Perkins recognizes that Jane embodies "every tomboy's fantasy" and therefore, "the process of feminizing her . . . is particularly painful"; yet she fails to ironize the film's insistence that Jane, "in finding true love . . . finds her identity and her femininity." In accepting the narrative intentions as fully realized, she can neither account for the queer residue of Doris Day's performativity nor analyze *against* the grain of narrative and ideological compulsion.[36] In tracking the persistence of the queer in *Calamity Jane,* I want to focus on the film's deployment of shaming as a tactic of normalization, of identity-consolidation, of converting the tomboy and potential lesbian into something approximating the heterosexual ideal of femininity. There are two kinds of shaming in this film, both of which hold up a mirror to the tomboy's body to mark it as inadequate and monstrous: the first is deployed through the male gaze and male discourse to instill a pervasive anxiety in Jane about her inadequacy; the second—which requires Jane's internalization of the derisive male gaze—is her own look at another woman's body and her measuring of difference. However, the queer ironies of lesbian performativity emerge most fully to subvert the wasting rigors of shaming, for Jane "sees" in the other woman's body *not* her identification but rather her difference, and her difference opens the field of desire. And the tentative recognition of this desire, rather than exorcising the spell of the butch, serves rather to intensify it. Thus, the narrative's deployment of shame to consolidate normative, "feminine" identity is subject to reversal, for if it does not *quite* succeed in shaping lesbian "identity," it queerly aggravates the fissuring of the subject, and leaves identity as suspended, problematic, to-be-constituted.

Sedgwick has recently argued that, whatever else the term *queer* might come to mean in the academy, no "amount of affirmative reclamation is going to succeed in detaching the word from its associations with shame and with . . . gender-dissonant or otherwise stigmatized childhood." Shame is a powerful affect, she argues, because it "delineates [identity] without defining it or giving it a content." As the first structuring experience of identity, shame, she concludes, "generates . . . the *question* of identity at the origin of the impulse to the performative, but it does so without giving that *identity-space* the standing of an essence. *It constitutes it as to-be-constituted.*"[37] It is useful in entertaining questions of performativity to consider shame not as a psychic experience from which the subject must recover but, in opposition to liberationist politics, as the ground that paradoxically promotes and problematizes—renders urgent and yet postpones—the consistencies of identity. If, as I argue, Calamity Jane's identity is precisely in suspension throughout the course of the film, then the mirroring operations of shame, and the performative of shaming, might be viewed as less the containment of gender trouble than its occasion.

Calamity Jane's instruction in feminine mystique occurs when the men in the saloon compete to acquire photographs of Adelaid Adams, a famous actress. In response to Jane's perplexed question, "What's a Adelaid?" Bill

Hickock initially waxes lyrical—"She's a hope, a dream, a vision"—and then, with a scathing look at Jane's body, insists that Adelaid "is everything a woman *oughta* be." Hickock returns to this tactic whenever Calamity's tomboy excesses turn from action to discourse: she can defend the Deadwood stage and "shoot injuns," but she isn't allowed the masculine prerogative of bragging. When he calls Calamity to account for her bragging, she draws her gun and inquires, menacingly, "Are you callin' me a liar again?"; Hickock quickly draws his own gun, shoots her gun out of her hand, and delivers the insult: "Why don't you ever fix your hair?" If these scenes of shaming hold up a mirror of the male gaze to Calamity's unregulated and uncertain body, a mirror in which she can recognize only inadequacy, they culminate in Hickock's directive that Calamity look at other women's bodies to understand how she might approximate the feminine. At the moment of her departure for Chicago—from whence she will supposedly bring back Adelaid Adams to perform in the saloon—Hickock advises, "When you get to Chicagey, notice the women, how they act and what they wear. Get yourself some female clothes 'n fixin's." Hickock's attempt at regulation is, however, already ironically and subtly compromised: having taunted Calamity with the impossibility of bringing Adelaid back to Deadwood, she has insisted, "I'll bring her, Bill Hickock—if I have to drag her back with my teeth!" And it is precisely the prospect of Calamity's sinking her teeth into Hickock's idealized feminine that marks the swerve, or perhaps the slippage, of queerness from gender to sexuality, from the tomboy to the lesbian.

In Chicago, Calamity Jane is both the subject of the queer look—gaping with amazement at women's bodies on the streets—and the object of the baffled look, when she is cruised by a prostitute who sees her—as what?: a man? an androgynous youth? a mannish woman? a lesbian? (fig. 4). In Chicago, Jane's gender and sexuality are open to question, which marks the unraveling of her previous casting as heterosexual tomboy. The queerest turn in the film, I would argue, occurs in Adelaid Adams's dressing room, where Jane encounters Adelaid's dresser, Katie Brown, who, in order to obtain employment in Deadwood, passes herself off as Adelaid. Now, a complex scene precedes Katie's meeting with Calamity, a scene in which Katie herself—who identifies with and idolizes the hyperfemme Adelaid—is shamed by Adelaid for her desire to be an actress, and scathingly dismissed as untalented and as possessing a body inadequate for spectacle,

4 On the streets in Chicago. Who is this woman and how does she see Calamity Jane?

a body not worth looking at. Consequently, the lesbian dynamics of this scene are double: Katie's identification with Adelaid prompts her to assume Adelaid's identity, to "play" her, and this identification is necessary to establish, in the course of the scene, Calamity's *dis*identification with this body, but her desiring swerve toward it. Although this is a crowded scene, the camera holds a long shot of Calamity's intense look at Katie's body and opens into a kind of courtship with Calamity's line, "Gosh a'mighty. You're the purtiest thing I ever seen. I never knowed a woman could look like *that*." Katie mistakes Calamity for a man until midway through the scene, and her response to this revelation is one of intense amazement, the opening of previously unrecognized possibility. I would argue that the scene is played as lesbian camp, in which the comedy of mutual misrecognition (Jane believes Katie is Adelaid, Katie continues to see Jane, queerly, as a man) takes the edge off, but cannot erase, the lascivious swerve of desire. Clearly, the intent of Calamity's encounter with the embodiment of the hyperfeminine is to mark another occasion of shameful self-recognition, but the effect—the queer performative effect—is one that galvanizes desire by interlining it with the recognition of difference, disidentification, a rec-

5 In Adelaid Adams's dressing room.

6 Little Closet on the Prairie: "A Woman's Touch."

ognition that cannot obviate shame but can recuperate shame as what Sedgwick describes as "a near-inexhaustible source of transformational energy." [38] The scene culminates in Jane's and Katie's look at their reflection in a literal mirror (fig. 5): Jane's self-recognition that "I reckon I do look a mite strange to a lady like you"—is itself transformed from a shameful occasion to one of emerging, if persistently incoherent, possibility.

The most spectacular instance of lesbian camp in *Calamity Jane*—a scene that, itself parodic of 1950s butch-femme roles, has been parodied by queer performance artists, most notably by Lypsinka—is the renovation of Jane's cabin, a sort of little closet on the prairie, into a site of domestic lesbian bliss, organized around the lyrics of "A Woman's Touch." This scene is predicated upon Katie Brown's abandonment of her Adelaid Adams impersonation and her recovery of her own "original" femme status: in order to keep male admirers at a respectable distance, she moves into Jane's foul cabin and transforms it, and Jane, into versions of frontier glamour (fig. 6). As is so often the case in this film, the intent of the song is subverted by the queer performativity of the cinematic image: the narrative intends Katie Brown to reconstruct Jane as heterosexual femme, but what ensues is rather the comfortable adjustment of Jane and Katie into classic butch-femme role-playing. Indeed, "a woman's touch" is intended as a metaphor for the 1950s ideal of feminine domesticity, but it swerves, uncontrollably, into a strikingly *literal* signification: the woman's touch in question is eminently legible as somatic, as highly erotic, as subverting the heterosexist compulsions of the narrative. Jane chops wood, paints, and remodels the bunk beds into what looks like a double bed; Katie cleans, cooks, and decorates. But as always, the tensions between the heterosexual requirements of the narrative and the queer performativity within the frame produce incoherence rather than uniformly coded identity. If, as an instance of lesbian camp, this scene parodies heterosexual domesticity to satirize its complacency, then its camp effect is surely doubled, for it also discerns the exaggerations of butch-femme role-playing within the 1950s lesbian subculture. In other words, it *"does" the lesbian to undo* her cultural stereotyping, to complicate her excessive marking. Kate Davy explains the queerly doubled performative address of such hijinks as staging "two seemingly contradictory positions: . . . [it] is not an expression of homosexuality and, at the same time . . . it represents a form of coming out. In the space of these contradictions lies the operating principle of Camp."[39] This scene, intentionally or otherwise, responds queerly to the rigidity of 1950s conceptions of butch and femme. According to Lillian Faderman, "when a young woman entered the subculture in the 1950s, she was immediately initiated into the meaning and importance of the roles, since understanding them was the *sine qua non* of being a lesbian within that group. . . . Being neither butch nor femme was not an option."[40] I want to suggest that *Calamity Jane* required a complex reception from its audience, whether straight, gay, or lesbian, because its queerness — its fissuring of identity coherence — engages not merely heterosexual conceptions of gender and sexuality but also an equally rigid lesbian imaginary of its historical moment.

Committed to semiotics and psychoanalysis, early feminist film theory was not attentive to the historically specific reception practices that have guaranteed the pleasures of recognition, of identification, for the lesbian viewer of classic cinema. Arguably, the elision of the lesbian filmgoer is but one consequence of this theory's indifference to history and identity politics: the work of Laura Mulvey and Mary Ann Doane, for example, resisted clear connection between "the female spectator" and the woman sitting in front of the screen, because the female spectator is a structural concept, not a person. Recently, revisionist cultural critique has attempted to restore specificity and agency to this curiously evacuated subject. Alexander Doty insists that traditional narrative films "often have greater potential for encouraging a wider range of queer responses than . . . clearly lesbian- and gay-identified films" because of their tendency to "create a space of sexual instability that already queerly positioned viewers can connect with in various ways." While the primary imperative of queer film criticism is, I believe, to expose the representation, the working-out of desire and identification in those sexually unstable spaces — and this is what I have attempted in analyzing the interlinearity of queer performativity and heterosexist requirements in *Calamity Jane* — the turn toward reception provides a valuable historical supplement that, quite apart from suggesting the resonance of cinematic spectacle with queer culture, brings the lesbian's look to visibility and restores it to particularity. Doty's suggestion that one "mention *Calamity Jane* to a group of thirty-to-forty-something American lesbians" might permit film criticism to chart the intersection of the cinematic moment with the historical moment, and thus provide evidence "that lesbian viewers have always negotiated their own culturally specific readings and pleasures."[41]

Such a project has been conceptualized by Andrea Weiss, who resists the emphasis on the roles of transvestism and masquerade assigned to the theoretical female spectator in classic feminist film theory: psychoanalysis alone, she maintains, cannot account for "the different cultural positioning of lesbians at once outside of and negotiating within the dominant patriarchal modes of identification." Weiss's interest in how self-identified lesbians responded to ambiguous cinematic performance — the work of

Garbo, Dietrich, and Hepburn in which "gestures and movements [are] inconsistent with the narrative"[42]—might take a queer turn when such questions are posed to women who do not identify as "lesbian." Jackie Stacey has conducted a remarkable survey of women filmgoers in Britain in the 1940s and 1950s, in which the theoretical emphasis upon the textual spectator has been replaced by the spectator as text. Stacey's interest in a wide spectrum of positionalities among women viewers resists what she perceives as the tendency in psychoanalytic and structuralist film theory to allow "little possibility . . . of the female spectator reading Hollywood films 'against the grain,' of seeing more than one meaning in a film text." The dominant trend in feminist film criticism, she argues, cannot allow a complex model of female desire or identification because it regards "textual meaning as fixed and the sexed subjectivities of cinema spectators are read off across a binaristic determinism." An important aspect of her project is to attend to historical instances of homoerotic desire in female spectatorship; moreover, Stacey's conceptualization of desire, in avoiding monolithic or totalizing sexual categories like "the lesbian," seems distinctly and currently queer. In attempting to "eroticize identification," to suggest that "identification between femininities contains forms of homoerotic pleasure," she argues not "that identification is the same as desire, or *only* contains desire," but seeks rather to "open up the meanings of both categories."[43] Accordingly, none of the respondents quoted by Stacey is self-identified as "lesbian," yet their reminiscences suggest the complex, often tentative implication of identity's predicate *to be* in both identification's *to be like* and desire's *to love the spectacle of likeness*.

The responses to *Calamity Jane* in particular, and to Doris Day's work in general, that are culled from Stacey's surveys indicate that lesbian desire and identification in 1950s fanship were frequently experienced as either "femme" devotion or "butch" imitation. While such iconic relations are highly selective—and certainly seem oblivious to the complication of identity categories achieved by *Calamity Jane*—they reveal much about the possibilities and limitations, the corporeal stylistics and discursive practices, that shaped and codified lesbian reception in that repressive decade. Alternately, such responses—in which "the lesbian" remains very much in suspension, signified but not explicitly realized or fully embodied—may well reflect not just restrictive subcultural roles and possibilities but their shaping effect upon the reception of the cinematic spectacle's own ambivalences, that is, the tensions between Doris Day's queer performativity and

Jane Canary's function within a heterosexist economy. Thus, one enthusiastic filmgoer—Veronica Millen—writes of "my fantastic devotion to my favourite star, Doris Day. I thought she was fantastic, and joined her fan club, collected all the photos and info I could. I saw *Calamity Jane* 45 times in a fortnight and still watch all her films avidly. My sisters all thought I was mad going silly on a woman, but I just thought she was wonderful, they were mad about Elvis, but my devotion was to Doris Day."[44]

While this woman's passion for Doris Day is remarkable in its intensity—she must have lived at the cinema night and day during that fortnight in the 1950s—what is perhaps most intriguing is her retrospective report of a disapproving, heterosexual gaze that attempted ineffectually to trivialize or to shame her desire. The repetitions in Veronica Millen's discourse are suggestive of the resistance, and persistence, of lesbian desire: if it is "mad" for a woman to go "silly on a woman"—this appears to have been the language her sisters directed against her—then their adoration of Elvis Presley was equally "mad." Millen's reversal establishes an equivalence between conventionally heterosexual and transgressively lesbian experiences of cinematic desire, and seems to locate queerness not so much in the gender of the object of desire as in the sheer excess of devotion.

While Stacey argues, correctly, that "the homoerotic connotations . . . are left implicit" in Millen's response, a lesbian cultural register is more strikingly evident in accounts of identification and corporeal imitation. Shirley Thompson, for example, writes that "Doris Day is the greatest and in the 50s she had a haircut called the 'Butch cut,' which I had to be like her."[45] Yet here, too, the currency of the signifier *butch* in the 1950s fashion system is by no means a transparent or univocal marker of the lesbian: as I observed in the context of Doris Day's body in performance, the tomboy is not incompatible with heterosexual positioning, and while she may hover on the threshold of the lesbian, the slide of desire—and of the androgynous sign—is slippery, not guaranteed. Cumulatively, the reminiscences presented by Stacey's survey are nostalgic; their discourses, though replete with lesbian possibility, are translucent, legible in diverse ways. Evidently, then, the project of historicizing the "lesbian" filmgoer is bound up with the subject's often indirect lexicon of self-representation, acquired in a different era, which is constituted perhaps, at least in part, by the ambiguities of the then current cinema. Connotation, according to D. A. Miller, is destined to remain a suspended mode of signification: it "excites the desire for proof, a desire that, so long as it develops within the connotative register, tends to draft every signifier into . . . the dream (impossible to realize, but impossible not to entertain) that connotation would quit its dusky existence for fluorescent literality, would become denotation."[46]

In charting the history of queer reception, it may be that nostalgia is not susceptible to an analytic will-to-clarity, that it generates but a partial glimpse, poetic and synecdochic. And what can be postulated about the curious fascination of these reminiscences—and of Doris Day's career—for the contemporary queer film critic, for myself? I began this project forty years after the release of *Calamity Jane* and shortly after Doris Day's seventieth birthday: such a project originates obscurely in one of identity's imperatives, namely, to foster an analytical relation to the decade in which one's subjectivity was distinctly shaped. Sometimes, oddly, such a relation depends upon one's personal absence from that cultural field. In Roland Barthes's account of what I would call queer nostalgia, the historical relation is conceptualized as a profoundly visual engagement with "the time when my mother was alive *before me*." For Barthes, the photograph of someone whose existence has somewhat preceded one's own embodies in its particularity "the very tension of History, its division: it is constituted only if . . . we look at it—and in order to look at it, we must be excluded from it." Ultimately, queer nostalgia recuperates the cultural and familial origins of the self, but is governed by the paradox between absence and a desire for presence, between reading one's nonexistence and recognizing the implications of one's positioning, one's coming-to-be. Barthes's response to photography is essentially a susceptibility to the ambivalent power of the connotative, synecdochic image: he "finds [his] mother, fugitively alas" in order to waken in himself "the rumpled softness of her crepe de Chine and the perfume of her rice powder."[47]

For me, watching *Calamity Jane* in the 1990s is an occasion to assemble my own synecdochic catalogue, to construct the genealogy of my own queerness: I remember, from around 1961, a drive-in cinema and the back seat of my father's Chevrolet Impala; I remember my mother's indulgence of my desire to *be* Doris Day. But I can make sense of this obscure and remote pleasure, this queer nostalgia, only by referring it to the critical paradigms I learned as an adult: thus, what comes to mind most immediately are not the songs I memorized from *Calamity Jane* or the little gun-and-holster set I played with endlessly, but rather Sedgwick's assertion that "for many of us in childhood the ability to attach intently to a few cultural objects . . . , objects whose meaning seemed mysterious, excessive or oblique in relation to the codes most readily available to us, became a prime resource for survival." [48] In short, to begin to reconstruct my own queer reception is, inescapably, to be suspended between different kinds of discourse: and somehow, that little boy in the back seat of that Chevrolet Impala in 1961 averts his eyes from my own searching look. What remains are fragments of self-invention, this continuing but inexplicable fascination with 1950s cinema, its connotative pleasure (including, perhaps, the strange coincidence that my mother's family name was Day), and the certainty of some strange accession to consciousness that Sedgwick calls "a resource for survival."

While *Calamity Jane* produces the queer body as spectacle, it also locates the queer look within the incorrigible subject, the look that recognizes and reads the excesses of the performative that are opaque to the straight viewership. In a narrative that consistently turns upon role-playing and mistaken identity, lesbian performativity is at one point measured against the much simpler touchstone of drag performance: the first spectacle we watch in the town's saloon is the conventional camp of a man cross-dressed as "Frances Fryer," attempting to pass as a "New York actress," singing a song about having a hive full of honey for the right kind of honeybee. The camera alternates between this ludicrous travesty and a close-up on Jane's knowing, discerning look. "Do you see what I see?" she asks Bill Hickock; his turn line—"She ain't very good lookin'"—indicates that the drag performance is illegible to him, that he cannot read the body beneath the sartorial signifier.

Against this straight incompetence, Jane delivers what is possibly her queerest line in the entire narrative: "That ain't *all* she ain't." The immediate point of this utterance is to confirm the power of the queer look, that it not only takes one to know one but it takes a better one to say it. But the implications of "that ain't *all* she ain't" resonate well beyond this scene to suggest the possibilities for mapping the treacherous gap, the space of reversal and undoing, that lies between the body in performance and the performative body. Here, I want to inflect Butler's insistence upon gender as corporeal theatrics through Sedgwick's grasp of the aberrant relation between identity's intentions and identity's representations. Finally, the cumulative effect of queer performativity is not simply the rupturing of the categories of heterosexual and lesbian. Rather, it brings to visibility, to the knowing look, the uncertain connection between doing gender and being gendered: for if volitional performance is predicated on the assumption that the performing body "ain't all," then performativity, always in excess of intention's illusions, suggests powerfully that the coherences of identity—that totalizing "all"—ain't.

NOTES

1   Wayne Koestenbaum, *The Queen's Throat: Opera, Homosexuality, and the Mystery of Desire* (New York: Poseidon Press, 1993), 90.

2   Doris Day performs this song, composed by Richard Rodgers and Lorenz Hart, in *Love Me or Leave Me* (1957, dir. Charles Vidor), based on the life of Ruth Etting.

3   Mandy Merck, "Travesty on the Old Frontier," in *Move Over Misconceptions: Doris Day Reappraised*, ed. Jane Clarke and Diana Simmonds (London: British Film Institute, 1980), 47.

4   Eve Kosofsky Sedgwick, "Queer Performativity: Henry James's *The Art of the Novel*," *GLQ* 1, no. 1 (1993): 2.

5   Molly Haskell, "Brando," *The Village Voice*, 26 July 1973, p. 74.

6   The most lucid refusals of queer critique are Terry Castle's "A Polemical Introduction" in *The Apparitional Lesbian: Female Homosexuality and Modern Culture* (New York: Columbia University Press, 1993), especially 11–15, and Leo Bersani's chapter, "The Gay Absence," in *Homos* (Cambridge: Harvard University Press, 1995). My work is enabled by Bersani's assertion that "a gay specificity doesn't commit us to the notion of a homosexual essence" (76); however, much of this work's hostility toward academic queer critique arises from the elision of "gay and lesbian studies" as a historical field, and queer theory as a deconstructive analytics.

7   Nathaniel Hawthorne, *The House of the Seven Gables*, in *Novels*, ed. Millicent Bell (New York: The Library of America, 1983), 351.

8   By *refusal*, I intend to signify something less consciously volitional than is suggested by *resistance*.

9   Eve Kosofsky Sedgwick, *Tendencies* (Durham: Duke University Press, 1993), 222.

10   Jane Clarke and Diana Simmonds, "A Chorus of Derision," introduction to *Move Over Misconceptions: Doris Day Reappraised*, 1–2.

11   Margaret Reynolds, "Introduction," *The Penguin Book of Lesbian Short Stories* (New York: Penguin Books, 1993), xxiv.

12   Mabel Maney, *The Case of the Not-So-Nice Nurse* (Pittsburgh: Cleis Press, 1993), 106.

13   Eve Kosofsky Sedgwick, *Epistemology of the Closet* (Berkeley: University of California Press, 1990), 197.

14   When Bacall's character first meets Douglas's, she obliquely foregrounds the lesbian possibilities of her rather indeterminate gendering, her ambiguous sexuality, by comparing herself to Day's blonde femininity, which she sees as "uncomplicated." "It must be nice to wake up in the morning and know who you are," she observes. This scene is included in the 1996 documentary based on Vito Russo's *The Celluloid Closet*.

15   Diana Fuss, introduction to *Inside/Out: Lesbian Theories, Gay Theories* (New York: Routledge, 1991), 3.

16   Judith Butler, *Bodies That Matter: On the Discursive Limits of "Sex"* (New York: Routledge, 1993), 122.

17   Jane Tompkins, *West of Everything: The Inner Life of Westerns* (New York: Oxford University Press, 1992), 4.

18   Ethan Mordden provides a useful and highly opinionated historical survey of 1950s musicals in his chapter, "The Energy Peters Out," in *The Hollywood Musical* (New York: St. Martin's Press, 1981). He claims that *Calamity Jane* was "one of Doris Day's few good roles" (191), but that it did not make much of an impression because it was not what "Day's public wanted from their favourite" (192)—an observation that is contested by recent historical work on women filmgoers, particularly Jackie Stacey's, which I take up later in my argument.

19   Judith Butler, "Lana's 'Imitation': Melodramatic Repetition and the Gender Performative," *Genders* 9 (1990): 1–2; original emphasis.

20   Ibid., 14.

21   I am indebted to Steven Bruhm for this witty description of Doris Day's opening performance.

22   Rebecca Bell-Metereau, *Hollywood Androgyny*, 2d ed. (New York: Columbia University Press, 1993), 90–91.

23   Mandy Merck points out that Doris Day's tomboy role "offers potential reconciliation as a transitional role, generally seen as pre-sexual, adolescent, rather than determinedly celibate or homosexual." Since such an identity is posited by the film as "temporal, rather than psychological," it "can be abandoned comfortably in the course of the narrative's time." But this film, like others in Doris Day's oeuvre, is unsuccessful in "closing off these contradictions." Since the tomboy role initiates "the phantasy of being other/more powerful than you are," it complicates any resolution that requires "the heroine's initiation into feminine subordination," an "outcome" that is "both asserted and denied in *Calamity Jane*" ("Travesty on the Old Frontier," 22–24).

24   This scene too appears in the documentary, *The Celluloid Closet*, and is perhaps the most important historical example in its work of exploring how gay men and lesbians locate ourselves in mainstream cinema.

25   Butler, *Bodies That Matter*, 9.

26 Judith Butler, "Imitation and Gender Insubordination," in *Inside/Out,* 18.

27 Butler, *Bodies That Matter,* 2, 10.

28 Butler, "Imitation and Gender Insubordination," 28.

29 Ibid., 15.

30 Butler, *Bodies That Matter,* 126.

31 Castle, *The Apparitional Lesbian,* 34, 11.

32 Alexander Doty, *Making Things Perfectly Queer: Interpreting Mass Culture* (Minneapolis: University of Minnesota Press, 1993), 15, 29.

33 Eve Kosofsky Sedgwick, "Queer and Now," in *Tendencies,* 8.

34 Eve Kosofsky Sedgwick, "Socratic Raptures, Socratic Ruptures: Notes Toward Queer Performativity," in *English Inside and Out: The Places of Literary Criticism,* ed. Susan Gubar and Jonathan Kamholtz (New York: Routledge, 1993), 131.

35 Molly Haskell, "An Interview with Doris Day," *Ms.* 4 (January 1976): 57.

36 T. E. Perkins, "Remembering Doris Day: Some Comments on the Season and the Subject," *Screen Education* 39 (summer 1981): 27, 30–31. Perkins writes a corrective response to the dossier compiled by Clarke and Simmonds for the British Film Institute, which, she claims, tends "to oversell those aspects of Doris Day's films which can be seen as instances of resistance or ideological incoherence but to underemphasize and leave uninvestigated ways in which such instances are ultimately used to validate ideology, and in fact are used to reassure us" (26).

37 Sedgwick, "Queer Performativity," 4, 12, 14; emphasis added.

38 Ibid., 4.

39 Kate Davy, "Fe/Male Impersonation: The Discourse of Camp," in *The Politics and Poetics of Camp,* ed. Moe Meyer (New York: Routledge, 1994), 140.

40 Lillian Faderman, *Odd Girls and Twilight Lovers: A History of Lesbian Life in Twentieth-Century America* (New York: Penguin, 1991), 168.

41 Doty, *Making Things Perfectly Queer,* 8, 12.

42 Andrea Weiss, "A Queer Feeling When I Look at You: Hollywood Stars and Lesbian Spectatorship in the 1930s," in *Multiple Voices in Feminist Film Criticism,* ed. Diane Carson et al. (Minneapolis: University of Minnesota Press, 1994), 336, 332. An example of such a response to Doris Day is Minnie Bruce Pratt's brief fantasy, "Pillow Talk," in *S/He* (Ithaca: Firebrand Press, 1995): "I had never imagined that [Rock Hudson] could be gay, that Doris Day could be a lesbian girl, or that I might be" (129). In Pratt's writing, the first and third person pronouns signify ambiguously, as the "I" slips between identification and desire.

43 Jackie Stacey, *Star Gazing: Hollywood Cinema and Female Spectatorship* (London: Routledge, 1994), 25, 29.

44 Quoted in ibid., 138.

45   Stacey, *Star Gazing,* 138; Thompson quoted at 203.

46   D. A. Miller, "Anal *Rope,*" in Fuss, *Inside/Out,* 129.

47   Roland Barthes, *Camera Lucida: Reflections on Photography,* trans. Richard Howard (New York: Farrar, Straus and Giroux, 1981), 64–65.

48   Sedgwick, "Queer and Now," *Tendencies,* 3.

Ellis Hanson

LESBIANS WHO BITE

ABJECTION AS MASQUERADE

Wait. My blood is coming back. From their senses. It's warm inside us again. Among us. Their works are emptying out, becoming bloodless. Dead skins. While our lips are growing red again. They're stirring, moving, they want to speak.
—Luce Irigaray, *This Sex Which Is Not One*

A woman is apparently addressing another woman in this passage, but is it a quotation from a French feminist manifesto or from a lesbian vampire flick? The text is from Irigaray's impeccably feminist essay "When Our Lips Speak Together," but it sounds like she has been watching too many midnight movies. Although films like *The Hunger* (1983) or *Daughters of Darkness* (1971) are greeted with ambivalence or downright hostility by most feminist film critics, I am struck by a certain covert attraction to the vampire myth, a certain identification with the creatures of the night, among even the most canonical of feminist theorists. I too have regarded the lesbian vampire with a degree of distrust: "The vampire lesbian, however, abounds explicitly in such films as *Blood and Roses, Vampyres,* and *The Hunger,* which may be related to the proliferation of 'fake lesbianism' in straight male pornography." [1] Or so I wrote, a number of years ago in a footnote to an essay entitled "Undead," on vampirism, psychoanalysis, and hostile representations of gay men with AIDS. The observation is true, in a limited sense. Vampire lesbians, surprisingly numerous in the cinema, invariably stalk their prey in films directed by men for whom the phrase "lesbian community" would appear to be a contradiction in terms. From what I can gather, virtually none of these films are acted, written, produced, or directed by lesbians, nor do they appear to be marketed specifically for lesbian audiences. Many of these films—among them *Blood and Roses* (1961), *Lust for a Vampire* (1971), *The Vampire Lovers* (1970), and *Carmilla* (1989)— are based, often weakly, on J. Sheridan Le Fanu's Victorian shocker, *Carmilla* (1872), and so they reproduce its plot, in which the predatory lesbian is tracked down and killed in the name of patriarchal virtue. The vampire lesbians themselves are a decadent species, slinky doyennes of haute couture with an inexhaustible appetite for the polymorphous perverse. When they make love to women, they are eminently on display, strangely posed, as though still a bit stiff from the crypt. The scenario is a familiar one in straight male pornography, in which lesbianism functions as an exotic form of foreplay and exhibitionism, produced primarily for a straight male market. Strictly speaking, I suppose, many of these vampires are not really lesbians at all; in a truly omnivorous fashion, they happily forgo the taste of a woman when an adventurous red-blooded man stumbles onto the scene. As in *Daughters of Darkness*, one of the classics of the genre, sex between women is not the only exotic spectacle on the menu: sadomasochism, necrophilia, fetishism, and male homosexuality also join forces with the usual bloodlust to generate sexual narratives that can be as ludicrous as they are inviting.

Nevertheless, I have to admit there is a great deal more to be said.

As I look again at lesbian vampire films, I am no longer struck by their misogyny, but quite the opposite. They do not always follow the predictable track-and-kill tradition of the vampire genre, and lesbian desire often functions as a destabilizing, even derailing, force in the paranoid narrative that seeks to demonize and contain it. Some of the more complicated examples of the genre present a number of entertaining and intriguing possibilities for lesbian and feminist fantasy. I have singled out three films in particular that offer new ways of thinking about that notorious cinematic stereotype, the lesbians who bite. The earliest is *Dracula's Daughter* (1936, dir. Lambert Hillyer), which has enjoyed a recent revival as classic lesbian camp in the spirit of films like *Queen Christina* (1933) and *Sylvia Scarlett* (1935). The others are a soft-core pornographic film, *Vampyres* (1974, dir. Joseph Larraz), and an equally steamy cult-classic, *The Hunger* (1983, dir. Tony Scott). While all three of these films partake of a politically dubious tradition of demonizing female sexuality, they also raise the attractive possibility of a queer gothic, rich in all the paradox and sexual indeterminacy the word *queer* and the word *gothic* generally imply. In fact, I am reproducing a long critical history of referring to these vampires as lesbians, even though their sexual identity—whether they have sex, whether they have a sexuality, whether it is primarily oriented toward women—is usually unclear. *Bisexual* would be a more useful term, I suppose, since it still enjoys, however improbably, a reputation for sexual indeterminacy. *Queer* has as yet an angrier and more playful ring to it, and it can more easily sustain the critique of sexual categories that has made it a privileged term among deconstructionists. Marjorie Garber, never one to blanch at the categorical confusion of *queer, bisexual,* and *lesbian,* is one of the few feminist critics to acknowledge the radical appeal of vampire films, however tenuously: "For the erotic and political purposes of the 'lesbian vampire' industry, bisexuality is sometimes—though not always—affirmatively queer."[2]

What does it mean when a paranoid narrative produces a queer vampire that it cannot kill? Does the gorgeous spectacle of the queer "lesbian vampire" appeal exclusively to a patriarchal male gaze? Cannot the anarchic behavior of the lesbians in these films be seen within the tradition of the queer outlaw or the feminist bad-girl? One thematic element that brings all three of these films together is their unique challenge to conventional notions of the cinematic gaze, which is typically coded as male in much feminist film theory. Far from reproducing the familiar pornographic regime of a male gaze that fetishizes the woman onscreen, even the lesbian woman, as a passive compensatory object, these films problematize the gaze, thematizing it as a central question. The gaze is forever in danger of appropriation and reconfiguration by the very lesbian vampire it seems to have dreamed into existence. If lesbian vampire films are an instance of patriarchy, it is a patriarchy in its decadence. Given their campiness and their humiliation of the male ego, many of these flicks should be far more appealing to gay men (as camp) and male masochists (as exquisite punishment) than to the patriarchal and sadistic "gaze" so familiar to us from much feminist film theory. Indeed, D. N. Rodowick has criticized Laura Mulvey's theoretical model of the sadistic masculine voyeur by pointing out the possibilities for male masochism in the cinematic fetishization of women. Carol Clover has pressed this critique even further to claim that cinematic horror is the genre in which male masochism is most evident.[3] In films like *Daughters of Darkness, Vampyres,* and *The Hunger,* men are little more than victims in a narrative contagion of lesbian vampirism from one woman to another, though male characters, no less than male audiences, may well be singing in their chains.

The question still remains, however: do these films offer pleasures that we might call lesbian or feminist? I think it time that we release the vampire lesbian from her marginal life, not only in my footnotes but in the sketchy remarks of those critics who have bothered to speak of her at all. Needless to say, however, the lesbian who bites, though commonplace in trashy films and novels, is highly unpopular in critical circles where her kind is likely to be discussed with any degree of scholarly rigor. She is often *femina non grata* even among feminists, who are wont to scorn her as a symptomatic expression of patriarchy. For example, in an essay that appeared about the same time as mine, the lesbian-feminist theorist Sue-Ellen Case claims to be tracking the lesbian vampire. And yet the few examples of vampire lesbianism that she offers are all dismissed with an impatient wave of her pen: "Whether she is the upper-class, decadent, cruel Baroness in *Daughters of Darkness* (1971; played by the late Delphine Seyrig, who was marked in the subculture as a lesbian actor), whose coercive lesbian sex act is practiced behind closed doors and whose langorous body proscribes the lesbian as an oozing, French dessert cheese; or whether she is the rough-trade, breast-biting Austrian lesbian vampire in *Vampire Lovers* (1970), or even the late-capitalist, media-assimilated lesbian vampire in the independent film *Because the Dawn* (1988), her attraction is (in) her proscription. Only the proscription of the lesbian is literally portrayed— the occult becomes cult in the repression."[4] Oddly, the only repression and proscription I find in this passage are Case's own. The first question that springs to mind is, of course, what is so bad about rough trade, breast biting, and oozing French dessert cheese? Case seems to be smacking her lips in protest. With "proscription" this attractive, who needs acceptance? Like Mina Harker, Bram Stoker's ever-vascillating New Woman, Case is a feminist in the throes of a strange trance; she scarcely knows whether to condemn her pleasure or to parade it.

In her essay "The Vampire Lovers," Andrea Weiss is also at best ambivalent. She is willing to recognize the appeal of camp humor in lesbian vampire films, but she is not on the whole amused. She falls back upon a clumsy application of Laura Mulvey's theories of sadistic male voyeurism and fetishization. For example, she describes at great length a scene from *The Vampire Lovers* in which two women get naked, chase each other around the room, and collapse into bed together. She believes that straight men eat this up, but women are left cold—a claim that is by no means self-evident. She speaks of fetishistic breast imagery and fetishistic camera angles, and she concludes, "Thus voyeurism and fetishism work together in this scene to contain and assuage the threat the vampire poses to the male spectator."[5] She appears not to have noticed, however, that there is no male spectator in her description, just two horny women and, in the audience, a dour feminist critic. A lesbian is watching a film in which two women do the nasty together, and all she can think about is men? The "male gaze" of camera angles is evidently stronger than we guessed, since it can even define the parameters of a feminist's pleasure. Weiss has theorized out of existence the possibility of lesbian fetishism and lesbian voyeurism and, I dare say, lesbian desire itself. She seems to have accepted without question the psychoanalytic presumption that women are incapable of fetishism, despite numerous feminist accounts to the contrary. As Pat Califia once wrote, at the height of the lesbian "sex wars," "In addition to being a sadist, I have a leather fetish. If I remember my Krafft-Ebing, that's another thing women aren't supposed to do. Oh, well. Despite the experts, seeing, smelling, or handling leather makes me cream."[6] Not surprisingly, Califia is the author of "The Vampire," a pornographic tale of lesbian s/m.

Nina Auerbach offers a much more historical critique of the vampire's appeal in her book, *Our Vampires, Ourselves*. She is charmed by *Carmilla*, but not by all films it spawned. She finds a warm and fuzzy feminism in Le Fanu's story and proclaims, rather improbably, that "the intimacy, the sharing, the maternal suffusion, were the essence, in the nineteenth century, of the vampire's allure."[7] Is she talking about *Carmilla* or *Cranford?* Why would anyone look to a vampire for improving lessons about "sharing"? She is half right. *Carmilla* is in part about maternal fixation and a Victorian "romantic friendship" between Laura and her supernatural houseguest, but as a vampire narrative it enacts the demonization of such notably chaste and respectable modes of homoerotic desire. Auerbach glides over the question of exploitation, violence, hypocrisy, betrayal, repression, and resentment between the two women in what is, after all, a strikingly Oedipal tale of sexual panic. She then faults certain film versions of *Carmilla* for being too pornographic. She trots out Mulvey's fetishism argument again, via Weiss, claiming that "lesbian vampire films in the aesthetic or commercial mainstream justify their existence by making gazing men, not desiring women, their subject."[8] She even invents a "drooling adolescent" who she claims is the primary audience for these films, and I presume she is not referring here to herself. What she thinks these vampire women are doing with each other if not desiring, I cannot say, but the tendency to project all sexuality onto men is certainly distressing, not the least because it is rarely justified by the films themselves or their audiences. Auerbach suggests that these movies have betrayed an originary feminist sentimentality that she attributes to, of all people, Le Fanu. This sweetness and nostalgia is apparent also in Jewelle Gomez's novel,

The Gilda Stories, in which, without a trace of ironic humor or camp, the author presents a rainbow coalition of lesbian-feminist vampires whose bite is not so much violent as simply edifying, a way of spreading a cult of peace, respect, love, and family through the ages. Her novel is certainly politically irreproachable in its sentiments. Nevertheless, the conception of desire is so anodyne that it cannot grapple with any of the more diffi-cult questions about sexuality that have made the vampire a stock figure in popular fantasy. Her vampires have no teeth. They are not dangerous, just misunderstood. When I taught this book in a lesbian fiction course, I discovered that my students were nodding off after the first chapter. Ironi-cally, in such revisionary efforts, feminists have disavowed the vampire and recast themselves as the new vampire hunters—sentimental, moralis-tic, and sweet (until, of course, they find someone who is misbehaving).

While lesbian vampire films are sometimes silly, they are never sweet. They are violent, fetishistic, and voyeuristic; they are man-eating and phallic; they are bruisingly butch and fabulously femme. Because feminist film theory has often, for dubious reasons, feigned an allergy to all these qualities, the lesbian vampire film has become one of its recurrent night-mares. Similarly, lesbians who have appeared in any way phallic—butch, masculine, leather-loving, dildo-wielding, father-identified—were held up to sisterly contempt throughout the seventies and eighties by feminists who regarded themselves as "woman-identified women." Even now, femi-nist theory, especially of the psychoanalytic variety, frequently disavows its own investment in what it calls the phallus, fetishism, and voyeurism, and Weiss and Mulvey Auerbach are very good examples. In *The Practice of Love,* Teresa de Lauretis has presented a theory of lesbian desire as a fetishistic perversion, a move that would appear to be a radical departure from this tradition; but even she seems to sneeze whenever she gets so much as a whiff of the phallus or even its humble anatomical sidekick, the penis. For de Lauretis, lesbians are fetishists because, in loving women, they have found an object through which they can disavow castration and recover the mother's body that has been denied them (the spectral Carmilla once again drifts through the room). Unlike the male fetishist, lesbians are not looking for a penis or a phallic substitute in another woman, nor for that matter on themselves. No, the phallus is apparently disavowed along with castration. The theory is, to use de Lauretis's own characterization, "far-fetched," not the least because—whether the approach be Freudian, Lacanian, or Kleinian—this mother's body is an object of desire and identification only because it promises access to a penis, in this case a particularly delectable one, envied by men and women both: the maternal penis. If there were no promise of a penis, then the protolesbian little girl would be, in a psychoanalytic framework, without motivation and without desire. De Lauretis has elected for herself an unenviable task: she would like to present a less phallocentric theory of lesbian desire (why bother?) through recourse to psychoanalysis, which is notorious for its presumption that desire is inherently phallic. In other words, her discussion of the disavowal inherent in lesbian fetishism requires a further disavowal, a theoretical refusal to acknowledge the full role of the phallus in her own theory. Like the male fetishist, who looks for the mere aura of the penis in a woman, de Lauretis's theory of lesbian desire requires that the phallus be there and not there at the same time. Naomi Schor ran into the same paradox nearly a decade earlier when she discovered that her own discussion of female fetishism sounded like the "latest and most subtle form of 'penis envy.'" Marjorie Garber has coined the term "fetish envy" to say in so many words that Schor was well-justified in her concern. De Lauretis quotes this phrase from Schor, as if to note the stink of penis envy were to exorcise it. She dangles this citation over the bosom of her own maternal argument as though she were donning a strand of garlic blossoms, but her phallocentric logic remains a tacit invitation to the very vampire she would disavow. Her book fails to describe lesbian fetishism precisely because it is busy enacting a far more Freudian version of it—though in this case the proper psychoanalytic term, as de Lauretis is aware, would be the "masculinity complex." What we never learn from any of these feminist critics, however, is why an investment in masculinity, fetishism, voyeurism, the phallus, or even a penis, necessarily creates a political problem. De Lauretis would have done better to discuss psychoanalysis itself as a fetishistic perversion—one that predicates desire on phallic presence, however veiled—and to leave the lesbians to their own devices.[9]

De Lauretis demonstrates with considerable theoretical rigor a problem that is already evident in a less articulate form in feminist critiques of the lesbian vampire: lesbianism has been constructed through feminism as a rejection of sexualities deemed for whatever reason to be the proper domain of men—which is to say, butchness, fetishism, voyeurism, phallic penetration, and s/m, to name a few. Paranoia inevitably ensues. Masculinity, here confused with misogyny, is even more monstrous when one is terrified of identifying with it. Thus, the lesbian film-critic, nothing if not a fetishist and a voyeur, disavows fetishism and voyeurism, disavows indeed an identification with men that her analysis at once invites and punishes, and the political or sexual gain is by no means always clear. The role of masculinity in feminist critiques of the lesbian vampire is often far more panicky than need be, given the role of men in the films themselves. Andrea Weiss, for example, is much offended by the dark and mysterious man who is sometimes shown hovering nearby during certain scenes of lesbian vamping in *The Vampire Lovers*. Auerbach has her knickers in a twist about him too, and she incorrectly identifies him as a vampire hunter. Both regard him as a patriarchal voyeur, and yet the film's narrative positions him as a satanic figure on the side of the vampire women. When they are defeated, so is he. The film encodes him as an enigmatic and subversive pervert, rather than a model representative of the Law of the Father. But the feminist critic is spooked, not by vampires but by her own theoretical framework. She is driven to paranoia by a psychoanalytic feminism that claims that the phallus is the enemy and the enemy is everywhere, a critical theory that, in one paradoxical gesture, incites her to search desperately for a nonphallic and exclusively female pleasure and prevents her from ever finding it.

Within the logic of such critiques, any lesbian who enjoys herself at a vampire movie must be suffering from patriarchal false-consciousness. To her credit, Weiss points out that lesbian audiences of *The Hunger* have spent a lot of time speculating about the lovemaking scene between Susan Sarandon and Catherine Deneuve, but she herself is relatively mute on the subject. Deneuve was more articulate when she said of her own dykon status, "*The Hunger* has a very strong image of beautiful women, so perhaps it is true. Suddenly, there was a woman looking like a woman and liking women. Yes, I showed you can be beautiful and be a lesbian."[10] The concept is simple enough to grasp, even clever in its punning on the word *like,* which can suggest desire and identification at once. A lesbian likes the gender she is like? According to a recent survey of cinematic tastes in the lesbian and gay magazine, *The Advocate,* this moment in *The Hunger* was deemed by female respondents to be their all-time favorite love scene between two women in a film. Much to the chagrin of *The Advocate,* Sharon Stone's noirish and vampy performance in *Basic Instinct* was voted the favorite representation of a bisexual woman. Evidently, the tastes of queer audiences do not necessarily follow the party line established by Vito Russo in *The Celluloid Closet*.[11] Nevertheless, this popular enthusiasm has been curiously inadmissible in lesbian film criticism, in which aesthetic and sexual pleasure is often cause for ideological panic. One of the perennial difficulties with much gay and lesbian film criticism is its cold shower of political correctness—its preoccupation with a narrow politics of representation and its search for so-called positive or accurate images, which, when they finally do appear, are often dull anyway. We moralize movies to death. We disavow fantasy in favor of social realism. We obsess about how we are seen rather than how we see. We are loath to enjoy ourselves, as long as there is a straight man somewhere who delights over the same images. Monika Treut, a queer filmmaker, provided a refreshing change of tone when she proclaimed that she did not give a damn whether men got off on her films, as long as women did.

In literature, where the vampire lesbian has been a popular romantic trope at least since Coleridge's "Christabel" (1816), critics have often spoken with a similar feminist disdain. Bram Dijkstra's account of vampire narratives as relentlessly misogynistic is typical of this approach. He speaks of the representation of women in these narratives as demonic and pathological, while the superior intellectual man is depicted as triumphant: "He must exorcise the inherently regressive, degenerate susceptibilities of woman with the broad sweep of his superior, light-born male intellect. The writers of contemporary Gothic novels, the makers of vampire movies, as well as the many men and women who are virtually addicted to these narratives, pronouncing them harmless fun or simply campy entertainment, are still unconsciously responding to an antifeminine sensibility established in its modern form and symbolic structure by the sexist ideologues among the nineteenth-century intelligentsia."[12] Well perhaps, but nevertheless, I have read Nordau, Lombroso, Charcot, and a great many other pseudo-scientific sages of fin-de-siècle social theory, and I have read Stoker and Le Fanu, Baudelaire and Swinburne. My amusement and fascination with vampire tales is far from historically naive, nor would I deem it misogynistic. The problem with Dijkstra's argument, apart from being hopelessly reductive and overstated, is that the author of such tales is not always a man or a female dupe, the vampire is not always a woman, nor is the vampire invariably hunted down and killed. Furthermore, the vampire is always more appealing and exciting than the men and women who hunt it. Dijkstra also fails to account for the evident appeal of vampire narratives among women readers—and women writers—except as self-hatred (the female decadent, Rachilde, is trashed in this way). In condemning contemporary gothic, he implicitly slights the accomplishments of a great many women writers (some of them lesbian, most of them feminist), among them Djuna Barnes, Joyce Carol Oates, Jamaica Kincaid, Jeanette Winterson, Anne Rice, Pat Califia, and Emma Tennant. He pathologizes an entire genre and its readers, in effect rendering them vampiric as might a modern-day Max Nordau. Even Nina Auerbach gives Victorian vampire tales more credit. In her book on women and the demon, she finds in the "monstrosity" of women in Victorian fiction not merely stigma but also a "celebration of female powers of metamorphosis." Furthermore, she writes, "when we actually read *Trilby*, *Dracula*, or *Studies on Hysteria* we are struck by the kinds of powers that are granted to the women: the victim of paralysis possesses seemingly infinite capacities of regenerative being that turn on her triumphant mesmerizer and paralyze him in turn."[13] No sentimental paeans to friendship there! Bonnie Zimmerman also writes of a potential for lesbian appropriation and spectatorial pleasure in vampire narratives, especially in the film *Daughters of Darkness*, where lesbian desire is represented as a seductive and irrepressible force. She is quick to point out that such a film is not necessarily feminist, but she further notes, "No attempt of man or god can prevent the lesbian from passing on her 'curse.' The effect of this transference is not at all horrifying, but rather amusing, almost charming, especially to a lesbian viewer."[14]

To delight in lesbian vampire films is not necessarily to ignore the political struggles of lesbians and other women. Obviously, the demonization of female desire is rampant in life, no less than in art. I am reminded of Betty Friedan's characterization of lesbians as the "lavender menace" in an effort to purge the National Organization for Women. Or, more recently, Jesse Helms's effort to block Roberta Achtenberg's presidential appointment by labeling her a "damned lesbian." The list goes on and on. In recent cinema, from *Windows* (1980) and *They Only Kill Their Masters* (1972), to the newer film noir, such as *Black Widow* (1987), *Poison Ivy* (1992), and *Single White Female* (1992), women's homoeroticism is virtually synonymous with violence and betrayal. In her book *Fatal Women*, Lynda Hart is understandably led to wonder why lesbian serial-killers are numerous in Hollywood but nonexistent everywhere else.[15] The vampire lesbian partakes of a long narrative tradition of the gothic in which homosexuality is always the unspeakable that is nevertheless spoken in a nightmarish fit of panic and horror. In this tradition, the lesbian is represented as spectral, demonic, brutal, unnatural, murderous, pathological, perverse, and a real bitch to the husband and kids.

But these are the least of her charms.

What I want to know is, why have some lesbians found these putatively homophobic and misogynistic narratives so entertaining? Why do I my-self sometimes find them fun, witty, moving, challenging, even liberating? Do these films not scream for appropriation by spectators who are lesbian, feminist, queer, or all three?

Eve Kosofsky Sedgwick, especially in her groundbreaking book *Between Men,* has offered what is in my opinion the most original feminist reading of the gothic—and certainly the queerest. In her view, gothic narratives often play on the anxious and always already transgressed erotic boundary between the homosexual and the homosocial in relations between men. Homosexual desire is therefore articulated in a panic, barely representable at all, and yet always, almost phantasmatically at the heart of the narrative. Homosexuals and homosexual desire become the scapegoats in a narra-tive whose erotic structure they have destabilized. In our own time, queer writers, filmmakers, and performance artists have been especially imagi-native in revising, subverting, and otherwise appropriating gothic style for their own purposes. "Gothic camp"—one could write a book about it—is a popular mode of short-circuiting the homophobic tendencies of the gothic novel while still retaining its creepy sensuality. Camp humor, as Susan Sontag has pointed out, is a powerful moral solvent. Gothic style, with its emotional effusion and its tendency to hysteria, is especially vulnerable. The vampire in particular has been for some time now the central figure of gothic camp. Francis Ford Coppola's lushly aestheticized version of *Bram Stoker's Dracula* (1992) and the no less lavish *Interview with the Vampire* (1994) are only the tamest versions of male homoeroticism as gothic camp. Outrageous humor reigns in this genre. We find the drag artist, Lipsynka, doing a fashion spread dressed in goth makeup and fangs. In the video *Stiff Sheets,* a drag queen dressed as a vampire ridicules the Roman Catho-lic Church's stand on AIDS. Andy Warhol's *Frankenstein* (1974) and *Dracula* (1974) turn the gothic into ridiculous queer pornography, as does Kevin Glover's film *Love Bites.* In *The Rocky Horror Picture Show* (1975), Tim Curry, in suitably goth erotic gear, celebrates himself as a "sweet transvestite from transsexual Transylvania." Charles Busch turns the gothic into a drag farce in the play *Vampire Lesbians of Sodom.* Vampire novels and gothic horror enjoy considerable popularity on the gay market. Consider, for example, Vincent Lardo's *China House* or Lewis Garrett's *The Living One*. In Jeffrey McMahan's novel, *Vampires Anonymous,* Andrew the gay vampire fights the forces of darkness in the form of self-hating vampires, a parody of self-hating gay men, who seek to cure themselves of their compulsion through a twelve-step program. Pam Keesey has collected two anthologies of lesbian vampire tales; the books were published by Cleis, a feminist press, and nearly all of the tales are written by lesbians, though admittedly the best of the lot is a reprint of *Carmilla*. Djuna Barnes's 1937 novel *Nightwood* must surely be the high literary benchmark of lesbian vampirism, if only for the final chapter in which an insane Robin Vote howls like a wolf in a dark and ruined chapel. Since I first wrote this essay, *Nadja* (1994) and *The Addiction* (1995), two of the most stylish and innovative films about women who vamp women, have premiered. There is also a lesbian gothic dimension to Monika Treut's s/m cult-film, *Seduction: The Cruel Woman* (1985), in which Wanda the dominatrix strikes ghoulish poses in a dripping dungeon, her very own waterfront whipping gallery. Enjoying a distinctively goth moment, Wanda lounges dreamily in an overflowing bathtub, her black tresses falling over her pallid shoulders as she awaits her new lover and victim, played by lesbian-feminist icon Sheila McLaughlin in black opera-length gloves. Never have lesbians looked quite so Yvonne DeCarlo.

The goth subculture itself is a work of gothic camp, a version of punk that is characterized by a rebellious sexual politics of androgyny and perversity. In a manner not unlike drag, the goths, who have raised films like *The Hunger* to cult status, take enormous pleasure in dressing up in elaborate gothic costume, with wild black hair and ghoulish white makeup. Their milieu is preeminently the late-night club scene, and their style is witty, tasteless, in your face, and not a little romantic. In their gothic playfulness they present an oppositional eroticism, a form of sexual theater, through which the radical queer can identify with the position of otherness and abjection she has inherited from a homophobic society. She can celebrate this position as a powerful site of fantasy and an ironic site of rebellion. She can mine the performance of gothic subjectivity for all the queer pleasures that are pathologized and execrated in the dominant culture. In her reading of *The Hunger,* Barbara Creed draws on Julia Kristeva's theory of abjection to describe the lesbian vampire as an example of the "monstrous-feminine." [16] She points out that abjection is always to some degree fascinating and attractive, though her own analysis focuses entirely on myths of blood, defloration, and menarche that are all quite nauseating. What amazes me about *The Hunger* and *Daughters of Darkness* is how fabulously chic everyone is in the film—the elegance of Catherine Deneuve and Delphine Seyrig, the trendy androgyny of David Bowie, the tailored sultriness of Susan Sarandon, the general ambience of luxury and leisure. Even the bloodier scenes are so aestheticized that they are sensual rather than repellent. Clearly, there is something more going on here than abjection. Vampire films present abjection as a masquerade, a glamorous appeal to the senses, that renders the monstrous, the outcast, and the lesbian, as a highly self-conscious mode of exoticism.

Like sentimentality, however, gothic camp does tend to drain the vampire of its more disturbing appeal. It is difficult to be ridiculous and still have bite. But in the best camp performances there is always something more than humor or parody. There is a disturbing sexual fantasy and a genuine identification with the parodied figure of abjection. The drag queen's impression of Bette Davis is never any good unless she really identifies with the more grotesque dimensions of the star's persona. Similarly, gothic camp has a sharper edge when it is clear that the artist is a little in love with the undead. In the best gothic camp, the anarchic and sadomasochistic possibilities of queer sexuality are still evident, in spite of the humor. Indeed, when Leo Bersani wrote of the "gay outlaw," the gay man whose desire is so asocial that he is ideologically unlocatable, he might have looked to vampire narratives for his examples, rather than to the gentlemanly Proust and Gide.[17] Bersani renders the term "gay outlaw" redundant, since he finds asociality inherent in all homosexual libidinal drives. I would say that, on the contrary, the gay outlaw, like the vampire, is a figment of the imagination, an aesthetic effort by no means attractive or even feasible for many gay men. To perform the role of the gay outlaw is to produce queerness as abjection, and vampire goths are especially good at it. They present abjection ironically as a masquerade, as a flirtation, and yet they always court the danger of becoming a mask without a face and losing themselves in a specifically queer fantasy of self-dissolution.

I think it is this enthusiasm for the paradoxical glamor of abjection, for fantasy and for style, that gives Anne Rice her enormous queer readership. Her prose cannot be dismissed as silly or entirely parodic like so much gothic camp can be. She sincerely identifies with the queer otherness of the vampire in all its violence and lawlessness. Vampirism is often a fashion statement in Rice's books, but it is also an alternative subjective condition, a queer site of fantasy where desire and sensation are peculiarly intense and where one can get away with murder. I think Rice deserves far more discussion than I can offer here, but I want to quote one passage in particular from her first novel, *Interview with the Vampire,* that I think will have resonance in my discussion of lesbian vampire films. Rice describes the transformation of a man named Louis into a vampire at the hands of another male vampire, Lestat. This explicitly homoerotic struggle is described as a violent passion, and the change it affords is a profound one, oddly reminiscent of a queer man's first euphoric experience of his queerness: " 'It was as if I had only just been able to see colors and shapes for the first time. I was so enthralled with the buttons on Lestat's black coat that I looked at nothing else for a long time. Then Lestat began to laugh, and I heard his laughter as I had never heard anything before. His heart I still heard like the beating of a drum, and now came this metallic laughter. It was confusing, each sound running into the next sound like the mingling reverberations of bells, until I learned to separate the sounds, and then they overlapped, each soft but distinct, increasing but discrete, peals of laughter.' The vampire smiles with delight. 'Peals of bells.' " [18] Here, the vampire is not simply an alien species to be hunted but an alternative subjectivity, an alternative mode of reception. In her revision of the paranoid and homophobic tradition of the gothic, Anne Rice, more successfully than any other writer, has grasped the pleasures of vampiric queerness. That this sort of revisionary writing has considerable appeal to queer audiences was made clear to me by a startling appropriation of Rice at an academic lecture. Sandy Stone, herself transgendered, was giving a lecture on her own rather camp and vampiric sexual politics.[19] She compared herself with Rice's Louis, describing how she looked at the other people at the conference with a perverse desire to feed, sensing their intensified beauty and the blood coursing through their veins. Transgendered subjectivity is for her a vampire persona, an altered state of feeling, a celebration of a queer hunger, and an identification with the position of abjection. In short, it is a different way of looking.

PICTURES BEHIND YOUR EYES

This is a chiller with plenty of ice; a surefire waker-upper in the theatre and a stay-awake influence in the bedroom later on.

—Review of *Dracula's Daughter* in *Variety*

If there is any lesbian vampire film that qualifies as classic camp, then *Dracula's Daughter* is it. Premiering in 1936 as a sequel to Tod Browning's highly successful *Dracula* (1931), the film was supposedly based on "Dracula's Guest" by Bram Stoker, though the two narratives have little in common but a female fiend. Because of its surprisingly explicit lesbian subtext and its ridiculous melodrama, *Dracula's Daughter* has enjoyed cult status in recent times. It would seem at first to have all the trappings of a typical misogynistic thriller of the slip-her-the-stake variety, but whatever the intentions of its makers, it reads more like self-parody. This camp dimension is probably its most subversive element, or it is at any rate the aspect of the film that reduces lesbian audiences to peals of laughter. Apart from its thirties campiness, however, the film marks some other interesting challenges to the misogynistic vampire genre. First of all, it is a parody of a psychoanalytic case study, since the vampire, Countess Marya Zaleska (Gloria Holden), has turned to the male hero, a psychologist named Jeffrey Garth (Otto Kruger), for assistance in controlling her "impulses." Through this play on the psychoanalytic session, the film is also able to foreground its own fascination with gender, desire, deception, and the gaze, even the very technology of filming itself. Like Freud's Dora case and his earlier *Studies on Hysteria*, *Dracula's Daughter* is eminently about "the daughter's seduction," the transferential battles between a good doctor-father, an evil dream-father, and a woman coded as a hysteric. The Countess starts out as Anna O., relatively pliant and eager to be well, but she ends up as Dora, snaring her doctor in a countertransferential game that threatens to overturn the psychoanalytic scenario and bring it to a premature end, as Dora ended her sessions, with a slam of the door—"an unmistakable vengeance on her part," or so Freud deemed it.[20]

The lesbian dimension of the film is another reminder of the Dora case. As is well known, Freud believed that his analysis of Dora went sadly awry in part because he "failed to discover in time and to inform the patient that her homosexual (gynaecophilic) love for Frau K. was the strongest unconscious current in her mental life." Having searched for the nature of Dora's hysteria in her relationship with her father, with her seducer Herr K., and even with himself, Freud discovers only too late what he fears should have been apparent to him much earlier, that Dora loved not Herr K., but Herr K.'s wife. In a recent book on gender and horror, Rhona Berenstein has discovered that there were efforts to censor the lesbian content of the film, but when I read the American reviews I find only obliviousness.[21] From what I can gather, the reviewers of *Dracula's Daughter* suffered from the same blindness as Freud, though they certainly had more clues. *The New York Times* made a joke of the film, presenting the Countess in purely heterosexual terms as a debutante. The headline reads "'Dracula's Daughter' Makes Her Debut at the Rialto and Proves She's a Chip off the Old Block," next to which is a glamorous, society-page photograph of Gloria Holden dressed in black. The film is given a good review as a "cute little horror picture," and the article ends with the line "Be sure to bring the kiddies."[22] Now, surely, any whisper of lesbianism in this film would have generated a scandal. But one cannot panic about something one has not noticed.

The Countess's lesbian seductions nevertheless provide some of the wittiest scenes in the film. Submitting at last to the need to feed, the Countess suddenly proclaims her intention to paint. She requires a model, and so she sends her funereal butler, Sandor (Freud's colleague Sandor Ferenczi, perhaps?), in search of girlflesh. He eventually finds some about to jump off a bridge. The girl, whose name is Lili, wonders at Sandor's intentions but agrees to go with him anyway. When the butch Countess gets darling Lili alone, she plies the girl with wine and a lingering gaze. Some truly priceless dialogue ensues, lines like, "I'm doing a study of a young girl's head and shoulders. You won't object to removing your blouse, will you?" or Lili's suitably naive questions, "Why are you looking at me that way?" and "I suppose you'll want me to pull down, won't you?" as she drops a strap from her shoulder. The Countess muses over the paleness of the girl's skin, mourning her apparent bloodlessness in strangely seductive tones. "Won't I do?" the girl asks, and the Countess replies, "You'll do very well indeed." She hypnotizes Lili with an enormous bauble of a ring, and when the girl screams, the camera cuts away to the grimace of an African mask hanging on the wall. A similar moment of lesbian thrills and chills occurs in the climactic scene of the film. The Countess has kidnapped Janet, Jeffrey's secretary, and has laid her out unconscious on a divan in her Transylvanian castle. In what must surely be the longest kiss never filmed, the Countess hovers lovingly over Janet, as the camera cuts away to Jeffrey, rushing into the castle to save her. The Countess hovers . . . and hovers . . .

slowly descending to kiss the recumbent Janet, but of course the actual clinch is interrupted by the endlessly delayed appearance of Jeffrey.

The Countess's lesbianism serves to distinguish her, like Dora, as the illicit seducer, the woman who—so it is discovered, only too late—fails to be a pliant object of the masculine look and is instead the furtive subject of a lesbian one. She is a creature of psychoanalysis in a number of other ways. Her vampirism is construed by Jeffrey as a neurotic impulse. She and Jeffrey both exercise their effects through hypnotism, a strategy Freud used in his early studies of hysterics in an effort to incite anamnesis. The African mask is vaguely suggestive of Freud's primitivism and his fascination for archaeological fragments. Another mask appears in a painting of a female nude, and in the castle there is a tapestry behind which a man is hiding. The emphasis on deception and masquerade suggests that the analytic gaze can misread and be willfully deceived. Vampires are deemed insidious precisely because one does not always recognize them for what they are, and the same has been said, of course, about lesbians. In this film, masquerade becomes especially troubling and impenetrable, pointing I think to anxieties about the filmic representation of femininity—is she what she looks like or not? The Countess goes out at night dressed like a Muslim woman, fully veiled but for her mesmerizing eyes, suggesting not only the peculiar fascination of the gaze but also the enigmatic and exotic "dark continent" of the Freudian woman, rendered in the familiar terms of colonial mystique. Jeffrey's office walls are covered with X-ray photographs, suggesting the power of science to render human subjectivity perfectly transparent (if somewhat ghoulish, in this instance); nevertheless, it is in those very rooms that the Countess, in a sly move, makes off with Janet right under Jeffrey's nose. The medical gaze examines the photographs and sees a medical condition rather than a skeleton, the traditional emblem of death; and when Jeffrey looks at the Countess, he sees a hysteric, not a lesbian, and certainly not the undead. Death and lesbian desire become tropes for what a perverse cinema can understand and a patriarchal science cannot. Like Freud, Jeffrey is imperious and aggressive with his "neurotic ladies," not only the Countess but also Janet herself, who pretends not to be in love with him. As the bearer of patriarchal authority, however, Jeffrey is hopelessly inept. He is annoyed to discover that he is dependent on Janet to tie his bow ties. His clinical interest in the Countess evolves into flirtation and unconscious obsession. The masculine gaze becomes the vehicle of its own entrapment. Jeffrey is betrayed by his own desire to see. The film is preoccupied with veiling and unveiling, seeing and failing to see, transference and countertransference, the very tensions that motivate the narrative suspense of the Dora case.

From the opening scenes, the Countess's vampirism, like Dora's hysteria, is conceived as a father fixation. The pretext for this theory of vampire etiology may well have been Freud's 1920 case study of a lesbian, in which he concluded that the subject's homosexuality was a function of her "masculinity complex" with regard to her father. But, as Lacan once remarked, the neurotic's wished-for father is the dead father. The film begins with a dead father, Dracula (and Renfield), run through with a stake in a dark alleyway by the good doctor-father Van Helsing. I will pass over for now the homoerotic implications of Van Helsing's dark and secretive deed and its attendant obsession. What is striking is the way the Countess's "impulses" are thereby construed in the language of an incest narrative. Dracula is the dead, silenced, mysterious father who nevertheless exercises a perverse influence over his daughter's behavior and her desire. In fact, Bela Lugosi was on the payroll for this film, although, eerily, he never appears in it. The vampire father is an influence from the beyond, as it were. The Countess feels she can be normal now that her father is dead: "I can lead a normal life now," she exclaims, "think normal things, play normal music!" Through a presumed act of betrayal in the distant past, however, the father continues to exercise a symbolic, controlling influence over the thoughts and behavior of the daughter, rendering her prey to strange erotic impulses. The Countess steals Dracula's dead body and, in a scene of ritual cremation, she assures herself that her father is indeed dead and can no longer influence her. In vampire lore, of course, the undead daughter should be free once the father is destroyed, but this film suggests that the incestuous influence of the father survives—and even thrives on—a proper burial. In a wonderfully melodramatic scene, the Countess sits at the piano with Sandor and has a go at playing "normal music." She hits a sentimental note and recalls a nostalgic scene with, of course, her mother. This defensive strategy should be familiar to us from Auerbach and de Lauretis. When she speaks of sweet shadows, however, Sandor reinterprets them as the shadows of death; the barking of dogs are reinterpreted as the howling of wolves; the birds become bats. With the slightest shift in the interpretive lens, the Countess's sweet maternal memory is darkened by its horrible paternal significance. The disavowal of her disavowal begins to crack. She bangs the piano keys with increasing passion. Later in the film, her perverse paternal identification complete, she will come out triumphantly: "I am Dracula's daughter!"

The broken social contract of incest and paternal identification, construed through the metaphor of lesbian vampirism, has made the Countess not a victim but a woman to be reckoned with, a woman whose obscure hunger places her, like the hysteric, oddly inside and outside the symbolic order at once. Her first session with Jeffrey Garth is a marvelous piece of pop-psychoanalytic nonsense in the best "You Freud, me Jane" tradition of films like *The Snake Pit* (1948) and *Marnie* (1964). Freudian camp is Hollywood's desperate attempt at assimilating the increasingly popular insights of psychoanalysis, and it is usually recognizable at a hundred paces by the heavy-handed use of word-association games, hokey dream sequences, silly jargon, and magical epiphanies that lead invariably to marriage and motherhood. The Freudian camp of *Dracula's Daughter* is no less blatant. We see it in the wistful way Gloria Holden repeats the word *release*, rendering it vaguely suggestive of orgasm rather than mental health. Or the inspired way she says phrases like "your strength against his," as she rallies her doctor to combat with her private demon. Or the professional tone by which he likens her problem to alcoholism and recommends that she "resist temptation." Above all, her neurosis is articulated as an uncontrollable sexual addiction, and Dracula is the source of this addiction. As in the Dora case, an aggressive scene of seduction is veiled by the peculiar pretensions of the analytic session.

The use of the hypnotism trope foregrounds this aggression and seduction as a struggle between two gazes that are opposed to each other and yet oddly similar. Both the Countess and Jeffrey make use of hypnotism, she with her shiny ring and he with a strange contraption of light and mirrors. Her hypnotism is construed as the feminine gaze, unspeakable, devouring, seductive, supernatural. His is the masculine gaze of science and analysis, an incitement to memory and confession, and therefore to mental health. The use of hypnosis would seem to be a reference to Freud and his hysterics. Hypnosis had also been, since the late nineteenth century, a popular method for "curing" homosexuality, for planting suggestions and aversions that would stimulate the patient's heterosexual responses.[23] Within the symbolic framework of the film, however, it is significant that both the ring and the machine project light into the eyes of a passive woman. Indeed, the ring is round and glassy like a camera lens, and the hypnosis machine, with its mirror and spinning lights, looks oddly like a film projector. Both the Countess and Jeffrey are closely associated with modes of representation and communication, she through her association with painting and books, he through more technological modes, such as the telephone, the telegraph, and the X-ray. In fact, when Janet is kidnapped, Jeffrey is able to muster a surprising technological force to track her down: not only the telephone and the telegraph but photography and radio as well, and the screen is filled with wires and machinery, the whole apparatus of modern communication. But it is the hypnotizing and visionary gaze of the cinematic camera that is at stake. The question is, who will appropriate the controlling and hypnotic gaze of the camera in this film? Will the dreamlike trance of the passive, cinematic spectator be determined by the feminized gaze of an erotic imaginary or the masculinized gaze of science, symbolic order, and temptation well-resisted? Clearly, the former is winning throughout much of the film. At the end of her session with Jeffrey, for example, the Countess, troubled by the mirrors in which she does not appear, is able to reject his suggestion that she submit herself to hypnosis. He is not much more successful with Lili after she has been hypnotized by the Countess. The hypnosis machine has very little effect on her "rambling, incoherent talk," and she finally dies in Jeffrey's care. He asks the girl to describe the "pictures behind your eyes," a repressed erotic discourse, essentially cinematic and yet unspeakable. When she speaks, it is from another world, a fragmented one, referring incoherently to the seduction she has just experienced. She addresses Jeffrey as though, ironically, he were the Countess, as if his machine were her ring, and indeed he seems to be engaged in a similar battle for control.

It is at this point that the tables seem to have turned. Like Freud, Jeffrey is a bit slow in recognizing his patient's motivations and even slower in recognizing his own—the countertransference. This part of the film reads like a fantasy of what might have happened had Dora not broken off the analysis when she did. The struggle between the psychologist and the vampire intensifies, and she intends for him to become her next victim. The Countess wants to lure him to Transylvania, and she poses as a willing hysteric in order to do it. She seduces him with the lure of knowledge, the truth as the truth about her desire. He demands from her "the entire truth," and she teases him with lines like, "I can't tell you. It's too ghastly," or "I'll make any confession." He is suspicious. He says, "You've told me all you dare." As Rhona Berenstein has remarked, "Although he earns his living as an analyst, Garth's powers of interpretation are worthless when it comes to vampires."[24] The Countess realizes she will have to kidnap Janet to get her way, and in an imperious aside, she says of Jeffrey, "I'll leave, and you'll go with me." And she is right. He does go to Transylvania, but not without suffering the accusations of others that he is himself "mad." The psychoanalytic session has reached the stage of negative transference and countertransference. As Freud writes of transference, "all the patient's tendencies, including hostile ones, are aroused," but in Dora's case, he must admit that he "did not succeed in mastering the transference in good time." He adds, "In this way the transference took me unawares, and, because of the unknown quantity in me which reminded Dora of Herr K., she took her revenge on me as she wanted to take her revenge on him. . . . Thus she *acted* out an essential part of her recollections and phantasies instead of reproducing it in the treatment."[25] The Countess, acting out her fixation on the evil dream-father, betrays the good doctor-father, and gets a piece of Janet in the bargain.

What is odd is the countertransference. Jeffrey has presumably come to Transylvania to save Janet, but he does not put up much of a fight when the Countess asks him to submit himself in Janet's place. He simply shrugs and lets her go for it. The doctor-hypnotizer becomes the hypnotized. The Countess is eventually killed, but not because of the superior knowledge and capability of the male hero. Rather, she is shot through with an arrow by Sandor, who is jealous (in an amusing cut, we see Janet twitch as the arrow penetrates the Countess's body). He would have shot Jeffrey as well were he not himself shot just in time by the police, who appear out of nowhere. The Countess is undone, then, only by her own kind, by the very betrayal at the heart of vampirism, and of course by the police, the always already on-the-scene representatives of the law. In this sense, *Dracula's Daughter* is a typical track-and-kill vampire movie. But the psychoanalyst, the one eminently "presumed to know" in this film, is the one who is finally most vulnerable, most perverse, the one whose own gaze ironically places him on the side of the woman whose gaze he desires to comprehend.

The final frame of the film is a still frame of the dead countess, her eyes wide open. As Roland Barthes has noted, the photograph is already on the side of obsession and death; "All those young photographers," he writes, "who are at work in the world, determined upon the capture of actuality, do not know that they are agents of Death."[26] This remark is especially suggestive in the context of this film, given Jeffrey's investment in photography and a medical discourse of "actuality." His X-rays give him the skeletons of the living, and his analytical session with the Countess eventually leads to her death and very nearly his own. Barthes also speaks of a photograph of a condemned prisoner of whom he writes, "he is dead and he is going to die,"[27] suggesting a defeat of time, an undead quality to photography itself that the lively motion of cinema seeks to counteract. The Countess becomes an eerie photograph, a frozen frame, within the normative cinematic narrative. Her dead gaze is familiar to us from a thousand poses, a thousand dead and vacant gazes, in fashion magazines and publicity stills. Despite itself, Hollywood was a little in love with death, admitting the cadaverous that inevitably haunts the glamorous. "She was beautiful," says the voice-over, "when she died a hundred years ago." Vampire films, like the masculine gaze itself, only ever experience the feminine as undead, uncanny, predatory, subversive: *Dracula's Daughter* ends not with Janet's docile and unthreatening beauty but with the Countess's undead face, now a glamor photograph, indistinguishable from the Hollywood ideal of femininity. As Bonnie Burns has written, "At the very moment that the Countess's death releases Garth from the entrancing power of the image, the image, in its potential as a disruptive lesbian eroticism, returns to haunt the cinematic apparatus."[28] The mask-like beauty of the Hollywood vamp, not only Gloria Holden but also Theda Bara, Greta Garbo, and Marlene Dietrich, often seemed to mix glamor with indefinable hints of lesbianism and sadomasochism. The female vampire may well represent a misogynistic effort to control that erotic power, but in this film it also represents the queer and insistent eagerness to indulge in it, to embrace the spectacle of abjection it has created, and to enter through the gaze the black-and-white dreamworld of the undead. There is something strangely triumphant in this final gaze of the Countess, something uncanny about her dead but open eyes, that keeps her desire in play at the end of the film.

THE *UNHEIMLICH* MANEUVER

Ted: "You intrigue me—and you worry me—because I don't understand you."
Fran: "Don't try to."
—*Vampyres* (1974)

The opening scene of *Vampyres* defines a cinematic gaze that is not only male but sadistic and pathological. Two naked women are making love on a bed. We hear the eerie and exaggerated sound of footsteps approaching from off-camera. The bedroom door opens, and a shadowy figure enters the room, presumably a man, judging from the outline of his fedora. He points a gun at the women and shoots them both dead. From this unpromising beginning, a vampire tale of lesbian rage and revenge unfolds. In the course of the film, the vampire couple, Fran (Marianne Morris) and Miriam (Anulka), pose as hitchhikers in order to seduce and dispatch a string of handsome male mashers. They also attack a couple who are camping in the woods nearby, and they excite the fascination of the homophobic wife in particular, who spends most of the film spying on them. As in *Dracula's Daughter,* the cinematic gaze is thematized as part of the film's preoccupation with eyes, spying, surveillance, and voyeurism. Unlike the earlier film, however, the vampire lesbians are seen as the victims of a paranoid homophobic gaze. The lesbians take vengeance on the men whom they have waylaid alongside the road and who regard them as amusing perverts or sexual objects. Although the lesbian or female bisexual betrays several men and a woman in this film, she does not betray the woman she loves (unlike *The Hunger,* for example, in which all the main characters are bisexual and they all betray everyone they love). In fact, the vampire lesbians in this film remain devoted to each other to the very end, and they actually survive the final credits. Their malice is the very vehicle of their bond.

An interesting point about *Vampyres* is its self-applied X-rating. The film is eager to excite the pornographic gaze that it then proceeds to thematize. *Vampyres* was produced at a time when pornographic markets were expanding rapidly and when the vampire was first making its appearance in porn, both as a *femme fatale* and an *homme fatal.* The film self-consciously incorporates certain generic aspects of straight porn. For example, in the opening scene, the women are completely naked and making love in a brightly lit room. When Miriam wishes to excite Ted (Murray Brown), the man she toys with throughout the film, she undresses in the fashion of a striptease to reveal black stockings and garters. Nevertheless, the film is not so much pornographic as low-budget art-house fare with a surprisingly sophisticated narrative structure. The director, like his vampire lesbians, seems to be exciting a sadistic homophobic gaze, only to render it problematic and even punish it through an equally erotic, equally sadistic return-gaze of lesbian revenge.

Indeed, one of the extraordinary things about this film is that the spectator is always aligned, rather uncomfortably, with the voyeuristic and murderous masculine gaze of the opening sequence. Although my own sympathy is always with the vampires, the camera often positions me as the murderer. Even so, the film is decidedly out of sympathy with him. The murderer's identity is obscured in the opening scene and, in fact, remains a mystery throughout the film. Our identification with him is already established, however, in that we too have been standing voyeuristically over the bed, watching the two women. The opening sequence functions ironically as a kind of primal scene, but this time it is not the baby wolf-child stumbling onto his parents screwing, pop on top and mom taking the abuse *a tergo,* to use Freud's quaint term. No, this time the father is left out in the hall, and boy is he angry. In fact, father takes the place of the child (male or female) as detective. This primal scene is continually replayed throughout the film, such that we are repeatedly identified with that sadistic and voyeuristic detective in the hall. We, too, pack a gun. There are moments, no less strange than the opening sequence, that seem to refer to our own voyeuristic gaze. While Ted is in bed with Fran, he is constantly paranoid. He is afraid he is being watched, and of course he is, by Miriam, but also by the camera, which self-consciously reproduces his lovemaking as a pornographic spectacle. We are at once the voyeuristic murderer and the vengeful lesbian. Even more curious is a shower scene in which we see Miriam kissing Fran. She warns Fran to kill Ted and stop playing around with him, then she kneels down to nibble at Fran's nether lips. Again, the scene is pornographic in style, with the shower brightly lit and Fran in the throes of orgasm. What is odd is that we are watching all this through the fronds of a potted plant, itself annoyingly obtrusive, as though we were spying—and we are. We are eavesdropping, hoping, as does Ted, to learn the intentions of these two women. Even stranger, there is no narrative justification for this camera position. Although a number of characters would like to be in our shoes, there is no one to whom this spying gaze actually corresponds, except ourselves. As Laura Mulvey would no doubt have said, the scene is fetishistic and voyeuristic. But it is also self-conscious. I find myself thrilling to this bold representation of lesbian desire, and yet I also find myself positioned as the uninvited guest, the unwelcome interloper who, like the murderer in the opening sequence, intrudes on these women with aggressive intentions of his own.

The theme of the "guest" is key in this film. Everyone is a guest, and no one has a home. At the heart of the film is the house—big, empty, gloomy, English, gothic—in which the lesbian couple was murdered and which they have now taken over as their haunt. Yet Fran speaks of herself as a guest in the house, and no doubt she originally was. She brings her men to the top of the house, telling them it is not her own, and she introduces them to the cozy room she claims is hers. She tells Ted, "I often receive guests," a line that he takes to be a coy reference to her promiscuity. Indeed, she offers her hospitality to every man who gives her a lift. They are the guests of guests. Ted is also a guest, not only in the house but also at the hotel in town. Harriet, the homophobic voyeur, encounters a sign on the grounds of the house, "NO TRESPASSING—PRIVATE PROPERTY," which she duly ignores, suggesting that she is a decidedly unwelcome guest. "It doesn't belong to you," her husband reminds her, even though he himself is yet another unwelcome guest, content to set up camp in a trailer that he has parked virtually in the backyard. In the final scene, an estate agent shows the house to an American couple—it is significant that they have come from abroad—though they are troubled by stories of ghosts. Everyone is a traveler in this film, and no one seems to have a home. This subversion of domestic life is part of Fran and Miriam's revenge. They render desire itself homeless while they secretly claim the house in which, as guests, they were killed. Their seductions are an invitation to others to wander from home, to trespass, to expose themselves on unfamiliar ground, and thereby to know the horror of dispossession.

The feminist message is evident. To be a lesbian is to be always entertaining uninvited guests, and yet to feel never quite at home. To be a lesbian is to submit against one's will to the dogma of what Adrienne Rich calls "compulsory heterosexuality." One submits to the gaze of the man on the make, the misogynist on the warpath, the female homophobe on the prowl. One entertains these various gazes, yet one is at great pains to find a room of one's own to which one can retire, feel safe, answer no questions, make no explanations. The vampire lesbians simply say, we've had enough. Go ahead. Take a look, take a long long look. All you see is all you get. We'll give you sex. We'll give you wine, a Carpathian wine, "feminine vintage." And when you are done, we shall eat you. We'll drain your blood and abandon your carcass in the road. Or we'll kill your husband and slash at your body with a knife. Or we'll let you wither slowly while, even more slowly, you learn to see what you have refused to see, a lesbian in the throes of a pleasure that does not respect you. This is not to say there will be no hospitality. "Does this kind of thing excite you?" Fran asks Ted in a moment of suspense, and the question seems to reverberate through the film. Of a knife, a man is asked, "Do you like it?" or of the Carpathian wine, "Do you like it? Everyone seems to like it." The question is always ironic, always spiked with mystery and polite aggression. But the time for explaining this mystery, this hunger for revenge, came and went a long time ago. Vampires never explain. When asked about Miriam, Fran demonstrates the queer art of telling the truth without actually revealing it: "She's my girlfriend. We've a lot in common and get on very well together." Entertaining guests has its limits, and confession has become one of them. "Is there a limit to the questions?" Ted asks, during a more general interrogation of Fran. Her response is polite: "There's a limit to the answers."

All of the victims of Fran and Miriam are in their own way guests, and yet each is replaying a familiar scene, the primal scene that marks the house and its haunting. Their curiosity is uncanny. They are wandering into the unknown, and yet oddly returning home. The last line of the film is spoken by the estate agent as he tries to make light of the ghost stories: "The murderer always returns to the scene of his crime." The line resonates in my mind with a peculiar irony, first because it is the murdered who keep returning in this film—the vampires themselves. The line is also ironic given the unrevealed identity of the murderer, not to mention the curious, almost contagious, dissemination of his gaze. Ted is identified with the murderer from the very beginning, when he is recognized at the hotel. "We haven't seen you down here in years," says an old man at the front desk. Ted tells him he is mistaken, but the man still retains an uncanny certainty. We are left with a suspicion that Ted is the murderer, returning to the scene after many years, but that suspicion is neither confirmed nor convincingly denied. As in Lacan, the gaze is other—it has a life of its own, it keeps turning up in the oddest places, and its traveling makes us nervous. In a scene that follows closely upon the opening murder sequence, Ted hears footsteps in the hallway outside his hotel room. With a twinge of paranoia, he bolts the door, then goes to the mirror and treats his eyes with eyedrops. Masculinity is in a panic in this film, and its gaze is sick. Our suspicions are further aroused, since it seems as though Ted remembers those footsteps from somewhere, and he knows what is supposed to follow. Or maybe he's just a little uptight, who knows? There is no limit to our questions in this film, but there is a limit to the answers. The script, like its vampires, never really explains its many secrets. When he picks up Fran, Ted has a momentary bout of *déjà vu:* "You remind me of someone I knew a very long time ago," he says, thus starting our detective wheels spinning again. Ted dismisses the thought, but not our suspicion. And yet nothing more is said on the subject.

Harriet has a similar paranoid experience while painting a picture of the house. Her painting is one way that she keeps the house and its two mysterious occupants under surveillance. Nevertheless, as she is painting, she begins to suspect that she herself is the object of a gaze, that someone is looking at her looking. Fran and Miriam approach, and Fran says something to Harriet that is mysterious and never explained: "I always knew we'd find each other. By this sign, I'll recognize you," and she draws an invisible mark across Harriet's forehead with her finger. Our detective wheels start spinning again. We presume she means by this enigmatic announcement that Harriet was the murderer and that she has returned to the house not by chance but by design. In fact, earlier, Harriet was frightened by a shout and a mysterious hand in the camper window, not unlike the scream and the shadowy hand that held the gun in the opening sequence. But nothing more is said of her guilt. Ted and Harriet seem to assume the position of the murderer. Each is coming home to a woman who is uncanny in her strangeness and her familiarity. This uncanniness recalls the German word, *unheimlich,* and Freud's explanation of it as the unhomelike, what is paradoxically most strange and most familiar because it represents a return to the primal domicile of the womb.[29] In this case, it seems to represent an uncanny return to the primal scene, the scene of the murder of which all the vampires' victims are strangely guilty, implicated as they are by their own obsessive gaze, if nothing else. As the victims of this *unheimlich* maneuver, the man in the hotel, Ted, Harriet, even ourselves as spectators, are made to feel a bit weird, since this home in which we are guests is strangely familiar. We are in need of more information. We wish Fran and Miriam would cough up a few facts for us. But they are not forthcoming with explanations. "There's a limit to the answers."

Of all the curious gazes, Harriet's is I think the most interesting. She is distinguished as the only woman who is attacked by Fran and Miriam. Furthermore, her gaze is marked as peculiarly feminine from the start. She is first seen with her husband driving along in a car. They pass Fran alongside the road, but do not stop to pick her up. Harriet has also noticed that Miriam is hiding behind a tree, but when she tries to tell her husband, he insists that she must be "seeing things." She cannot understand why there would be a second woman in hiding, and she begins to obsess about her. Her husband is still dismissive, saying things like "You must have been

dreaming" or "You've got to convince yourself that you were dreaming"—
the classic male hysterization of any woman's perspective that fails to harmonize with his own. In this way, Harriet is marked as neurotic, and yet
we too have seen what she has seen. There is also no small hint of lesbian
panic in Harriet's obsession. Why should she get all worked up about seeing two women where there should be only one? She cannot take her eyes
off the women. Their every appearance outside her camper is an event for
her, and her gaze is anything but approving. Her homophobia is confirmed
when she sees Fran and Miriam dash through a meadow at dawn. "It didn't
look normal," Harriet says. "It gave me a strange feeling." To make sure
the word *normal* jumps up and hits us between the eyes, Harriet later says,
"No normal person would live in a place like that." Hers is a classic homosexual panic—a terror that makes her curious about the abnormal women,
makes her want to get a closer look rather than run away. She must indeed be seeing things, seeing precisely what others miss, a glimpse of the
lesbian desire that she sees precisely because, in some mysterious way, she
has already seen it. Fran and Miriam have already seen that she has already
seen it. They know she was fated to meet with the lesbian vampire. They
have made her a marked woman, though we are not quite sure why. But a
lesbian, or even a vampire, she will never be. Her desiring gaze, like that
of the male murderer, can be articulated only through her panic.

In the end, Harriet is brutally murdered by the vampires, as is her husband. In fact, Ted is the only victim of the vampires who survives, but he
survives only at their whim. He discovers some of the secrets of the vampire lesbians bit by bit, or rather bite by bite. At one point, in an anemic
daze, he is even obliged to look on helplessly as Fran and Miriam lose
interest in his naked body and have sex with each other beside him on the
bed. At daylight one morning he simply stumbles off, rather pathetically,
like the cliché of the sheepish enthusiast of the pornhouse who slinks off
in his raincoat. Fran and Miriam make their usual mad romantic dash
across the graveyard, running from the rising sun. Like a pair of sardonic
dominatrixes, they debate whether they should make a last minute effort
to do him in: "But we can't let him get away alive!" They give it a miss. But,
with the curious dissemination of his *curious* male gaze, a guilty voyeurism that infects the audience no less than the characters in the film, I am
left wondering of whom they speak when they say "him."

CRUISING FOR A BRUISING

Tom: "I think you should see a doctor."

Sarah: "I am a doctor."

— *The Hunger* (1983)

In these lines from *The Hunger,* it is clear we have come a long way from *Dracula's Daughter,* where the vampire lesbian was the object, or rather the target, of a hostile medical gaze. Sarah Roberts (Susan Sarandon) plays a medical researcher on the verge of a breakthrough discovery that might help to reverse the aging process. Her work, as popularized in her book and a television interview, excites the interest of a vampire, Miriam Blaylock (Catherine Deneuve), whose companion John (David Bowie) has suddenly begun to decay after a few centuries of youth. Eventually, Miriam realizes she has to tuck John away in a coffin in the attic along with her other lovers, and she chooses Sarah as her next partner in crime. She seduces Sarah away from her lover Tom, and in a steamy sex scene that was groundbreaking for the representation of lesbians in mainstream cinema, Miriam infuses Sarah with vampire blood. Sarah, however, rejects her passive role in the relationship. She double-crosses Miriam, buries her alive in a casket much like John's, and takes her place as vampire lesbian, luring mortal women away from their men.

Although daring in many respects, *The Hunger* might still be regarded as misogynistic in ways typical of the vampire genre. Much of the problem stems from the screenplay's reliance on Whitley Strieber's antifeminist novel, published in 1981, in which lesbianism is mined purely for shock value and Sarah's dedication to her career is presented as aggressive and unwomanly. Like the vampire narratives of the fin de siècle, both Strieber's novel and the film are very much about the New Woman, in this case a generation of ambitious and well-educated female professionals whose burgeoning numbers have excited a great deal of nervous media scrutiny over the past two decades. In Strieber's novel, Tom seeks to rescue what shreds of conventional femininity remain in Sarah's character, while Miriam is the vampiric woman who appeals to all of Sarah's most aggressive instincts. Tom loses, but then Sarah recognizes the error of her ways and commits suicide. The film, however, seeks to undermine Strieber's attitudes in a number of ways. First of all, Sarah is seen as triumphant in the end; indeed, she is rewarded for her ambition, her iron will, and her professional brilliance. The men in the film are dull and ineffectual, and Sarah's lack of sexual interest in Tom becomes a running joke. Sex between women is portrayed as sensual and beautiful, rather than just weird.

Calling anyone a blood-sucking fiend is, of course, never a nice thing to say; nevertheless, I think *The Hunger* represents a disruptive queer pleasure that is neither homophobic nor misogynistic. The film's popularity among the goth crowd should tip us off to its oppositional appeal. If we view *The Hunger* through the lens of a certain strain of lesbian feminism that emphasizes gentleness, love, family, growth, and healing, then things begin to look grim. Surely, the adherents of the "positive images" campaign, which still preoccupies much lesbian and gay film criticism, find little to admire here. If we turn the lens a notch, however, and view the film through a lesbian identity that insists on its own subversive otherness, its adventurous demand for sexual pleasure, its promiscuity, its funky sense of style, its disregard for neoconservative "family values" and conventional femininity, and its celebration of its own physical and intellectual power, then this film is infinitely more entertaining. Miriam becomes radically seductive and dangerous, a romantic sexual outlaw rather than an abusive menace. Furthermore, the music, the nightclubbing, the makeup and clothing of the two women look forward to the "lipstick lesbian" style of recent years. In fact, *The Hunger* was widely ridiculed by most reviewers as being absurdly chic. One writer quipped, "The new eroticism may therefore rely less on the clash of wills than on the contrast of surfaces and fabrics"[30]—if only this claim were true! Nina Auerbach also faults the film for being a very eighties celebration of consumerism and a competitive business ethos that leaves room for only one lesbian at the top. Materialist critics as vampire hunters . . . there is something relentlessly Victorian about their moral piety. To turn Auerbach's perspective a notch, one might also say that this film is a very feminist meditation about the fear of female economic autonomy and the fear of women who choose to enter arenas of traditionally male competition. The representation of the rich, ambitious, disturbing, glamorous, exceptionally autonomous lesbian has a tradition of its own in mainstream cinema, from Barbara Stanwyck in *Walk on the Wild Side* (1962) to Candice Bergen in *The Group* (1966) to Sharon Stone in *Basic Instinct* (1992). In a number of vampire flicks, especially *Blood and Roses* and *Daughters of Darkness,* a decadent aristocratic lesbian chic is central to the film's appeal. In *The Hunger,* glamor appears to be a way of distinguishing lesbian or bisexual desire as more intense, more sensuous, more stylish. The opening scene in particular is remarkable for its incorporation of rock-video style—loud music, dazzling lights, violent imagery, frenetic jump-cuts, confusing juxtapositions—at a time when MTV was still an innovation. The rest of the film has all the exaggerated sensuality of a perfume ad, complete with classical music, museum pieces, and beautiful people moving in slow motion. The soundtrack offers eerie amplification or distortion of sounds: resonating voices, the exaggerated thump of car tires crossing a bridge, the beating of a heart, the reverberation of a scream. *The Hunger* is a cinematic echo of Anne Rice's notion of vampire subjectivity, a dreamlike otherness of aggravated desire and intensified perception.

Another sexual dimension of *The Hunger* is its investment in sadomasochism—its leather, its attitude, its top-bottom dynamics, and its eroticization of pain. The film appeared at about the same time as the lesbian s/m debates, which culminated in 1982 not only with Samois (an outspoken organization of leather dykes) and the s/m manifesto *Coming to Power* but also with the regrettable feminist diatribe *Against Sadomasochism*, whose numerous gentle and loving contributors sought in so many words to slip Samois the stake. Although lesbian s/m places enormous emphasis on safety and consent, accusations of rape, however ludicrous they may be, are always going to hover around the more violent extremes of s/m pornography and fantasy. In the literalizing critiques of s/m, fantasy can scarcely be said to exist: s/m is false-consciousness, rape as sexual orientation. For some viewers, *The Hunger* is problematic in that the blood-wedding between Miriam and Sarah appears to be coercive, and yet the film subtly constructs a narrative of sexual panic in which Sarah is pursued by the lesbian vampire only because—whether she realizes it or not—she is in dire need of her. Those lesbians who are willing to distinguish between actual rape and s/m fantasy might find that this film, with its volatile female master/slave dynamic, crackles with sexual tension. "You belong to me! We belong to each other!" Miriam exclaims, with flawless attitude. Sarah runs from the scene in a panic, but Miriam knows she will be back because they share a peculiar hunger. As one reviewer wrote, "The already notorious lesbian seduction scene between Deneuve and Sarandon would have been more effective if there had been somewhat less complicity,"[31] but her complicity is precisely the point. Although she will later betray Miriam and replace her as top girl, she first looks to Miriam to bring her out, to seduce her, to make her perform the unspeakable. In the sadomasochistic logic of most vampire films, the need to feed goes arm in arm with the need to bleed.

For those women who do not include rough-trade breast-biting on their agenda, *The Hunger* offers other points of interest. The preoccupation with the gaze, not to mention the various technologies of representation and surveillance, from photographs and videotapes to television and security monitors, places *The Hunger* in the tradition of thematizing lesbian looks in vampire films. From the opening scene in the nightclub, the vampiric gaze is foregrounded as an intensified mode of lesbian and bisexual desire. In short, the vampiric gaze is about cruising. In the club, Miriam and John scope for their prey through funky shades, as they are cross-cut with the goth group Bauhaus performing in a wire cage, then cross-cut confusingly with Methuselah the monkey lashing out at Betty the monkey in Sarah's experimental research cages. Miriam and John pick up a pair of bisexual fashion-victims in black leather and whisk them back to the lair. The cruising continues, as there seems to be some misunderstanding about who is going to do whom. The woman flirts with Miriam but is lured away by John. At one point, she dances seductively, or tries to, in front of a brightly lit screen, like a cinema screen, suggesting the art-house pornographic voyeurism the film seeks to excite.

All the technological gadgetry in the film is intended to capture a look. The film is obsessed with looks in the sense of gazes, but also looks in the sense of fashions, appearances, poses—looks also in the sense of good looks, of finding an attractive partner with whom one can spend eternity. Cameras, televisions, and monitors are of course the modes of a controlling gaze, but they can also capture and control a look, a glance, an image. They can freeze-frame a youthful and beautiful look, as in a fashion photograph. The technology of the gaze is again in the service of the undead. Like cinema itself, this technology overturns the presumed superiority of reality to fantasy, since it is often the photographic images that seem more intensely true. Images reveal the truth. They reveal what one is. Sarah treasures her research videos because they reveal the truth about aging; John's violin student, Alice, notices how awful he looks only when she sees him in the photograph she takes with her camera; Miriam discovers that John has fed on Alice only when she finds a photograph of the attack; and when Miriam infuses her blood into Sarah, we see medical imaging of blood coursing through her veins. The cinematic camera itself, never more than in this film, valorizes fantasy, making all the supernatural promises of the vampire: eternal youth, eternal beauty, eternal life, eternal fixation in the past. The camera as a controlling and desiring gaze is evident in the monitor at the Blaylock's door, which allows them to see their guests without being seen. There is also the television on which Miriam watches an interview with Sarah and the monitor through which Miriam secretly gazes at Sarah during a public book-signing. These technical gazes are not unlike Miriam's power to "touch" other people, to commune with and influence others through telepathy. She uses her telepathic touch as a kind of hypnotic suggestion, implanting erotic fantasies in Sarah's mind. This touch is likened to a phone call whose ring no one but Sarah can hear. The technological gaze of *The Hunger* is almost always, for the vampiric, a preying and illicit look, and for the human, the revelation of a secret, the view to another world, the fatal lure of everlasting life. Even in the case of Sarah's research, which reveals as much about her own vampiric desires as about the secrets of aging, the gaze functions most powerfully at the level of fantasy.

This gaze of fantasy, though always bisexual, can be male as well as female. The casting of David Bowie as the vampire John was especially ingenious, given his own media image of punk, androgyny, and bisexuality. The film is fascinated by his eyes and his glances. Sometimes his gaze takes a turn through technology, as when he looks at Alice through the monitor in the doorway. Mirrors also seem to function, like technology, to position erotic fantasy on the side of the undead. John's sizes up a hospital worker in a men's-room mirror, just as Miriam can sometimes be seen only in the mirror (when, for example, she cruises Sarah in the bathroom or a trick in the elevator). In traditional lore, the vampire is not supposed to appear in mirrors or in photographs, since it has no soul, no original essence to be copied, but in *The Hunger* the vampire is the very creature of mirrors and photographs: pure otherness, pure image, pure fantasy rendered visible and palpable through the peculiar postmodern erotics of technology. As a technologically produced image, the vampire is also the very embodiment of betrayal. Like mirrors, like photographs, like the cinema, the vampire is seductive in its promise of the truth, of communion with the other, of an aggravation of longing for everlasting youth. The vampires are the very embodiment of cinematic image-making, the lure of the image itself. But the promise of the vampire, like the promise of the image, cannot be kept. John is finally betrayed by Miriam, tricked into believing she was offering eternal youth, when all she really had to offer was eternal darkness. He is condemned to decay forever in a coffin, a fate worse than death. Sarah rejects Miriam's seductive promise, but her rejection is only a further betrayal, a betrayal of betrayal, that condemns Miriam to the coffin in her place. Bisexuality becomes the preferred mode of this betrayal, not the least because it is already popularly associated with hedonism, with narcissistic gratification, and with a promiscuous prowling from lover to lover and from gender to gender. In this film, bisexuality represents the wish to be the subject of the promise, to be the alluring locus of an everlasting life even if it turns out to be an everlasting undeath. This queer vampire embodies seduction in the age of technological reproduction.

For much of the film, Miriam is the only master of the gaze. She is the Other looking back at us. Catherine Deneuve's aura of coolness, mystery, and deception is ideal for such a role. Everything mechanical, from telephones to Mack trucks, is on her side. Technology stages a queer and vampiric rebellion precisely because it is on the side of the Other, the undead. John is most pitiable in his failure to assume that place. He is the seduced, though fabulous for a time. The scenes of his decay are especially moving, in that his gaze is one of desperate fantasy in search of eternal life—even more desperate than Sarah's or Miriam's. In close-ups of the wrinkles forming around John's eyes, even as he sits in the waiting room of Sarah's hospital, we recognize the very gaze of fantasy itself in decay. "Look at me!" he exclaims, but to look has become unbearable. It is no doubt symptomatic of my own looking, my own fantasy life, my own implication in the sexual panic of my time, that these scenes in *The Hunger* read oddly like an AIDS narrative to me. John excites my identification, my anxiety: the young, promiscuous, nightclubbing bisexual suddenly finds that his body is falling to pieces because of his own unusual blood, because of a strange illness he does not understand. The woman who has been his partner for centuries searches in vain for a cure. Finally, the man, in a pathetic state of decay, begs her to assist him in suicide: "Kill me, Miriam! Release me!" She refuses, with the eerie lines, "Their end is final, ours is not." She sadly stows him away in a coffin in the attic alongside her other lovers, similarly in decay—"all of you, all my loves," amid the voices of an angelic requiem—portrait of a promiscuous queer vampire in the age of AIDS, fated to perpetual mourning or to a sudden but protracted physical decay. I am certainly not surprised that AIDS is the eternal darkness that I discover within the promise of pleasure in this film. I am scarcely permitted to dream otherwise.

The vampiric gaze between women in the film is, by contrast, a far more humorous and sensual affair. After being "touched" and gazed at by Miriam through various cameras, Sarah finally confronts the vampire face-to-face.

Her very eagerness and anxiety about Miriam is evidence of her increasing desire. They flirt a while, drink sherry, and discuss antiques. This bit also excites my identification, though not my anxiety. The sexual tension builds, as Miriam plays the "Flower Duet" from *Lakmé* on the piano. Sarah clues into the lesbian overtones of the music right away. She bluntly asks if Miriam is making a pass at her, to which the vampire responds coolly, "Not that I'm aware of, Sarah." In a moment of inspiration, Sarah promptly spills her sherry down her left breast, which allows her to take off her shirt, which allows her to hop in the sack with Miriam and make love to her with the "Flower Duet" warbling in the background. Delibes's opera resonates well with the lesbian narrative of the film. Although it attempts a critique of British imperialism, *Lakmé* is nevertheless an exquisite example of French orientalism at its most voluptuous, and this exoticism contributes to the decadent chic of the film. Furthermore, the duet is a love song between two women, the princess Lakmé and her slave, Mallika. We sense a spark of masochistic submission so crucial to *The Hunger,* as Mallika humbly and fondly unclasps the jewels from her mistress's body and places them on a stone table within the secluded sanctuary where they sing. Even the biting, through which Miriam infuses her blood into Sarah, recalls the dazzling and poisonous datura blossoms, whose menacing presence during the "Flower Duet" foreshadows Lakmé's suicide when she nibbles them in the final scene. The opera is ostensibly about Lakmé's conflict between her duty to her father and her love for the English soldier, Gerald, so that within this heterosexual traffic in women the lesbian interlude is simply gratuitous—and yet it is the most beautiful piece of music Delibes ever wrote. With hands and voices joyously entwined under a bower of jasmine and roses, they sing of the boat in which they depart together, wending its way languorously on the gentle tide. The love scene in *The Hunger,* which is itself a secretive interlude between two women who are already committed to men, is true to the lush sensuality of the "Flower Duet" that drifts over it. The two women are filmed through blowing white veils, which reveal and conceal them, suggesting not only the marriage veil (which first appears in a flashback of Miriam as she promises everlasting life to John) but also the fetishistic paradox of revealing and re-veiling that is typical of cinematic seduction. Like the fronds of the plant in the shower scene in *Vampyres,* the veils thematize our looking, or rather our voyeuristic peeking, at two women who are engaged in an illicit sexual act together.

From this scene, in which Miriam bites Sarah and infuses her with vampire blood, the film makes a droll cut to an image of a knife slicing through a rare steak. Sarah is eating in a restaurant with her lover, Tom. In this scene, the lesbian gaze is an illicit look, a gaze of fantasy that is more real than reality. Sarah is in a state of lesbian panic, as suggested by a sadomasochistic blood-metaphor: Miriam's vampire blood is battling with Sarah's human blood for dominance over Sarah's body. The human blood is losing, and Sarah feels pangs of hunger that will not be satisfied in the usual fashion. The steak comes to represent heterosexual desire, her love for Tom in particular. She desperately gorges herself, only to throw up in the toilet afterward. The filming of the conversation between Sarah and Tom is especially witty. He is aggressively nosy, and she is snippish and vague. There is no end to his questions, but there is a limit to her answers. While he is interrogating her, she is glancing at a nearby swimming-pool and picturing to herself a fantasy of the lesbian frolic that he is slowly beginning to suspect. She is constantly looking to one side and envisioning those "pictures behind her eyes," a heretofore unrepresented scene of two women splashing around naked in a pool. The interpolated scenes are a fantasy, a telepathic "touch" from Miriam perhaps, or a Lakmé-like daydream, and yet her fantasies displace the real scene of her conversation with Tom. The voyeuristic shots of Miriam and Sarah in bed together are reclaimed in this scene as not only the fantasy of the cinematic spectator but also Sarah's own fantasy about herself. In other words, the voyeuristic gaze is reframed as specifically lesbian. Meanwhile, Sarah hardly hears a word that Tom says. Even later, when she begins to panic, lesbian desire is construed as an overwhelming pleasure, a sidelong glance, cruising out of the corner of her eye. Unlike Harriet in *Vampyres,* however, we are convinced that, with a little prodding, Sarah would make a really hot dyke. Her lesbian panic, her internalized homophobia, is articulated metaphorically as a fear of the vampire when she eventually learns the truth about Miriam. She runs from Miriam and tries to hail a taxi. She settles for a pay phone, and tries to call Tom. But technology is already on the side of the undead, and she cannot get through to him in time. Her face is reflected in the polished chrome of the telephone, another uncanny mirroring that marks her passage into pure image. She has a vision of Miriam outside the phone booth, accompanied by the impatient voice of the man who has been waiting for the phone. "How 'bout it lady?" he says, but his temporarily disembodied male voice is immediately reconfigured as lesbian, as a sexual come-on, within the context of her vision of Miriam. Although lesbian desire is articulated in classic paranoid fashion as vampirism, as narcissism, as sadism, as betrayal, as an eating disorder, even as drug addiction (the man presumes she is a junkie), the pleasure this film affords, its very suspense, lies for me in Sarah's slow realization of her own lesbian desire as she gives in to it.

The Hunger is only the most artful in a tradition of vampire films whose sexual politics have left many lesbian feminists feeling ambivalent, if not wholly disgusted. These films seem to carry on a tradition of demonizing lesbians. I doubt that lesbian solidarity and empowerment were an issue in the making of any of these films, and I have never seen a cinematic vampire lesbian demonstrating for reproductive rights, volunteering at a battered-women's shelter, or reading Audre Lorde. Nevertheless, the films I have discussed do not always adhere to the simplistic cinematic tradition of depicting lesbians as monsters to be tracked down and dispatched. I find an enormous potential for queer narrative pleasure in these films. When *The Hunger* comes to its notoriously confusing end, I thrill to see that Sarah has not committed suicide in a fit of homosexual panic, but continues on into eternity, seducing women from the side of their faithful men, seducing woman after woman. She is getting away with murder, but the film seems to be on her side, in spite of itself. The final frames are surely wide open to interpretation: Sarah, having seduced another woman, looks off the terrace of a high-rise apartment, gazing at a vast urban emptiness, a panorama of orange twilit sky, while the music of Miriam's piano mixes with the wailing of Miriam's cries in her coffin. The scene is generally read as the cruel but strangely appealing triumph of her vision, but a vision of what? We could read her vision in classic psychoanalytic terms: she may see an eternal emptiness, the hollowness behind the mirror of a sadistic and narcissistic gaze. We could read it in materialist terms: she may see the really swanky view promised to the woman, alone of her sex, at the top of the professional ladder. But her look seems to me to defy such a facile critical distance. It is a projection, an emblem of cinematic fantasy itself embodied in the gaze of the queer woman. It bears a promise, though the promises of the vampire are always deceptive. No doubt she must be seeing things, and not just the rolling credits that we see. We should not underestimate this gaze at a gaping technicolor space—an emptied space that returns our curious look and is not unlike the blank screen of cinema itself, an eternal possibility for fantasy already suspiciously on the side of the undead.

NOTES

1   Ellis Hanson, "Undead," in *Inside/Out: Lesbian Theories, Gay Theories,* ed. Diana Fuss (New York: Routledge, 1991), 338.

2   Marjorie Garber, *Vice Versa: Bisexuality and the Eroticism of Everyday Life* (New York: Simon and Schuster, 1995), 99.

3   D. N. Rodowick, *The Difficulty of Difference: Psychoanalysis, Sexual Difference, and Film Theory* (New York: Routledge, 1990); and Carol J. Clover, *Men, Women, and Chain Saws: Gender in the Modern Horror Film* (Princeton: Princeton University Press, 1992), especially 206, 222.

4   Sue-Ellen Case, "Tracking the Vampire," *Differences* 3, no. 2 (1991): 15. In a more playful mood, Case does claim that the fanged kiss of the lesbian vampire brings the chosen one "trembling with ontological, orgasmic shifts, into the state of the undead" (15) —whatever that means.

5   Andrea Weiss, *Vampires and Violets: Lesbians in the Cinema* (New York: Penguin, 1992), 93.

6   Pat Califia, "A Secret Side of Lesbian Sexuality," reprinted in *S&M: Studies in Dominance and Submission,* ed. Thomas S. Weinberg (New York: Prometheus Books, 1995), 141. "The Vampire" appears in Califia's collection, *Macho Sluts,* as well as in Pam Keesey's first lesbian-vampire anthology, *Daughters of Darkness.*

7   Nina Auerbach, *Our Vampires, Ourselves* (Chicago: University of Chicago Press, 1995), 59. Bonnie Zimmerman has a tendency toward the same sort of feminist sentimentality. She was the first to make an argument (with abundant qualifications) for these films as camp and as feminist revenge fantasies, but then she rather improbably admires the figure of Delphine Seyrig in *Daughters of Darkness* for being motherly and benign and for dissipating the gothic atmosphere.

8   Ibid.

9   Teresa de Lauretis, *The Practice of Love: Lesbian Sexuality and Perverse Desire* (Bloomington: Indiana University Press, 1994); see also Naomi Schor, "Female Fetishism: The Case of George Sand," in *The Female Body in Western Culture,* ed. Susan Rubin Suleiman (Cambridge: Harvard University Press, 1986), especially 371; and Marjorie Garber, "Fetish Envy," *October* 54 (1990): 45–56. For an excellent overview of the debates about female fetishism—an overview that does not ignore empirical evidence—see Lorraine Gamman and Merja Makinen, *Female Fetishism* (New York: New York University Press, 1995).

10 Quoted in Judy Wieder's interview with Catherine Deneuve in *The Advocate,* 25 July 1995, 53.

11 Gerry Kroll, "The Bad and the Beautiful: Results from *The Advocate*'s 1996 Hollywood Survey," *The Advocate,* 20 August 1996, 38–39. Regarding their findings about *Basic Instinct,* Kroll writes, "We've steeled ourselves to the pos-

sibility of letter after venomous letter coming to our offices." The hint of vampirism in the word *venomous* is certainly instructive, especially since his reaction makes no sense, given the evidence of the poll he is presenting. Who are all these venomous queers, and why do they not like movies about other venomous queers?

12 Bram Dijkstra, *Idols of Perversity: Fantasies of Feminine Evil in Fin-de-Siècle Culture* (Oxford: Oxford University Press, 1986), 340.

13 Nina Auerbach, *Woman and the Demon: The Life of a Victorian Myth* (Cambridge: Harvard University Press, 1982), 17, 65.

14 Bonnie Zimmerman, "Daughters of Darkness: The Lesbian Vampire on Film" (1981), in *Planks of Reason,* ed. Barry Keith Grant (Metuchen: Scarecrow Press, 1984), 161.

15 In her book, *Fatal Women: Lesbian Sexuality and the Mark of Aggression* (Princeton: Princeton University Press, 1994), Lynda Hart discusses the popular representation of lesbians as extremely violent. Her chapter on Aileen Wuornos is especially relevant here (135–54).

16 Barbara Creed, *The Monstrous-Feminine: Film, Feminism, Psychoanalysis* (New York: Routledge, 1993), 59–72.

17 Leo Bersani, *Homos* (Cambridge: Harvard University Press, 1995), 113–81.

18 Anne Rice, *Interview with the Vampire* (1976; New York: Ballantine, 1989), 20.

19 Stone presented at the "Unnatural Acts" conference at the University of California, Riverside, February 1993. Nina Auerbach was also in the audience, and she attributes to Stone a degree of sexual dissidence that she deems impossible in lesbian vampire films. In *Our Vampires, Ourselves,* Auerbach astutely observes, "Because they glide on the margins of activity, Sandy Stone's vampires dissipate rigid structures of gender and received identity, freeing their acolytes to 'celebrate the change, the passing of forms'" (181).

20 Sigmund Freud, "Fragment of an Analysis of a Case of Hysteria," in *The Standard Edition of the Complete Psychological Works of Sigmund Freud,* ed. James Strachey (London: Hogarth Press, 1955–1974), 7:131.

21 Rhona J. Berenstein, *Attack of the Leading Ladies: Gender, Sexuality, and Spectatorship in Classic Horror Cinema* (New York: Columbia University Press, 1996), 24–28.

22 *New York Times,* 18 May 1936, 14.

23 There are recent case studies in which hypnosis is still used in this way. In one case, published in 1986, a married man, complaining of a "chink in his armor," appealed to a psychiatrist to free him from his homosexual "impulses." "He evidenced little resistance to hypnosis and agreed to the hypnotherapy treatment to help him not to act on his homosexual impulses, appropriately terminate his homosexual relationship, and strengthen his heterosexual feelings toward his wife." The case study ends with an announcement of the patient's

"increased and satisfying relations with his wife 'about once or twice weekly,'"
thus demonstrating perfectly the continuing role of modern psychiatry in the
enforcement of monogamy and compulsory heterosexuality. The title alone of
this study speaks volumes. See Michael Jay Diamond, "When the Knight Re-
gains His Armor: An Indirect, Psychodynamically Based Brief Hypnotherapy
of an Ego-Dystonic Sexual Impulse Disorder," in *Case Studies in Hypnotherapy*,
ed. E. Thomas Dowd and James M. Healy (New York and London: Guilford
Press, 1986), 73, 79.

24   Berenstein, *Attack of the Leading Ladies*, 94.

25   Freud, "Fragment of an Analysis," 139, 140, 141.

26   Roland Barthes, *Camera Lucida: Reflections on Photography*, trans. Richard
Howard (New York: Noonday Press, 1981), 92.

27   Ibid., 95.

28   Bonnie Burns, "*Dracula's Daughter:* Cinema, Hypnosis, and the Erotics of Lesbianism," in *Lesbian Erotics*, ed. Karla Jay (New York: New York University
Press, 1995), 196–211. Burns's essay offers a psychoanalytic reading of the hypnotism theme in the film with respect to the tension between a lesbian gaze
and a lesbian spectacle.

29   Sigmund Freud, "The 'Uncanny,'" *Standard Edition*, 17:219–56.

30   Andrew Sarris, review of *The Hunger, Village Voice*, 10 May 1983, 100.

31   Ibid.

Michelle Elleray

HEAVENLY CREATURES IN GODZONE

Merata Mita, a New Zealand filmmaker discussing the body of films made by Pākehā in the context of those made by Māori, says this about Pākehā settler identity:[1]

> The notion of the white man or woman at odds with his/her environment, with his/her country and himself/herself, has been the theme of many New Zealand films. . . .
>
> What I find curious is the way that these films repeatedly fail to analyze and articulate the colonial syndrome of dislocation that is evident in such works. What appears on the screen are the symptoms of a deeper malaise . . . [and] what becomes clear in the body of work mentioned is the absence of identity and how driven by fear and repression these films are.[2]

Absence of identity, fear, repression—these terms, spoken here in the context of settler identity, invoke a history of homophobic discourse. Such resonances between sexuality and nationality are central to Peter Jackson's *Heavenly Creatures* (1994).[3] Embedded in contemporary New Zealand concerns, the film provides a critique of 1950s Anglophilia and homophobia, a critique that is invested in the symptomaticity of Mita's "colonial syndrome of dislocation," rather than an enactment of it. What Mita's and Jackson's commentaries demonstrate is the presence, alongside the milk-and-honey mythology of New Zealand as Godzone (God's Own Country), of Pākehā ambivalence about their status in relation to the land. In *Heavenly Creatures* this has parallels in and reverberations for lesbianism insofar as nationality and sexuality intersect: Pauline's desire for Juliet cannot be separated from her Anglophilia, and viewers' reception of New Zealandness in the film determines their reaction to the lesbianism.

Peter Jackson and Fran Walsh's screenplay is based on real events leading to the violent murder in 1954 of Honora Rieper in Christchurch, New Zealand. However, while I occasionally refer to historical details, I focus on the film's representation of the social issues and progression of events. The murder of Mrs. Rieper is committed by her daughter, Pauline, and her daughter's friend, Juliet Hulme, and a central consideration of the film is the disparate nature of the two girls' backgrounds. The Riepers are a working-class New Zealand family, but Pauline makes friends with the upper-middle-class Juliet through their mutual adoration of Mario Lanza and their shared experience of gruesome childhood illnesses. Juliet's family has recently shifted from England into Christchurch's high-society circles when Dr. Hulme became rector of Canterbury College; the class disparity between Juliet and Pauline is therefore reenacted through national differences, differences that Pauline seeks to transcend as she adopts the Hulme family as her own. Having established the friendship, the two girls immerse themselves in their shared fantasy worlds, known as the Fourth World and the Kingdom of Borovnia, and assume the heterosexual roles of various imaginary characters in their increasingly lesbian relationship, while John, Pauline's previous lover, is abandoned. Eventually Dr. Hulme suggests to the Riepers that Pauline should be examined for incipient lesbianism by his friend, Dr. Bennett, who is "the ideal man to set her back on track" and thereby rescue Juliet from Pauline's "rather unwholesome attachment." In the face of family alienation, the Hulmes' impending divorce, and the threat of separation Pauline and Juliet face, the girls' division between imaginary and real life collapses, allowing them to rationalize the murder of Pauline's mother in order to achieve the "reality" of their fantasized future together.

Pauline and Juliet's relationship, which I read at various points in terms of lesbianism, parodic romantic friendship, and mateship, radically alters the parameters of Pauline's world. Their closeness at first glance only *appears* to erase the national and class delineations of the Rieper and Hulme families; the film is in fact propelled by the erasure of that which is local, domestic, and inevitably aligned with New Zealand. Thus, by focusing on the connections between the settler's relation to nationalism and lesbianism in *Heavenly Creatures*, I read Pauline and Juliet's relationship through precisely the New Zealand context, which Pauline, in particular, seeks to eradicate and which in turn fails to accommodate Pauline and her sexuality.

LOCATING NEW ZEALAND

The 1950s film clip that provides the opening shot of *Heavenly Creatures* presents New Zealand as a location that requires explanation to a presumed overseas viewer, although Christchurch is recuperated as familiar through its faithful re-articulation of Oxonian Englishness (a cathedral, a college with "shadowed cloisters," a boat punting on the river), an Englishness that is taken as normative and therefore does not itself need explanation. But Jackson reverses the viewer's perspective with the introduction of Juliet on her arrival at Christchurch Girls' High School. Juliet counteracts her recent New Zealand residency in Hawkes' Bay with the assertion, "I am actually from England," and is then explicitly located as fantastically foreign through the headmistress's comment that, "Juliet has travelled all over the world, and I'm sure she's very eager to share her impressions of exotic lands across the seas with the girls of 3A." In this way, Juliet is attributed with a privileged cosmopolitanism, and claims an Englishness unsullied by her sojourn in the colonies, in opposition to the New Zealand schoolgirls stuck at the bottom of the Pacific puddle.

In tandem with his introduction of Juliet to the viewer as exotically English, Jackson eschews Eurocentric romances of remote South Sea islands. Instead, *Heavenly Creatures* presents New Zealand as ordinary, domestic, and mundane—a drabness that Pauline encapsulates, especially in contrast to Juliet. Pauline is marked in the film as "the New Zealander" by her recognizably local accent, which accentuates her social distance from the Hulmes and thus elaborates the contrast between Pauline and Juliet, and by her proximity to Kiwiana (those everyday objects comprising a nostalgic or kitsch iconography for contemporary New Zealanders), which provides the filmgoer with symbols of a national identity also inflected by class difference. Insofar as the period has been described as "characterized by a consolidation of [New Zealand] popular culture,"[4] Kiwiana constitutes the markers for a local identity to which Pākehā can lay claim. The Kiwiana onscreen is seen in relation to Pauline, and all but one of the objects appear in her home, thereby reiterating the interconnections of Pauline, New Zealand, and the everyday: when Juliet comes to tea at the Riepers, pikelets are served; Dad announces that the diary Pauline is given for Christmas is from Whitcombe and Tombes, an early publisher of New Zealand texts; the frontispiece of Pauline's diary carries an advertisement for Edmonds (a New Zealand brand name) with their "Sure to Rise" baking products; a poster of a kiwi hangs on the wall of Dr. Bennett's office; and when Mrs. Rieper is angry with Pauline, what better way of showing her mood than slapping down that infamous New Zealand breakfast—a bowl of soggy Weetbix.

However, if in the film Pauline is aligned with all things New Zealand, or more specifically, all things Pākehā, the drive of the film and the actual historical events are mobilized by Pauline's rejection of New Zealand for a mythologized England,[5] which is enacted through Jackson's use of maternal figures in the shipboard sequence of *Heavenly Creatures* that appears before the opening credits. A series of intercut shots entwine the aftermath of the murder and the projected voyage to England, when close-ups of blood-spattered legs running through mud are then aligned with nostalgically sepia-toned close-ups of the same legs, now clean, running along the deck of a ship. The shipboard sequence culminates in two shots: in the second-to-last, Juliet is shown in the foreground of the frame calling out "Mummy," which Pauline then repeats from behind, suggesting her desire for incorporation within the English Hulme family. Furthermore, in the last shot this familial incorporation is situated against the necessitated absence of the local landscape: a loving Dr. and Mrs. Hulme are shot from behind as they gaze at the receding New Zealand shore. Jackson then cuts to an apparent replica of the previous shipboard shot as the blood-streaked Pauline and Juliet run toward the camera with Juliet in front, only now Pauline pushes past Juliet to fill the frame and cry, "It's Mummy," this time the New Zealand one, "she's terribly hurt." The juxtaposition of the two mothers underlines a double narrative in the film — one of a nostalgic return to Mother England, the other of a prosaic maternal New Zealand to be violently disavowed.

SETTLER SPACES

Settler identity is what one postcolonial academic refers to as an "inauthenticity in the landscape," which in itself "becomes a source of meaning"; or, to put it another way, the crisis that crystallizes identity for the settler subject is "the anomaly of being native in what was still seen as alien land."[6] Settler subjectivity is therefore marked by the settler subject's contingent relation to his or her geospatial locality: the far-flung colony designated alien, foreign, or exotic by English-centered views of the Empire, is in fact the domestic space occupied and lived through by the settler. The exigencies of this situation are made explicit through the settler subject born and raised in the colony for whom the landscape is familiar as domestic space, but who lives in a society where institutional affiliations, cultural references, hierarchical status, and global locations are understood via the centrality of an unknown, imaginatively constituted England. Thus the term *settler* signals the inability of the binarism "colonizer-colonized" to fully account for those people who, through an opening historically constituted by the processes of colonialism and deeply imbricated in colonialism's culture, live the peripheries of the British Empire as their reality rather than as a romanticized space of some cultural Other, while nevertheless understanding their society through the English culture in which they are no longer local participants. The settler is found at the interface of cultural references and physical landscape, where the space imaginatively occupied by the settler is not necessarily the space physically occupied, while any identity formations in relation to the local landscape are necessarily ambivalent insofar as the land is inscribed with the violence of colonialism. In the New Zealand context this violence is apparent in the history of land wars, raupatu (land confiscation), and treaty issues, such that any identification with the land by settlers must sit alongside the land's prior and continuing location in the spiritual and social world of the tangata whenua (indigenous peoples).[7] While the historical events on which *Heavenly Creatures* is based preclude a discussion of settler-indigene relations,[8] I wish to emphasize here the colonizing relation of the settler to the tangata whenua in order to preempt any erasure of these power relations through a slippage back into the colonizer-colonized binarism, where the settler occupies the latter position in relation to the colonial metropole.

The settler's oscillation between a metropole and periphery circumscribed by imperialism is dramatized in *Heavenly Creatures* when Juliet and Pauline read the Biggles books and then act out versions of them. Biggles was a flying ace, "virtually a British cultural icon, representing all things decent, upstanding, and Imperial,"[9] and the titles of the Biggles books flashing onscreen remind the viewer of the girls' location in a society that expected children in the South Pacific to place themselves imaginatively within the mores, scenery, and history of England. One of the Biggles books is in fact set in the South Pacific, so that identification with the hero for the New Zealand child involves seeing the geographically local as culturally other.[10] It is this imaginative orientation through English culture that Jackson takes into account when visualizing the girls' Borovnian fantasies: "The buildings and houses I kind of wanted to make clichéd medieval, because that's what [Pauline and Juliet] would have imagined them to be like. . . . they would have imagined something they would have seen in English picture books about the English countryside."[11]

In *Heavenly Creatures,* the most obvious marker of the settler's negotiation of spatiality—of location and dislocation—is the ship, through its evocation of distance, travel, and geographic mediation. Ships in New Zealand are emblematic of arrival and subsequent settlement, and as such are built into the nation's mythologies, but if from a New Zealand point of view the ship symbolizes arrival, what is the status of the departing ship? Or more pertinently for this film, what is the status of the New Zealand settler on a ship departing for England? If the person heading from England out into the Empire is clearly designated as English, his or her designation is not so obvious upon return to the metropolitan center, the subject instead being marked by residence in the colonies. In other words, it is the negotiation of distance—of movement between the metropole and periphery of Empire—that identifies the individual as either an English or a settler subject. The settler becomes a white Other, recognizable as formerly English, but now marked as not *of* England. While this distinction between English and settler subject remains somewhat murky when it is the same person who both leaves and returns to England via the colony, such ambiguity disappears when the return is enacted by the next generation. In that early shipboard scene then, Pauline's call to and adoption of the English mother, Mrs. Hulme, is precisely what cannot be realized because her own immigrant mother has, literally and figuratively, given birth to Pauline as a New Zealand subject.[12]

Juliet's Englishness, while used structurally by Jackson to contrast with Pauline's New Zealandness, is not as substantial as her accent would suggest. Her position is neither completely that of the settler subject nor the English subject, for while born in England, much of her childhood has been spent in the former British colonies of the Bahamas and New Zealand due to illness, and South Africa is the home planned for Juliet by her parents in the wake of their divorce. For Juliet too, England is a distant, idealized place, but unlike the Riepers, she has never settled in settler space, nor was her settler status enforced by her being born in a former colony. It is thus the English-born Juliet who is authorized to construct the Anglophilic fantasy that the two girls inhabit, whereas it falls to Pauline to erase the New Zealand settler identity she comes to resent, through the murder of her mother. Juliet's complicated relation to Englishness is highlighted when she takes a school assignment on the Windsor family and presents the Borovnian royal lineage instead, thus mocking settler society's adulation of British royalty, while privileging a fantasy that takes as its foundation exactly that European formation. Juliet's mockery of the Windsors in the film had a serious parallel in the 1954 murder trial when, as an indictment of the girls' general nonconformity and antisocial behavior, the prosecution pointed out that "[d]uring the Queen's visit [Juliet and Pauline] made no attempt to see the Queen or the decorations." [13]

The rejection of settler identity on Juliet's part is apparent in the scene where the two girls go on holiday to Port Levy, just outside Christchurch, at which point a family crisis provokes Juliet's transformation of the New Zealand landscape into the imaginative panorama of the Fourth World. When Juliet is faced with the threat of being left in New Zealand while her parents return to England, a threat that is potentially one of becoming the settler subject, she runs away across the brow of a hill. At this point, Jackson uses a rotating aerial long-shot projecting a hilly range dwarfing Juliet, swirling and encircling her in her attempts to run away, such that the landscape itself threatens to engulf Juliet. But she immediately retaliates by imaginatively transforming these brown New Zealand hills into a world embellished with fountains, doves, and unicorns, all clichés from the English romance tradition. As the Biggles books have trained her to do, Juliet privileges a Eurocentric imaginative space over the physical reality of her New Zealand surroundings.

LESBIAN SPACES

Shots of doors and entrances gather a cumulative weight with regard to access to, or closure of, significant spaces in *Heavenly Creatures*. When visiting the Hulmes' house for the first time, Pauline is shown hesitating at the threshold, reluctant to step further into the living room, until Juliet sweeps her into her arms for a dance and they circle around the living room to the strains of Mario Lanza. Thereafter, the camera's location inside the Hulmes' house emphasizes Pauline's penetration into this salient space, so that the status of the girls' relationship is registered through Pauline as she, sometimes gingerly, at other times exuberantly, moves along hallway passages to rooms where Juliet's welcoming arms await. In this map of entrances leading to passages that end in enlarged spaces—that is, a morphologically female spatiality—the previously divided Pauline and Juliet embrace.

Such spaces of entrance and union are linked to the girls' fantasy world in the early stages of their friendship when a sandcastle becomes the site of Borovnian sexual escapades between the imaginary Charles and Deborah. This sandcastle scene also restates the significance of doors that mark openings to sexualized spaces. When the entrance doors to the sandcastle crash open, the camera, standing in for the mounted Charles, takes the viewer thundering up a narrow stairway passage and through doors that lead to a bedroom. Accompanying this visual trajectory is Pauline and Juliet's narration, telling us that while Deborah waits in a "private boudoir," Charles "smells her scent from fifty paces and urges his steed onwards," finally arriving at the prominently displayed bed where he "ravish[es] her." As a coda, Juliet adds, "I bet she gets up the duff [i.e., pregnant] on their first night together!" This sandcastle scene is then echoed in the sanatorium scene when Pauline visits Juliet: the same initial crash of opening doors signals Pauline's haste as she runs along narrow passages, passages that eventually open up into a space containing Juliet where the two girls hug and kiss. The girls' friendship thus acquires the sexual innuendo of the parallel sandcastle scene, while the heterosexual knowledge displayed in relation to Charles and Deborah gets homosexualized when, for the period of Juliet's quarantine, the two girls assume the characters of these Borovnian lovers in order to maintain and extend their own relationship.

The film's emphasis on doors forced open and opportunities created for entrance, is juxtaposed with two scenes highlighting closed doors, both of which are aligned with unsympathetic professional men. The first instance occurs after Dr. Bennett suggests to Pauline, "perhaps you could think about spending more time with boys," to which Pauline responds with the fantasized phallic thrust of a Borovnian sword through Dr. Bennett's abdomen. We are then shown an unfortunately unscathed Dr. Bennett as he escorts Pauline out of the consulting room and ushers her mother in, followed by a close-up that highlights the closing of the door to the consulting room. The closed door excludes Pauline from the site of her medical classification, while the viewer cuts to a parody of 1950s homophobia in the extreme close-up of Dr. Bennett's stuttering efforts to pronounce a diagnosis of "h-h-homosexuality."

The second instance of the visual closing of avenues and entrances occurs after the revelation of the Hulmes' impending divorce. An outside shot of Dr. Hulme standing at the doorway of his home watching an off-screen Pauline is followed by a shot of her biking away—the first time we have seen her departing from the Hulmes'—while she states in a voice-over, "Dr. Hulme is the noblest and most wonderful person I have ever known of." But for the viewer the adulation in this declaration is visually punctuated, or punctured, by the following close-up of the Hulmes' front door slamming shut. In a wider context, these closed doors carry the resonances of social restrictions around gender and class, but here, as the doors lock Pauline out, they also mark the attempts to contain the lesbianism with which the previous rushing through doors is associated.

There is another lesbian space the girls occupy, which is imaginary rather than physical, a space where they create room for "going through the saints," these particular saints being various male movie-stars. Filmed in golden light, the scene establishes the girls' manipulation of a heterosexual mandate as Pauline morphs into Orson Welles before s/he bends down to kiss Juliet. As Welles mediates between shots of first Juliet, then Pauline, in sexual raptures, *Heavenly Creatures* demonstrates Pauline and Juliet's use of the imaginative space offered by film in order to screen, in the opposing senses of that word, their own fantasies.

In contrast to the gold-lit passion of lesbianism, Pauline's sexual encounter with John is filmed in low light, with close-ups of John's strained face contributing to the scene's farcical nature. This division of sexuality into lesbian romance and heterosexual dinginess is emphasized by intercutting the scene of heterosexual sex with shots of Pauline waking and searching through Borovnia for Juliet, while the rhythm of the cuts accelerate to keep John's imminent orgasm to the fore. In a reversal of the Orson Welles fantasy that enables lesbian sex to take place, here Pauline mediates the reality of heterosexual sex by searching for Juliet in the fantasy land of Borovnia, and in doing so Pauline inverts heteronormative romantic conventions. Heterosexual sex is marked by subterfuge, as Pauline sneaks up the back fire-escape to John in the middle of the night, while dogs root around in rubbish bins below; in contrast, Pauline wakes to the sunny flower-filled fields surrounding the medieval castle of chivalric romance, a castle in which she pictures herself finding and claiming Juliet.

John disappears from the film when his Borovnian counterpart, Nicholas, is summarily executed. As he departs from the castle, John/Nicholas reaches down for a ring set with a pink gem, at which point the portcullis comes crashing down on his neck and the gem dislodges to roll to the feet of Pauline and Juliet. The two girls look at the gem, which is foregrounded in the frame, as a voice-over reads out a poem from Pauline's diary in which two girls, one with "hatred burning bright" in her eyes, the other whose eyes glitter with "icy scorn . . . contemptuous and cruel," are the two "heavenly creatures" of the film's title, who proclaim their bond in the face of "fools." The poem ends with the line, "[a]nd these wonderful people are you and I," as the camera trails up a bed to show Pauline and Juliet asleep, curled in each other's arms.

The location of the pink gem at the fantasized death of a heterosexual lover and a poem about the superiority of two entwined females, is crucial in reading Honora Rieper's death scene. The same pink gem, having been dropped by Juliet for Mrs. Rieper to notice and pick up, provides a distraction that enables the girls to beat her to death with a brick. This is the first time an object from the girls' fantasy world has traversed through to their real world, thereby signaling to the viewer a breakdown in the division between the two realms that allows the girls to perpetrate the murder. Thus, it is the trajectory of the pink gem, with all its concomitant sexual innuendoes, that enables the imaginary scene of erasing heterosexuality to become the real scene of killing the New Zealand mother.

MATESHIP IN THE BUSH

A recurrent setting in *Heavenly Creatures* is the bush, an icon of the New Zealand landscape, which figures a test of settler adaptation through the ability to survive off the land. We first encounter the bush when the BBC accents of the opening clip voice-over distort into the sound of crashing branches, and the camera, standing in for both the viewer and the two girls, stumbles through bushes and along a path to the accompaniment of screaming on the soundtrack. In this instance, the bush is a placeholder for a terror from which the girls are running away, a terror that is later revealed to be the violent murder of the New Zealand mother.

In the events chronologically prior to this matricide, however, the bush is the site of Pauline and Juliet's deepening relationship. As such it invokes mateship, the Australasian category of homosociality that historically evolved out of the bush lore of early male settlers, who sought companionship together in the face of the new land's hardships. Mateship thus serves as the social correlate to the bush's geographical space, and is a specifically male category; in *Heavenly Creatures,* on the other hand, it is Pauline and Juliet, with arms around each other, clad in their underwear, and deliriously happy, who are mates in the bush. Jackson places Pauline and Juliet face-to-face with the bush's traditional male occupant when a bemused man of the land, the prosaic, manual-laboring, taciturn but friendly Kiwi bloke, raises his hat to the two girls in their bra and knickers.

This encounter effects a visual transfer of cultural categories through the movement from one shot in which the Kiwi bloke invokes a tradition of mateship (although conspicuously without a mate himself), to the next shot in which the two girls, standing arm-in-arm, enact that mateship.[14]

The significance of mateship to the 1950s society in which Pauline and Juliet lived is reflected in the central place acorded to Frank Sargeson's short stories on this topic in the newly established canon of New Zealand literature. While Sargeson's stories, like those of his Australian counterpart, Henry Lawson, present mateship as a conflicted category involving betrayal and violence alongside male bonding, the popular reception of mateship saw it as unambiguously positive. In New Zealand's literary tradition, mateship tales were a form through which Pākehā came to understand themselves as a settler society with a domestic culture grounded in the local landscape, rather than as an English satellite. This binarism of masculine New Zealand mateship and a feminine English romanticism is used by Sargeson when he writes that masculine literary realism, of which he is a chief exponent, is to supplant the earlier writing by women whose flights of fancy present New Zealand in English terms.[15] Because of the girls' gender then, *Heavenly Creatures*'s momentary incursion into mateship is unsustainable, and thus Pauline and Juliet do not have available to them mateship's social approbation and cloaking form when Dr. Hulme says, "it's the intensity of the friendship that concerns me." I say "cloaking" because Sargeson, himself gay, is able to present in his own writing the proscribed but nevertheless evident slippage between mateship and male homosexuality.[16]

Pauline and Juliet's relationship follows a progression in which Pauline leaves the New Zealand scene of mateship in the bush—a category that has no room for her as a female, let alone as a lesbian—and moves toward the English Juliet. In the process she occupies the chivalric fantasies of medieval kingdoms Juliet has constructed, and takes on the Hulmes' values, which are at odds with her own familial background. The schoolgirlish giggles of Pauline and Juliet scampering through the undergrowth are contextualized by shots at the beginning and end of the film in which the two girls run through the bush after murdering Pauline's Mum. The bush marks for the viewer the extent of Pauline's dislocation as she moves from being at home in the New Zealand landscape, to murdering the mother who designates New Zealand as the place of Pauline's self-location.

When Mrs. Rieper, Pauline, and Juliet go for an afternoon outing, two key terms aligned with New Zealand—the *bush* and the *mother*—come together for the first time in the event of the murder; previously, Mrs. Rieper has not been seen within the New Zealand landscape, appearing instead in the home and its backyard, or medical offices and hospitals. The buildup to the murder is symbolically marked by a literal descent when Mrs. Rieper, Pauline, and Juliet pick their way down a muddy track in the bush. As the trio walk down in single file, Mrs. Rieper is between Pauline and Juliet and oblivious to the glances passing between them, a position that marks her dual function as an apparent intervention in their relationship, and as an innocent caught within their violent bid for a fantasized freedom. Having arrived deep in the bush, Pauline and Juliet beat Mrs. Rieper to death and the two hysterical girls then reascend the track, to appear finally at the top of the hill covered with mud from the bush and blood from Pauline's mother. At this point the film refers back to its nonchronological beginning, and retrospectively explains why the viewer's first encounter with the bush saw it aligned with terror.

KIWI FRUITS

In *Heavenly Creatures*'s most radiant lesbian scene, Pauline writes of her and Juliet's "hectic night going through the saints," that it was "wonderful, heavenly, beautiful and ours." But the nights are not solely theirs, as we see at the end of the "Heavenly Creatures" poem when the camera moves up from the sleeping girls' peaceful world to reveal Dr. Hulme lurking on the outside of the darkened window above them, staring in like a stalker while lightning and thunder mark his morbid presence. We then cut to him standing on the Riepers' doorstep in a trench coat and brimmed hat pulled low, as the door opens to allow him and his views on lesbianism in, and marks the beginning of doors shutting Pauline out. Within the Riepers' living room, Dr. Hulme insinuates that Pauline is the lesbian of the couple and a wayward influence on Juliet, thereby designating lesbianism as simultaneously solitary and potentially contagious.

The national and the sexual merge in Pauline, our nexus of New Zealandness, with her establishment in this scene as the sole bearer of lesbianism, a designation that, in Dr. Hulme's homophobic rendering of the term, is connected with the hierarchies of class and former colonial relations. While part of Juliet's sexual allure for Pauline is her Englishness,

Dr. Hulme relegates lesbianism to Pauline, that is, to the New Zealand-ness for which she stands. At this point, settler society's representation of England as the source of cultural authority and the center of categoriza-tion for Pākehā society enables the English Dr. Hulme to be the purveyor of knowledge who is able to name the lesbian as such. On Jackson's part however, this authority is undermined by the campy stalking shots that introduce the insinuation of lesbianism. The scene's low-angled shots of Dr. Hulme and high-angled shots of the Riepers parallel many of those of Juliet and Pauline respectively, replicating and emphasizing the relative class and national power positions, but in a double move, Jackson's sym-pathetic rendering of Pauline's lesbianism upends the class and colonial hierarchies implicit in Dr. Hulme's opinion of "that Rieper girl."

Dr. Hulme suggests Dr. Bennett as a suitable medical professional for Pauline, and the examination scene in particular provides a filmic link be-tween the national and the sexual in *Heavenly Creatures,* as Dr. Bennett discloses to Mrs. Rieper her daughter's homosexuality. The scene com-bines an evocation of 1950s homophobia with an ironized comment on the medicalization of lesbianism as an illness, a comment that is encap-sulated within the specifically New Zealand iconography of the national bird, the kiwi. Using his now familiar technique of a series of crosscuts in dialogue with one another, Jackson switches focus between Dr. Bennett and Mrs. Rieper. On the one hand, we have a series of shots in which the doctor, having finally managed to say *homosexuality,* proceeds to induct Mrs. Rieper into 1950s homophobia with the phrases, "it's not a pleasant word," "it can strike at any time," and "mental disorder." On the other hand, there is a series of three shots centered on Mrs. Rieper: in the first we have a head-and-shoulders shot of her, while in the top left corner of the frame the bottom of a poster is visible, slightly out of focus, on the wall behind; in the second shot the camera has pulled back from her slightly to reveal the phrase "Eat Fruit Daily" on the bottom of the poster; and in the third shot the frame is diagonally split between Mrs. Rieper and the full poster, revealed to be New Zealand's national bird constructed out of fruit and carrying the slogan, "Be a Healthy Kiwi."[17] By means of the double entendre on fruit as both an edible object and a queer, the slogan tying healthiness to national identity through the promotion of fruits is ironi-cally juxtaposed with the medical pathologization of Pauline as a lesbian.

DISLOCATIONS

The New Zealander screenwriter and director, Peter Wells, describes himself growing up "a provincial pouf, a queer on the furthest perimeter of a Eurocentric map,"[18] a comment that connects homosexuality with critiques of Eurocentricity through a parallel with settler identity. The interconnections are made more explicit when Wells relates his personal experience of the 1950s:

> Cinema offers a liberation, perhaps particularly potent to a Pakeha New Zealander, of a post-War generation: for New Zealand culture in my youth defined itself in terms of certain rather drab values: self reliance, sense, strength—masculine values, defensive and aggressive in the same awkward posture.
>
> . . . Lyricism was like a missing heartbeat, a last note. The very power of cinema comes from the fact that it provides the poetry that is essential to the human condition. . . . That it was borrowed from other cultures did not, immediately, strike me as a dislocation: perhaps because all life at that time seemed a dislocation—for what else could it be to a Pakeha child growing up homosexual in a society which itself had such an insecure identity?[19]

Having located 1950s New Zealand as a masculine space, Wells goes on to articulate the necessity for escape this provoked, such that he, like Pauline and Juliet, sought the power of images. In tying his experience of film explicitly into Pākehā and homosexual identity, Wells reintroduces Merata Mita's term of *dislocation,* having extended it beyond references to colonialism alone.

Dislocation stems from an inability to believe or participate fully in an identity that society mandates as desirable, normative, and stable, but dislocation itself is not necessarily the problem. Rather, the problem is the imperative to achieve the illusion of a stable location, that is, to evade dislocation by aiming instead at the self-satisfied exclusionary stability of an imperial Britain or a homophobic heterosexuality, a stability achieved through the erasure of anything that would challenge the naturalization of its centrality. Mateship, for example, began as a local attempt to locate Pākehā in the landscape and was explicitly directed against the dislocation of importing English cultural categories, but the effort to locate a stable identity resulted in significant erasures: a failed erasure in the attempt to distance mateship from male homosexuality, but a more successful erasure of women and women's relationships from the canonical history of Pākehā literature. Similarly, efforts to locate Pākehā as local to New Zealand have a history of negating Māori as the indigenous people, and thereby also erasing the violence of colonial relations that enable Pākehā to claim New Zealand as home.

The dislocation of 1950s New Zealand settler society, whereby Eurocentric culture is privileged over local experience and imaginative life is routed through a fantasy of England, makes more comprehensible the breakdown of the division between fantasy and reality for Pauline and Juliet that results in Mrs. Rieper's murder. It also provides a framework for the girls to privilege the sexualized fantasy life they share together over the reality of heterosexual imperatives, so that in extending their relationship, Pauline and Juliet use the structure already provided by settler society of privileging Englishness over New Zealandness, fantasy over reality. Thus the scene where Pauline assumes Orson Welles's persona in order to make love to Juliet provides an integral link between settler and sexual identities, for "going through the saints," the girls' mode of performing lesbian sex through a heterosexual paradigm, parallels the process of the settler whose reality is mediated through another culture's symbolism and categories.

This parallel trajectory of lesbianism and the settler reflects the failure of 1950s New Zealand society to accommodate either a national identity for Pākehā, or a sexual identity for the lesbian. However, a delineation is necessary here between Pauline's desire for the Englishness that Juliet represents —which in turn necessitates a rejection of New Zealandness—and *Heavenly Creatures's* location of Pauline as the New Zealander for the viewer. The national and the sexual are intertwined in *Heavenly Creatures,* and such intersections reveal both historical and contemporary attitudes toward lesbianism as a nationally inflected category. For Pauline and Juliet, their relationship is associated with English chivalric romance, while for Dr. Hulme it is relegated to New Zealand lower-class degeneracy; but this alignment is then further elaborated through the contrast between the medical pathologization of Pauline as the solitary lesbian, as enabled through her nationality and class, and Jackson's use of New Zealand icons in the "Be a Healthy Kiwi" poster to pass ironic comment on such pathologization.

Because of the intersection of the two categories of New Zealander and lesbian established in the film, the viewer cannot reject Pauline's lesbianism without rejecting her New Zealandness as well, and to reject her

New Zealandness would be to recapitulate the trajectory that sees Pauline murder her mother. *Heavenly Creatures* encourages the viewer to refuse Pauline's settler Anglophilia, which results in the murder of the New Zealand mother; instead, we are enjoined to locate her in New Zealandness. Insofar as the national and the sexual merge in Pauline, any endorsement of Pauline's New Zealandness necessitates an acceptance of her lesbianism, for the film structurally aligns homophobia with the destructiveness of Anglophilia. Jackson takes Pauline's repression and denial of her settler status, and presents it paralleled in, and magnified by, 1950s attitudes toward homosexuality, so that what is denied as aberrant is reversed and instead made constitutive of identity. Thus, rather than an anomaly to be repressed and vilified by New Zealand society, lesbianism in *Heavenly Creatures* is seen to be integral to evaluations, representations, identifications, and even the establishment, of the national itself.

NOTES

1   *Pākehā:* New Zealander(s) of European descent. When I use the term *settler,* in the context of this essay only, I am referring to relations between British and Pākehā New Zealand society, and not to any of the other New Zealand immigrant groups. *Māori:* used from the mid-nineteenth century to designate the various indigenous tribes of New Zealand as a collective unit.

2   Merata Mita, "The Soul and the Image," in *Film in Aotearoa New Zealand,* ed. Jonathan Dennis and Jan Bieringa (Wellington, New Zealand: Victoria University Press, 1992), 47.

3   *Heavenly Creatures* cast: Sarah Peirse (Honora Rieper), Melanie Lynskey (Pauline Parker), Kate Winslet (Juliet Hulme), Clive Merrison (Dr. Hulme), Diana Kent (Mrs. Hulme), Simon O'Connor (Mr. Rieper), Gilbert Goldie (Dr. Bennett), and Jed Brophy (John/Nicholas).

4   Stephen Barnett and Richard Wolfe, *New Zealand! New Zealand!: In Praise of Kiwiana* (Auckland, New Zealand: Hodder and Stoughton, 1989), 9.

5   This renunciation of the local is exemplified by the real Pauline's relation to her New Zealand accent, as Julie Glamuzina and Alison Laurie note in their discussion of Pauline's diary: "on one occasion [Pauline] recorded with delight that another passenger on a bus asked her how long she had been out from England. On another occasion she was very pleased when 'a girl who sat at the same table as us in a milkbar', said 'how beautifully I spoke English, that I almost had an Oxford accent, what a refreshing change it was, and several other very pleasing things'" (Diary entries for February 21, 1954 and May 29, 1953,

respectively. Qtd. in Julie Glamuzina and Alison Laurie, *Parker & Hulme: A Lesbian View* [Auckland, New Zealand: New Women's Press, 1991], 46).

6   Elleke Boehmer, *Colonial and Postcolonial Literature: Migrant Metaphors* (New York: Oxford University Press, 1995), 221, 213.

7   *Raupatu:* usually refers to contested government acts of land confiscation after the 1860s land wars, confiscations that were enabled through the 1863 New Zealand Settlements Act; "treaty issues" refers to government obligations under the Treaty of Waitangi, a document signed in 1840 between Britain and Māori chiefs. *Tangata whenua:* literally "people of the land," the term is used to designate Māori as the indigenous people of Aotearoa New Zealand.

8   I say this, first, because settler-indigene relations were not an aspect of the murder case itself, nor the events leading up to it; and second, because this is not surprising in a city such as Christchurch where urbanization of the Māori community was not yet a significant demographic phenomenon. Glamuzina and Laurie provide an account by a Māori elder that reads the murder in terms of Māori spirituality. However, this appears to be additional, rather than integral, to their own reading.

9   John D. Porter, et al., *The* Heavenly Creatures *FAQ*, ed. John D. Porter (1995). Available at <http://www.helix.net/~adamabr/Section_3/TOC3.html>, 3.1.18 [accessed June 17, 1996].

10   Captain W. E. Johns, *Biggles in the South Seas* (London: Oxford University Press, 1940).

11   Peter Jackson, quoted in Howard Feinstein, "Death and the Maidens," *Village Voice,* 15 November 1994, 60.

12   I refer to Pauline's mother as "immigrant" because the real Mrs. Rieper was born in Birmingham, England, and arrived in New Zealand when she was eighteen (see Glamuzina and Laurie, *Parker & Hulme,* 36). This is never explicitly stated in the film, but is instead marked by Mrs. Rieper's accent, which is not as strong as Pauline's.

13   Quoted in Glamuzina and Laurie, *Parker & Hulme,* 93, apparently from transcripts of the trial. Queen Elizabeth II visited New Zealand shortly after her coronation, the first reigning monarch to do so. Pauline's equivalent of Juliet's mockery of royalty is of course her derisive comments about Sir Edmund Hillary.

14   My thanks to Jolisa Gracewood for calling this scene to my attention.

15   For a discussion of this while attending to Sargeson's homosexuality in the context of New Zealand literary masculinity, see Kai Jensen, "Holes, Wholeness and Holiness in Frank Sargeson's Writing," *Landfall* 44, no. 1 (March 1990): 32–44, and Jensen, "'A Poet Quite as Large as Life': Literary Masculinity in New Zealand 1932–1960," *Landfall* 45, no. 2 (June 1991): 206–24.

16   See, for example, "I've Lost My Pal," "That Summer," and "The Hole that Jack

Dug," in *The Stories of Frank Sargeson* (Auckland, New Zealand: Penguin, 1982), 30–34, 145–227, 243–50. Sargeson also discusses (covertly) the slippage between homosociality and homosexuality in relation to Australia's foremost writer of mateship tales in "Henry Lawson: Some Notes after Re-Reading," *Landfall* 20, no. 2 (June 1966): 156–62; rpt. in *Conversation in a Train and Other Critical Writing*, ed. Kevin Cunningham (Auckland, New Zealand: Auckland University Press and Oxford University Press, 1983), 119–25.

17   Rather unfortunately for my reading of *Heavenly Creatures*, the modified version of the film formatted for video slices this catchphrase off the top of the screen.

18   Peter Wells, *The Duration of a Kiss* (London: Minerva, 1995), 200.

19   Peter Wells, "Glamour on the Slopes," in *Film in Aotearoa New Zealand*, ed. Jonathan Dennis and Jan Bieringa (Wellington, New Zealand: Victoria University Press, 1992), 174–75.

QUEERING THE REEL

Sexual Politics and Independent Cinema

Jean Walton

WHITE NEUROTICS, BLACK PRIMITIVES,

AND THE QUEER MATRIX OF *BORDERLINE*

INTRODUCTION

In 1930, a group of white modernist poets and critics collaborated on an ambitious film project that is unique for its self-conscious attempt to combine avant-garde cinematic techniques with racial and sexual politics, its deployment of psychoanalytic assumptions about neurosis, sublimation, and the unconscious, and its symptomatic disclosures of its makers' own desires and identifications. Titled *Borderline,* the film was the result of the collective work of imagiste poet H.D. (Hilda Doolittle), her lesbian companion, Bryher (Winnifred Ellerman), and H.D.'s bisexual lover, Kenneth Macpherson, who had married Bryher in order to conceal his affair with H.D. This domestic and artistic ménage-à-trois (which H.D. referred to as a "composite beast with three faces")[1] formed a collective called the POOL group, and, based in Switzerland, they published books, edited the film journal *Close-Up* from 1927 to 1933, and made four experimental films, of which *Borderline* seemed to be the most significant.

It is striking that *Borderline* has not received more attention, given that it featured not only H.D. and Bryher in principal roles but also Paul and Eslanda Robeson, who were persuaded by the POOL group to take a week out of their heavy touring schedule to shoot the film in Switzerland. It was Paul Robeson's second film role since he had appeared in Oscar Micheaux's *Body and Soul* (1924). *Borderline* is an expressionistic depiction of the racial tensions that develop in a small European village when two couples, one white, one black, work out the interpersonal problems that follow upon the white man's sexual involvement with the black woman. In the "libretto" that was passed out at initial screenings of the film, the white couple, Thorne and Astrid, are described as "highly strung, their nerves . . . tense with continuous hostility evoked by Thorne's vague and destructive cravings."[2] Adah, played by Eslanda Robeson, has been living as Thorne's lover, sharing rooms with the white couple in the mountain village where the film is set. The opening scenes hint at her rupture with Thorne; she prepares to depart, suitcase in hand, while Thorne reacts violently, throwing a ceramic figurine onto the floor. Adah's husband, Pete (played by Paul Robeson) has arrived in the village, prompting her to end her interracial affair; the film focuses on the violent aftermath of this breakup. As Pete reconciles with Adah in a series of outdoor scenes, Astrid, played by H.D. herself, and Thorne (Gavin Arthur) quarrel until Astrid is stabbed to death. The drama between the two couples is intercut with, and sometimes enters into, scenes of racist bigotry on the part of the villagers set in the public space of the Hotel's café, which is presided over by a very butch-looking, cigar-smoking Bryher as the café manageress, a femme-styled Charlotte Arthur as the barmaid, and a gay-coded piano player acted by film critic Robert Herring. Astrid's death leads to further mob-like racist hatred on the part of the townspeople, until Adah voluntarily leaves, and after receiving orders from the mayor to depart, Pete follows her. Overall, the film takes an attitude of critical irony toward the racist triumph of the townspeople; it seems to imply, however, that Thorne has undergone a transformation as a result of the events, and he is given the most privileged subjectivity by the end of the film.

In her analysis of a contemporaneous text on the other side of the Atlantic, Nella Larsen's *Passing,* Judith Butler asks:

> what would it mean . . . to consider the assumption of sexual positions, the disjunctive ordering of the human as "masculine" or "feminine" as taking place not only through a heterosexualizing symbolic with its taboo on homosexuality, but through a complex set of racial injunctions which operate in part through the taboo on miscegenation. Further, how might we understand homosexuality and miscegenation to converge at and as the constitutive outside of a normative heterosexuality that is at once the regulation of a racially pure reproduction?[3]

If psychoanalysis is partially responsible for the "heterosexualizing symbolic" that regulates racial, gendered, and sexual identity, then Larsen's *Passing,* according to Butler, is "in part a theorization of desire, displacement, and jealous rage that has significant implications for rewriting psychoanalytic theory in ways that explicitly come to terms with race."[4] As the cultural production of a group of white modernists consciously working within psychoanalytic paradigms, *Borderline* complements texts such as Larsen's, bringing into the realm of visual representation (and thus into our critical purview) both the heterosexualizing and racializing effects of psychoanalysis. As Butler puts it, "though there are clearly good historical reasons for keeping 'race' and 'sexuality' and 'sexual difference' as separate analytic spheres, there are also quite pressing and significant historical reasons for asking how and where we might read not only their convergence, but the sites at which the one cannot be constituted save through the other."[5] *Borderline* is, I would suggest, invaluable for its significance as a site for exploring not only the convergence but indeed, the interdependency of constitutions of "race," "sexuality," and "sexual difference." The film has received brief treatment in studies of H.D. and Robeson, in film histories, and in at least one survey of lesbians in cinema. However, no single analysis of the film has adequately accounted for its problematic imbrication of sexual and racial identity, nor for its evidence of how the "queering" of modernism was, at least in some quarters, constructed as an exclusively white prerogative.[6]

In a more extended examination of *Borderline,* placing it in the biographical, film historical, psychoanalytic, and racialized contexts already outlined by film historian Anne Friedberg, H.D. scholar Susan Stanford Friedman, and film critic Richard Dyer, I will explore it partly as a "film à clef" that exhibited the preoccupations of its collaborators and their fixations, obsessions, and aspirations. More importantly, I will consider it as a cultural document that testifies to a gendered modernism whose queered configurations could not be separated from its presuppositions about racial difference. As I have argued at length elsewhere, the Robesons are clearly constructed as the "natural" or primitivist heterosexual couple of the film, and are explicitly contrasted with the overcivilized, therefore neurotic, white hetero couple.[7]

Less obvious is how this black/white binary is inflected by the presence of the queer-coded white characters in the film: the lesbian couple and the gay piano-player function both as mediators between the straight white and black couples, and as disapproving but ineffectual observers of the mob-like racist villagers. As a psychoanalytic exercise, the film seems to suggest a series of racialized tropes on the theme of (Oedipal) civilization and its discontents. In the overcivilized white couple, the film presents a degenerate or "dipsomaniac" version of oedipality: Astrid and Thorne may be white and may be heterosexual, but insofar as heterosexuality is based on repressed homoerotic impulses, this couple is subject to the neurosis that will eventually end in Astrid's death. Two alternatives to white hetero neurosis are offered by the film: on the one hand, there is the hetero but black couple, who is outside the vicissitudes of the white symbolic (but also apparently outside the realm of subjectivity altogether); on the other hand, there are the white but homosexual characters, who haven't repressed the homoerotic, and hence are "mentally stable" by comparison to the white hetero couple.

A critical analysis of the film's racialized sexual politics must be preceded by a biographical account of the interrelationships of the POOL group, as well as a reconstruction of the psychoanalytic assumptions that informed its aesthetic and political agenda, in particular, the ideas about sexual repression, neurosis, and civilization to be found in Freud's study of Leonardo da Vinci, as well as his essay " 'Civilized' Sexual Morality and Modern Nervous Illness."

THE *POOL* GROUP

Her complex sexual and domestic arrangements have made H.D. a particularly rich figure for feminist and lesbian revisions of modernist literary history. But less has been written about how the POOL group's transgressive sexual politics were crosscut by their psychic investments in, and aesthetic representations of, racially delineated figures of the Other as black. A short history of H.D.'s erotic and affectional affiliations in the years just preceding the shooting of Borderline will help us to understand the tensions and contradictions that no doubt determined the film's peculiar sexual and racial dynamics.

Critics agree that H.D.'s most enduring relationship was to Bryher who, in the intimate early years of their romantic involvement, agreed to undertake the care and upbringing of H.D.'s daughter, Perdita, and who continued to be H.D.'s primary companion even during her affairs with men throughout the rest of her life. Bryher had been preceded in H.D.'s lesbian affections by Frances Gregg, with whom H.D. was in love as a young woman. By the mid-twenties, H.D. was in a mutually sustaining relationship with Bryher, was friends with Gregg (who, according to Friedman, "still magnetized [H.D.] with her intensity"),[8] and had just become sexually involved with Kenneth Macpherson.

It should be noted, however, that the liaison with Macpherson was not a conventionally heterosexual one. In the first place, according to Friedman, their relationship was "initially triangulated by the role Gregg played in the formation of the affair."[9] Gregg had been previously involved with Macpherson, and it was through her that H.D. came to know him: "her presence was very much evident in the attraction of H.D. and Macpherson. 'K and I talk much of Frances,' H.D. remembered in 'Autobiographical Notes.' . . . In part, the charismatic, gifted, boyish, and bisexual Macpherson had taken Gregg's place."[10] In a reversal of the usual patriarchal arrangement, then, Macpherson became an object of exchange between women; his valency as the erotic focus of H.D.'s affections was established via the previous lesbian attachment between the two women. Moreover, if H.D. was simultaneously dismayed and yet compelled by a pronouncement she had read by Freud somewhere that "women did not creatively amount to anything or amount to much, unless they had a male counterpart or a male companion from whom they drew their inspiration,"[11] then she could both comply with and challenge such an assumption by choosing Macpherson as her "male" companion in the late twenties. Indeed, according to Friedman, before collaborating on Borderline, Macpherson and H.D. each wrote novels that "reflected" each other insofar as both were "bisexual, ultimately homoerotic novels of development whose style and narrative structures are mirror images of each other."[12] Thus if Macpherson was H.D.'s "male counterpart," it was not so much because his "maleness" or masculinity provided an opposite for H.D.'s femininity but rather because his homoeroticism became a point of identification for her own, an identification that formed the basis of their artistic creativity.

Friedman speculates that by this time, H.D. and Bryher were "profoundly attached and loyal to each other, bonded in a primary relationship, probably not (or no longer) sexually engaged with each other, and open to other erotic attachments."[13] Bryher agreed to marry Macpherson, partly to screen his affair with H.D. (his parents had wanted him to marry an heiress, and "as the daughter of England's richest man, Bryher fit the bill"),[14] and partly (as in her previous marriage to Robert McAlmon) to maintain her freedom from her family. She and Macpherson eventually officially adopted Perdita, and the unorthodox family settled in Switzerland.

Friedman's account of the eventual deterioration of this arrangement during and after the filming of Borderline begins to suggest how this story of sexual and marital "passing" was inflected (or, in Friedman's version, perhaps infected is a more apt term) by a simultaneous story of cross-racial desire:

As Macpherson's [novel] *Poolreflection* anticipates . . . he became res-
tive in a heterosexual relationship with an older woman and turned increasingly to younger men. Fascinated by black culture in both Harlem
and expatriate communities like Capri, Macpherson fell in love with
a black cafe singer, Toni Slocum, and later a black tubercular youth
whom he (with Bryher's money) cared for. The crisis came in December of 1930 with "the Toni drama in Monte Carlo—and the charm of
the original spell of K is broken[."] . . . Enthralled by Toni, Macpherson
forgot to meet H.D. at the train and to keep "arrangements" with her.[15]

Elsewhere, Friedman summarizes the demise of the ménage as follows:
"Sixteen years younger than H.D., Macpherson was something of a talented
drifter when H.D. met him in 1926. . . . both H.D. and Bryher believed in
and nurtured his talent, even after he began pursuing liaisons with young
black men in 1929. Supporting him emotionally and financially, they urged
him to focus his talents and to pursue the film career Pabst offered. But,
by 1930, Macpherson's creative drive began to dissipate, finally dissolving into neurosis by the early 1930s."[16] In effect, though Friedman does
not emphasize this, Macpherson's marriage to Bryher, indeed, perhaps his
sexual relationship with H.D., also functioned to cover the highly transgressive nature of his homoerotic relationships with black men. No doubt
inadvertently, Friedman gives the impression in this last account that Macpherson's downfall is due to the persistent consummation of his queer,
cross-racial desires, desires that are in conflict with the development of
his talent. We are told that H.D. and Bryher nurture this talent "even after"
he becomes involved with black men. This involvement continues until
his creative drive begins to "dissipate, finally dissolving into neurosis by
the early 1930s." It would seem as though the racial purity of the creative
ménage-à-trois is infected or corrupted by blackness in this account, as
Macpherson shifts from sublimating (via aestheticized images of Robeson),
to consummating, to symptomatizing his cross-racial desire.[17]

That (white) creative drive might "dissipate" and "dissolve" into (white)
neurosis is a primary underlying assumption in the representational and
extradiegetic dynamics of *Borderline*. Indeed, in her pamphlet on the film,
H.D. seems especially concerned to shore up the discursive distinctions
that will prevent Macpherson from undergoing just such a transformation.
Her strategy is twofold: on the one hand, explicitly to compare Macpherson with Leonardo da Vinci, and on the other, implicitly to contrast him

with Paul Robeson. As a Leonardo figure, Macpherson is located firmly at the site of enunciation of the film, a producer and manipulator of its psychoanalytic complexities, but not (as in the case of its white hetero protagonists) pathologically subject to them. Robeson, on the other hand, is located, by virtue of Macpherson's expertise, within the interior of the pro-filmic world, and has as little agency over its direction and shape as the neurotic white characters who are caught up within its diegetic space.

Given that H.D. was an active collaborator in the making of *Borderline,* and especially, with Bryher, in its editing, feminist scholars have been perplexed by her self-effacement in the pamphlet, which lavishes all credit for the film's virtues on Macpherson. She gushes about how watching him at work is "like watching a young gunner alone with his machine gun. It is as if one knew all the time the sniper would at the last get him. But it is a privilege, in no small way, to stand beside just such a rare type of advanced young creative intellectual."[18] Generally speaking, says H.D., the "advanced and intellectual film-director," like Macpherson, "must be mechanic, must be artist, must be man, must be warrior" (*B,* 115). It becomes difficult to see H.D. as radically re-gendering modernism in passages like these. As Susan Stanford Friedman remarks: "Instead of writing the female body . . . H.D. appeared to promote in *Borderline* a modernity in which the phallus is the precondition and expression of creativity." Indeed, in anonymously publishing the pamphlet, H.D. "effaced her own role as catalyst and her achievement as the best-known and hardest-working artist in her immediate circle." This can be understood, according to Friedman, if we see the pamphlet as "something of a love letter to a lover already gone, one that projects the role of disciple/lover admiring the artistic genius of the director/beloved."[19]

I would suggest, however, that H.D. does more than simply, as Friedman puts it, fall "into the conventions of the romance plot, eager to enact the part of the hysterical woman, captured on screen by the camera gaze of the male director."[20] For H.D. praises Macpherson as "mechanic . . . artist . . . man . . . warrior" precisely to the extent that he is like Leonardo da Vinci who, as "world's greatest 'artist' must have a try at everything" (*B,* 115). H.D.'s insistence on constructing Macpherson as a modern-day Leonardo subverts what might otherwise indeed be an unattenuated phallic (and hetero) version of his masculinity.

It must be remembered that by the late twenties, and especially for those who were steeped in the discourse of psychoanalysis, Leonardo had been officially "queered," as it were, by Freud's study of him in *Leonardo da Vinci and a Memory of His Childhood*.[21] As H.D. would certainly have been aware, the Leonardo in Freud's study is a Leonardo whose considerable artistic achievements are intimately connected with a primarily homoerotic libido. For Freud, the problem at hand is to discover the extent to which Leonardo's homoerotic desire had undergone repression on the one hand (resulting in neurosis) and sublimation on the other (resulting in his creative powers). As Diana Fuss notes:

> In Freud's enthusiastic estimation, Leonardo was the 'rarest and most perfect' homosexual type, the 'ideal' homosexual—ideal because he sublimated his homoeroticism into acts of adventurous intellect and breathtaking artistry. 'Ideal' homosexuality can only be achieved, paradoxically, through its own ruthless repression. The artist's 'frigidity' and 'abstinence' . . . serve as the very precondition of his genius; Leonardo embodies for Freud 'the cool repudiation of sexuality' . . . , a man whose every passionate impulse has been rerouted into an 'insatiable and indefatigable thirst for knowledge[.]'[22]

Thus, when H.D. claims that "juxtaposition of 'Leonardo' with 'modern screen art' is neither as inept nor as ironical as it may seem at first glance" (*B*, 112); when she links "divine Leonardo-like curiosity" and "intensive Leonardo-esque modernism" with Macpherson's "cadaverous frame getting more thin, his grey-steel eyes getting more glint and fire" (*B*, 113); when she tells us that "Mr. Macpherson, like Mr. da Vinci is Hellenic in his cold detachment, his cool appraisal, his very inhuman insistence on perfection" (*B*, 113), we must assume that it is not just Leonardo-as-Renaissance-genius that is being reincarnated here, but Freud's Leonardo-as-repressed/sublimated-homosexual, whose creative genius *and* potential for failure are both defined in relation to an underlying queer eroticism. If Macpherson's homoeroticism was a powerful point of identification for H.D., it was also the impulse that seemed to draw his attention away from her, and toward the black men who had by this time become the primary focus of his sexual desires. The pamphlet, then, could be seen as H.D.'s (failed) attempt to conjure a Leonardo-like Macpherson: still driven by a homoerotic libido, yet ruthlessly repressing or sublimating it (the distinction is no clearer in Freud's text than it is in H.D.'s) in the service of high filmic art.

As we will see, Robeson, both in H.D.'s pamphlet and in the film, serves as the material evidence of this sublimation; he attests simultaneously to the cross-racial trajectory of the male homoerotic gaze, and to the "artist's" transcendence of sexual desire. Robeson's body is discursively positioned in the film as the "natural" (black) flesh that sets into motion the (perverse) desires of the white characters, yet this same body is repeatedly fetishized (in much the same way that the white female body is fetishized in classic cinema) partly to ward off its perceived threat, partly to demonstrate the artistic genius of the filmmaker as "sculptor." While H.D. stresses the professionalism of both Macpherson and Robeson, it is only Macpherson, as director, whose artistry seems to have necessitated conscious planning, intellectual engagement, and technical know-how. Robeson may be an "artist of high repute," but his is an unreflective, untutored talent: "Mr. Robeson had only to step before the camera and the theme flowed toward him as many small streams toward that great river. Mr. Robeson is, obviously the ground under all their feet. He is stabilized, stable, the earth. Across Mr. Macpherson's characterization of Pete, the half-vagrant young giant negro, the fretting provincialism of small-town slander and small town menace move like shadows from high clouds" (B, 112). In this passage, where she ostensibly illustrates the "relative professional experience and inexperience" of the members of Borderline's company, H.D. seems unable to keep her focus on Robeson's professional status as a conscious performer, and readily confuses him with the character he plays, or indeed, with the metaphorical force this character is meant to bear in the film: we move from "Mr. Robeson" to "great river" to "ground" to "earth" to "Pete" to "half-vagrant young giant negro." These last two designations refer not so much to Robeson's depiction of Pete but to Macpherson's "characterization" of him. In other words, even Robeson's "professionalism," when it is not mythologized, "belongs" in a sense to Macpherson. Robeson is the raw material out of which Macpherson makes high art:

> Light flows over a face. . . . There is a bronze forehead and the eye sockets are gouged out just this way; there is a concentration of shadow here, a plane of light here. You see a face, perhaps at most you see a pleasing portrait. You may even murmur "Gauguin." . . . You do not realize that that face has been moulded, modelled by an artist, that those lights have been arranged, re-arranged, deliberately

focussed. . . . Macpherson sculpts literally with light. He gouges, he reveals, he conceals. All this not by accident, not automatically but with precision and deliberate foresight. (*B*, 115)

Robeson merely steps before the camera; Macpherson is the true modernist artist in the scenario, the "steel-glint" of his "rapacious grey eyes" (*B*, 114) discerning where and how Robeson's "eye sockets" are to be "gouged out just this way." Not only does Macpherson wield the phallic sculpting chisel he also plies the "keen knife-blade of indigenous intrepidity" (*B*, 112), and has metaphorically "cut apart dead arms and dead hands to see what nerve centres really do look like" and "probed down and down with a little sharp implement" to "discover by its valve formation, why the human heart should beat so" (*B*, 113). Most importantly, he handles the sharp blade of montage, of the "cutting and fitting of tiny strips of film" as it is edited into its final form (*B*, 119):

> The minute and meticulous effect for instance that Mr. Macpherson achieves with Pete, the negro and the waterfall, or the woman Astrid with the knife, are so naturalistic, I should say so "natural" that they seem to the uninitiate, sheer "tricks" or accidents. The effect of the negro, Pete, against the waterfall is achieved by a meticulous and painstaking effort on the part of the director, who alone with the giants of German and Russian production is his own cutter and will not trust his "montage" to a mere technician, however sympathetic. (*B*, 118–19)[23]

In H.D.'s text, the image of a steel knife-blade figures as a positive phallic emblem of Macpherson's filmmaking skills; but inside the fantasy world of the film itself, knife imagery is negatively weighed as the dangerous phallic cutting blade of white, civilized neurosis. However, whether in the film, or in H.D.'s discussion of it, never is the knife, and its associations with the phallus, ever constitutive of black subjectivity.

BLACK PRIMITIVES AND WHITE MODERNISM AS NEUROSIS

If H.D.'s pamphlet on *Borderline* emphasizes a Macpherson whose homoeroticism has been successfully sublimated, making him the "artist par excellence" who "sees with the eye and what he sees, he portrays," caring "no more for you or me than Leonardo did for King Francis or the merchant husband of Mona Lisa" (*B*, 112), then the film depicts at least three male counterparts to this idealized figure of sublimation: Thorne, as the "degenerate dipsomaniac" whose repressed sexuality has resulted in his modern neurosis; the unnamed pianist whose overt coding as gay makes him representative of a homoeroticism that is not repressed, though perhaps sublimated (since he is the only "artist" in the film); and Pete, whose blackness-as-primitivity seems to relegate him altogether outside the realm of either repression or sublimation. Such a sexual and racial parsing of masculinity derives its logic from another of Freud's texts on the question of repressed and sublimated homoeroticism, his 1908 essay, " 'Civilized' Sexual Morality and Modern Nervous Illness."

In this article, Freud first summarizes Ehrenfels's distinction between " 'natural' and 'civilized' sexual morality," in which "natural" sexual morality is "a sexual morality under whose dominance a human stock is able to remain in lasting possession of health and efficiency" and "civilized" is "a sexual morality obedience to which . . . spurs men on to intense and productive cultural activity," but under whose domination "the health and efficiency of single individuals may be liable to impairment." Freud then identifies the single most injurious effect of "civilized" sexual morality to be "modern nervous illness," or more specifically, "psychoneurosis." [24] That our civilization, as Freud says, is founded on the suppression of the "sexual instinct" has two important corollaries:

> It [sexual instinct] places extraordinarily large amounts of force at the disposal of civilized activity, and it does this in virtue of its especially marked characteristic of being able to displace its aim without materially diminishing in intensity. This capacity to exchange its originally sexual aim for another one, which is no longer sexual but which is psychically related to the first aim, is called the capacity for *sublimation*. In contrast to this displaceability, in which its value for civilization lies, the sexual instinct may also exhibit a particularly obstinate fixation which renders it unserviceable and which sometimes causes it to degenerate into what are described as abnormalities. (*SE*, 9:187; original emphasis)

In Freud's account, it is not just any sexual instinct that is either suppressed or sublimated by civilization but specifically those which afford pleasures outside of the reproductive function, including, most notably, homoerotic instincts. Indeed, elsewhere in this article, and in keeping with his study of Leonardo, Freud notes, "The constitution of people suffering from inversion—the homosexuals—is, indeed, often distinguished by their sexual instinct's possessing a special aptitude for cultural sublimation" (*SE*, 9:190). The model outlined by Freud in this essay, whereby sexual morality is divided into "natural" and "civilized," and whereby "civilized sexual morality" gives rise to neurosis on the one hand and cultural achievement on the other, has been overlaid in *Borderline* by a racialized schema, where, unsurprisingly, blacks find themselves on the side of the "natural," and whites on the side of the "civilized." We have already seen how H.D. constructs Macpherson-the-director as white civilized sublimator of homosexual libido. What remains to be demonstrated is how the other side of repressed white libido within "civilized" morality plays itself out within the diegesis of the film itself. As I have noted elsewhere,[25] *Borderline* is predicated on a black-white racial continuum, with Astrid/H.D. and Pete/Robeson occupying opposite poles. That they are meant to be linked contraries is implied by the fact that they never appear in the same frame, nor even in the same scene, together, as though they belong to two racially distinct worlds. "Clatter montage," as a technique to enter the minds of characters, is used almost exclusively with these two characters, as though their minds are most in need of contrastive juxtaposition. H.D. emphasizes this in the passage I quoted above, where (in two separate scenes) Pete's face intercut with the waterfall and Astrid's face intercut with the knife are offered as exempla of the film's significant use of montage. According to H.D., Astrid's dagger is to be taken as an explicit symbol of the "modern nervous illness" that marks the white couple as "borderline" and constitutes the fundamental way in which they differ from the black couple: "The giant negro is in the high clouds, white cumulous cloud banks in a higher heaven. Conversely, his white fellow men are the shadows of white, are dark, neurotic; storm brews; there is that runic fate that 'they that live by the sword shall perish by the sword.' Or as here applied, 'they that live by neurotic-erotic suppression shall perish by the same'" (*B*, 112). As a "giant negro" most insistently photographed against natural backdrops (clouds, trees, waterfall, hillside), Pete/Robeson occupies a pre-civilized, therefore pre-neurotic realm, where sexual impulses are imbued with an earthy and godlike innocence. Astrid, on the other hand, lives so much "by the sword," which is to say, is so marked by her "neurotic-erotic suppression," that she does, indeed, literally die by that same sword. Adah, constructed by H.D. as a "mulatto woman," occupies the untheorized middle-ground between black and white, and indeed, is the token of exchange that eventually gives rise to what might be interpreted as primarily a homosocial bond between Pete and Thorne if it were not for the presence of the overtly queer-coded characters in the film. Arguably, *Borderline*'s primary concern is with the exiling of the black couple and the racist mechanisms by which the village community reconstitutes its "purity." But the presence of the lesbians and the gay piano player in the film inflect this explicit theme of white supremacy with a subtler one of cross-racial homoerotic desire and identification. Before the black characters are abjected from the film, its central female characters are dispensed with, as though they have merely been obstacles to the true erotic exchange of the text, that between Pete and Thorne.

As I suggested in my introduction, the characters in the film make up three distinct couples or groups, each one occupying a representative position within the natural/civilized, homo/hetero, healthy/neurotic world sketched out in Freud's "Modern Nervous Illness" essay: Thorne and Astrid are white, civilized, and are repressing their homoerotic impulses, hence are hetero but neurotic; Pete and Adah are black but outside the "civilized" world of the white characters, hence not susceptible to "neurotic-erotic suppression"—their sexuality is just somehow innocently hetero; and the hotel manageress, the barmaid, and the pianist are white and civilized, but insofar as they are coded as a butch/femme lesbian couple and a gay man who expressly desires Pete, we are to assume that they are *not* repressing their homoerotic impulses, hence are, like the black couple, healthy despite their white/civilized status. These three groups do not remain static throughout the film, but metamorphose in relation to each other, so that a new couple is established, then ruptured, by the end of the film: that of Thorne and Pete.

In the pages that follow, I'd like to explore this story of what Richard Dyer calls "love and the death of love between the two men."[26] In one of the film's most prolonged and strangely paced scenes, Thorne, as the "libretto" puts it, "breaks his way into Pete's room, but seeing Adah and Pete together, he realises that they belong indeed to each other." As usual, the plot summary is misleading, especially insofar as it omits to mention the role played by the butch manageress and the pianist in this crucial scene. It should be noted here that the queer-coded characters are featured very prominently in the film, especially in the many scenes set in the café, where the barmaid dances, flirts with patrons, pours drinks, empties ash-

1   The manageress (Bryher, *left*) and the barmaid (Charlotte Arthur, *right*) look on as Astrid (*not shown*) gives a racist tirade in the café (courtesy of the Beinecke Rare Book and Manuscript Library, Yale University).

trays, affectionately ruffles the manageress's hair, and admonishes Astrid and other racist townspeople for their bigotry; the manageress smokes her cigar, brandishes a mop, keeps the books, and generally casts a businesslike eye on her patrons (fig. 1); the piano player gazes longingly at Pete, or at the picture of him propped on his piano, flourishes a long cigarette-holder, sometimes dances the Charleston across the room, and visually punctuates every scene with "diegetic" piano music, providing a kind of "jazz age" aura to the film (fig. 2). Yet, while H.D. expostulates at length in her pamphlet on the psychological borderline status of the white couple, and the racial borderline status of the black couple, she remains silent about the sexual borderline status of the hotel employees.[27] On the one hand, this could be taken as a closeting on H.D.'s part, characteristic of her general reluctance to publish her overtly homoerotic autobiographical novels of the period. On the other hand, it implies that the homoerotic relationship of the les-bian couple, and the homoerotic desire of the pianist, are so normalized in the film, even though they are queer people among straight people, that (at

least within the fantasmatic realm of the film's world) they do not constitute
the kind of "social problem" attending what H.D. calls "black people among
white people" (*B*, 110), and hence need not be commented on as significant
"borderline" cases. How, then, are they deployed within the film in relation
to those characters who *do* occupy what H.D. terms "borderline" status?

To approach this question I will consider how the film's interior settings
are divided into three significant spaces: the adjoining rooms inhabited by
Thorne and Astrid; Pete's single room in the hotel above the café; and the
café itself, which is linked to Pete's room by way of a staircase. As a couple,
Thorne and Astrid are in part defined by the "private" space of their rooms,
in particular by the photos, prints, and curios on their walls, and the newspapers, playing cards, books, phonograph and records, knife and a stuffed
sea gull strewn about the floor and tables. This is the space to which they
retreat between scenes of public interaction, and it helps to delineate their
shared occupancy of the realm of "white" civilization. The same is true
of Pete, and later Pete and Adah, with regard to the somewhat less private space of his room in the hotel. His flowered wallpaper connects this
room with the exterior settings in the countryside, marking his space as

2 The pianist, played by Robert Herring (courtesy of the Beinecke Rare Book and
Manuscript Library, Yale University).

the "natural" and the "pre-civilized" (his room is nowhere near as cluttered with the accoutrements of industrialized modernity). The manageress and the barmaid share their "space" not only with the other queer-coded character, the pianist, but also with anyone who comes into the café. Never do we see the lesbian couple in something like a "private" space, where we might have access to the dynamics of their relationship when they are not in public view. By the same token, the rapid montage technique used to probe the minds of other characters, to enter their "private" psychic space, is never used on the queer characters, as though to indicate that there is nothing "repressed" to be exteriorized through filmic-psychoanalytic technique.[28] The film offers no "private" space of definition for them, only the public space of the café, which is nevertheless more consistently asserted as "their" space than anyone else's. They are the proprietors of this public space, the purveyors of its atmosphere, accommodating all other couples and characters as they pass through it on their way to and from their respective private spaces.[29] The public matrix of the film, then, is a homoerotically defined space; only its peripheries, those private rooms belonging to the two couples, are hetero-coded. Hence, one might say that the hetero interactions of the film, including the racist jealousy exhibited by Astrid, and Pete's angry punch aimed at a villager who seems to have insinuated something about Adah, are "hosted" by the queer-delineated space of the café, and that the film's conventionally "straight" plots are eventually queered by their trajectory through that space.

THRESHOLDS AND PRIMAL SCENES

I want now to consider two occasions when the occupants of one of the private spaces crosses through the "queer matrix" of the hotel café and attempts to enter the other private space. The two episodes are quite different. The first is the one I introduced above, when Thorne bursts into Pete and Adah's room. Prior to this scene, we have witnessed a kind of double reconciliation of the black couple; once on the hillside, where they wander in apparent contentment, and then in Pete's room itself, where Pete has just returned with fuel for the oil stove. Shots of Pete and Adah talking in the "intimacy" of their room (fig. 3) are intercut with shots of the butch manageress eavesdropping from the stairway, her hand poised at her ear. Eventually, Pete and Adah embrace; in a reaction shot, the manageress stops listening and, with a satisfied smile on her face, begins to descend

3 Pete and Adah (Paul and Eslanda Robeson) in a moment of intimacy in their room. Adah holds the small hand mirror (courtesy of the Beinecke Rare Book and Manuscript Library, Yale University).

the stairs. When she reaches the café, she seems to convey her satisfaction to the piano player via a look of serenity. He receives this communication either with indifference or disappointment, turning to his sheet music and sitting down to play a new song while the camera emphasizes the photo of Pete propped beside him. It would seem that Pete and Adah's intimacy is not only housed but also monitored by the queer ménage in the café.

Shortly, Thorne rushes into the café, then through the doorway that leads to Pete's room upstairs. The manageress follows him, and after some hesitation, so does the pianist. The camera cuts to the interior of Pete's room, where Pete is seated on the bed; Adah stands near him, looking into a small hand mirror. The door bursts open as Thorne forces his way into the room. But Thorne proceeds no further than the doorway, as though the scene that confronts him, the black couple in a moment of intimacy, has frozen him in his tracks. Indeed, given the anxiety and paralysis that seems to take hold of Thorne, we might suspect that this scene is structured like a primal scene, where a child is at once fascinated and terrified by the sight of his parents engaged in sexual intimacy. Freud observes that such a "primal phantasy" is a "phylogenetic endowment" in which

> the individual reaches beyond his own experience into primaeval ex-
> perience at points where his own experience has been too rudimen-
> tary. It seems to me that all the things that are told to us to-day
> in analysis as phantasy—the seduction of children, the inflaming of
> sexual excitement by observing parental intercourse, the threat of cas-
> tration (or rather castration itself)—were once real occurrences in the
> primaeval times of the human family, and that children in their phan-
> tasies are simply filling gaps in individual truth with prehistoric truth.
> (SE, 16:371)

It is as though the POOL group has transposed the "primaeval" and the "prehistoric" onto the racially differentiated other: by opening the door onto the space of black sexuality, Thorne peers through to his own pri-maeval past, where the parents in question are marked by the blackness of pre-civilization. Strangely enough, this irruption onto a racialized "primal scene" inaugurates the homoeroticization of Thorne's hitherto neuroticized libidinal impulses. Ostensibly, of course, according to the rudimentary plot structure of the film, Thorne has come in search of his concubine, Adah, seeking to take her back from Pete. But this hetero convention is quickly obscured by the strange immobility that settles upon the scene, as an in-creasingly erotically charged standoff between Pete and Thorne demands our attention.

Thorne's intrusion into the room (this door seems perpetually accessible to all who want to open it) is conveyed through an accelerated montage se-quence of brief shots: the door of the room bursts open; four brief close-up shots present Thorne's face from slightly different angles; a brief shot shows Pete sitting on the bed and Adah standing behind and to the left of him, holding up the small hand mirror; another close-up shows Thorne's face, followed by brief astonished reaction-shots of Adah's and then Pete's face; a cutaway low-angle shot from behind of the manageress and the pianist has-tening up the stairs; close-ups all around again of Pete, Adah, and Thorne, and finally a mid-shot of Thorne, the manageress, and the pianist, framed as a trio in the doorway. The editing decelerates at this point, to give us longer shots of each character, as they slowly begin to act and react. Indeed, time seems to stretch out, as the camera records long takes of Thorne's face, his chin ducked, his forehead glistening, his eyes fixed downward, perhaps on Pete's stockinged feet, which we are shown in close-up, as he in turn reaches for his shoes under the bed, and begins to put them on. For the rest of the scene, Adah recedes to the background as Pete rises, approaches Thorne, and engages in a drawn-out staring match with him. If Thorne has remained at the threshold, it is partly because his shoulders and jacket are gripped by the manageress and the pianist. Presumably, they have followed Thorne to intervene in case of violence, yet, they seem now to join in the voyeuristic gazing into the private space of the black couple. Indeed, given that he has already been marked by the fetishized photo on his piano as having an (eroticized) interest in Pete, the pianist's presence in this scene serves in part to inflect Thorne's gaze with homoerotic overtones.

Two-shots of Thorne and Pete, standing face-to-face, interspersed with close-up shot-reverse shots of each of them delineate the remainder of their contemplation of each other; as Thorne's face becomes more and more tormented, streaming with perspiration, Pete's becomes more relaxed and unperturbed. Their mutual mesmerization is intercut with close-ups of the hands of the manageress and the pianist, pulling Thorne with all their strength. It is as though Thorne's paralysis has spread to them; they too get caught up in the homoerotic showdown, and pull as they might, are unable to budge Thorne from his spot. We also see a brief close-up shot of Adah's eye, reflected in her small hand mirror, as though she has by this time been banished to a self-enclosed, narcissistic space-off.

Finally, the manageress and pianist are able to pull Thorne back into the hallway, at which point, the trance is broken and he flees down the staircase. The manageress makes a gesture of accomplishment by thrusting her two fists downward in front of her, nods to Pete, and closes the door to his room, as though to assert her agency as protectress of the black characters' private domain.

The susceptibility of this space to white intrusion, however, is established not only by this scene but by two others; an earlier one in which the barmaid opens the door on Pete to tell him Astrid is trying to reach him by telephone, and a later one in which the manageress brings news to Pete of Thorne's acquittal. The penetrability of the "black" domain, and indeed, its serviceability as a source for the white characters' transformation, contrasts sharply with the relative impermeability of the "white" domain as represented by Thorne and Astrid's rooms.

This impermeability, particularly with respect to the black characters, is clearly demonstrated in a scene that stands as a formal counterpart

4 Astrid (H.D.) confronts Thorne (*not shown*) just prior to her death. (courtesy of the Beinecke Rare Book and Manuscript Library, Yale University).

to that of Thorne's irruption into Pete's room, insofar as this later scene shows the black couple's failed attempt to enter Thorne and Astrid's room. Prior to this scene, a dagger-sized knife has featured in most of the action depicted in Thorne and Astrid's rooms. Early in the film, Thorne fidgets nervously with this knife, pointing its tip into his palm, thrusting it into the wooden floor, and pressing it vertically against his nose and forehead. Later, in his lengthy confrontation with Astrid, he sharpens a pencil held at pubic level, as though to underscore the knife's significance as a phallic signifier—one that Astrid is about to appropriate (fig. 4). Shortly after, she takes the knife from the table, and brandishes it threateningly at Thorne, slashing his face and hand. In the scuffle that ensues, the two of them fall in a confused motion across the table and onto the floor. We gather by the next shots, in which Thorne looks dazedly at his bloodied hands, and then at Astrid, lying unresponsive on the floor, that Astrid has been stabbed by the ubiquitous knife. This is the point, presumably, at which (as H.D. has written in the pamphlet): "'they that live by the sword shall perish by the sword.' Or as here applied, 'they that live by neurotic-erotic suppression shall perish by the same.'" If both Thorne and Astrid have been "living by the sword" as a result of their "neurotic-erotic suppression," it is only Astrid who technically "dies" by this same sword, thus taking the fall for the vicissitudes of "civilized" sexual morality. That "neurotic-erotic suppression" is here figured as a woman's unauthorized appropriation of the phallus suggests that the very decadence of whiteness-as-neuroticized-heterosexuality is linked to the gender transgressions of the white woman, but not to the racial transgressions of her male counterpart. In any case, the elaboration of phallicism in the constitution of white subjectivity is a private affair, reserved for white eyes only.

Shortly after Astrid's death, while Thorne mops confusedly at the blood on the floor, Pete and Adah are shown approaching the door to the white couple's rooms. Hearing their knock at the door to the outer room, Thorne rushes over and locks the door to the room, crouching near it soundlessly while Pete and Adah knock, call out, look around themselves in bewilderment, and try the door handle in vain. Clatter montage technique is then applied to black and white hands gripping the handle on either side of the door, as one- or two-frame shots of each hand are spliced together in a flickering juxtaposition that emphasizes once again a face-off between the two men, this time stressing the barrier that separates them. The scene thus formally repeats the potentially homoerotic coupling of the men that had been established in the scene of Thorne's irruption into Pete's room. However, it also functions as the obverse of that scene insofar as Pete is prevented from entering Thorne's room. Thorne throws open Pete's door when he wants to see Pete; Thorne locks the door when he does not want to be seen by Pete. Thus, while Thorne can at first quite easily penetrate the private space of the black couple, they, in turn, are effectively barred from entry to the private space of the white couple. Another kind of "primal scene," the scene of the white woman's death, as a result of phallic "civilized" and neuroticized heterosexuality, remains hidden from their view; they can neither be traumatized by it, nor stand as material witnesses to the crime, even though it is the event that will lead to their ejection from the village.

By the time Pete and Thorne encounter each other again, both women have disappeared from the diegetic space of the film. In the scene I have just described, the black and white hands, separated as they were by the locked door that sequesters and protects the private space of white neurosis, could only be "joined" by the mechanical device of rapid montage. In the final meeting between Thorne and Pete, the hands are foregrounded once again, clasped in an exaggerated icon of black reconciliation with white. On the surface of it, and according to the film's "libretto," Pete and Thorne "both realise that what has happened has been beyond them, and brought about by external circumstances — that enmity has been among others, and they themselves mere instruments for its consummation." Enmity (like love) can be, and has been, consummated, and they have been the instruments for this consummation. This handshake then would seem to constitute a counter-consummation, an agreement to defy compulsory enmity between black man and white man as it is prescribed by a racist culture.

Yet, this scene is preceded and informed by a brief but suggestive shot in which the pianist, having heard of Pete's impending departure, takes the photo of Pete that has been propped on his piano throughout the film, gazes at it longingly, tucks it in his wallet, and puts the wallet in his breast pocket. If the photo has functioned throughout as a signifier of his homoerotic desire for Pete, it would seem that this is the moment where that desire must go "undercover" in a sense, and be secreted before it is effectively transferred to Thorne in the next scene.

The juxtaposition of white and black hands on either side of the locked door in the scene following Astrid's death retrospectively takes on an aura of pathos in the final handshake scene; it is not Thorne's white hand that has prevented Pete's black hand from opening the door. Rather, "enmity among others" is responsible, an enmity configured, through the women, in a saga of heterosexual jealousy playing on mob-like racist bigotry. The hands may not clasp until the women have been removed from the field of identification and desire. In their scene of forgiveness, a two-shot presents Thorne on the left and Pete on the right as they face each other (fig. 5); a shot-reverse shot sequence shows each face smiling and gazing upon the other, until Thorne extends his hand. When the camera cuts to a close-up of the clasped hands, their positions are reversed, with black hand on the left, white hand on the right, suggesting an interchangeability between the two men in keeping with the 1920s coding of homoerotic desire as narcissism. Immediately following this scene, as though to remind us that it has been "accompanied" and inscribed all along by the gay pianist's overt homoerotic desire, we see a brief close-up of his hand gliding in a flourish across the piano keys.

5 Thorne (Gavin Arthur, *left*) and Pete (Paul Robeson, *right*) in their final scene of forgiveness (courtesy of the Beinecke Rare Book and Manuscript Library, Yale University).

CONCLUSION

As I have suggested, it is finally Thorne's subjectivity that is privileged in the diegetic realm of *Borderline;* if he has survived the "sword" of "neurotic-erotic suppression," it is by virtue both of the white female counterpart who has "perished" for him, and of the black male counterpart who has served as a catalyst for the circulation of white homoerotic desire. In the final moments of the film, shots of Pete waiting on the train platform are intercut with shots of Thorne sitting alone on a hillside. It would seem that Thorne is more affected by the loss of Pete than the loss of Astrid; affected in the sense that something of Pete has been "transferred" to him via the interrupted trajectory of their counter-consummation. Thorne now serenely inhabits the forested terrain of the countryside that had previously been deployed to signal Pete's oneness with "nature"; no longer marked as white by frenzied and aimless movement, he sits, motionless, contemplating the scenery that lies before him. If white hetero neurosis is susceptible to a cure, then, it would seem to be via the simultaneous appropriation

6 Director Kenneth Macpherson (*left*) and Paul Robeson (*right*) taking a break during the shooting of *Borderline* (courtesy of the Beinecke Rare Book and Manuscript Library, Yale University).

of Pete's blackness-as-pre-civilization on the one hand, and of the pianist's homoerotic desire on the other.

Indeed, understood as a "film à clef," *Borderline* features each of its primary white collaborators in multiple roles, and translates the story of "white civilized artistic sublimation" into "white civilized neurosis." If H.D. advocated the sublimation of cross-racial desire—both her own and Macpherson's—Astrid, as one of her representatives in the film, serves as a cautionary example of the neuroticization of that desire. But it is as though H.D. had to split off the lesbian part of herself, and give it a second representative in the film: the barmaid who, like H.D. in real life, is paired in the film with Bryher-as-manageress (indeed, on first viewing, audience members have often confused the barmaid with Astrid). Macpherson also appears in two guises in the film: as the gay piano player, played by Robert Herring, a man who, like Macpherson, was a gay film critic sexually attracted to black expatriots and figures of the Harlem Renaissance,[30] and as Thorne, whose apparently hetero interest in Astrid and Adah is eventually displaced by the developing cross-racial bond with Pete. Pete, however, remains static with regard to both his "natural" pre-civilized state and the unproblematized heterosexuality that accompanies it. Indeed, while he functions as the object of the homoerotic desire of the white men (the pianist, Thorne, and indeed, Macpherson himself as Leonardo-the-director), this function is perhaps contingent on the fixity both of his heterosexuality, and of his blackness-as-pre-civilized state; he is thus made serviceable as the "primitive" to which the white neurotic and artist alike can turn for a dose of revitalization.

Arguably, *Borderline* transgresses the heterocentric cinematic conventions of the period, and attempts to present an antiracist politics that is inextricable from a "queered" modernist aesthetic.[31] But in the process, it reserves psychological depth and complexity only for its white characters, constructing the black characters as the primitivized others, the prehistorical background against which the white psyche may be laid bare through its own artistry. In the imaginary of *Borderline's* white collaborators, there is no black neurosis, no black homoerotic desire, and (perhaps as a result) no black Leonardo. Moreover, in the hands of the POOL group, Freud's model of modern neurosis, with its (homo)sexual roots, proves to be a decidedly white model, bound to a very specific history of racist exploitation, colonialism, and the guilt of the white modernist.

NOTES

1   Quoted in Susan Stanford Friedman, "Modernism of the 'Scattered Remnant':
    Race and Politics in the Development of H.D.'s Modernist Vision," in *H.D.:
    Woman and Poet,* ed. Michael King (Orono, Maine: National Poetry Foundation, 1986), 98.

2   The one-page "libretto" is reprinted in Anne Friedberg, "Writing About Cinema: *Close-Up,* 1927–1933" (Ph.D. diss., New York University, 1983), 150. It
    should not be confused with the much longer interpretive pamphlet that H.D.
    published after the film's release, entitled "*Borderline.*" I should note that my
    plot summary here is as much a result of reading the libretto as of watching
    the film itself; *Borderline's* disorienting, expressionistic style of editing makes
    it difficult to establish a clear narrative even on second and third viewings of
    the film itself. Yet, the fact that they distributed a plot summary at screenings
    of the film suggests that the POOL group considered the details of the narrative important to understanding the film as a whole, and that the libretto was
    integral to the viewing experience.

3   Judith Butler, *Bodies That Matter: On the Discursive Limits of "Sex"* (New York:
    Routledge, 1993), 167.

4   Ibid., 182.

5   Ibid., 168.

6   Film scholar and historian Anne Friedberg, in her dissertation and articles
     on the POOL group, has provided the most exhaustive sources for informa-
     tion about the genesis, artistic conception, psychoanalytic underpinnings,
     and (white European) reception of the film. While Friedberg helpfully con-
     textualizes the film by bringing together relevant contemporaneous texts on
     psychoanalysis and cinema, innovations from Eisenstein and Pabst, debates
     about the representation of blacks in Hollywood film, and European reviews
     of the film when it was released, she offers no extended analysis of the film
     itself. See "Writing About Cinema: *Close-Up, 1927–1933*," "On H.D., Woman,
     History, Recognition" *Wide Angle* 5, no. 2 (1982): 26–31, and "Approaching
     Borderline," in *H.D.: Woman and Poet*. H.D. scholar Susan Stanford Friedman,
     in the course of her extraordinarily detailed and meticulous accounts of H.D.'s
     life and work, makes the most serious attempt to establish H.D.'s racial poli-
     tics vis-à-vis her modernist contemporaries, drawing most notably from her
     fictional and critical texts, including "*Borderline*," the long interpretive essay
     that followed the release of the film in pamphlet form. Even as she brings into
     view some fascinating evidence about how racial assumptions informed H.D.'s
     (gendered) modernist aesthetic, however, Friedman is mainly concerned to
     exonerate H.D. of overt racism, and says almost nothing about *Borderline*
     itself, except as H.D. referred to it in her pamphlet. See *Penelope's Web: Gen-
     der, Modernity, H.D.'s Fiction* (New York: Cambridge, 1990), and "Modernism
     of the 'Scattered Remnant.'"

     Richard Dyer, focusing on Paul Robeson's role in the film, provides per-
     haps the most shrewd analysis of *Borderline*'s deployment of "blackness," and
     acknowledges as well its depiction of secondary queer characters; but since
     his discussion of the film constitutes only a small section of a long chapter
     that covers the multiple ways in which Robeson's image was appropriated and
     commodified throughout his entire career, Dyer can say little about how race
     and sexuality are co-delineated in the film. See Dyer, *Heavenly Bodies: Film
     Stars and Society* (New York: St. Martin's, 1986). See also Martin Bauml Duber-
     man's excellent biography of Paul Robeson (New York: Knopf, 1988) for an
     account of the Robesons' collaboration with the POOL group. For a brief ac-
     count of the lesbian couple in the film see Andrea Weiss, *Vampires and Violets:
     Lesbians in Film* (New York: Penguin, 1992).

7   See Jean Walton, " 'Nightmare of the Uncoordinated White-folk': Race, Psycho-
     analysis, and *Borderline*," *Discourse* 19, no. 2 (winter 1997): 88–109.

8   Friedman, *Penelope's Web*, 133.

9   Ibid., 132.

10   Ibid., 133.

11   H.D., *Tribute to Freud* (Boston: D. R. Godine, 1974), 149.

12   Friedman, *Penelope's Web,* 133. For a discussion of *HER,* H.D.'s unpublished homoerotic novel of the late twenties, see Susan Stanford Friedman and Rachel Blau DuPlessis, "'I had two loves separate': The Sexualities of H.D.'s *HER,*" in *Signets: Reading H.D.,* ed. Friedman and DuPlessis (Madison: University of Wisconsin Press, 1990), 205–32.

13   Friedman, *Penelope's Web,* 228.

14   Ibid., 230.

15   Ibid.

16   Ibid., 17.

17   For a historical overview of interrelationships between black and white lesbians and gay men during the 1920s, see Eric Garber, "A Spectacle in Color: The Lesbian and Gay Subculture of Jazz Age Harlem," in *Hidden From History: Reclaiming the Gay and Lesbian Past,* ed. Martin Duberman, Martha Vicinus, and George Chauncey Jr. (New York: New American Library, 1989), 318–31. See also James Smalls, "Public Face, Private Thoughts: Fetish, Interracialism, and the Homoerotic in Some Photography by Carl Van Vechten," *Genders* no. 25 (spring 1997): 144–94.

18   H.D., "*Borderline,*" in *The Gender of Modernism: A Critical Anthology,* ed. Bonnie Kime Scott (Bloomington: Indiana University Press, 1990), 113. Further references to this work will be abbreviated *B* and given parenthetically in the text.

19   Friedman, *Penelope's Web,* 18.

20   Ibid.

21   Sigmund Freud, *Leonardo Da Vinci and a Memory of His Childhood,* in *The Standard Edition of the Complete Psychological Works of Sigmund Freud,* trans. and ed. James Strachey (London: Hogarth, 1953–74), 11:63–137. All further references to Freud will be abbreviated *SE* and given parenthetically in the text, along with volume and page numbers.

22   Diana Fuss, *Identification Papers* (New York: Routledge, 1995), 87.

23   According to Friedman, Macpherson did in fact "trust" at least some of the editing to H.D. and Bryher when he became ill and could not finish it himself. One wonders if H.D.'s reluctance to admit that she also wielded the editing knife is in any way linked to the fate that befalls Astrid, the character she portrays in the film, who, after all, dies as a result of wielding the knife.

24   Sigmund Freud, "'Civilized' Sexual Morality and Modern Nervous Illness," *SE,* 9:181, 182, 185–86.

25   See Walton, "'Nightmare of the Uncoordinated White-folk.'"

26   Dyer, *Heavenly Bodies,* 132.

27   When she does mention the lesbian couple, they are interpreted, through Thorne's eyes, as an "allegory of drink" (the barmaid) and of "sordid calculation" (the manageress); no reference is made to their status *as* a couple (*B,* 123).

28 Or as filmmaker Abigail Child has put it: "[The barmaid and the manageress] are lively and playful, loyal and guarded. The portrayal of the cafe in general has a liveliness that is not seen outside it. The public space seems to exist outside the symbology that defines the white and black characters that carry the moral argument of the film. Freed from symbology, the homosexual couple is allowed some life, a mobility of expression not seen by the film's leads. It is as if their space is exempt from the apparatus of psychoanalysis, and thereby freed of the heavier melodrama and fixed gestures that dominate the life of the 'unconscious,' the life taking place in the rooms upstairs" ("A Flight to Unity: Modernist Aesthetics in the Film *Borderline*," unpublished manuscript).

29 Child has delineated these spaces in a similar way: "It is in the cafe's public space, a place of exchange, where the anonymous public interacts with the film's characters. This space I conceive as a kind of *consciousness,* leading to what we might call, the rooms of the mind or the *unconscious* that are built off of it. The rooms play out the interior lives of the black and white heterosexual couples respectively, while the public arena serves as a mixed zone where all enter freely, pass through and out of, are overheard. Significantly, this is also the zone of the homosexual, the '*border type*'" ("A Flight to Unity"). As I have noted, H.D. never comments on homosexuality *as* "border type" in her pamphlet, though Child is correct to note its "border" status in the film.

30 Friedman, "Modernism of the 'Scattered Remnant,'" 100.

31 See *Close-Up* 5, no. 2 (1929) (a special issue devoted to race and cinema) for an understanding of the POOL group's attempts to intervene in racist filmmaking practices in Hollywood and British film traditions.

Matthew Tinkcom

SCANDALOUS!

Kenneth Anger and the Prohibitions of Hollywood History

Kenneth Anger's achievements in filmmaking continue to sustain his status as one of the leading proponents of avant-garde cultural production, but Anger's writings remain largely neglected by critics and historians of the cinema. In films such as *Fireworks* (1947), *Scorpio Rising* (1964), and *Inauguration of the Pleasure Dome* (1954), Anger forges an aesthetic vision that interweaves groundbreaking innovations in film style, some of the earliest alternative cinematic depictions of male homosexuality, and the occult and its accompanying countercultures, while his film experiments continue to influence younger film and video producers in the present moment, not least among them Martin Scorsese, in his much-lauded use of popular music as scoring, and John Waters, in his investigations of marginal subjects within the "trash aesthetic." As J. Hoberman has written, "*Scorpio Rising* points the way towards *Easy Rider* and *L.A. Plays Itself, American Graffiti, Mean Streets* and every MTV video ever made."[1] Yet, Anger's rendering of Hollywood history, found in his *Hollywood Babylon* volumes, has remained almost entirely unexplored. In some measure, critical neglect of the *Babylon* volumes may stem from the perception that these volumes, or the "Holy Babies" as Anger has referred to them, are ancillary to his film productions, or even more dismissively, his published writings may appear as accessories to the production of Hollywood publicity. While it is indeed true that part of the appeal of *Hollywood Babylon* resides in its shocking and provocative use of tabloid imagery and gossip, Anger's project in the books is not simply one of compiling the detritus of Hollywood's long history of love affairs gone sour, "perverse" sexualities, and gruesome suicides. Worth remembering is that Anger situates his materials in the context of an important argument about the role of Hollywood cinema in contemporary American life. Further, the antagonistic stance toward Hollywood found in the *Babylon* books appears not from a left or Marxist interrogation of capitalist corporate production, the more customary venues for critique, but from Anger's camp sensibilities and his intense fandom of Hollywood cinema, which allow him to investigate the industry's compulsively heteronormative representations.

Beginning with the 1950 J. J. Pauvert edition of *Hollywood Babylone* (in French) and continuing through the various editions appearing in the United States from the mid-1960s onward, Anger offers a critique of Hollywood, and his is a critical project that derives from his position as a fan. Further, Anger writes from within the discursive strategies of gay male camp, strategies of dissemblance, subterfuge, and ironic play.[2] Because of these countervailing tendencies within his work (Anger's critical eye toward Hollywood's near-total exclusion of images of homoerotic desire, his loving embrace of Hollywood iconography), we witness in the *Babylon* volumes a simultaneous delight in the gossip in which Anger traffics and use of gossip-driven fan accounts to rethink the status of Hollywood as a purveyor of purportedly "wholesome" entertainment; Anger interrogates Hollywood in the context of his vast fan knowledges and fan devotions. Similar to the interpretive work of many fans, his version of Hollywood is forged in tension and in concert with official and unofficial publicity apparatuses, for Anger is first a fan of the Hollywood cinema, *if* fandom is conceived as those practices that allow popular cinema's followers to engage with the publicity of the industry while also inventing their own readings of its limits to address their frequently marginal status. By marginal, I mean to suggest that most fans are hardly in a position to shape the meanings of the Hollywood cinema from the vantage point of industrial production. *Hollywood Babylon* stands as counterhistory to an idealized Hollywood offered both by journalistic enterprises that are aligned with the industry (think of *Entertainment Tonight's* endless nostalgic parade of "old Hollywood" stories) and by figures seemingly remote from Hollywood (House Speaker Newt Gingrich's invocations of *Boy's Town* [1938] as a model for civic reorganization).

In order to understand how Anger goes about the work of interrogating the monolithic construction of "Hollywood History,"[3] it is crucial to understand his position as a gay camp fan of the subject matter. Gay fandom has historically differed from other fan practices as they are described by critics such as John Fiske and Janice A. Radway,[4] in that gays have often had to be comparatively discreet in how they appear as fans, and thus have deployed camp rhetorical strategies in order to circulate their writings. One question, though, that repeatedly arises in regard to fan culture is whether fandom is not solely a compensatory practice, in that fans illuminate the moment of capital's almost complete saturation of the cultural sphere, where studios, record companies, and publishers profit directly from the ways that subjects choose to cope with their own alienation from the making of the cultural commodities that they consume. This argument has particular repercussions for gay fans, in that they appear complicit with the invisibility that Hollywood and contemporary conservative and homophobic social discourses on dissident sexualities seek to encourage.

At the same time, fandom has sometimes lent itself to celebratory descriptions of subjects who fashion their own readings of popular culture. For example, Judith Mayne comments that Radway's work in *Reading the Romance* evidences a high degree of projection on the part of the author, wishing as she (Radway) may that the female romance readers whom she interviews are agents of a different variety of feminism than that of the academy. As Mayne observes, "I doubt seriously, for instance, that the Smithton women [Radway's ethnographic subjects] would agree with the necessity of understanding the reading of romance fiction in the categorical terms of critique or celebration."[5] Mayne's question is not one of whether Radway's interview subjects are "genuine" feminists in need of the critical terms with which to understand how they are addressed by the publishing industry but rather is a query of the extent to which we might often wish fans to display a particular form of resistance to the industrial modes of production and distribution. This is no small matter; as Mayne suggests, "I do not say this in order to imply cynically that no alternative positions of spectatorship are possible, but rather to suggest that one of the most persistent myths of spectatorship (and of theory) that has perturbed and in many ways hindered the analysis of spectatorship is the belief that it is not only possible, but necessary, to separate the truly radical spectator from the merely complicitous one."[6] While Mayne describes the predicament of attempting to conceive of historical subjects as complex and contradictory (that is, as inhabiting everyday life), the degree to which she resorts to characterizing readers of romance fiction, and indeed all recipients of popular forms, as "spectators" tells something about the legacy of a particular theoretical insistence on viewers' engagements with those forms as always appearing to create "proper" and suitable subjects for capital within patriarchal constructions of femininity. By thinking of the consumers of popular culture as "spectators," we fall into the habit of prioritizing cinema viewing, and especially the attendance of narrative studio film, over and above other activities that are implied by fandom (reading fan magazines, collecting star images, fantasizing, and daydreaming). Further, the theoretical models for addressing film culture, which are gathered under the name of *spectatorship,* can have the effect of forming too rigid a binarism of male/active and female/passive, where there seems little room for the mobility of sex/gender difference to afford a larger variety of responses to popular culture.

Miriam Hansen suggests that one of the most powerful figurations of Laura Mulvey's still-provocative theory of the film viewer, that of the transvestite, has been seriously neglected. Hansen comments that "the figure of the transvestite suggests that female spectatorship involves dimensions of self-reflexivity and role-playing, rather than simply an opposition of active and passive. The perceptual performance of sexual mobility anticipates, on a playful, fictional level, the possibility of social arrangements not founded upon a hierarchically fixed sexual identity."[7] Situating the fascination of Rudolph Valentino in the 1920s in relation to racist, nationalist discourses of the period, Hansen suggests that women fans became interested in Valentino precisely to the degree that he offered a vision of ethnic, "non-American" male sexuality beyond the current Hollywood fare. In addition, a male star such as Valentino offered a figure in whom women fans may have fancied some likeness (his "foreign" polished effeminacy), while simultaneously fantasizing themselves as objects of his seduction; hence, viewer responses among Valentino's women fans may have been characterized by the sexual mobility (i.e., transvestism) to which she alludes. Importantly, Hansen does not seek to rescue Valentino as an emblem of an imaginary utopian space, but rather seeks to "delineate the contours of a female subjectivity, with all its contradictions and complicity, in the institution of cinema and the text of film history."[8] The intertwined nature of such "contradictions and complicity" that arise within fan devotions do not dispel, in the case of Valentino, the importance of racism, homophobia, and nationalism, which helped to define his image and through which the star came to have a following, but do suggest the complexity of female fan responses as they reveal shifting definitions of femininity, sex, and consumerism.

We should heed Mayne's advice and not try to wish the complexity of viewers' experience on behalf of a chimerical "free zone" of reception; likewise, we should also wonder why "compensatory" fan practices might so quickly be disallowed. When we recall "compensation" as not only that which serves as an equivalent (its more usual monetary and legal sense) but also that which offsets an error or defect, as in the case of fandom's compensatory power, we recognize that while fans do not garner substantial financial profits from their fan labors, they do draw attention to how official forms neglect their social presence. The fact that fans do not transform the culture industries at the level of altering them as capitalist enterprises does not, at least to me, disallow the potential of fans to shape their own readings and the subcultural networks that value those readings. Equally, fan labors redirect and refashion the value-potential of star publicity beyond corporate profit itself: we detect the importance of fan labors in the industry's attempts to exploit fan formations by reincorporating (some, but not all of) those efforts into the product.

One remarkable aspect of the phenomenon of gay viewership should then be noted, namely, that gay male fan discourses on popular cinema are not simply coincidental to the forging of gay languages and social circles; cinema and popular culture more generally have been vital to the very forming of those things in the first place. As Mayne observes, "the question is not what characterizes gay/lesbian spectatorship as common responses to film texts, but rather what place film spectatorship has had in the cultivation of gay/lesbian identity."[9] That is to say, when we address gay spectatorship, we cannot assume a fully developed gay identity in advance of a gay-inflected commentary upon cinema; the relation between film—and in this particular discussion, Hollywood film—and gays is a dialectic in which neither of those two categories, Hollywood cinema or gay identities, can be seen as stable and unchanging.

One of the most striking challenges posed by the fan writing of *Hollywood Babylon* is that of a contemporaneous readership that would have been actively interpreting the innuendo and dissemblance in these texts. As the historical moment of their writing recedes from us, the possibility of discovering such readings becomes more remote, but I take this as an indication of their power in the moment of their appearance. No scandal, to my knowledge, accompanies the gay authorship of these texts, although the history of *Babylon*'s publishing, with its initial appearance remote from Hollywood, suggests that camp responses to Hollywood star iconography could for a long period only inhabit the margins of film culture.[10]

The *Babylon* volumes dwell upon failed marriages, masked sexual "perversions," and the panoply of suicides found among the lives of the Hollywood film colony, but these salacious features of Anger's work can eclipse his overall vision of Hollywood, one that he pronounces at the outset of the project in 1959. Even as he invokes the prurient fascination of stars' lives, Anger reminds us that the traditions of Hollywood cinema revolve around titillation and gossip, and, even more provocatively, each instance of a new scandal carries with it the power to offer some "new" revelation about Hollywood heretofore unseen—not simply the novelty of an emerging scandal, but the sense that a larger dimension of film culture might be glimpsed through the star scandal. Citing the scandalous images of Theda Bara and Louis Glaum, and hinting at D. W. Griffith's propensity for "très jeunes personnes," Anger writes of the more recent scandal involving the murder of Lana Turner's boyfriend, Johnny Stompanato, by her daughter Cheryl: "there's nothing astonishing about these [recent events], for the winds of scandal flare again from the pinnacle of the American film industry: the prominent trial 'Hollywood versus *Confidential*,' the sensational drama of Lana Turner with her own gigolo-gangster, write themselves perfectly into the traditions of the American cinema."[11] Referring to the libel suits brought by Dorothy Dandridge and Maureen O'Hara against *Confidential* magazine in 1957, Anger locates the recent reportage surrounding Stompanato's murder within a longer history of Hollywood scandal. It is Anger's overarching project to show how scandals have long been a staple feature of the commercial cinema's production of its own sense of the lurid. For Anger, the sense that the litigation surrounding *Confidential* might seem to have heralded a transformation in the accountability of the tabloid press only, in fact, served to show how deeply embedded fan gossip and the discourses of secrecy and revelation that underpin gossip were circulated within the larger setting of popular cinema and its reportage. That is, the *Confidential* trials revealed in more spectacular fashion what had long been crucial to Hollywood's appeal—namely the perverse, the other, the "unnameable" dimensions of gossip. In a subsequent American edition, Anger notes that the public discourses of scandal after the *Confidential* trial changed significantly, but only in the degree to which they saturated other domains of star production, for stars could financially benefit from the admission of their sins and had much to lose from their *exclusion* from the uses of gossip and tabloid excitement. Anger suggests that, after Maureen O'Hara's suit against *Confidential* was settled, stars "started coming out with their own 'tell-all' autobiographies. Why let others cash in on their private lives when they could rake in the bread for themselves?"[12]

Despite numerous revisions of the first volume of *Hollywood Babylon* through its various editions, it has retained a historical sense of the complicated long-term bond between the scandal-driven press reportage and the studios that appeared to be repressing scandal.[13] Read as a fan's history of film colony gossip and scandal, then, it is significant that the various editions of *Hollywood Babylon* open with accounts of the scandals that inaugurated the earliest moments of Hollywood star-driven tabloid culture.[14] Among these are the 1920 suicide of Olive Thomas, the 1921 death of Virginia Rappe (allegedly at the hands of Fatty Arbuckle), and the 1922 murder of director William Desmond Taylor. Referring to the spectacular treatment of these events in the popular press of the 1920s, Anger claims that "the 'star system' was born: at once the dogma and rites of this new cult were established, the entire world fell into step with it. In France, Scandinavia, Germany, Italy, Japan and in India, the cinema relied upon the 'cult of personality' and this formula assured its fortunes."[15] The fortunes of Hollywood, we learn, are not simply pinned to the creation of a star system, a version of Hollywood history that the industry itself has long liked to circulate, but more specifically, as Anger would have it, to the creation of the star-scandal system. This insight allows Anger to read Hollywood publicity, from its earliest moments, as a history in which stardom and scandal are closely linked and, indeed, constitute one another within the ideological field of popular culture, and it is in particular scandalous sexualities that form a large part of Hollywood's dynamics of production. *Babylon* depicts the event of the star scandal as emerging in sync with the screening of the cinematic image and the formation of a star system within the studios. Star gossip, movie magazines, film attendance, and fantasy about stars, all form, according to Anger, part of a larger network through which Hollywood has been responsible for the creation of contemporary notions of sexuality, wealth, consumerism, and class mobility within the global setting for the Hollywood product.

Indeed, one of the most important features of *Hollywood Babylon* is its insistence that what Hollywood produces is a larger constellation of social meanings than can be apprehended in terms of a particular film and its exhibition. Anger disrupts an opposition between accepting Hollywood *films* as ratifying a wholesome, normalized set of traits (heterosexuality, proper bourgeois values, familialism) and Hollywood *gossip* as a secondary phenomenon that occasionally undermines such depictions through its devotion to stars. Rather, *Hollywood Babylon* refuses to isolate gossip as a lesser feature of star lore, and perversely reads Hollywood backward through its gossip in order to interrogate the too often prioritized (and idealized) notion that Hollywood only sought to suppress its own power to titillate. In the 1959 edition of *Hollywood Babylon,* for example, Anger reprints as an appendix the Censorship Code with an accompanying epigraph from Saint Matthew, warning that "if your hand is an object of scandal, cut it off." Anger seems to have anticipated Michel Foucault's notion of the production of contemporary sexualities through their apparent prohibitions, the net effect of the Code's presence in *Babylon* demanding that we perceive censorship as signaling the presence, and not the omission, of contentious sexual representations (but not only that: criminality, blasphemy, alcoholism). Of course, as the paradoxical scriptural injunction reminds us, the problem of locating scandal in relation to the whole "body" of Hollywood (to cutting it off) is that gossip's energies and enthusiasms derive from the fascination with scandal that is allegedly redressed, but in fact may only be heightened, by censorship.

Anger offers a reading of Hollywood through its own allegedly prohibited history. One strategy for recuperating such a suppressed history appears in his lavish illustrations, taken from Hollywood publicity, scandal sheets, and his own private archive. While the text details myriad Hollywood love affairs, bouts with alcohol and careers in demise, the graphics do not accompany Anger's writings as chunks of evidence, so much as they invite the reader to conjecture about the connotative possibilities for reading them in the ways that Anger suggests are possible.[16] For example, in a chapter in *Hollywood Babylon II* entitled "Odd Couples," Anger offers staged studio publicity shots of housemates Cary Grant and Randolph Scott, which might have appeared as "innocent" depictions of two stars enjoying domestic pleasures as two of Hollywood's most eligible bachelors, the captions intoning "Cary and Randy: at home, at the pool, harmonizing and out at the fights." Nowhere does Anger suggest that Grant and Scott might have been lovers (a long-standing Hollywood rumor that survives today),[17] but such a conclusion is left to the reader through her or his interpretation of the photographs as more than just cheerful publicity about the joys of bachelor life, but also a record of gay coupledom within the strictures of Hollywood censorship. I would hazard that part of the appeal of *Hollywood Babylon* resides in its unwillingness to trace specifically the valences of unarticulated desires and repulsions that many of the images attempt to evince in the books' readers. While Anger captions many of the photos with tongue-in-cheek (and let's say it: often bitchy) commentary, the effect of these comments is one that invites the reader to try to imagine the alternative "straight" reading of the material, an exercise in which the ideological fissures of star imagery begin to open up with dizzying effect.

One might object to the *Babylon* books in that they seek to claim knowledge of the private domains of the lives of Hollywood stars and can only substantiate such knowledge through innuendo. Such literal readings of the books fail to account for the fact that the *Babylon* books assume a familiarity on the reader's part with the practices of reading and sharing gossip, practices that form part of Hollywood's own impulse to profit from gossip-driven knowledge. In the 1965 American edition, Anger offers a definition of stardom that situates scandal centrally within the industry and locates the star icon as an effect of fans' desires to know more than the censored versions of publicity can supposedly reveal:

> the Hollywood religion—"Star Worship"—of the Heavenly Bodies began when the flicker-figures doffed their anonymity, taking each a made-up name (obligatorily euphonious—Bunny, Dove, Pretty, Sweet), matched with a made-up personality, and a colorful, spicy "private affair"—necessarily an enormous snow-job—the whole teetering structure supported by press-agents' handouts, planted news items, slush-and-gush fan-magazines, and studio-inspired fan-clubs. The desires and frustrated appetites of the fans were focused into an awesome kind of bug-eyed, Beatlesque, frenzied worship; ready to erupt at any public glimpse of the idol in the flesh, and, more pertinently, conditioned to *pay* and *pay* and *pay* for his shadow at the box office.[18]

By citing earlier moments of star production in conjunction with more recent events (in this case, the contemporaneous appearance of Beatle fandom, but other examples might be substituted: Madonna, Michael Jackson, Tupac Shakur), Anger seeks to articulate fan practices and the economics of studio profit ("*pay* and *pay* and *pay*") that accommodate them. Throughout the *Babylon* project, we repeatedly discover Anger's treatment of the spectacle of Hollywood scandal as continuous with filmgoing, leading us to an important question: that of whether gossip, be it produced seemingly in concert with or against Hollywood reportage, should be seen as transgressive of other versions of Hollywood history. If the industry is structurally predicated upon the inclusion (which *appears* as an exclusion) of scandal within its own publicity-driven discourses, then are fan knowledges, as we see them played out in *Hollywood Babylon,* necessarily at odds with what the industry might wish for the reception of its product.

To my mind, this problem is illustrative of the strictures that confront "marginal"[19] recipients of cinema of all sorts, gay men not the least among them, and which need to be theorized in such a way that allows for a subtle interplay between fan knowledges and the industry's recognition that such knowledges circulate beyond the control of the industry. It is not simply the case, within Anger's reading of Hollywood public-relations materials, that the studios generated a singular and monolithic set of representations, and then subsequently all spectators accommodate themselves as they might within particular discursive limits; instead, scandal and tabloid culture indicate those most contentious of matters that the industry might not necessarily address in its more central texts (i.e., the films) but do address in other productions, say of stardom within tabloids and gossip magazines. Anger illustrates those traits of Hollywood life that could not appear on the big screen, at least to the extent that the use of drugs and alcohol, extramarital and promiscuous sex, and blackmail and a host of other crimes, could not appear in conjunction with the articulation of star images within Hollywood films. (Of course, both before and after the implementation of the Hays Code, Hollywood adapted to the Code while appealing to audience interest in those phenomena.) Anger recognizes, though, the fascination with sexual perversity and criminality in relation to stars' "real" lives, as they were imagined in gossip and in the scandal-driven tabloid press that Anger dwells on.

Having suggested that *Babylon* functions primarily as a gay fan textual production of Hollywood history, it is important here to clarify that many of the books' strategies for recalling Hollywood lore take part in the gay male camp habit of focusing upon female star iconography, and it is telling that scandalous sexuality is thematized in *Babylon* around one primary topic: female (largely heterosexual, but sometimes lesbian) erotic pleasure.[20] Despite the books' many references to the homoerotic dimensions of male stars' private lives, read as an exercise in fan textual production, *Hollywood Babylon* centers its concerns with the status of female sexuality and sexual pleasure. The appearance of this theme as an organization of the books is not all that surprising, given the situation of Hollywood within the terrain of contemporary sexualities; what is surprising is the degree to which Anger does not link female sexuality with narratives of dissolution and demise. Despite contravening treatments of the matter to be found within conventional Hollywood film history, which focus on the containment of female sexuality, Anger offers the possibility of finding representations of "prohibited" sexualities within the very materials of Hollywood star discourses that do not wholly condemn such sexual pleasures. For Anger, many of Hollywood's most important female stars circulated as powerful images of how sexual and social regulation and questions of power are sent askew in the wake of images of female star icons.

The portrayal of female sexuality within *Babylon,* in fact, attributes the dissolution of heterosexual marriage to that institution's failure to accommodate pleasure on the woman's part. Anger reverses the usual depiction of marital breakup, seeking to understand how marriage denies sexual pleasure, particularly that of women, rather than seeing divorce as the fault of an excessive female sexuality. In his relatively lengthy treatment of Mary Astor's relationship with George S. Kaufman, Anger fixes his discussion around the discovery of Astor's diary. There, Astor wrote of her relation to Kaufman in detail, and her subsequent "downfall" arose from her husband's discovery of the diary and use of it in their divorce proceedings.

Although she was, through the litigious circulation of her diary, held hostage to the demands of proving herself a "respectable woman," Astor eventually was awarded custody of her daughter and given property rights. Anger's account, driven through his impulse to endorse Astor's extramarital sexual pleasure, concludes with the fact that her career did not suffer in the aftermath of the scandal but in fact flourished; as Anger crowingly comments, "it is significant to note that Mary Astor's screen career *did not* go glimmering after all this torrid exposure. Hollywood took note, as it was confirmed that Mary's box-office had actually *climbed* after all the to-do over her carefully noted love life."[21] This latter fact, not lost on Anger, draws our attention to the relation between the press's rendering of a female star's nonmarital erotic life and her continued popularity at the box office, for such publicity served to ratify the star, within her offscreen (but widely reported) private life, as an emblem of erotic pleasure for whom marriage became an institution of control and prohibition. Astor's career did in fact flourish after the revelation of her affair with Kaufman, much in the same way (as Anger reminds us) that other stars' careers were bolstered through scandal: Robert Mitchum's marijuana-possession arrest of 1948 and Errol Flynn's 1942 rape trial (in which he was acquitted), serve to remind that scandals can launch a new career and revitalize an old one.

Within the gossip-driven accounts of the lives of female stars, there were of course limit-cases, and for Anger's work the regulation of what could be depicted within Hollywood, both on and off the screen, appears in his handling of two figures, Mae West and Frances Farmer. West became a contentious figure within Hollywood because, according to Anger, she used her motion-picture vehicles as a venue in which to play out her unapologetic delight in her own body and those of her favored muscle-boys. Paradoxically, if West staged herself publicly as an icon of feminine sexual self-delight, she carefully orchestrated her private life in order to avoid scandalous reportage, all the while creating an even greater speculation about her erotic prowess; Anger remarks that, "while Mae has never been known to lack male company, and has always shown a marked preference for boxers and body-builders to actors and playboys, she has always been most careful to draw the shades."[22] Drawing the shades on her offscreen relations would not be enough to counter the innuendo that her onscreen presence came to galvanize. West became a central figure for the industry's censorship codes, and from Anger's account emerges the paradox of gossip: lowering the shades is always potentially (within the realm of fantasy) a way of raising them. Nevertheless, Anger's rendering of West deliberately avoids situating her as a figure of abjection; writing in 1965, he delights in the fact that "today, as always, the one-and-only Mae West could say: 'It's not the men in my life that counts—it's the life in my men.'"[23]

Counterposing the figure of West for Anger is that of Frances Farmer, the Hollywood actress whose career ended abruptly in 1942 with a drunk-driving violation. Anger recounts in detail the events leading to this star's exile from Hollywood through prisons and mental hospitals; the chapter on Farmer, "Daughter of Fury: Frances, Saint," offers a hagiographic account of an artist involuntarily unable to control her antagonism to the police, courts, psychiatrists, and other agents of the contemporary institutions that legislate and patrol ideals of appropriate femininity. While Hollywood itself later attempted to resurrect Farmer as a figure of independence and powerful femininity, Anger records the demise of her career in order to understand how the industry has consistently handled its talent: by insisting on the allure of its stars, but disavowing them when they prove too much of a liability.

On the whole, *Hollywood Babylon*'s distinction from other forms of star discourse arises in its insistence on retrieving the biographies of such "failed" stars as Mae West and Frances Farmer as significant for having been *both* those things: as stars and as failures whom the studios were unwilling to support at the moment in which they appeared to be risks. To hear them described by Anger, the lives of Astor, West, and Farmer are triumphs over the hypocrisy of Hollywood politics, where the studios actively recruited nonconforming talent in order to garner box-office profits, all the while remaining unwilling to support, legally or otherwise, these figures when they erupted outside the boundaries of propriety. Yet, these women have hardly remained staples of Hollywood star canons from its classic period, and in fact enjoy a status mostly within a "trash" aesthetic of Hollywood cinema to which Anger has been pivotal.

In this regard, it seems that *Hollywood Babylon* may confuse its own version of stardom (a celebration of degeneracy and the perverse) with the supplanting of another (wholesomeness, glamour), and one response to Anger's writings might be to insist that he "merely" glorifies the nasty and brutish goings-on of the film colony. Although Anger's emphasis on stardom as a site of contestation over what stars mean to viewers replicates the very spectacle he seeks to undercut, focusing on this inclination loses sight of the fact that fan-produced texts, which I understand *Hollywood Babylon* to be, function within and against the powerful and far-reaching star discourses of the industry's own invention.

Within the *Babylon* project's tendency to celebrate its own version of morbid stardom, it evokes camp fandom as a powerful strategy for demystifying star-production through the latter's own terms. By quoting so heavily from trade-press articles, Hollywood gossip, and publicity photographs, *Hollywood Babylon* appropriates the materials of star discourse and often emulates them; yet *Babylon* interrogates stardom, as a site of scandal, in order to convey how little Hollywood production of the star commodity has changed since the first scandals in the 1920s.

Inhabiting the contradictions of star culture, Kenneth Anger embraces the individualizing and personalized notions of stardom while simultaneously reminding his readers of the industry of which stars are a significant feature—and I am not convinced that this has been an unimportant project. To the degree that the *Hollywood Babylon* books have succeeded, within a popular venue, in making visible the camp fan who doubts the motives of the film industry and the primacy of its self-depiction, the "Holy Babies" project retrieves the debris of Hollywood in order to make sense of fans' alienation from the false promises and bogus claims of star culture. In the closing of the first volume of *Babylon,* Anger quotes from a bit of Hollywood's own pathos-laden self-description:

I walk along the streets of sorrow
The Boulevard of Broken Dreams
Where Gigolo—and Gigolette
Can take a kiss—without regret
So they forget their broken dreams
You laugh tonight and cry tomorrow
When you behold your shattered schemes
And Gigolo—and Gigolette
Wake up and find their eyes are wet
With tears that tell of broken dreams . . .[24]

These lines, excised as Anger notes from the 1934 Warner Bros. production of *Moulin Rouge,* offer a now-clichéd rendering of the film colony's ambivalence around stardom and its allure. And yet by citing them so prominently, Anger points to the ways that Hollywood occasionally can acknowledge that, indeed, it has known all along how complicated and desperate its product is.

NOTES

1   J. Hoberman, *Vulgar Modernism: Writing on Movies and Other Media* (Philadelphia: Temple University Press, 1991), 175.

2   Camp has emerged in the past thirty years as a significant feature of critical theory and historical work on gay subcultures, and even its definitions are disputed. Nevertheless, one can understand camp heuristically as a signifying practice that emerges in gay male urban subcultures in the past century, a practice that emphasizes irony, artifice, and performance. In Chris Jones's succinct definition, camp is "a critical attitude which involves looking at texts less as reflections of reality than as constructed sets of words, images and sounds at a distance from reality. The attitude involves irony or detachment when considering this distance" (Jones, "Lesbian and Gay Cinema," in *An Introduction to Film Studies,* ed. Jill Nelmes [London: Routledge, 1996], 264). See also Andrew Ross, "Uses of Camp," in *No Respect: Intellectuals and Popular Culture* (New York: Routledge, 1989), 135–70; Susan Sontag, "Notes on 'Camp'" in *Against Interpretation* (New York: Farrar, Straus and Giroux, 1964), 275–92; Eve Kosofsky Sedgwick, *The Epistemology of the Closet* (Berkeley: University of California Press, 1990), 150–57.

3   Anger seems to be addressing the popular journalistic account of Hollywood, witnessed in the pages of *Photoplay, Confidential,* and other fan magazines; more contemporary versions can be found in the pages of *People, Enter-*

tainment Weekly (the upscale publishing venues), as well as the *Globe, Sun, National Enquirer,* and *Weekly World News.*

4   Fiske's and Radway's immensely important contributions to the discussion of fandom demonstrate that fans actively shape the meanings that they derive from the objects of their fan devotions (Madonna fans, in Fiske's studies; popular-romance readers, in Radway's work) even as they encourage discursive and material limits to their participation in the creation of popular culture. But the fans whom Fiske and Radway describe seldom are called upon to conceal the particular concerns that fandom allows them to express, in the way that camp allows gays to comment upon mass culture without being named as perverse or dissident subjects. Nevertheless, it seems to me that Fiske and Radway offer what are the sustaining questions for current work on fan culture; Fiske's analysis of the coterminous economies of fandom to those of the industry, and Radway's ideological critique of the complexities of fan affective investments have suggested a variety of avenues for subsequent work on fan culture. See John Fiske, *Understanding Popular Culture* (Boston: Unwin Hyman, 1989), 69–102, and Janice A. Radway, *Reading the Romance: Women, Patriarchy, and Popular Literature* (Chapel Hill: University of North Carolina Press, 1991). For other readings on this topic, see Jane Feuer, *Seeing Through the Eighties: Television and Reaganism* (Durham: Duke University Press, 1995); Henry Jenkins, *Textual Poachers: Television Fans and Participatory Culture* (New York: Routledge, 1992); and Jackie Stacey, *Star Gazing: Hollywood Cinema and Female Spectatorship* (London: Routledge, 1994).

5   Judith Mayne, *Cinema and Spectatorship* (London: Routledge, 1993), 84.

6   Ibid., 86.

7   Miriam Hansen, *Babel and Babylon: Cinema and Spectatorship* (London: Routledge, 1993), 84.

8   Although she does not expand upon this insight, Hansen does offer that Valentino seems to have had a gay following, her primary form of evidence residing in Anger's tribute to the star in *Hollywood Babylon.* The citation of Anger does not so much demonstrate that a significant gay cult of Valentino existed during the star's ascendancy as much as it forms a moment through which Anger is typically referenced as an ethnographic resource. Nevertheless, Hansen implies an important affinity between gay camp fandom and female fans' culting of Valentino, inasmuch as they offer readings of a star contrary to what might be expected.

9   Mayne, *Cinema and Spectatorship,* 166.

10   The question of gay discourses as having only inhabited the margins of representation, that is, the question of the metaphors of invisibility, becomes increasingly important for gay theory and history. Robert J. Corber, in fact, argues that invisibility was not the problem for gay writers such as Gore Vidal,

Tennessee Williams, and James Baldwin, but rather that their writings failed to coincide with, and indeed antagonized, all variety of orthodox politics—left and right—of the 1950s. See Robert J. Corber, *Homosexuality in Cold War America: Resistance and the Crisis of Masculinity* (Durham: Duke University Press, 1997).

11   Kenneth Anger, *Hollywood Babylone* (Paris: J. J. Pauvert, 1959), 8. Translation mine.

12   Kenneth Anger, *Hollywood Babylon* (New York: Bell Publishing, 1975), 266.

13   Gossip forms an important part of the experience of alterity; yet gossip in its relations to everyday life, popular culture, and representation has been little theorized or historicized. Despite the obvious intractability of the topic in its capacity to be verified—it is hard to "prove" gossip, and that's indeed the point—the subject deserves greater attention. For treatments of the topic, see Patricia Mellencamp, *High Anxiety: Catastrophe, Scandal, Age and Comedy* (Bloomington: Indiana University Press, 1990), and Patricia Meyer Spacks, *Gossip* (Chicago: University of Chicago Press, 1985), for two considerably different feminist treatments of the subject.

14   The publishing history of the *Hollywood Babylon* volumes is as labyrinthine as anything described in their own pages. The first edition appeared in France in 1959, while an English version appeared in 1965. By the mid-1960s, some of the recent events to which Anger had drawn his readers' attention in the first edition had lost their immediacy and were deleted. Further, Anger revised the volume extensively in each of its subsequent printings, and while the tone and argument of the book remain largely intact, many of the illustrations that contained graphic nudity were omitted for the American edition, which was issued in softcover. When *Hollywood Babylon II* was published in 1984, it contained several portions from the first French edition that American readers had never seen before in combination with new materials. As with his film work, Anger's projects can seldom be said to be completed, returning as he does to rework older materials. One photo in *Hollywood Babylon II*, a photo of Marlon Brando, is captioned "why is he laughing? He knows that I can't print the indiscreet photo of *him*" (Anger [New York: Dutton, 1984], 284–85), suggesting the promise of perhaps a third volume.

15   Anger, *Hollywood Babylone* (1959), 10. Translation mine.

16   The similarity between Anger's use of photographs and illustrations to abet the reader's critical powers and those offered by way of leftist critique are striking. John Berger, for example, structures *Ways of Seeing* as a pedagogic exercise in which the reader is invited to analyze uncaptioned reproductions of Western figure painting through critical terms of property, class, and gender difference, forging a dialectic of interpretation through written text and photo-reproduction. Similarly, Anger provides his reader with star photo-

graphs whose meanings become unstable when analyzed in the spirit of his commentary, for we can consider how even Hollywood's own official discourses host a variety of interpretations and responses. See John Berger, *Ways of Seeing* (London: British Broadcasting Corporation and Penguin Books, 1977).

17 For a compendium of Hollywood gossip, whose legitimacy is ostensibly authorized by the author's claim to gay identity, see Boze Hadleigh's *Hollywood Babble-On*, which sustains long-standing gossip about stars. Indeed, the volume's punning title signals its debt to Anger as integral to gay commentary on Hollywood. Hadleigh's book purports simply to be quoting stars as they gossip about each other, thus attempting to validate the authenticity of the material and claiming truth-value because such gossip is said to have its origins within Hollywood. Boze Hadleigh, *Hollywood Babble-On: Stars Gossip About Other Stars* (New York: Birch Lane Press, 1994). Steven Cohan's unpublished work on Judy Garland listservs and Web sites suggests in fact that fans do not necessarily seek adjudication from Hollywood for what can be deemed proper and improper gossip; rather, fans negotiate the truth-value of every claim about a star in relation to the body of gossip *and* official discourses, sometimes preferring alternate readings of a star over the available official ones.

18 Kenneth Anger, *Hollywood Babylon* (Phoenix: Associated Professional Services, 1965), 21.

19 I call attention to the effects of labeling such subjects as "marginal" (that is, not central to Hollywood production) because gay viewers may not have been explicitly addressed as the industry's intended audience, but through gossip and anecdotal history insert themselves into the circulation of star imagery.

20 I am here momentarily cleaving sexuality from other illicit practices, such as alcohol bootlegging and suicides, although virtually every "forbidden" subject intersects with another at some moment in *Babylon;* alcoholics have affairs, stars emerge from unhappy alliances to take their lives, and so on.

21 Anger, *Hollywood Babylon* (1965), 198.

22 Ibid., 217. For an account of West's fascination as sexualized female star icon and her status as a camp feminist emblem, see Pamela Robertson, *Guilty Pleasures: Feminist Camp from Mae West to Madonna* (Durham: Duke University Press, 1996).

23 Ibid.

24 Ibid., 295.

Jim Ellis

QUEER PERIOD

Derek Jarman's Renaissance

Another Country (1984, dir. Marek Kanievska) opens with the camera moving up a river toward a British public school in the 1930s. Intercut with this intensely pastoral vision are scenes of a young journalist arriving at a dingy, memorabilia-laden, Moscow flat to interview British traitor and homosexual Guy Bennett about his schoolboy past. *The Last of England* (1987, dir. Derek Jarman) opens with Jarman sitting at his desk writing, accompanied by a voice-over about memory. This scene is followed by another in which an actor, Spring, destroys a copy of Caravaggio's *Profane Love* (a prop from Jarman's *Caravaggio* [1986]): "Spring kicks the painting and masturbates over it. It's a love/hate relationship. Meanwhile I'm filming and this is not a passive camera but a cinematic fuck, my shadow falls across him" (*LE*, 190).[1] A comparison of these two beginnings points to the difference between two cinematic approaches to the past, between what we might designate the gay period film and the queer period film. For the former, as for the conventional period film in general, the past is always another country, a site of lost plenitude invested with nostalgia. The period film offers the chance to speak with the dead, to revisit an imagined past of grace, simplicity, and noble suffering. Queer period, on the other hand, offers no such nostalgic consolations. While Jarman may have wanted to fuck with the dead, to "find a dusty old play and violate it" (*QE2*, preface), he only ever wanted to speak to the living.

Jarman's vision of history and of art is a decidedly activist one: he repeatedly stated that he made his films for himself and his community, and his engagement with historical subjects is often an attempt to wrest them away from the official guardians of the past, in order to secure a happier future. As he says in *Queer Edward II*, "I have a deep hatred of the Elizabethan past used to castrate our vibrant present" (112). Time and again in his journals he scornfully remarks on the British film industry's obsession with period films: he lambasts *Chariots of Fire* (1981) as a "damp British *Triumph of the Will*" (*DL,* 197), "jingo, crypto-faggy Cambridge stuff" (*LE,* 112), and he renames *Brideshead Revisited* (1981) "Brideshead Recidivists" (*DL,* 14). The 1980s in Britain saw a resurgence of what Andrew Higson has named the "heritage film": period films that revisit privileged texts, eras, or sites of English nationalist tradition.[2] The hugely successful *Chariots of Fire* was widely seen as the beginning of a new British film renaissance, which would later include the Merchant-Ivory Edwardian fantasies, the various Raj treatments, and World War II homefront dramas. The end of the decade saw the emergence of Kenneth Branagh and Emma Thompson, who would shepherd this merchandizing of nostalgia into the 1990s. Although heritage films were by no means the only British cinema product of the 1980s, they certainly seemed to dominate them. When the film industry declared 1985 "British Film Year," in an attempt to lure the public back to the theaters, thirteen of the twenty-one films chosen for attention were period.[3]

Jarman doesn't do period, at least not in the conventional manner. His films of the Renaissance are clearly for the present, and insistently reference the present, whether it is Elizabeth Welch singing "Stormy Weather" to a crew of hunky sailors in *The Tempest* (1979), the OutRage activists in *Edward II* (1991), or the typewriters and motorcycles in *Caravaggio.* Jarman distinguishes his approach to history from that of the heritage film by placing it in a tradition that includes Caravaggio's approach to historical subjects. The heritage film, on the other hand, is the heir of the " 'scientific,' archaeological method" of Poussin and David, where "painting turned into an obsessive catalogue of detail" (*Ca,* 45): "*Brideshead Revisited* or *The Draughtsman's Contract* are the archaeological field in the way that they are visualised. It seems to me that the other tradition is one in which the past is always contemporary, in the sense that the past is always the present. So when Caravaggio painted biblical scenes they were always of people of his period, and all the medieval pictures are like that. It's only a recent tradition that creeps in by the way of someone like Poussin who does it properly and makes it look like Rome."[4] Jarman sees the difference between these two approaches as an ideological difference, and certainly it operated in that way in the British heritage film of the 1980s. *Chariots of Fire,* one of Ronald Reagan's two favorite films that year, "chimed in with the craving for some sort of national revival, the theme of Margaret Thatcher's election campaign two year's previously."[5] The film's "main narrative of class exclusion was one of middle-class entitlement, and amid the patriotic excess of the Falklands-Malvinas war, the film's critique became tantamount to a Thatcherist parable."[6] At the other end of the decade is Kenneth Branagh's *Henry V* (1989), which, although labeled a "post-Falklands" war film, is really only "post" in the sense that it came after, its purported antiwar message amounting to the banal conservative credo that war is hell but it builds character. Branagh and Thompson consulted Prince Charles on the portrayal of the king, which many have read as a portrayal of Branagh himself: the apotheosis of Thatcherite individualism.[7]

The ideology of period films, however, is not solely (or even largely) attributable to their narratives. Regardless of the politics of the source texts or even the script, the visual pleasure offered by period detail in these films swamps whatever critique they may originally have had. Higson notes, for example, that "in the adaptations of the Forster and Waugh novels, contemporary social satires and comedies of manners are transformed into period pieces"[8] through the standard period treatment. When we remember that the "obsessive catalogue[s] of detail" (*Ca,* 45) that are the hallmark and the chief appeal of the period film are most often the fetishes of a faded imperial glory, the inescapably conservative nature of the genre becomes clearer. Jarman's refusal to provide the visual pleasures of period, whether through an aggressively antirealist mise-en-scène, or the pointed use of anachronistic props and language, both circumvents and implicitly critiques the trap that is almost constitutive of the genre.

If there were such a category as the queer period film, Jarman would have to be recognized as its foremost practitioner. The theory behind this sort of film would be similar to the historiographical principles outlined by Rosi Braidotti: "Following Foucault, I see resistances as a way of politically activating counter-memories, that is to say, sites of non-identification with or non-belonging to the phallogocentric regime. . . . Thus, the political function of the intellectual is closely linked to her/his capacity to bypass or deconstruct the linearity of time, in a set of counter-genealogical moves."[9] Jarman's films of the Renaissance constitute a series of such counter-memories, which function as challenges to the nostalgic, Thatcherite construction of England's glorious past in the cinema of the 1980s. Colin MacCabe notes that "For Jarman the investigation of what it is to be English is inseparable from a reworking of the controlling myths of the English Renaissance,"[10] since these myths form the core of English nationalist sentiment. This reworking of the Renaissance takes several forms. The most obvious of these is to choose key Renaissance texts—Shakespeare's sonnets or *The Tempest*—and "improve" them (as he says of his *Edward II*), in order to contest the dominant readings. This contestation is often accomplished by disrupting the narrative in order to allow other narratives to emerge, and pointedly including anachronisms that point to the history of the text's transmission. Jarman also reworks or restages Renaissance aesthetic forms, most obviously painting in *Caravaggio,* but also the sonnet sequence in *The Angelic Conversation* (1985) and the masque in *Edward II.* Yet another strategy for reworking the Renaissance, and one that will be of central interest to this essay, is to invoke unorthodox Renaissance discourses that are marginal to the usual account of the period. For Jarman, the discourses of Neoplatonism, hermetism, and alchemy were potent sources of counter-memories with which to resist homophobic constructions of the past and the present.

Although critics often draw attention to Jarman's interest in alchemy and the ideas associated with it, few go on to explore what precisely attracted him to this unorthodox world and what use he may have made of it. Before turning to the films, I will discuss some of the Renaissance texts that interested him and speculate on how they may have surfaced in his work. This will be followed by detailed discussions of an earlier and a later film: *The Angelic Conversation* (1985), Jarman's film of Shakespeare's sonnets, and *Edward II* (1991), his adaptation of Marlowe's play. In *The Angelic Conversation,* Jarman's interest in alchemy as an alternative art is relatively explicit, as it was in other films he made around this time. In *Edward II,* the explicit references to alchemy are gone, and he takes up instead the masque, a theatrical form closely linked to alchemy and hermetic thought that strives to erase the boundary between the real and fictional. What these films share is an activist approach to history and an appropriation of Renaissance knowledges incorporated at the level of technique. The appropriation of these texts and knowledges constitutes a counter-genealogy, a challenge to the dominant construction of the present through the redeployment of discourses of the past.

ALCHEMICAL CONJUNCTIONS

In his earlier films, Jarman invokes the early modern practice of alchemy for a wide range of reasons: as a parallel for his own artistic practice and artistic community, as a source of metaphor and technique, but most importantly perhaps, as an earlier example of an art form that is explicitly

interested in transformation. Thus, although Jarman was certainly interested in the "homosexual" figures and texts of the Renaissance, the early
modern personalities populating his texts and films are more often phi-
losophers of one form or another: Neoplatonists, hermetists, alchemists,
heretics. John Dee held for Jarman the most fascination, appearing in one
way or another in *Jubilee* (1977), *The Tempest, In the Shadow of the Sun*
(1980), and *The Angelic Conversation*. Marsilius Ficino appears frequently in
his writings, as do Cornelius Agrippa, Pico della Mirandola, and Giordano
Bruno (one of whose texts the young Caravaggio reads with his patron,
Cardinal Del Monte, in Jarman's film). Alchemy is occasionally invoked by
Jarman as a metaphor for his own art: film, he writes, is "the wedding of
light and matter—an alchemical conjunction" (*DL*, 188). This connection
is made more directly in *The Tempest*, where Prospero's alchemical draw-
ings are actually images of cameras: "On the floor the artist Simon Reade
drew out the magic circles that were blueprints of the pinhole cameras he
constructed in his studio next to mine at Butlers Wharf" (*DL*, 188). Jarman
sees the Renaissance alchemists and hermetists as an embattled group on
the fringes of sixteenth-century society, practicing an esoteric art under the
constant threat of persecution. The accusations of witchcraft and sodomy
that were inevitably made against them connect them in Jarman's imagination with early modern sexual minorities: "In the cities, people must have
identified in underground groups; leading to rumours of covens, celebrat-
ing 'wild' sexual acts" (*DL*, 21).

The conditions of production and exhibition of Jarman's early films resemble in a way this demimonde of the alchemists. These films, he says,
were "home movies, an extension of my father's and grandfather's work.
The difference, of course, is that they don't record family life" (*LE*, 54).
At least not conventional family life: like Jack Smith's *Flaming Creatures*
(1963), Jarman's Super-8 films are made with and for a small group of initiates. "What I discovered in film was community. I discovered my world
in film. I wasn't the director in those Super-8 films in that sense. I merely
directed the camera." [11] Even in his later films, this interest in his community remained. Of *The Last of England* he wrote: "I would never say I am
making this film for an audience: that's very dishonest. It would be true
to say I am making this film for myself with my collaborators, we are the
community" (*LE*, 197). This film ends with the image of a boat full of refu-
gees rowing off in stormy seas into the dark, perhaps the most poignant
evocation (among many) of marginal or embattled communities in Jar-

man's films.[12] For Jarman, modern-day queers are the heirs of the heretical and sexually suspect alchemists.

Alchemists and queers share more than simply marginality, however. The secret language of the alchemists becomes for Jarman an example of a potent counterdiscourse that parallels queer film practice. At the end of *Jubilee* Queen Elizabeth sighs, "Oh John Dee, do you remember the whispered secrets at Oxford like the sweet sea breeze, the codes and countercodes, the secret language of flowers?" (*DL*, 252). Jarman explains that "Part of my interest in the magician John Dee was his pre-occupation with secrets and ciphers. Why this obsession with the language of closed structures, the ritual of the closet and the sanctuary? the prison cells of Genet's *Un Chant D'Amour,* the desert encampment of *Sebastiane;* Anger, insulating himself with magick, screening himself off" (*LE,* 60). In a 1985 interview he remarks, "I think of the area of magic as a metaphor for the homosexual situation. You know, magic which is banned and dangerous, difficult and mysterious. I can see that use of magic in the Cocteau films, in Kenneth Anger and very much in Eisenstein. Maybe it is an uncomfortable, banned area which is disruptive and maybe it is a metaphor for the gay situation."[13] These comments throw into question Tony Rayns's claim that "the alchemical equations and symbols that pepper [Jarman's] paintings and films co-exist rather awkwardly with the overtly gay elements, as if they were secretly intended to dignify what would otherwise be straightforward carnal representations."[14] John Collick is more judicious in his assessment of Jarman's interest in alchemy, linking it to more general countercultural movements. He argues that "The rediscovery of ancient myths and belief systems like alchemy and magic during the 1960s and 1970s was one of the many nostalgic attempts to create a homogeneous and liberating counterculture in the face of an alienating mass culture."[15] Although Jarman may have participated in a more general rediscovery of alchemy and related pursuits, his interest in it differs significantly from, for example, Anger's use of the "black magick" of Aleister Crowley. The use to which Jarman puts alchemy is by no means nostalgic (although it was certainly countercultural) and is in fact one of the queerest aspects of his work. Recognizing this, however, requires some further elaboration of Jarman's understanding of hermetic thought.

In *Dancing Ledge,* Jarman recalls explaining Frances Yates's *Art of Memory* to someone he picked up while cruising. Although Yates's versions of the Renaissance and especially of John Dee have recently been challenged

as overly syncretic, Jarman's understanding of alchemy and the Renaissance magus seems closely related to hers.[16] Yates and those scholars associated with her at the Warburg Institute established the dominant frame
for understanding Renaissance hermetism and alchemy and their relation
to Neoplatonism. These critics emphasized the centrality of hermetic philosophy to Neoplatonism, both of which were introduced into fifteenth-
century Florence through the translations of Marsilius Ficino. Hermetic
philosophy was based on the texts of Hermes Trismegistus, wrongly assumed to be a contemporary of Moses: "These texts aroused considerable
interest because they presented a particularly exalted conception of man
as a semi-divine intermediary between the divine and the terrestrial and
as capable of creating his own nature, the key to which was the practice
of magic for both power over the created world and the attainment of
spiritual communion."[17] This hermetic conception of man as semidivine
had its most famous and influential statement in Pico della Mirandola's
Neoplatonic "Oration on the Dignity of Man," and magic gained a certain
legitimacy by association.

Like Yates, Jarman sees in Ficino the conjunction of various aspects of
the Renaissance: a revolt against the orthodoxies of Catholicism and Aris-
totelian scholasticism, a legitimation of ancient pagan arts and knowledges,
and the Neoplatonic validation of male same-sex desire. He writes that "In
the 1430s a fourteen-year-old boy could be burnt at the stake for an act of
sodomy—this would not happen in Florence again. Platonism confirmed
that it was right and proper to love someone of your own sex" (Ch, 58).
This new acceptance of sodomy is for Jarman connected with a more general revolution in thought, which shocked medieval Christian orthodoxy:
"Ficino translated Plato in the Platonic Academy and initiated the Renaissance, which uncovered the old gods, rescuing them from the abandoned
gardens, placing them back on their pedestals. The Neoplatonic garden re-
instated the old polytheism, charting a path through the psyche in groves
and arbours, terraces and temples. Here, pageants and parties, statues and
fountains, conceits and practical jokes were set to music and fireworks"
(Ch, 66). This last sentence recalls Jarman's own early Super-8 films such
as "Picnic at Ray's" (1975), "Gerald's Film" (1976), "Removal Party" (1976),
and "Jordan's Dance" (1977), which are often records of "pageants and
parties . . . conceits and practical jokes . . . music and fireworks." He sees
in the hermetic belief in the interconnectedness of all things an acceptance

and celebration of the diversity of creation, a philosophy that for him contrasts sharply with the restricting confines of contemporary British culture.

The hermetists envisioned the universe as a vast system of correspondences and hierarchies, ruled by the influence of the stars, and ultimately
by God or the One behind the stars. Everything in the universe was composed of the four elements of earth, air, fire, and water. The hermetic
science of alchemy attempted to alter the composition of these elements
in a substance, and thus transform the substance itself. Natural magic, a
pursuit closely related to alchemy, worked by manipulating the secret correspondences between things to draw on the power of the stars. In a 1651
translation of Cornelius Agrippa's *De Occulta Philosophia* (a copy of which
Jarman owned, and which appears on Prospero's desk in *The Tempest*),
Agrippa introduces the subject by saying that

> Magick is a faculty of wonderfull vertue, full of most high mysteries,
> containing the most profound Contemplation of most secret things,
> together with the nature, power, quality, substance, and vertues therof,
> as also the knowledge of whole nature, and it doth instruct us con-
> cerning the differing, and agreement of things amongst themselves,
> whence it produceth its wonderfull effects, by uniting the vertues of
> things through the application of them one to the other, and to their
> inferior sutable subjects, joyning and knitting them together thor-
> oughly by the powers, and vertues of the superior Bodies [the stars].[18]

As a result of these correspondences, "things under *Mars* are good for
the head, and testicles, by reason of *Aries,* and *Scorpio.* Hence they whose
senses faile, and heads ake by reason of drunkennesse, if they put their
testicles into cold Water, or wash them with Vinegar, find present help."
The hyacinth "has a vertue from the Sun against poisons, and pestiferous
vapours; it makes him that carries it to be safe, and acceptable; it con-
duceth also to riches, and wit; it strengthens the heart; being held on the
mouth, it doth wonderfully cheer up the mind."[19] The hermetists used
the plants, stones, animals, times, or persons connected with a star to call
down its influence to heal the sick or help the well.

According to Ficino, the images of things also contain a healing power,
an idea that would have an obvious appeal to Jarman, who trained as a
painter. Yates discusses Ficino's instructions for painting an image of the
world on a ceiling, so that after gazing upon it, a person will better appre-

hend the true nature of the universe: "By arranging the figure of the world and its celestial images with knowledge and skill, the Magus controls the influence of the Stars."[20] This belief in the power of images is at the heart of the arcane memory system constructed by Giordano Bruno, for whom "the classical art of memory . . . has become the vehicle for the formation of the psyche of a Hermetic mystic and Magus. The Hermetic principle of reflection of the universe in the mind as a religious experience is organised through the art of memory into a magico-religious technique for grasping and unifying the world of appearance through arrangement of significant images."[21]

The hermetist technique for changing perception through the correct combination of images provides another perspective on the techniques used in Jarman's longer experimental films, *The Last of England* and *The Garden* (1990), as well as shorter works such as *The Queen Is Dead* (1986), a promotional film made for the Smiths. In all of these, Jarman uses video technology to juxtapose or superimpose images, often contrasting images of flowers with images of industrial decay. This is not to say that Jarman learned montage from Giordano Bruno rather than, say, Eisenstein and Anger, but rather that the particular combinations of images he uses are reminiscent of hermetist thought, adapted, of course, to a queer perspective. A sequence of *The Queen Is Dead,* for example, combines in rapid succession images of a blue boy, a burning car, suburban streets, and Piccadilly's statue of Eros, and superimposes the silver silhouette of a flower on the rotating figure of an angel against a backdrop of swimming goldfish. While these experimental works are all more or less non-narrative, they are at the same time determinedly political, attempting precisely to alter the viewer's perception of the world through the combination of significant images. This technique of commingling images becomes a new memory system for Jarman, a way of reactivating or appropriating a much older counterdiscourse.

Central to Jarman's appropriation of hermetic image systems are flowers. Flowers are for Jarman persistently associated with memory; poppies, the archetypal flower of remembrance, appear in virtually every film. In hermetic thought, flowers are often used as therapy or prophylaxis. In the films, flowers come to signify a therapeutic form of memory, a memory associated with desire. In the sequence of *Aria* (1987) directed by Jarman, flower petals rain down as an old woman remembers love; in *The Last of England,* the Spenser Leigh character remembers the Tilda Swinton character in a field of flowers; in *Jubilee,* Elizabeth and Dee reminisce about the language of flowers, Dee declaring "Sweet Majesty, to me you are the celandine now as then before, balm against all melancholy" (*LE,* 252). *Modern Nature* further consolidates these connections, using traditional lore on the significance of flowers to trigger both memory and political commentary. As Jarman observes of the painters Gilbert and George, "like them, I can find strength in flowers, boys and childhood memories" (*MN,* 91). These alternative arts of memory are crucial for the survival of the community, as is suggested by the subtitle of Jarman's most overtly political volume of autobiography, *At Your Own Risk:* "A Saint's Testament."[22]

While Jarman is returning to older discourses, it is not due to nostalgia or a perverse intellectual dilettantism but rather to reclaim certain sites for the construction of a queer subjectivity in the present. Jarman's interest in alchemy is not simply antiquarian, nor does he use it as a source for quaint iconography. It stands rather as an oppositional knowledge system that celebrates the diversity of creation and that occupies a metonymic relation both to the Neoplatonic celebration of same-sex desire, and to an approach to representing history that is, for Jarman, exemplified by Caravaggio's historic paintings. The Renaissance art of memory becomes for him a way of activating counter-memories and sites of non-belonging to the phallocentric order (to recall Braidotti's formulation). At the same time, Jarman finds in the alchemists and the practice of magic a way of imagining his own artistic community, a tradition of gay filmmaking that includes Eisenstein, Cocteau, Genet, and Anger.

THE ART OF MIRRORS

The Angelic Conversation is part of a trinity of early films, including *The Tempest* and *Jubilee,* that challenge the nostalgic construction of the twin pillars of the English Renaissance, Shakespeare and Elizabeth. In particular, *The Angelic Conversation* picks up what has always been the most potentially disruptive part of Shakespeare's canon, the homoerotic sonnets addressed to the young man, and flaunts their unorthodoxy. Although these three films are very different, each use the Elizabethan period as a point of contrast, all conjuring up in one way or another the figure of John Dee, mathematician, astronomer, antiquarian, hermetist, and alchemist.

A contemporary of Elizabeth I, Dee corresponded with her under the reign of Mary and acted as a consultant to her government during her reign. History has not been kind to the reputation of Dee, principally because of his association with alchemists and his attempts with the alchemist and scryer Edward Kelley to converse with angels. Scrying was a relatively common (although not entirely respectable) practice of "seeing visions in smooth or reflective surfaces,"[23] such as mirrors and obsidian plates. (Jarman, it might be argued, updates this practice to include movie screens.) Scrying inevitably brought with it charges of necromancy, which dogged Dee's final days and sealed his reputation for centuries. Frances Yates began a rehabilitation of Dee, calling him a "Prospero who touches the Elizabethan age at almost every point,"[24] and historians of science are beginning to reevaluate his role in the development of mathematics, navigational arts, and astronomy. In both *The Tempest* and *Jubilee* Jarman follows Yates in linking Prospero and Dee: Prospero carries a staff topped by Dee's hieroglyphic monad, an occult sign that Dee believed contained all the wisdom of the universe. In *Jubilee* Dee's angel Uriel is renamed Ariel, who responds to Dee's commands by quoting Shakespeare. Contemporary critics have taken this one step further, calling Jarman himself a latter-day magus.[25]

Jubilee begins with Elizabeth summoning Dee and asking him to show her the future. Through a flash in a mirror, Ariel brings the queen and her retinue to a postapocalyptic London where law and order have been abolished, the entertainment industry runs the world, and a small band of murderous female punks and queers roams the streets, killing cops and glam rockers. Peter Wollen argues that the film "is a protest against the whole horrendous notion of the 'second Elizabethan age', the backdrop of national grandeur and creativity against which Britain's economic and cultural decline was played out for twenty-five years."[26] Filmed in 1977, *Jubilee* can be read as something of preemptive strike against the heritage industry of the 1980s.

In *Jubilee* the flash in the mirror is used to show Elizabeth the future. C. L. Whitby notes that "the use of mirrors (catoptromancy) and of crystals (crystallomancy) were the most popular methods of divination in the sixteenth century."[27] The flashing mirror, which Ariel holds over his crotch, is an image that gets repeated in the films that follow, and one whose significance for Jarman could well stem from his reading of Dee: "optics plays a crucial role in Dee's magic as well as in his astrology because of the conformity of natural causes to the laws of optics. Dee points out that, 'if you were experienced in catoptrics you would be able, by art, to imprint rays of any star much more strongly upon any matter subjected to it than nature itself does,' which practice is 'the greatest part of natural magic.'" [28] The mirror in the film is used on the level of narrative as an unorthodox device for transmitting secret knowledges, and the flash in the camera's eye functions to physically affect the audience in an unorthodox way of transmitting experience. What does not come from Dee, of course, is the placement of the mirror on the angel's crotch. This recalls the conjunction of alchemy as an alternative knowledge and the queer filmmaker as producer of alternative knowledges about desire.

Reading Ariel as a cipher for a heterodox conjunction of knowledge and desire may help to explain the significance of the flashing mirror in Jarman's film of Shakespeare's sonnets (the title of which, *The Angelic Conversation*, Jarman credits to the alchemist Dee). Angels are frequently if obliquely associated with gay desire in the experimental films, whether it is Ariel with his shining crotch, the statue of Eros in Piccadilly Circus (a famous rendezvous for hustlers), or the angelic lovers here. In the book after which Jarman names his film,[29] Dee relates his many conversations with the angels, consultations that he undertook when, he says, "At length I perceived that onely God (and by his good Angels) could satisfie my desire, which was to understand the natures of all his creatures."[30] Jarman's *Angelic Conversation* is similarly undertaken due to his dismay at the failure of conventional wisdom, as well as the British film industry, to comprehend diversity. It is an attempt, Jarman said, to explore new psychic landscapes on film, or as Dee might have said, to understand the nature of all God's creatures.

Like *The Tempest*, *The Angelic Conversation* has a way of collapsing history into the present moment. In *The Tempest* the costumes "are a chronology of the 350 years of the play's existence, like the patina on old bronze" (*DL*, 196). In *The Angelic Conversation* a selection of Shakespeare's sonnets provides an oblique commentary on a series of hallucinatory images that range from young men meeting in a Renaissance garden, to the hulks of burning cars and radar towers. The anachronism is not simply used here to suggest the relevance of the past text to the present, or to make parallels between two periods, or even to insist upon the presentness of the past, although it does do all of these. By including the intervening years, both films engage with their primary texts as cultural productions with histories of transmission and reception. These histories become inescapably part of the object itself. The approach is thus genealogical, rather than the archaeological method of Poussin or Greenaway.

If Jarman's method is to engage with the received, palimpsestic text in the present, rather than an imaginatively reconstituted archaeological text, it will be useful to specify what the dominant tradition of reading the sonnets has been. As Eve Kosofsky Sedgwick notes in *Between Men,* the sonnets have traditionally been interpreted in a dehistoricized, novelistic way:

> *The* tradition of the Sonnets is the tradition of reading them plucked from history and, indeed, from factual grounding. There are all the notorious mysteries of whether they are a sequence, when they were written, to whom and to how many people addressed, how autobiographical, how conventional, why published, etc., etc. To most readers of the sequence, this decontextualization has seemed to provide a license for interpreting the Sonnets as a relatively continuous erotic narrative played out, economically, by the smallest number of characters — in this case four, the poet, a fair youth, a rival poet, and a dark lady.[31]

Jarman's answer to this decontextualization of the sonnets is not to stage a return to their original moment, even if this were possible. History is restored in some way, but as with *The Tempest,* it is the history of the sonnets themselves that is restored, not the historical moment of their inscription. This relation to history is visualized in the opening sequence, where a young man in contemporary dress looks out through the diamond panes of a Tudor house. A similar condensing gesture occurs toward the end of the film, when a man in suit, carrying a fan, walks through the gardens of an Elizabethan mansion.

Sedgwick argues that the early sonnets addressed to the young man take place within a homosocial context akin to that of the Greeks, and in that sense cannot truly be considered as "homosexual," at least insofar as that term is inevitably understood as being opposed to heterosexual: "The Sonnets present a male-male love that, like the love of the Greeks, is set firmly within a structure of institutionalized social relations that are carried out via women: marriage, name, family, loyalty to progenitors and posterity, all depend on the youth's making a particular use of women that is not, in the abstract, seen as opposing, denying, or detracting from his bond to the speaker."[32] Studies by Alan Bray and Lorna Hutson of the configurations of early modern male friendship tend to confirm Sedgwick's judgment that male friendship was an openly eroticized relation of mutual economic and social benefit.[33] The interruption of the dark lady into the sonnets shows what happens when an actual woman intervenes, and becomes the focal point in a Girardian erotic triangle, where the rivalry between the men is perhaps the strongest relationship. Jarman's film disrupts the possibility of such an erotic configuration occurring; in his film the dark lady is represented by one of the two lovers, now in a dark suit, holding a fan. None of the sonnets read are from the early group urging the young man to marry, or the latter group concerning the perfidy of the dark lady.

The sonnets are read not by one of the actors onscreen, who seem to represent the poet and the young man, but by Judi Dench, in an offscreen voice-over. Jarman explains, "I asked Judi Dench to read them, I wanted a woman's voice so there was no confusion. If I had used a man's voice it would have seemed that one of the young men was talking about the other. One of them would have the dominant voice, and I didn't want that to happen, so the voice became that of an observer, leaving the imagery autonomous" (*LE,* 143–45). There is clearly more at stake here in Jarman's description of his reconfiguration of the dramatis personae than simple gender-blind casting. The dark lady is, in one sense, written out of this film, but then, as Sedgwick observes, "The dark lady is, for the most part, perceptible only as a pair of eyes and a vagina" in the sonnets.³⁴ Making the speaker's voice feminine in a film that focuses on the homoerotic sonnets may work to resist the circuit of homosociality that these sonnets describe. The more typical film scenario is reversed as the bodies of the young men become the erotically invested objects of the gaze and the woman is granted the agency of the voice. Thus the woman in this film is not the conduit of desire between man but rather a dissociated voice for it. At the same time, the voice becomes a reminder of the alienation of image and text, and the inaccessibility or opacity of the images onscreen.

Jarman's reconfiguration of the sonnets partly works to resist the circuit of homosociality, but also in a sense recognizes that the particular scenario of desire traced by the sonnets is no longer possible. The erotic bond between the poet and the young man, which in the sonnets is not seen as mutually exclusive to a heterosexual relation, has given way to a society in which no erotic bonds between men are sanctioned, a fact that is registered by the constant presence of the radar towers looming over the lovers in Jarman's film. "Destruction hovers in the background of *The Angelic Conversation;* the radar, the surveillance, the feeling one is under psychic attack; of course we are under attack at the moment" (*LE,* 133). But the interest in the sonnets does not stem from a nostalgia for a homo past, as the homosocial bonds of the sonnets are strongly implicated in misogyny. The film disengages the homoerotic elements of the film from their historical context, in order to counter these attacks that are occurring in the present. This rewriting is precisely the refusal of nostalgia: there is no attempt to film a historically authentic version of the poems, even if the history used were that of Sedgwick rather than E. M. W. Tillyard. History is told for the present, and Judi Dench is speaking rather than Shakespeare. The film's dislocation of imagery and voice means that we have no direct access to the consciousness of any of the figures onscreen. No novelistic readings of these figures are possible.

This disjuncture is important because it resists another narrative that Joel Fineman locates in the sonnets, a narrative of subjectivation and heterosexualization, of the formation of the protomodern individual who is, it hardly need be added, male. This is accomplished, Fineman argues, by Shakespeare's reconfiguration of the poetry of praise from a poetics of homogeneity to one of heterogeneity, which profoundly alters the speaking subject of the poems and subsequently of literary history. This move from the singularly ideal to the corrupted heterogeneity, which is also a shift from the visual to the verbal, parallels the move from the love for the young man to the more complicated love for the dark lady. In so doing, argues Fineman, "Shakespeare in his sonnets invents the poetics of heterosexuality," by which, he says elsewhere, "I meant to specify a necessarily misogynist desire."[35] At the same time, Shakespeare invents what Fineman calls a poetic subjectivity: he argues that "the subject of Shakespeare's sonnets experiences himself *as* his difference from himself."[36] The rupture from the self that carves out his interiority occurs because he desires what he despises, the dark lady. The poetic subjectivity that Fineman sees Shakespeare creating is possible only through the intervention of the fantasy of the dark lady, who is as corrupting and duplicitous as language itself.

If, according to Sedgwick and Fineman, the sonnets record a heterosexualization of the male subject and, for Fineman, one of the first historical emergences of that subject, this is precisely the narrative that Jarman resists in *The Angelic Conversation*. In fact, it could be said that the film resists narrative altogether. Although Jarman has called the film a love story, it is not a love story in the usual sense. He gives a more descriptive account elsewhere, saying it is "A series of slow-moving sequences through a landscape seen from the windows of an Elizabethan house. Two young men find and lose each other. The film ends in a garden" (*DL*, 133). In terms of information about the characters, this is pretty much all we get. They never speak and are not given names. Their actions are not explained, no motivations or thoughts are ever given, except perhaps in a removed way by the soundtrack. If anything, they resist any attempts by the audience to know them in any but the most banal sense or to construct for them an interiority. Performing enigmatic tasks, gazing at sights beyond the camera's range, or, most pointedly, using a mirror to shine light back into the camera's eye, they refuse to come into the range of the viewer's comprehension. What is the point of the refusal? Part of it is specifically to avoid the illusion of the self-presence of the speaking subject of the sonnets, with an interiority constructed via the misogynist fantasy of the woman. But a more immediate reason for this refusal of access is specifically to avoid getting caught in the information systems of the masses, the hostile surveillance by the combined forces of the state and the dominant culture that is represented by the radar towers. The flashing mirror, as we have seen in *Jubilee*, transmits an alternative knowledge. Slipping under the radar in this way is a necessary survival tactic: to avoid the confining definitions of selfhood that limit the queer subject, if one is ever to end up in the garden.

This refusal of narrative, in particular the narrative of a heterosexual subjectivation, is complemented by the formal aspects of the film, through the way in which the images of the lovers appear. In order to get the particular effect he wanted, Jarman filmed *The Angelic Conversation* using a Super-8 camera running at high speed. The film was then projected at slow speed, which brings the speed more or less back to normal, and refilmed by a video camera, sometimes using color filters. The final product was then transferred to 35mm film stock. The result of the altered film speeds is to produce an effect something like a very rapid slide show. While the speed is normal, the action is quite clearly the concatenation of moments or of single frames, rather than a smoothly continuous motion. According to Jarman, "The single frame makes for extreme attention, a concentration that is voyeuristic. Time seems suspended. The slightest movement is amplified. This is the reason I call it 'a cinema of small gestures'" (LE, 146). The structure that Jarman describes is in fact very like that of a sonnet sequence: a concatenation of lyrical moments that seem to produce a narrative. In the film, however, attention comes to be focused more on the texture and the production of each moment, instead of on the illusion of motion that the combination of these moments produces; this effects, in another way, the refusal of narrative. This attention to the textuality of the moment is further emphasized by the graininess that is the product of all the image transfers. One effect of this image processing is to foreground the role of production, in this case the production of history: both history itself, and the history of the self.

If the way in which Jarman shot *The Angelic Conversation* draws attention to the production of narrative and of history, it can also work to transform it. This is hinted at in Jarman's explanation in *Dancing Ledge* of how he shot a particular segment of the film *In the Shadow of the Sun*: "This section is brought to a close with some refilmed footage off the screen at the Elgin Cinema in NYC of *The Devils*—the final moment when Madeleine escapes from the claustrophobic city of Loudun into the world outside, over the great white walls; but now, in my version, she walks into a blizzard of ashes" (130). We get a similar sort of thing happening at the end of *The Angelic Conversation,* where the image of the blossom gradually obliterates the image of the radar tower; a way of "cauterising" the "hovering, external violence" that lurks around the edges of the film. Jarman's remarks about *The Devils* are telling, however, because they address not just the *how* of image transfer or transformation but the *why:* in one version Madeleine escapes the city of Loudun, "but now, in my version, she walks into a blizzard of ashes." Evidently, more is altered in this process than just picture quality. By reprocessing an image we can change its meaning, its consistency, its texture, and its essence: a process that could well be called alchemical. In alchemy Jarman finds a powerful art of memory and transformation, which he translates into a filmic method for constructing alternative gardens of desire.

RESCUING EDWARD II

Jarman scorned the pretense to objectivity of the period picture, saying that his *Edward II,* for example, "resembles the past as any 'costume drama' (which is not any great claim)" (*QE2,* 86). In claiming for his films the same status as any other costume drama, Jarman is obviously not saying his films are authentic renditions of the past, but rather that the mainstream costume dramas are every bit as political as his more overtly activist revisionings of the past: "Filmed history is always a misinterpretation. The past is the past, as you try to make material out of it, things slip even further away. 'Costume drama' is such a delusion based on a collective amnesia, ignorance and furnishing fabrics. (Lurex for an Oscar)" (*QE2,* 86). Rather than looking to the Renaissance for a lost utopia of male desire, he uses it as a site of resistance to normative culture. Nowhere is this clearer than in his "improved" version of *Edward II.*

Edward II is a much-edited, rearranged version of Marlowe's play. It begins, as does the play, with the return of Gaveston, the king's lover, from exile and the resulting controversy among Edward's advisors. Jarman drops much of the political intrigue in order to focus squarely on the peers' attempts to separate the lovers, as they do by eventually killing Gaveston and imprisoning Edward. The role of Mortimer is increased to represent all of the peers, and the role of Isabella, the queen, in the peers' campaign is made less equivocal in the film. The play is reduced to a four-character drama, observed by a fifth: Edward, Gaveston, Isabella, and Mortimer battle it out in front of the eyes of the boy Prince Edward. With the exception of Prince Edward, none of these characters fares too well in the film version. Gaveston and Isabella come off as particularly monstrous, although all four commit brutal acts of violence. Jarman notes at one point in his shooting diary, "Andrew is not playing Gaveston in a way that will endear me to 'Gay Times'" (*QE2*, 20). Thuggish, petty, and vengeful, Gaveston brutalizes the bishop who arranged his exile, humiliates Isabella, and antagonizes the peers. Isabella is initially a sympathetic character, but through her rejection by Edward, her rough treatment at the hands of Gaveston, and the manipulations of Mortimer, she turns into a steely monster that is part Lady Macbeth (wringing her hands when ordering the execution of Edward) and part Lady Thatcher. When the time comes to kill Edward's brother, Kent, Isabella bites his neck and drinks his blood. This transformation is echoed by the portrayal of Gaveston in exile, after his humiliation by the bishops, as he crouches, howling like a werewolf, in the rain. Critics quite understandably labeled the portrayal of Isabella as misogynist, although it would perhaps be more productive to see her evolution in the film as a record of the deformations of a misogynist society, just as Gaveston's thuggishness is due at least in part to the homophobic society he rails against.[37]

As in *The Tempest* and *Caravaggio,* the costumes, props, and sets are a deliberate mix of time periods. In *Edward II,* these citations are pointed. Mortimer wears a British soldier's uniform and reads a copy of *Unholy Babylon,* a book about the Gulf War; the order to banish Gaveston is written on House of Commons stationery; the peers' forces are contemporary riot police. The costumes were much commented upon in the reviews, particularly those of Tilda Swinton, who appears in a different designer dress in every scene. (J. Hoberman remarked that "since everyone is . . . a raving fashion plate, it gives the impression of being filmed in a Soho emporium like Comme des Garçons.")[38] Both the showy costumes and the anachronistic props tend to forestall any possibility of the audience relating to this as a period film. Nor are they offered the usual period story. Although there is a narrative, the film works more as a series of tableaux. In many ways the film is much closer to a Renaissance masque than to a Renaissance play.

In Marlowe's *Edward II,* Gaveston declares upon being initially recalled to London:

> I must have wanton poets, pleasant wits,
> Musicians, that with touching of a string
> May draw the pliant king which way I please;
> Music and poetry is his delight,
> Therefore I'll have Italian masques by night,
> Sweet speeches, comedies and pleasing shows,
> And in the day when he shall walk abroad,
> Like sylvan nymphs my pages shall be clad,
> My men like satyrs grazing on the lawns
> Shall with their goat feet dance an antic hay. (1.1.50–59)

Bruce Smith notes that the entertainment that Gaveston describes resembles a masque performed in 1575 at Kenilworth for Elizabeth I.[39] In the script, Gaveston says the last five lines as a voice-over while a bodybuilder with a snake performs for the camera. Presumably this is an example of the sorts of entertainments that Gaveston will stage. Edward and Gaveston's lavish spending on their amusements is later one of the causes of discontent for the nobles. Mortimer complains that "The idle triumphs, masques, lascivious shows / And prodigal gifts bestowed on Gaveston, / Have made thy treasure dry" (2.2.157–59). Jarman differs from Marlowe in actually showing some of these masques and lascivious shows. The king and Gaveston are entertained at various points in the film by a pair of male dancers (from the dance company DV8), a poet reading Dante, Annie Lennox singing, and a string quartet playing a tango. Not only does the film show these elements of the masques but there are also a number of ways in which the film incorporates aspects of the form to become a kind of masque itself.

A Renaissance masque was an amalgam of dance, spectacle, and a fairly minimal script. Usually designed to be performed only once, masques featured extravagant costumes, perspective sets, and expensive stage machinery. Characters were often a mix of allegorical, mythical, and historical figures, and the story was generally a Neoplatonic allegory involving a conflict between order and disorder, which would be resolved in a dance that joined audience and actors. D. J. Gordon argues that "The audience's participation is crucial; even if they do not join in the dance, they join in the play. They are bound together by their capacity to understand, and the masque . . . functions to define their identity too, to assert their existence as a social group."⁴⁰ Although the function of the masque was generally to flatter the sovereign, masques were occasionally used as a vehicle for critique. In any case, they were always concerned with asserting a particular moral vision. Stephen Orgel argues that "The chief characteristic of the masque . . . is that it was an occasional production and appealed to its audience in a very special way. It attempted from the beginning to break the barrier between spectators and actors, so that in effect the viewer became a part of the spectacle. The end toward which the masque moved was to destroy any sense of theatre and to include the whole court in the mimesis—in a sense, what the spectator watched he ultimately became."⁴¹ The masque was also a form, according to Frances Yates, that was associated with hermetism and alchemy. She argues that "the masque is a case in which the connection in the Renaissance mind between magic and mechanics finds expression."⁴² Prospero, the great magus whom both Yates and Jarman saw as a depiction of John Dee, stages a betrothal masque for Miranda and Ferdinand in *The Tempest*. John Dee himself staged a masque-like theatrical performance at Trinity College, Cambridge, that earned him the reputation of conjurer.

It is not difficult to understand Jarman's attraction to this aesthetic form, with its assertion of a moral vision, its topical nature, and its attempt to erase the border between spector and spectacle. Colin MacCabe argues that Jarman had repeatedly attempted a "filmic subversion of the relations between representation and audience,"⁴³ a subversion he believes Jarman comes closest to achieving in *Edward II*. Seeing the film as a form of masque provides a context for some of its more anachronistic elements, the inclusion of Annie Lennox and the OutRage activists. Jarman's staging of the masque in his version of *The Tempest* provides the precedent for Annie Lennox's appearance in *Edward II*. In the earlier film, Jarman replaced the goddesses Ceres, Iris, and Juno in Prospero's masque with Elisabeth Welch singing her signature tune, "Stormy Weather," to a crew of sailors. Lennox is likewise associated with the song she sings: she had previously recorded "Ev'ry Time We Say Good-bye" for the Red, Hot & Blue AIDS benefit, and had asked Jarman to make the video. He was too sick at the time, but the video then turned into what is clearly a tribute to him. In the video, Lennox sings while home movies from Jarman's childhood (which also appeared in *The Last of England*) are projected onto a screen. In the video Lennox is obviously singing to and about Jarman, as she is, perhaps, in the film. Her appearance in *Edward II* thus imports into the film certain associations with Jarman and with AIDS, which further complicates the film's mode of address but clarifies that the film is on one level about what it means to be queer and/or HIV-positive in the oppressive climate of 1980s Thatcherite Britain.

This brutalizing, oppressive society is actualized in the film by the mise-en-scène, and by the way Jarman and his co-writers rearrange the script. As in *Caravaggio,* Jarman intersperses the death scene throughout the film. Although the audience may not realize it, the film opens with Edward already in prison, with Lightborn, the executioner, reading aloud the note that summons Gaveston from exile. Edward snatches the note back from him, and repeats the opening lines of the play: "My father is deceased. Come, Gaveston, / And share the kingdom with thy dearest friend." On "kingdom," Edward casts a baleful glance at the dungeon, suggesting kingdom and dungeon are coextensive. The repeated "returns" to the ending function like the radar tower in *The Angelic Conversation,* as a reminder of the violence that is always hovering nearby. After a couple of these flash-forwards, which establish the location of the prison and the identity of the executioner, Jarman plays scenes in the dungeon that do not take place there in the play. These scenes merge with the general prison-like atmosphere of the sets: a series of empty, cavernous rooms with stone walls and dusty floors, with the lighting making every scene seem to take place at night or underground. Figures are framed against these walls by long static shots, and posed in very formalized, almost geometrical, tableaux. By turning the film itself into Edward's prison, Jarman makes the simple but necessary point that gays still do not have equal rights and that homosexuality is still criminalized. But starting the film in the dungeon with Edward and Lightborn adds another dimension to the film. The persistent return of the ending raises the question as to what one does with a death foreknown. How does one act in the face of one's own imminent demise? Which is to say, the return of the ending turns the film into an allegory of AIDS, and more particularly, of Jarman's very public HIV-positive status. The film itself stands as one response to the challenge of being HIV-positive in the 1980s. In response to the question, "You're a pessimist?" Jarman responds in terms that are reminiscent of the tone of the film: "Not at all. The act of making the film is the opposite. I'm not cowering in this room,

I'm going down fighting, that's optimistic. This is war, it doesn't matter if I lose the battle, someone else will win the war" (*MN*, 167).

As with the anachronisms, the foregrounded and then disavowed ending provides a commentary on the play's reception history and its place in contemporary culture. The speech that begins "My swelling heart for very anger breaks" (sequence 46) takes place with Edward standing in the pool in the dungeon. (In the play, Edward's final place of imprisonment is the castle's sewers.) On the wall behind him is projected the shadow of Lightborn. This scene cuts to shots of Lightborn with a welding torch, heating the poker, and then to a scene of Mortimer with prostitutes. Mortimer is tied up, lying on his stomach, while the prostitutes grind their stilettos into his back and pull back his head with a leash and collar. The parallel to Edward's execution is clear, and can be read in one way as a commentary on the appeal of the play to straight audiences, and their prurient delight in the spectacle of the "poetic justice" meted out to this infamous "homosexual." This can, of course, be paralleled to the tabloid press's obsessive, prurient interest in gay sex and the concomitant punitive attitude toward HIV-positive gay men, both of which are documented by Jarman in *At Your Own Risk*. By relegating Edward's execution to the status of dream, Jarman denies the audience the sadistic pleasure that fuels much of the interest in the play.

This intervention in the text is made on behalf of the OutRage activists, who come to play the role of Edward's (nonviolent) forces in the war against the peers. The psychological violence of the prison of homophobia is matched by the violence of the state repression, as the protestors are first beaten and then executed against a wall. Along with Annie Lennox's performance, the OutRage activists are the most jarring and insistent intrusions of the present into the film, although they can both be linked to Renaissance theatrical practice. D. J. Gordon notes that the masquers were in no way concealed by their costumes. The characters they portrayed were meant to be continuous with their identities, a conjunction that functioned to draw attention to the topicality of the allegory. The masquers were from the same world as the audience, a point that would be emphasized in the final dance. When the film reveals at the end that it is a performance staged for the activists, it makes sense to read their earlier entrance into the fiction as the masquers, the forces of good who do battle with the anti-masquers, as emblematic of all that threatens civil society.

There is a sense in which the OutRage activists are fighting not for

Edward but for their history: "In our film all the OutRage boys and girls are inheritors of Edward's story" (QE2, 146). This battle for history, and the use to which histories are put, takes place in the present, in what is a clear filmic illustration of Walter Benjamin's sixth thesis on the philosophy of history, that "In every era the attempt must be made anew to wrest tradition away from a conformism that is about to overpower it. . . . Only that historian will have the gift of fanning the spark of hope in the past who is firmly convinced that even the dead will not be safe from the enemy if he wins."[44] Remembering that Kenneth Branagh's Thatcherite *Henry V* was released less than two years earlier makes the urgency of this struggle even clearer. The battleground on which the protestors are fighting could not be more appropriate: in addition to storming the police, the activists are, in effect, storming the BBC who, with British Screen, produced *Edward II*, and who are home to the most institutionalized reading of Renaissance texts, the BBC Shakespeare. It is to the invading forces that Jarman gives the film, the final shot tracking across a sea of seated protestors, as if to suggest that the play was a performance staged for them. This final shot thus echoes the gesture made in the final paragraphs of *At Your Own Risk*:

> I am tired tonight. My eyes are out of focus, my body droops under the weight of the day, but as I leave you Queer lads let me leave you singing. I had to write of a sad time as a witness—not to cloud your smiles—please read the cares of the world that I have locked in these pages; and after, put this book aside and love. May you of a better future, love without a care and remember we loved too. As the shadows closed in, the stars came out.
>   I am in love. (119)

Edward II, too, ends in love. In a creative act of disavowal, Jarman stages the famous execution as a dream sequence, and replaces it with a scene of the executioner, Lightborn, throwing away the poker and embracing Edward. Future queer lads are represented by the young Edward, dancing in partial drag to the "Dance of the Sugar Plum Fairies" on top of a cage that holds Isabella and Mortimer. Prince Edward is, like the activists, principally an observer in the film, although he does intervene in the end to imprison his father's captors. For the most part, however, he wanders through the film with a flashlight, occasionally shining it into the camera as if to take up the heritage of Ariel in *Jubilee* and the lovers in *The Angelic Conversation*.

Edward is and is not executed, but what remains is the possibility of love. The disavowed ending of Marlowe's play is emblematic of the odd mixture of sadness and defiance that infuse the film, and indeed, much of Jarman's later writings. The past—both his and England's—is not a lost utopia but more often a record of brutality and defeat. There are nonetheless moments of joy that can be rescued, and even moments of defeat can be used as a site for the mobilization of a community of desire and resistance. It is the role of the queer period film to seize these moments, and to provide an alternative art of memory for this community. Jarman's screen, like Ariel's mirror, is a surface with which to conjure the future.

NOTES

1   Quotations from Jarman's written works are cited in the text with the abbreviations listed below:

DL: *Dancing Ledge,* ed. Shaun Allen (London: Quartet Books, 1984).

Ca: *Derek Jarman's Caravaggio* (London: Thames and Hudson, 1986).

LE: *The Last of England,* ed. David L. Hirst (London: Constable, 1987).

MN: *Modern Nature: The Journals of Derek Jarman* (London: Century, 1991).

QE2: *Queer Edward II* (London: BFI, 1991).

AYR: *At Your Own Risk: A Saint's Testament* (London: Hutchinson, 1992).

Ch: *Chroma: A Book of Colour—June '93* (London: Century, 1994).

2   Andrew Higson, "Re-presenting the National Past: Nostalgia and Pastiche in the Heritage Film," in *Fires Were Started: British Cinema and Thatcherism,* ed. Lester Friedman (Minneapolis: University of Minnesota Press, 1993), 109–29. See also Tana Wollen, "Over our shoulders: nostalgic screen fictions for the 1980s," in *Enterprise and Heritage: Crosscurrents of National Culture,* ed. John Corner and Sylvia Harvey (London: Routledge, 1991), 178–93.

3   "Not one film was included by any of those 'uncomfortable' directors noted for their highly critical look at today's Britain. No *Jubilee,* no *Britannia Hospital,* no *Babylon,* no *Ploughman's Lunch;* no woman director's work, though Sally Potter's *The Gold Diggers* was eligible; no truly low-budget work by an independent director except *The Draughtman's Contract.*" (Alexander Walker, *National Heroes: British Cinema in the Seventies and Eighties* [London: Harrap, 1985], 270).

4   Derek Jarman, "Imaging October, Dr. Dee and other matters: An Interview with Derek Jarman," interview by Simon Field and Michael O'Pray, *Afterimage* 12 (1985): 55. For a less interested comparison of the historical methods of Jarman and Greenaway, which situates them in a tradition of modernism, see Peter Wollen, "The Last New Wave: Modernism in the British Films of the Thatcher Era," *Fires Were Started,* 35–51.

5   James Park, *British Cinema: The Lights that Failed* (London: B. T. Batsford, 1990), 144. Sheila Johnstone mentions the Reagan preferences and the marketing of the film in "Charioteers and Ploughmen," in *British Cinema Now*, ed. Martyn Auty and Nick Roddeck (London: BFI, 1985), 99–110.

6   Geoff Eley, "The Family is a Dangerous Place: Memory, Gender, and the Image of the Working Class," in *Revisioning History: Film and the Construction of a New Past*, ed. Robert A. Rosenstone (Princeton: Princeton University Press, 1995), 23.

7   For a reading of Branagh's *Henry V* in the context of British politics, see Graham Holderness, "'What ish my nation?': Shakespeare and National Identities," *Textual Practice* 5, no. 1 (1991): 74–93. See also Robert Lane, "'When Blood is Their Argument': Class, Character and Historymaking in Shakespeare's and Branagh's *Henry V*," *ELH* 61 (1994): 27–52.

8   Higson, "Re-presenting the National Past," 120.

9   Rosi Braidotti, "Revisiting Male Thanatica," *Differences* 6, nos. 2/3 (1994): 201.

10   Colin MacCabe, "A Post-National European Cinema: A Consideration of Derek Jarman's *The Tempest* and *Edward II*," in *Screening Europe: Image and Identity in Contemporary European Cinema*, ed. Duncan Petrie (London: BFI, 1992), 10.

11   Jarman, "Imaging October," 49.

12   Jarman's creation of a community through his filmmaking leads to interesting interfilmic relations: the actor who plays Borgia Ginze in *Jubilee* plays the pope in *Caravaggio* and Caliban in *The Tempest*; Madonna and child from *The Garden* become Isabella and Prince Edward in *Edward II*. Recognizing these relations, of course, means entering into the coterie that these films depict.

13   Jarman, "Imaging October," 58.

14   Tony Rayns, "Submitting to Sodomy: Propositions and Rhetorical Questions about an English Film-maker," *After-image* 12 (1985): 63–64.

15   John Collick, *Shakespeare, Cinema and Society* (Manchester and New York: Manchester University Press, 1989), 102.

16   For a good introduction to the place of Dee in early modern intellectual history, as well as a reevaluation of Yates's work, see Nicholas Clulee, *John Dee's Natural Philosophy: Between Science and Religion* (London and New York: Routledge, 1988). See also William H. Sherman, *John Dee: The Politics of Reading and Writing in the English Renaissance* (Amherst: University of Massachusetts Press, 1995).

17   Clulee, *John Dee's Natural Philosophy*, 4–5.

18   Henry Cornelius Agrippa, *Three Books of Occult Philosophy . . . ,* trans. J. F[rench] (London, 1651), 2–3.

19   Ibid., 66, 48, 52.

20   Frances A. Yates, *Giordano Bruno and the Hermetic Tradition* (London: Routledge and Kegan Paul, 1964), 75.

21   Frances A. Yates, *The Art of Memory* (Chicago: University of Chicago Press, 1966), 229.

22   On Sept. 22, 1991, Jarman was declared "Saint Derek of Dungeness of the Order of Celluloid Knights," by the London chapter of the Sisters of Perpetual Indulgence, in recognition of his films, books, activism, and his "very sexy nose." See *AYR*, 117–18.

23   C. L. Whitby, "John Dee and Renaissance Scrying," *Bulletin of the Society for Renaissance Study* 3 (1985): 26.

24   Frances A. Yates, "A Great Magus," in *Ideas and Ideals in the North European Renaissance: Collected Works, Vol. 3* (London: Routledge and Kegan Paul, 1984), 52.

25   Kate Chedgzoy, *Shakespeare's Queer Children: Sexual Politics and Contemporary Culture* (Manchester: Manchester University Press, 1995), 197.

26   Wollen, "The Last New Wave," 47.

27   Whitby, "John Dee and Renaissance Scrying," 28.

28   Clulee, *John Dee's Natural Philosophy,* 66–67.

29   As far as I can tell, Jarman was mistaken in referring to Dee's book as *The Angelic Conversations.* The original title is *A True and Faithful relation of what Passed for Many Yeers between Dr. John Dee . . . and Some Spirits,* ed. Meric Casaubon (London, 1659).

30   Quoted in J. L. Heilbron, "Introductory Essay," in *John Dee on Astronomy,* ed. and trans. Wayne Shumaker (Berkeley: University of California Press, 1978), 15.

31   Eve Kosofsky Sedgwick, *Between Men: English Literature and Male Homosocial Desire* (New York: Columbia University Press, 1985), 29.

32   Ibid., 35.

33   Alan Bray, "Homosexuality and the Signs of Male Friendship in Elizabethan England," in *Queering the Renaissance,* ed. Jonathan Goldberg (Durham: Duke University Press, 1994), 40–61. Lorna Hutson, *The Usurer's Daughter: Male Friendship and Fictions of Women in Sixteenth-Century England* (New York and London: Routledge, 1994).

34   Sedgwick, *Between Men,* 36.

35   Joel Fineman, *Shakespeare's Perjured Eye: The Invention of Poetic Subjectivity in the Sonnets* (Berkeley: University of California Press, 1986), 17; Joel Fineman, *The Subjectivity Effect in Western Literary Tradition* (Cambridge, Mass.: MIT Press, 1991), 224.

36   Fineman, *Perjured Eye,* 25.

37   The charges of misogyny may well be the product of two key features of all of Jarman's films: his project of exploring on film the gay male psyche, "the part of the garden the Lord forgot to mention" (*MN,* 23), and his critical, non-utopian portrayal of sexuality in general: "It's hard to fight against passion,

for whatever it wants it buys at the expense of soul" (*LE*, 248). Although both of these are well-known aspects of Jarman's films, this has not led critics to attempt to understand in more complicated ways Jarman's portrayal of the relations among the sexes. Colin MacCabe's otherwise interesting reading of *Edward II* will serve as an example of this tendency: "The film is much more unambiguous in its misogyny than any of his other work. In that gay male dialectic where identification with the position of the woman is set against rejection of the woman's body, *Edward II* is entirely, and without any textual foundation, on the side of rejection. For Marlowe, as for his age, the love of boys was merely the ultimate sexual transgression, not in any sense an alternative to heterosexual sex. It is here that Jarman does violence to his source, making Edward's passion for Gaveston a consequence of his inability to be roused by the queen's body in a truly chilling scene at the beginning of the film" ("Throne of Blood," *Sight and Sound* [Oct. 1991]: 12–13]). (I must admit to being unfamiliar with the gay male dialectic of which MacCabe speaks, and fail to see even in what sense it is dialectical.) The scene to which Mac-Cabe refers (sequence 10 in the published script) occurs in the film well after Gaveston has returned, after more than one romantic scene between the lovers; moreover, Edward's passion for Gaveston predates his marriage to Isabella and the birth of Prince Edward. It is not entirely clear, therefore, why MacCabe has chosen to understand the scene, or indeed, the etiology of Edward's passion for Gaveston, in this way. There is, further, strong textual foundation for Edward's rejection of Isabella and his obsession with Gaveston. Early in the play (in lines that appear in the film) Isabella complains that "my lord the king regards me not / But dotes upon the love of Gaveston" (1.2.49–50). In the same scene Edward pushes her away, ordering "Fawn not on me, French strumpet; get thee gone" (1.2.145). Isabella later observes that "never doted Jove on Ganymede / So much as he on cursed Gaveston" (1.4.180–81). Whatever the vicissitudes of Renaissance desire, clearly, in Marlowe's play, Edward desires Gaveston to the exclusion of everyone else.

In trying to understand MacCabe's reading of *Edward II*, it may help to remember Jonathan Goldberg's claim that there are times when analyses "of complicities between male homosocial arrangements and misogyny" are "made in the effort to delegitimate male-male sexual relations, and when the defense of women turns out to be a defense of heterosexuality" (Introduction to *Queering the Renaissance*, 8). Certainly this would seem to be the case in MacCabe's lopsided description of Renaissance sexuality, in which homosexual sex gets historicized as "merely" a transgressive thrill, while heterosexual sex is, well, heterosexual sex, as experienced through the ages. Finally, it should be pointed out that *Edward II* is by no means blind to the fact that gay men are not immune to misogyny, but it insists upon understanding this in a broader context, as I suggest above.

38 J. Hoberman, "Prisoners of Sex," *Village Voice,* 24 March 1992, 57.

39 Bruce R. Smith, *Homosexual Desire in Shakespeare's England* (Chicago and London: University of Chicago Press, 1991), 212.

40 D. J. Gordon, "Roles and Mysteries," in *The Renaissance Imagination,* ed. Stephen Orgel (Berkeley: University of California Press, 1975), 21.

41 Stephen Orgel, *The Jonsonian Masque* (Cambridge: Harvard University Press, 1965), 6–7.

42 Frances A. Yates, *Theatre of the World* (London: Routledge and Kegan Paul, 1969), 86.

43 MacCabe, "A Post-National European Cinema," 14.

44 Walter Benjamin, *Illuminations,* ed. Hannah Arendt, trans. Harry Zohn (New York: Schocken Books, 1969), 257.

Amy Villarejo

FORBIDDEN LOVE

Pulp as Lesbian History

The New *Pocket* Books that may revolutionize New York's reading habits.

Today is the most important literary coming-out party in the memory of New York's oldest book lover. Today your 25 cent piece leaps to a par with dollar bills.

Now for less than the few cents you spend each week for your morning newspaper you can own one of the great books for which thousands of people have paid from $2 to $4.

These new Pocket Books are designed to fit both the tempo of our times and the needs of New Yorkers. They're as handy as a pencil, as modern and convenient as a portable radio—and as good looking. They were designed especially for busy people—people who are continually on the go, yet who want to make the most of every minute.

Never again need you say, "I wish I had time to read" because Pocket Books gives you the time. Never again need you dawdle idly in reception rooms, fret on train or bus rides, sit vacantly staring at a restaurant table. The books you have always meant to read "when you had time" will fill the waits with enjoyment.

—*New York Times* advertisement, June 19, 1939

New York, time, leisure, urban anxiety, leaps of value, book loving, and coming out, condensed neatly at the debut of a new commodity: these will be the subjects of this essay, which moves from the mass-market paperback of the 1940s to 1960s, to a relatively recent film that returns us to them, and more specifically to the fantasies of (lesbian) history they invoke, the 1992 film financed by the National Film Board of Canada, *Forbidden Love* (dir. Aerlynn Weissman and Lynne Fernie) (fig. 1). If we had the time to read *Forbidden Love* as something like a pulp *film*, we would be ushered toward a set of questions about pulp's specificity, its transformations across media, its specularization of the clandestine. If we had time to read more closely, we might focus on a single sequence at the outset of *Forbidden Love,* which begins with a titillating track across the covers of a group of forties and fifties mass-market paperbacks: *Women of Evil, The Girls in 3-B, Satan's Daughter, Women's Barracks, How Dark My Love, Duet in Darkness, Private School, Queer Patterns.* The tracking shot then cuts to individual shots (ending in tight focus) of exemplary covers: *Queer Patterns* and *Women's Barracks* (again), *Girls' Dormitory, Man Hater,* and *Lesbians in Black Lace.* If we had time to examine these covers (for the sequence is brief), much less to read these books, we might wonder how they become ethereal proxies for *defining* what is generally at stake for lesbian and gay historiography in its incessant return to the fifties, and how these lurid covers and titles, in particular, therefore function not only as a form of history but also as a visual form of static classification, of synchronicity, in *Forbidden Love.* And if we had time to displace the paradigms of history that mark the synecdoche "Stonewall" as a rupture between the period of "twilight lovers," shame, and shadows these novels evoke and that of self-proclaimed enlightened urban lesbian "identity" the film boasts, we might begin to probe the nature of history as commodity, affectively invested and circulated as value, within the vast matrix of postwar American culture.

But what gives us time, according at least to the logic of the advertisement, is the new commodity, which envelops and distributes, fills and makes time. The commodity, the mass-market paperback, is time's design; design gives time, and design sets value "leaping." Crises of value inhere in time's design: no wonder that the most frequent word used to describe the covers of mass-market paperbacks of the forties and fifties is *salacious,* "to leap." The advertisement heralds the mutation of value along contradictory axes, both tied to the problematic of speed, time's new rate of motion, in the city: on the one hand, the book as commodity remains tied to literary value (only obliquely summoned, however, through reference to "great books") yet promises class mobility, and, on the other, the book now will serve an ancillary if not competing function, produced by acceleration and deceleration within modernity itself, of "filling time," "killing time," "occupying time" when urban isolation (stasis) threatens to engulf.[1] An encapsulated morsel of the modern moment, the new commodity thus conjures a reader: not a book reader but a reader of mass publications (newspapers, magazines, and the new paperback), an isolated, modern, urban creature beset with anxieties (fretting, busy, loath to be dawdling idly or staring

1 *Forbidden Love*
(courtesy of Women
Make Movies).

vacantly) that will be soothed by this new product. And time's design as
paperback produces the masses themselves: this Pocket Book reader will
become a comrade-consumer in the "paperback revolution."

What, though, is the "queer pattern" (if there is one) in the web of design, books, modernity, cinema, history, and value? The paperbacks on
display in the film *Forbidden Love* share a lesbian "theme" (or so it would
appear from their covers and titles that these novels are "about" lesbians), and there are gay-themed counterparts, though fewer of them, that
partake of the same tropes of torment, shame, sin, lust, and shadows in
their titles and cover illustrations. As a literary or filmic critical gesture,
however, isolating those books (or films) with identifiable lesbian or gay
themes against a presumed-stable heterosexual majority results in three
layers of misguided analysis. First, thematic analysis in its hermeticism
ignores the social determinations of textual production. Second, the isolation of lesbian- or gay-themed novels severs their connections with other
forms of social abjection (delinquency, alcoholism, nymphomania, and the
like) that are central to their history and regulation. And third, there is a
convergence of the critical gesture of isolation with the postwar social pro-

duction of isolation (addressed in the advertisement itself), a convergence that further sequesters critical commentary from the domain of the popular within which its subject is located. If there is a queer pattern to see, at work, it emerges from the industrial context of these novels' production, from the ties binding lesbianism and homosexuality to allied perversions and practices, and from the matrix of postwar popular culture.

To militate against such thematic treatments, it is necessary to see the novels themselves (as material products as well as "literary" or "popular cultural" texts) as artifacts of postwar and Cold War culture, evoking dominant concerns with anxiety and paranoia, while they, at the same time, are products of industrial innovation and the reorganization of mass consumers and mass taste. Central to their emergence, heyday, and decline *are* codings of sexuality, of emergent urban conflicts and sexualized enclaves (and therefore of suburban mythologies), and of work and leisure (of sexuality as a component of both, and therefore of time's design through Fordist industrial organization but also nostalgia for sedimented myths of nineteenth-century pastoral idylls). Yet the "form of appearance" of sexuality is caught within a set of dense determinations, within lingering forms of mass literature from the previous century, pre-war conceptions of the city (including contradictory responses to the "great migration" of the 1920s), and massive reorganizations of leisure. What would it mean to read within this matrix?

The novels both appeal to and shape what Antonio Gramsci calls "common sense": a conception of the world that "contains Stone Age elements and principles from a more advanced science, prejudices from all past phases of history at the local level and intuitions of a future philosophy."[2] The challenge in understanding the novels "in a Gramscian way"[3] is to make visible the tentacles of common sense, its modes of transformation, and its complex determinations within the conjuncture. Indeed, what may be occluded by a certain fidelity to Gramsci (the tendency to historicize his writings) is his insistence on the mutability of institutions, the speed of transformation of the social landscape, and the consequent need to develop flexible critical methodologies to track the lines of metamorphosis of "popular" and mass culture.[4] Gramsci's comments on the intellectual *function,* on Americanism and Fordism, his attention to cinema as powerful popular-cultural force, and his awareness of the molar as well as molecular dimensions of sexuality demonstrate his capacity to turn a critical eye on emergent forms, and reading "in a Gramscian way" provides a begin-

ning point for an analysis of these mass-market paperbacks and their contemporary circulations and translations, including their cinematic movement. While some have recently been critical of the polarizing nature of
(mis)readings of Gramsci,[5] it is possible to retain his insights into the strati-
fied and heterogeneous nature of popular-cultural forms while articulating
his work with Marxist critical projects of recent decades. In particular, it
seems crucial to assess the specific ways in which "the fantasy world [of
the popular novel] acquires a particular fabulous concreteness in popular
intellectual life,"[6] and, consequently, to examine the particular modes of
sensation, adventure, affect, and emotion that these novels embed not only
in their ostensible content but also as commodities that circulate now.

PULP FICTION

Gramsci's oxymoron, "fabulous concreteness," beckons us toward this dy-
namism, which seems structurally constitutive of pulp. If, as narrative,
Quentin Tarantino's 1994 *Pulp Fiction* returns to the world of temptation,
violence, and redemption of 1940s mass-market paperbacks (straddling
realism and escapism, a binary we will trouble later in the essay, in its
fixation on drugs, mobsters, and crooked boxers), as phenomenon it re-
kindled John Travolta's flagging career, stimulated older modes of naming
alienation and prurience, and strengthened the petit bourgeois populist
imaginary associated with the "new independents," whereby the unofficial
knowledge of the renegade video-store clerk is validated as superseding
that of the outmoded corporate marketeer, the Hollywood mogul. Easily
commodified (if Routledge titles and mass-market reissues are any indication), pulp has entered the mainstream at alarming speed as the new
postmodern buzzword, despite the longtime interest in pulp novels by
collectors and bricoleurs interested in twentieth-century cultural debris.
Aligned with but not equivalent to camp and kitsch, pulp seems to secure
at minimum some mode of circulating and transforming abjection, bad
taste, outrageousness, criminality, and despair, but it does so, historically
at least, at the level of the cover (artifact and metaphor), to which we turn
briefly by way of defining pulp fiction.

    Robert deGraff launched Pocket Books with the *New York Times* adver-
tisement above. While, according to Janice Radway, deGraff has wrongly
been heralded as the initiator of the paperback's "second revolution" (she
contends that Mercury Books, and their line of Mercury Mysteries begun

in 1937, deserve the honor), the influence of deGraff is nonetheless uncontestable.[7] His initial list included ten books, a hodgepodge of titles ranging from classics to best-sellers, mysteries to self-help.[8] What unified this eclectic group was the books' design: a uniform size, a recognizable imprint colophon (Gertrude the Kangaroo), high-quality print and binding, and eye-catching cover illustrations under a Perma Gloss coating (which, in many cases, endures sixty years later). Despite the differences among deGraff's and Pocket Books' imitators, the paperbacks published from 1939 to the late 1950s are significant for the purposes of this essay precisely for the cover: as analytical touchstone, as signifier (though unreliable) of their "thematic" interests, as historiographic text, as source of titillation or fascination, and, importantly, as focal point of industrial organization.

What does a cover do? Its foremost function is to lure the potential reader at the "point of sale," the moment of transaction between retailer and consumer. But, moving from publisher to distributor to retailer, the cover has traveled through a number of ancillary functions before that crucial encounter. At the design stage (the focus of much of Geoffrey O'Brien's *Hardboiled America*), the publisher's art director and stable of artists create an image "appropriate" (a troubled idea) for the book in question, and in that design stage are involved labors of artistic creation, layout, self-censorship, and promotional decisions. In the development of marketing schemes for mass-market paperbacks in the early 1940s, deGraff made a decision that erased the gap between a potential and an actual mass audience: he devised a distribution system that went outside the parameters of hardcover distribution to retail bookstores, and he instead employed independent distributors (IDs), who sold newspapers and magazines to drugstores, corner stores, and the like. This strategy promised Pocket Books a truly mass audience, not concentrated in the larger cities and not limited to higher-income hardcover buyers. The cover underwent a second transformation at the stage of sale from publisher to ID: it had to represent the promise of a new title, without accompanying page proofs (except in the case of anticipated best-sellers). Frequently on the basis of the cover alone, IDs selected the titles they would promote to their customers; they would, therefore, favor some illustrations over others, since they could not include every title of every imprint in their offerings. While O'Brien sees the importance of the cover art in determining a book's future as an occasion to elevate the artists themselves to active producers of cultural taste (a worthy claim), what I want to remark about the cover's function at this stage is the weight of the "economic" function, the place the covers occupy within the circulation of value, ensconced within the cover itself, to the exclusion of the "content," of Shakespeare's five tragedies or of *Seven Footprints to Satan*. Of course, the IDs' knowledge of the novels' "quality" is not limited to the cover alone, but its *functional* role in distribution at this moment, consonant with the uniformity of design, troubles the distinction between "quality" and "trash" on the basis of "content."

After the cover performs its marketing function to distributors, it moves to retailers, who place the book on display: in racks designed to fit the uniform size of the paperbacks, and, more important, in groupings suggested by the imprints' signifiers of genre. It would not be an overstatement to suggest that design determines genre and that genre likewise fractures the coherent category of the author. As with the color-codings of Albatross's line, the mass-market paperbacks of the "second revolution" were distinguished by genre on the cover itself: a Red Arrow Thriller or Dell Mystery or, more familiar to scholars due to its longevity and Radway's study, a Harlequin Romance. The cover art sought to confirm the genre designation (keyhole conventions for mysteries, gothic palaces lurking in the background for romances), and the imprint's name and colophon become indices of generic division along with the image. Many publishers issued series, and most of the imprints numbered their volumes for reference, with the effect of enhancing the pattern of repetitive consumption of a single imprint. Retailers, too, chose their stock from distributors' selections on the basis of covers (though retailers were more often sold blocks of titles dependent upon distributors' earlier choices, a practice that was soon contested). But in the hands of retailers, the cover later came to serve yet another function: as a substitute for the book itself upon return. After a number of days, if a mass-market paperback fails to sell, a retailer may return only the cover for reimbursement of the book's price by the publisher (a practice instituted to save money on shipping costs of returns). At this stage, then, the final step (in the case of the commodity's failure) in the loop, which returns us to publisher, the cover is a metonym, a substitution for the book's total value: the physical book remains (to be read, to be traded, to be illegally resold), but it has shed its value within the sphere of legal circulation.

The cover thus organizes the movement of the commodity from publisher to distributor to consumer. However, as Marx stresses in the second volume *Capital,* in a chapter entitled "Circulation Time," the form of appearance of value (of productive capital, of money capital, and of commodity capital) mutates at each step of the cycle from circulation to production and back to circulation.[9] Rather than a linear model, such as one might deduce from the direct movement of the book from publisher to consumer, Marx emphasizes a multilayered model, wherein at every synchronic freezing of the movement, the form of appearance of value is distributed over productive, money, *and* commodity capital. Mediating the cycle is time: when a number of books, for example, are unable to be sold as commodities, they are stalled as value in the commodity form, which cannot be returned to the publisher as money capital to reinvest in the next production cycle, and yet money capital must be available to reinvest in production, and productive capital must also be available to continue production until it, too, can be replaced. The cover, as we have remarked, stands in for the death of the commodity (its death only *within* the circuit of capital) at its final destination, and returns to the publisher as a signifier of his loss. Marx stresses two elements in the second volume of *Capital* that are crucial to understanding the cover at every "stage" (which is not a misnomer only in the freezing of what is in Marx's model continuous) of the cycle of production-circulation-consumption: the social character of the commodity (reified through fetishistic relations) and the role of time in determining value's form of appearance. Recall Marx's restatement of fetishism in the second volume: it "transforms the social, economic character that things are stamped with in the process of social production into a natural character arising from the material nature of these things,"[10] replacing social relations with relations among things. The *predication* of the fetish is substitution; the *effect* of fetishism is stasis, the freezing, reifying (thing-ifying) of a process wherein elements truly acquire significance or meaning only in relation to their functions over time. Marx is at pains to emphasize function over the categorical imperative, time and social processes over the stagnancy of fetishistic bourgeois economy. What is important to remark in his treatment of function, moreover, is that *from within the capitalist mode of production of value itself,* each element of capital value mutates at any given time. This mutation, in the world of the mass-market paperback, happens "under the cover."

UNDER THE COVER: SALACIOUSNESS REGULATED

The most frequent adjectives used to describe the covers of mass-market paperbacks of the 1940s and 1950s are *lurid* (a pale yellow, metaphorically associated with ghostliness, the unknown or the mysterious) and *salacious,* stitching the "leap of value" (where a quarter becomes a dollar) to the leap into the forbidden, the voyeuristic, the prurient, or the streets (where one does not "properly" belong). For whom and by whom is this leap made possible? There is little record of publishers' internal comments on the covers' design, but, in *Hardboiled America,* O'Brien develops an archaeology of the mass-market paperback cover through interviews with publishers and the few artists whom he was able to find. What O'Brien uncovers is the relative devaluation of the cover at the level of individual "artist": while a few of the imprints included the name of the artist along with the cover art or on a blurb, most of the artists went unacknowledged, and, indeed, most of the original cover art was destroyed by the publishing houses years after the penchant for original illustration waned. O'Brien argues, "Of all the things that may be considered when looking at this art, personal style is probably the least significant."[11] What is more significant—and available—for analysis is at the more general iconographic level: conventions that developed over the course of the mass-market paperback's life from 1939 into the 1950s. From the highly stylized conventions of the mystery novel, whereby the cover simply reduced to the barest possible degree the pertinent narrative features (a formalist rendering of a cat, or the central position of the falcon in the first cover of *The Maltese Falcon*), to the more airbrushed "Deco-style" covers and back-cover extensive "maps" of mysteries developed by Dell, the cover artists tended to adopt recognizable patterns and styles repeated by a number of imprints.

The hallmarks of the covers taken collectively are, of course, memorable scenes of sex and violence: scantily clad women behind diaphanous flowing skirts holding cigarettes or guns (most often pointed toward men, but occasionally threatening each other), scenes of the streets, men in trenchcoats, pools of blood and murdered corpses, tenements, piles of cash, public parks, blond sirens, hotel rooms, docks, and so forth. The colors are bold, and indeed often "lurid" in its literal sense, yellow or chartreuse (integral to fifties design).[12] This iconography intensified in the early years of the 1950s in order to combat declining sales: "Art Deco abstractions and cityscapes . . . gave way very quickly to photographic realism and expanses of bare flesh."[13] No matter whether the cover illustrated a "classic" by James Baldwin, a hard-boiled mystery by Chandler, or an exposé of life in a women's prison by an unknown (unrenowned or anonymous) author, the covers partook of the same imagery despite the ostensible "content." The correspondence, moreover, between the covers' illustrations and the books' narratives or themes was slight (the limits of the "appropriate"), so much so that the conventions of cover illustration took on lives of their own and became amplified into the 1950s. To the extent that the covers were an index of industrial innovation (product differentiation), they obeyed the market dictum that "sex sells," a trend that had the paradoxical effect of flattening distinctions between covers, genres, and imprints.

It was during the early 1950s that the "excesses" of the covers (more flesh, more blood, more "realist" depictions of the sordid worlds the novels investigate) became indicators of the novels' lessened value measured against literary standards popularly understood. That is, the more the covers became what they were, or the more they obeyed the conventions that distinguished them from hardcover literature, the more they fell into disrepute. If the monetary "leap of value" promised by the Pocket Books advertisement elevated the mass-market paperback to the status of the hardcover, where a quarter became a dollar, the covers came to signify a fall in moral value, which resulted in a call for the law. In 1952, a Congressional committee (a Select Committee on Current Pornographic Materials, known as the Gathings Committee) was convened to investigate the conjunction of sex and violence that the covers signified.

The Gathings Committee was charged with investigating mass-market paperbacks, magazines, and comic books that were pornographic in nature and threatened the nation's health. In a rhetoric determined both by Cold War anxiety over popular morality and by the recent regulations of the film industry (in the Hays Code and the Paramount decision of 1948), the committee, relying on literary-critical and medical "experts," sought to establish an "innocent" national readership prone to the dangers of corruption, which they condensed in a delicious list: obscenity, violence, lust, use of narcotics, blasphemy, vulgarity, pornography, juvenile delinquency, sadism, masochism, perversion, homosexuality, lesbianism, rape, and nymphomania.[14] These readers, of course, were themselves products of the industrial organization that spawned the paperbacks, but they nevertheless had to be saved by state intervention or industrial self-regulation, as had motion-picture spectators with the Hays Production Code and Paramount decision.

The form of regulation concealed the crisis to be regulated: the committee, unable to attack the books' content directly due to First Amendment protection and debates over the difficult legal parameters of obscenity, produced and investigated allegations, not charges, of "block-selling" and monopoly against the distributors, the American News Company in particular, of the mass-market paperbacks. As with the Paramount decision, which dismantled monopolies (vertical integration) of the film industry four years earlier, the Gathings Committee invoked the nature of autonomous copyright violation in the practice of block-selling. In the words of the Paramount case, the District Court held block-booking illegal for the reason that "it adds to the monopoly of a single copyrighted picture that of another copyrighted picture which must be taken and exhibited in order to secure the first."[15] Moreover, "Where a high quality film greatly desired is licensed only if an inferior one is taken, the latter *borrows quality* from the former and strengthens its monopoly by drawing on the other. The practice tends to equalize rather than differentiate the reward for the individual copyright."[16] Block-booking or block-selling, in other words, violates the boundaries of value, the preservation of quality, and opens the field of cultural production to "inferior" copyrights, or perverted and sinful paperbacks. The task of the committee, then, was to establish a legal field: it could not level charges per se but could suggest arenas in which current law could be enforced, or in which new laws were necessary to regulate pornography. What the regulation of blind- and block-selling was meant to effect, however, was a shift from the constraints of obscenity law, with its First Amendment allegiances, the taint of "censorship," and its problematic focus on content, to the seemingly more malleable nature (and entrepreneurial spirit) of copyright protection under antimonopoly law—but "content" haunted the proceedings, again "under the cover."

Obscenity law, as summarized in the Gathings Committee Report, is founded upon the impossibility of citation. The more obvious dimension of this founding paradox is that any selection or quotation found to be obscene within the meaning of a judicial decision cannot be reproduced within the report itself: "to include these quotations herein would be to disseminate obscenity which would therefore result in making this report pornographic."[17] This modest disclaimer is, however, belied by the evolution of obscenity law from its common-law rule in *Regina v. Hicklin* (1868) to the "modern" rule set down in *United States v. One Book Called "Ulysses"* (1933).[18] In the common-law rule, "the test of obscenity is this, whether the tendency of the matter charged as obscene is to deprave and corrupt those whose minds are open to such immoral influences, and into whose hands a publication of this sort may fall."[19] The test applied "to the passages of

the writing which were charged as obscene without viewing them in relation to the remainder of the writing, and without considering the intent
with which they were written by the author."[20] By contrast, the *Ulysses*
case (a case based on the violation of the Tariff Act) "was an attempt to
point out that indictable 'obscenity' must be 'dirt for dirt's sake,' and not
just vulgarity without considering its relationship to the rest of the text":

> in any case where a book is claimed to be obscene it must first be de-
> termined whether the intent with which it was written was what is
> called, according to the common phrase, pornographic, that is, writ-
> ten for the purpose of exploiting obscenity. . . . the meaning of the
> word "obscene" as legally defined by the courts is: tending to stir the
> sex impulses or to lead to sexually impure and lustful thoughts . . .
> whether a particular book would tend to excite such impulses and
> thoughts must be tested by the court's opinion as to its effect on a
> person with average sex instincts—who plays in this branch of legal
> inquiry, the same role of hypothetical reagent as does the "reasonable
> man" in the law of torts.[21]

The "modern" or federal rule thus not only produces a new normative
sexual legal entity (whose "average sex instincts" must be established by
expert psychological criteria) but it reopens obscenity to intent and to
context, two related and notoriously slippery, if not undecidable, analytic
arenas.

Who identifies an "obscene" passage and how? How is it possible to
mark the obscene, the salacious, the vulgar, "dirt for dirt's sake" from the
literary as such, especially when the "content," as we have seen, is already
an effect of a substitution, where the cover comes to signify, to circulate, to
stand in for the whole complex of genre differentiation, marketability, appeal, and encodings of the relation between the subcultural and so-called
mainstream readership and of the relation between the mass readership
constituted by a popular form and the standards of high literature, artistic integrity, and the like? What is at stake here and what the Gathings
Committee's report struggles to contain, to my mind, is the social or legal
regulation of metonymy or synecdoche itself, which is another name for
the complex of reading as a social activity (the chain of substitutions traced
by authorship and address beneath the "cover"). The report presents, in a
remarkable nutshell, an ensemble of excesses produced by this effort at
containment. First, it makes visible the contamination of the literary by

the judicial and vice versa, resulting in the necessity of jury trials where the judge and jury become not only the "hypothetical reagents" posited in the *Ulysses* opinion but also "common sense" literary critics who, in a distinctly American vein, refute the highbrow erudition of "experts," as well as the minority report's contention, regarding both aesthetic and moral value, that "it is not the province of any congressional committee to determine what is good, bad or indifferent literature. This carries with it echoes of thought control."[22] Second, the report reveals the insidious nature of biographical evidence and "representative" positions and politics, when one opinion favorable to the dissemination of certain novels is refuted by the allegation that the judge's impartiality is impaired by his ownership of stock in a publishing company, or where the children of the House Representatives on the committee become the "average readers" representing the populace in committee testimony. Third, it foregrounds the incommensurability of capitalist innovation and the regulation of "morality," where the practices of block-selling are the logical consequences of an industrial expansion that cannot itself be regulated. And finally, it marks the unstable nature of the signature measured retrospectively by literary "integrity" and by the prominence of pseudonyms and anonymity in the field of pulp fiction, where a potentially obscene portion of a novel is identified by the literary-critical insight of a judge, who discerns that the "filthy scatological portions are written in a bluntly different and distinct style from the pretentious metaphysical reflective manner of writing, otherwise."[23]

The novels in large measure treat the investigative nature of modern society, "thematizing" the encounter between the law and its subjects across a wide domain of emergent social categories, all of which become *signified* through sexual iconography on their covers, and the committee's concern is unified not by the singular focus on "sexuality" but instead on a hypothesis through which the report generates a stable text on the one hand and a hypostasized readership on the other (despite the extent to which that statis is threatened by the discursive apparatus of legal regulation sketched above). The decidability of both poles of the author-readership relation rests on the cover, in the language of the minority report: "The committee has rightfully observed that the covers of many of these volumes are extreme and in bad taste. We agree with that observation. There is no doubt that in many instances the covers do not reflect the content of the book and are designed to promote sales by catering to the sensational. The book, however, must not be confused with the cover."[24]

How is it possible to prevent such confusion? It is difficult to find a terminology that adequately characterizes the assumptions on which this hypothesis of separability rests in relation to the audience it presupposes both within the choke hold of the moral and everyone else outside it, and in relation to the practices of reading it presupposes for this populace; these can be shorthanded as *questions* of authorship, genre, and address. The dangers in citing the language of the report are in reproducing a surface/depth model of ideology that the metaphor of the cover appears to solicit but belies, as well as falling into the psychologism or psychoanalytic language that characterizes pathology.[25] On the one hand, the committee activates the fear (which persists now with television regulation or proposed self-regulation) that readers understand these novels, say, about "narcotic abuse," as instruction manuals, "how to" books on how to shoot heroin, smoke pot, or snort cocaine: the novels "describe the pleasures of narcotics, how to use them, how to use the needle." So too do they "expand upon homosexuality, and one book advises or supports polygamy, and any number of books deal with lesbianism and nymphomania."[26] Yet, on the other hand, the committee hears and approves testimony that tests the implicit class and gender bases of the hypothesis (that those most prone to corruption are women, children, and others disempowered due to their social position outside, for whatever reason, the comfort of the middle-class nuclear family).

If it is the case that the Gathings Committee's report struggles to contain the signifying capacities of the covers, the extent to which the covers betray the ostensible content, level distinctions between "quality" and "inferior" copyrights, disrupt socially sanctioned and industrially necessary codings of value (legitimizing perverse and pathological challenges to hegemonic practices), then we can begin to develop a critical rejoinder to the report's stress on the counterhegemonic potential of these novels. The committee is not so much operating within the nexus of "realism" versus "escapism," a binary that has miscalculated the social function of the reading of popular literature, as Modleski and Radway have shown, but more within an anxiety over what is at stake in the *visualization* of perversion (through highly conventionalized iconographic repertoires). If the covers are seen to be excessive, they excessively present to sight (something we struggle to name as lurid or salacious) that which cannot be calculated or contained in the moral, aesthetic, and political arithmetic that subtends the law. Within the dynamic of capital, pulp fiction appears to be a processing, or translating, or machinic transformation, of a variety of non-normative products of modernity and urbanity through the industrial inscription of *sex;* this transformation is then subsumed into a specular stasis that is tamed through the category of sexuality, and non-normative sexuality in particular. That is to say, "sexuality" can be understood as a substitution for containment itself, since what is visualized can be dissected, taxonomized, regulated, or policed.

The undecidable dimensions of authorship and address trouble the condensation of meaning *within* the category of sexuality per se, even if it is understood to be operative within a specific historical moment as discourse. Foucault's vigilance against the liberatory sloganeering beneath the banner of sexuality needs to be augmented by an investigation into the visualization of sexuality as an alibi for the slippages it struggles to contain. *Forbidden Love* provides a "case study" for such an investigation.

POPULAR CULTURE AS LESBIAN HISTORY

In the United States, New York City vies with San Francisco as a mythographic mapping of dyke nirvana, homosexual heaven, the capital of the "queer nation." The myth, of course, has a basis in social reality: the postwar expansion of urban gay culture, the reproduction of New York as a center for intellectual and artistic activity, the incipient demands for "gay rights" in the late 1960s through activist groups with competing ideological demands. This siting of New York is certainly not new or recent; indeed, New York, through Greenwich Village and through its synecdoche "Stonewall," has for some years now functioned in common sense as the mark of a rupture, the sign of a break, in lesbian and gay history and cultural expression. The contemporary myth dubbed "pre-Stonewall," as Angela Weir and Elizabeth Wilson describe it eloquently and at length, is comprised of mixed horror and nostalgia, a "kitsch dystopia":

> On the one hand, we have been inundated with fifties pastiche—from Levi jeans advertisements to films, from sharp haircuts to dark-red lipstick, from pop graphics to golden oldies. The world that is thus recreated is deeply romantic—sexuality is hedged about with prohibitions, passions both personal and political are hidden, secret, threatening. A wonderful style exists to express this, a combination of Paris Left Bank and Greenwich Village, Jean Gabin and Audrey Hepburn, out-

lawry and bohemianism to set against the uptight heterosexuality of tight-waisted fashions inspired by Christian Dior. On the other hand, we re-create the period of the Cold War, the nuclear threat, McCarthyism, spies, treason, fear, while according to our feminist folk myth, all women were pushed back into the home, all gays were persecuted; there was no chink of radical light at the end of the tunnel.[27]

Elements of this contradictory myth (which in its descriptive points of reference alone limits the "we" it invokes considerably) persist even in historiographic accounts that challenge the conception of the fifties as a period of seamless conservatism and conformity.

More recently, however, lesbian and gay historians and ethnographers (including John D'Emilio, Allan Berubé, and Elizabeth Lapovsky Kennedy and Madeline Davis) have emphasized the post–World War II years, if not years earlier as well, as creating the possibility for lesbian and gay relationships in embryonic gay communities in large American cities (such as New York and San Francisco, in particular). That dissent was alive in this period is confirmed *retrospectively* by the eruption we call "Stonewall," an event that shorthands a number of translations (themselves fabrications) that found contemporary gay and lesbian politics and culture: from shame to pride, from isolation to community, from silence to activism. None of these translations is complete or adequate, yet we are steeped in the iconography of this caesura: the signposts of the Village's Gay St. (featured on the cover of Ann Bannon's novel, *Beebo Brinker*) and Christopher St., images of gay men and lesbians spilling into the streets, butches and femmes huddled over tables in cozy bars, clones cruising, queens dragging, bikes gleaming. The street becomes, in effect, a specific street, the iconography emptied of the dialectic of hiding and disclosure that produced it in the first place. This iconography, indeed, overwhelms the recent fiction film by Nigel Finch, *Stonewall* (1996), notable only for its ability *not* to treat any single component of the matrix "Stonewall" in adequate detail but in dreamlike fashion to invoke the entire ensemble. And in the years "post-Stonewall," films have recirculated and re-created the heady energy of that inaugural moment: of massed gay and lesbian bodies in the streets, of public seduction and exuberant sexuality, of collective, active, and loud demands for survival and well-being, even in the face of the most profound threats to them. Some, including B. Ruby Rich, have called this the "new queer cinema," and others have rightly, I think, been hesitant to celebrate a repertoire of images that are mainly white, highly commodifiable to mainstream audiences, and anchored in rights-based discourses of political activism.[28] This is nonetheless a dominant vision of gay and lesbian "metropolitan life," a universalizing image that is more easily disseminated through the organs of the relatively recent national lesbian and gay culture-industry, not coincidentally based in New York. What I want to emphasize here is not the measurement of these myths against "concrete reality," but the sense in which they circulate in order to bestow a form of retrospective continuity upon contemporary cultural and political struggles that are *not* unified within the iconography of that mythology and the forms of historicizing the myths solidify.

John D'Emilio and Estelle Freedman are among those historians who characterize the postwar years as creating the possibilities for a new gay subculture, emphasizing the extent to which, during the 1920s and 1930s, "the resources for naming homosexual desire slowly expanded."[29] Alongside massive immigration, the penetration of psychoanalytic and psychiatric language into popular culture, euphemisms that circulated through "the so-called race records,"[30] and fictional characters in novels such as *The Well of Loneliness* and plays such as *The Captive,* lay the ground both for emergent gay identities and erotic experiences in urban centers. These parallel movements suggest to D'Emilio and Freedman that "World War II was something of a nationwide 'coming out' experience."[31] By "nationwide," they agree that "what appeared as a deviant form of sexual behavior on the fringe of society now seemed to permeate American life," as evidenced by the paperback pulp novels of Ann Bannon and Paula Christian, which "offered easily available images of self-affirming lesbian love."[32] There are a number of conflations here that bear mention: the undifferentiated role of Broadway plays, British novels, psychoanalytic theory, and African American music in producing a national (read, New York and white) gay culture, as well as the repetition of coming out into a public sphere that is unmarked by the competing cultural designations that appear to make it possible.

In D'Emilio and Freedman's *Intimate Matters* there appears a still photograph of a pulp cover, *Chris,* subtitled "Life in the Limbo of Lesbianism, An Intimate Story of the Third Sex Told with Tenderness and Unblushing Honesty." Passing over the alliterative bravado, allusion to Hirshfeld and earlier conceptions of lesbianism, and cover art, the authors note: "Many of the lesbian pulp novels appealed to male voyeurs as well as to lesbians."[32] D'Emilio had earlier distinguished between regressive and progressive pulps, citing a survey by Barbara Grier for the early lesbian publication of the Daughters of Bilitis, *The Ladder*. D'Emilio notes, "How was one to know that inside the covers of *Guerilla Girls, The Savage Salomé,* and *The Twisted Ones* could be found, according to Grier, 'interesting, sympathetic studies' of lesbian characters?"[34] By 1966, one, or at least Barbara Grier, knew: lesbianism, she reported for *The Ladder,* had achieved a "complete integration" into the American mainstream.[35] Grier's conclusion is based on a calculation of the declining number of "lesbian" paperbacks from 1964 to 1966 (161 to 104), and also on her own evaluations of the relative "sympathetic" nature of the characters within those novels.[36]

While there is no doubt that certain versions of lesbians were circulating widely by 1965, we see that, with *Chained Girls* (1965) as well as the efflorescence of lesbian pulps, the "popular" picture of lesbianism that emerged during this period is significantly domesticated by the historical glance backward that desires coherent support for a contemporary emancipatory narrative. The most significant effect of this domestication is that the "public" sphere broadly sketched by commercial iconography is uncontaminated by division, by antagonism, and most of all by the transformations of capitalism during this crucial period (as seen through the mutations of the "cover" as fact and metaphor, as nexus of exchange and signifier of a differential of sex that continues to haunt regulatory efforts). One can read the uses of the past that rely on these codings of lesbianism's presence as directly contributing to the current reconsolidation of lesbian and gay "identity" as consumer positions that succumb to the imperatives of the market and the contours of demography, identity positions that have forgotten their alliances with the most abjected regions of the street (racial conflict coded through the threat of cultural miscegenation). The contemporary film, *Forbidden Love,* is exemplary of a "cinematic use of the past"[37] to reconfirm contemporary myths of continuity.[38]

FORBIDDEN LOVE: A DIAMOND IN YOUR POCKET

Within this narrative of progress, films repetitively fabricate a history of isolation and exclusion, marginalization and vulnerability, hidden pleasures and lurking dangers of the twilight and shadows. *Forbidden Love* is one such re-creation. It tends to reproduce both poles of the contradictory myth sketched by Weir and Wilson: that is, a cherished, melodramatic, and contradictory preservation of the shadows and twilight of a lesbian past and the public dangers exterior to it, as framed by conceptions of social progress. The glances both backward and forward in the film produce a tension of history, since the specificity of the twilight past is universalized to anticipate the coherent and inclusive present, a coherence torn asunder by its attempt to "include" women of color in its present and to banish questions about sex as labor, sex as imbricated with exchange.

Briefly, *Forbidden Love* is a National Film Board–financed hybrid documentary, organized loosely around the phenomenon of lesbian pulp fiction. The film takes two routes in addressing these novels: it builds its own four-part "forbidden love" girl-meets-girl narrative within the film, the opening and closing segments of which frame the documentary, and it uses the novels as a starting point for "talking head" interviews with older Canadian dykes who recollect their experiences with the emergent urban lesbian culture in Canadian cities (Vancouver, Toronto, Montreal) during the 1950s. Intercut with the interviews are the requisite personal photographs of the women in their youth, as well as an entire newsreel that purports to disclose the ideological construction of women in the decade: as workers and consumers (in some version of suburban hell) in tension with dominant conceptions of femininity. The combination (of these so-called historical texts, with the lesbian pulp narrative, with the interviews) produces an eclectic text that lurks behind the mode of historicizing I have just sketched.

First, then, the film gestures toward substantial questions about the *function* of lesbian popular culture invoked through the lesbian pulp novels both as narrative impetus and as historical phenomenon. The film's initial tracking-shot of the novels, which I mentioned at the beginning of this essay, is followed with stories of lesbians gleefully picking those novels coded as lesbian (through their titles and cover art) off the shelves of local drugstores and with an interview by Ann Bannon, the leading auteur of lesbian pulps, recounting her fantasmatic romance with the Village. Shots of the novels are subsequently intercut to punctuate, to add support for, the memories of the women interviewed. According to the film, then, the function of the novels is to fabricate, through widely disseminated representations, a collectivity out of isolated individuals whose longings, desires, sexual practices, glances, clothing, bodies, roles, jobs, and fantasies incline them toward something that is odd, queer, homosexual, lesbian, "resistant" to the totalizing burdens of heteronormativity. As Bannon suggests, the books "reached out and connected with women who were very isolated and sequestered almost in little towns across the country. . . . [this is] the reason why paperback originals which did deal with the lesbian theme became so valuable to so many women."

To *recirculate* these novels as affirmative celebrations of lesbian identity is, as we have seen, again to reduce the complexity of social relations to the register of sexuality, to read them, in effect, as realist representations of lesbian lives rather than fantasy worlds wherein "home — and indeed everything about everyday life — [is] subordinated to the fierce dictates of sexual desire."[39] What we need to probe is the "fabulous concreteness" (Gramsci's oxymoron) these conceptions assume, whereby the twilight of isolation comes to carry with it (represented by the myths of the Village and the street) resonances of outlawry, rebellion, and ritual excluded from most white middle-class women's lives during the decade of the 1950s. The film thus offers popular-cultural nodal points for attaching danger and excitement to a hallucinatory past fraught with the contradictions arising from the desire to locate contemporary lesbianism within a sphere of galvanizing liberatory politics.

Bannon, a talking head in the film, remembers her first encounters with Village life, where she escaped from her husband and children for fodder for her Gold Medal originals: "It [the Village] mattered to me, and therefore it was imprinted on all my senses as something to take away with me and keep and use and mine it for my subsequent writing. . . . As my grandmother would say, it was like a diamond in your pocket. You carry it forever, and it feeds the stories." The metaphor is equally apt for characterizing the role of film or the paperbacks: a gleaming, solicitous commodity shaken from its productive constraints or structural determinations and affectively ensconced as historical memory.

LESBIANS UNDER THE COVER(S)

Forbidden Love, though, borrows the pulp paperback for its own "cover." First, its promotional materials (poster, T-shirt, video box, advertisements) feature a contemporary rendition of a lesbian pulp cover. Featured boldly in the Women Make Movies video catalog, the film has been the most aggressively marketed title of their "lesbian" list and has consequently found an audience at festivals and within academia above other titles in the catalog. The cover, then, continues to beckon to us at the "point of sale," though now in parasitic fashion, seizing the cachet of pulp fiction for a conventional documentary form. Second, it borrows its narrative frame from a 1950s pulp novel; the narrative's mainstays—the lesbian Laura leaving her now-heterosexual girlfriend for the city, the encounter with the butch Mitch in a bar, romantic dancing and drinking in Mitch's apartment leading to foreplay, and the final erotic encounter—partake in the stylized iconography of the 1950s described by Weir and Wilson (including a Fonz-like moment at the bar's jukebox).

This text under the cover raises a second set of questions about the role of documentary as historiography, and the relation of narrative to historical memory and "evidence" in *Forbidden Love*. The film's fictional narrative of "forbidden love," subtitled the *"unashamed* stories of lesbian lives," is the most explicit revelation of the film's "take" on the pulp novels and lesbian culture of the 1950s. It corroborates the commonsense understanding that we have moved from shame to pride, from isolation to affirmative connection, and the visual evidence for these translations comes (pun intended) in the final installation of the narrative: the love scene between Laura and Mitch, when Laura unashamedly declares that she is a lesbian. But the film disclaims its own role as historiography in a title at its end: *"Forbidden Love* presents the story of lesbians whose desire for a community led them on a dangerous search for the few public beer parlours or bars that would tolerate openly 'queer' women in the 1950s and 1960s. It is not intended to be a survey or overview history of lesbians in Canada; indeed, most lesbians were forced to live intensely private lives, often isolated from one another. This film, like all lesbian and gay histories, is meant to contribute another fragment, another telling, as we break the silence of our lives." The metaphor of the fragment structures lesbian and gay historiography, within an additive logic whereby any contribution merely augments its predecessors, and the subaltern speak partially, yet truly, to replace the silence, and shame, of hiding. A number of routes of analysis open here: Eve Sedgwick's work on shame in her article, "Queer Performativity: Henry James's *Art of the Novel*," is one road we might follow in unpacking the various affective registers condensed in the concept-affect shame (the coding of the body, the constitutive role of shame in identity-formation, etc.), which pose challenges to the "(always moralistic) repression hypothesis."[40] Without recharting the specific contours of her argument, I would second her impulse to resist the recoding of Foucault's critique of the repression hypothesis as "subversion" and rather to face the force of that critique in the persistence of its residues or its denial. Another route, toward the same end, involves asking after the exclusions the narrative makes in producing "unashamed" contemporary identity.

These exclusions involve, above all, race and labor. *Forbidden Love* carefully "includes" two talking heads in its multicultural panorama of lesbian "herstory": Amanda White and Nairobi Nelson, Native and Costa Ricana Quebecer, respectively. Both are framed in significantly different fashion from the white women in the film; rather than filmed at home, on the couch (with cats, of course), Amanda is set against a wall of Native wood sculptures, which are shot in tight focus to cue her appearance, while Nairobi is interviewed in a dimly lit nightclub as a visual reminder of her career as a cabaret singer. The film recognizes that the pulp paperbacks do not generally chart a multiracial world, so that when a cover appears with an African American woman on it (*Duet in Darkness*), its iconography prompts a cut from a lingering shot of that cover to Nairobi's interview. Nairobi's appearance is also signaled by stills of her band's promotional posters. No Native equivalents exist, and Amanda's appearances are therefore generally cued by mention of the street, since Amanda's story focuses on her experiences as a lesbian torn between Native culture and white culture, experiences that drove her into street life.

The film's specular marking of Nairobi and Amanda functions to reduce the challenges the two women provide to the seamless universalism of the film's historical and narrative re-creation; they are reminders that the urban lesbian culture of the 1950s and 1960s the film retrieves is not simply white and middle class but dependent upon white and middle-class fantasies (based on glimpses of experience) of danger and outlawry associated with people of color and street life. Yet, within the mode of the fragment, they are present as corrective, as visual evidence that the film is not committing a parallel sin. But Amanda's story in particular seems to suggest otherwise: it is she, uniquely, who names the fantasmatic back on whom this version of lesbian history rides, first in the early stages of her recounting, in her first interview. After rejecting the constricting options of Native culture to go to the white man's school, she observes about "this" white culture the pressures of patriarchy represented by the patronym, yet she hopes that with a woman she would find a relationship untarnished by repressive power. "So I thought," she says. Caught within the interstices or clashing schemes of value-coding of two cultures, Amanda finds refuge in street life.

Several interviewees provide colorful and detailed descriptions of lesbian and gay bars in Toronto and Vancouver during the 1950s. Most vivid are their memories of dirt: dirty toilets, cockroaches, cigarettes stubbed out on the floors, and "dirty," "wicked," or "dangerous" neighborhoods (cross-streets) in which the bars were located. Dirt thus becomes a synecdoche for the wicked, dangerous streets, which, in turn, are substitutions for street life, prostitution, and outlawry. The movement of the editing shapes a pattern: Carol describes the "beautiful people" of her set on the beach, in whites, with yachting caps, picnics, wine, and "posh Toronto," in an interview that then introduces the second segment of the pulp narrative, set in a lesbian bar that appears cozy, clean, and embracing. Stephanie then recalls both her fear and elation at finding the New Fountain, in an area replete with drunks and drug addicts—"really skid row." And Amanda finds herself on the bottom rung of this ladder of the lesbian socius: "I knew nothing about skid row. All I knew was that it was home to me, it was just like home. There were Native people around, people were drinking and all of that . . . , and I felt comfortable there." Later, she remembers her discomfort in the lesbian bar, the Vanport, in Vancouver: the women looked like men, and "it was hurtful, too, because everybody was either drunk out of their mind or stoned out of their mind, and to me what I was trying to run away from was exactly this."

The geography of the idyllic interior represented in the pulp narrative gives way to a cartography of exclusion, territoriality ("it was like animals, almost, like lions, it was that fierce"), brawls, rigid roles, and policed sociality, unsettlingly aligned with the streets on which the bars were located. Both visually and through the metaphorics invoked to describe bar culture, *Forbidden Love* starts to resemble *Chained Girls,* the discourse of self-affirmative disclosure veering toward the discourse of medico-social regulation, and the abject figure of that slippage is now exteriorized in the street embodied by Amanda. But it is again Amanda who reminds us that the street is a site of labor, labor performed predominantly by lesbians: "most of the people working in the street—in drugs, prostitution, dancing—were lesbian women. They wouldn't identify themselves as lesbian, it was an unwritten code." We are returned to the displacement of the pulp cover, where the predication of identity-formation as represented by bar culture in the 1950s seems to rely on the exclusion of work that cannot be coded as "lesbian," but which nonetheless is fetishized as outlawry, rebellion, a generalized otherness coded simultaneously as racial, affective (excitement, danger), and political.

Lois Stuart and Keeley Moll offer two poles of this operation's dimensions, positions that indicate the mobile nature of affective coding. On the one hand, Lois understands the heightened and intensified identifications with street life as modes by which lesbians embraced their outcast status, accepting marginalization as strength: "If you're going to live a double life, then live a double life!" Lois carried an eight-inch dagger, strived toward butch magnificence, and enjoyed accentuating the contrast in her leisure/sexual/social life from the normalized femininity and heteronormativity that characterized her working hours. The film relishes her energy, spunk, humor, vigor, and, most of all, her continued engaged politics around the body, which are retrospectively seen to emanate from her earlier butch stylizations. The closing interview with Lois takes place on the street, but now as the site for a pro-choice march ("What do we want? Choice. When do we want it? Now!"). In voice-over and then in her home, Lois observes: "If you aren't mistresses of your bodies, you're a slave. That's what slavery is. . . . I think post-menopausal women should run the world!" Though we might agree with this suggestion, Lois's implicit assertions of current strength as derived from her past are supported by a chorus of the other women. Stephanie is now a Metropolitan Community Church minister threatened by arson and murder against church members and the single mother of a strong, antihomophobic daughter; Amanda is off the street thanks to a friend who recognized her education. The film translates the women's past courage (as Stephanie says, "to be what we were, flaunting the law, doing something slightly illicit") into affective support for their contemporary engagement.

In Stephanie's final comments, we find the equation on which the film's history relies: being equals doing, and in Keeley Moll's closing interview, we hear its undoing as faulty arithmetic, while a more dangerous version substitutes in its place: "I think that not being able to move through society as a human being and a person without [sic] dignity isn't exciting. I think maybe robbing a bank is exciting, but not being an outcast because you have preferences that the majority don't have. That's not exciting. . . . I don't want to be harmed, I just want to have nice social contacts. I just want to have fun. . . . I don't want to sit at the back of the bus. That sucks." Keeley is the only interviewee associated with the country, on a farm with a horse in Alberta. This closing segment is shot with Keeley resting against a post of her isolated cabin and is privileged as the final word in that it precedes the final installment of the pulp narrative: the sex scene followed by Mitch and Laura's morning coffee, and a voice-over guiding this last in-stallment that jubilantly announces Laura's proud realization that she is a lesbian. *Being means.* As with the previous installments, the scene blends from freeze-frame into a stylized re-creation of a pulp cover, stressing the *unashamed* stories of lesbian love. Jimmie Rodgers and then the Fleet-woods' "Come Softly to Me" play as the credits roll.

Is Laura "our" Rosa Parks?[41] Has fun in the country replaced even the slightest of engagements with those lesbians working in an unwritten code on urban streets? Or are these questions unauthorized, improperly ad-dressed to a fragment that disclaims its social force? If we are to make any sense of what being a lesbian means, I think we have to ask them even as we are made possible by a signifier caught within their denial. The ques-tion invokes the relation of affect to subject predication, the encrypting of value, and the overwhelming mobility of cultural forms specularly and spectacularly condensed in static conceptions of identity. Let us remem-ber: (1) Lesbian bar culture has been and is involved in the production of racist enclaves, hallucinations of urban life that depend for their existence on street culture (drinks, drugs, sex work, and pornography), and street culture provides a sense of "outlawry" but in turn is denied or disdained by white lesbians seeking "community"; (2) The labor of the streets, particu-larly sex work, is often performed by lesbians (see, for example, *Straight for the Money* [1993] by Hima B.), and the predication of these women's sociopolitical subjectivity is precisely that labor, which has been hitherto overlooked by bourgeois lesbian culture; (3) The participation in subcul-tural leisure activities does not guarantee a politics, much less an antiracist agenda or awareness of the competing determinations of political subjec-tivity; (4) When we think that we are "odd girls out"—on the town, into the streets—we must re-map the streets of that town, which has always belonged both to capital and to struggles we do not see in our lesbian chic finery.

The pulp cover as visual condensation of popular-cultural domestica-tion helps us to forget, as does a certain form of analogizing gay and lesbian struggles with the history of integration and the civil rights move-ment, finessing the violent appropriation of an origin as solidarity. If pulp seems to mark a desire for outlawry more generally, if it seems to privi-lege a mode of transformation (not subversion) of dominant codes, it does not do so by escaping the confines of representation, only by reworking, within generic and industrial constraints, routes of travel within culture.[42]

The contemporary recirculation of pulp, moreover, coexists with other appearances of the lesbian that, in the obverse direction, flee the streets to no less fraught or contested enclosures.

NOTES

1 Susan Stewart's brief and brilliant discussion of the book collection in *On Longing: Narratives of the Miniature, the Gigantic, the Souvenir, the Collection* (Durham: Duke University Press, 1983) touches upon this transformation: "In the realm of market competition," Stewart suggests, "speed is the auxiliary to consumption, and the rapid production and consumption of books, their capacity for obsolescence in material form, necessarily seems to transform their content" (33). The crisis thus effected for the bourgeois reader is one of value-attribution (a crisis I argue in the longer form of this essay), which is then displaced onto the value-coding of normative sexuality in the 1950s debates over mass-market paperbacks.

2 Antonio Gramsci, *Selections from the Prison Notebooks,* ed. and trans. Quintin Hoare and Geoffrey Nowell-Smith (New York: International Publishers, 1971), 324.

3 Stuart Hall, "Gramsci and Us," in *The Hard Road to Renewal: Thatcherism and the Crisis of the Left* (London: Verso, 1988), 161. Hall's oft-cited caution against "pluck[ing] up this 'Sardinian' from his specific and unique political formation" to solve the problems of the late twentieth century is worth repeating in light of the abuses to which Gramsci's notes have been subjected in recent "theory." It is precisely the "revolutionary character of history itself" (162) that Gramsci discovers and Hall cherishes in his writings, the insight that history is above all dynamic.

4 See Marcia Landy, *Film, Politics, and Gramsci* (Minneapolis: University of Minnesota Press, 1994).

5 Eve Kosofsky Sedgwick and Adam Frank, in a long footnote to their introductory essay in *Shame and Its Sisters: A Silvan Tomkins Reader* (Durham: Duke University Press, 1995), attribute the binary question "is [a given cultural manifestation] subversive or hegemonic?" to certain misreadings of Foucault. While I share their impatience with the mantra-status of this question in cultural studies, it seems important to note how Gramsci's affiliation with the immensely tangled and powerful concept of hegemony (and subsequent readings of Gramsci, by Stuart Hall and other "Birmingham" figures) become effaced through contemporary intellectual history. The imperative for reading "in a Gramscian way" is not so much to resuscitate Gramsci but rather to bring the many strands with which "hegemony" is imbricated in Gramsci's

work (the distinction between the state and civil society, the function of the intellectual, the mobile nature of cultural forms, among others) to bear on questions of cultural analysis. My reading, however, involves an analysis of the affect "shame" indebted to their volume and Sedgwick's work elsewhere. Carol Stabile has similarly attributed to Gramsci faults that more properly lie with his readers, such as John Fiske, in her article "Resistance, Recuperation, and Reflexivity: The Limits of a Paradigm," *Critical Studies in Mass Communication* 12 (1995): 403–22.

6   Antonio Gramsci, *Selections from the Cultural Writings*, ed. David Forgacs and Geoffrey Nowell-Smith, trans. William Boelhower (Cambridge: Harvard University Press, 1985), 350.

7   Janice Radway, *Reading the Romance: Women, Patriarchy and Popular Literature* (Chapel Hill: University of North Carolina Press, 1984), 27.

8   The first ten titles were: *Lost Horizon* by James Hilton; *Wake Up and Live!* by Dorothea Brande; *Five Great Tragedies* by William Shakespeare; *Topper* by Thorne Smith; *The Murder of Roger Ackroyd* by Agatha Christie; *Enough Rope* by Dorothy Parker; *Wuthering Heights* by Emily Brontë; *The Way of All Flesh* by Samuel Butler; *The Bridge of San Luis Rey* by Thornton Wilder; and *Bambi* by Felix Salten. Cited in Thomas L. Bonn, *Under Cover: An Illustrated History of American Mass Market Paperbacks* (New York: Penguin Books, 1982), Bonn's history is as fine as Geoffrey O'Brien's *Hardboiled America: The Lurid Years of Paperbacks* (New York: Van Nostrand Reinhold Company, 1981) and Lee Server's *Over My Dead Body: The Sensational Age of the American Paperback: 1945–1955* (San Francisco: Chronicle Books, 1994).

9   Karl Marx, *Capital, A Critique of Political Economy*, vol. 2, trans. David Fernbach (New York: Penguin Books, 1978), 326–33.

10 Ibid., 303.

11 O'Brien, *Hardboiled America*, 47.

12 See Karal Ann Marling, *As Seen on TV: The Visual Culture of Everyday Life in the 1950s* (Cambridge: Harvard University Press, 1994), especially p. 40. Marling's dizzying and extremely fun discussion of Mamie Eisenhower and popular fashion emphasizes the significance of color as "a symbol of the shock of the new," and color palettes as modes for displacing the rigidity of sexual coding of pinks and blues in an emergent generational divide and battle during the decade.

13 O'Brien, *Hardboiled America*, 38.

14 "Report of the Select Committee on Current Pornographic Materials," House of Representatives, Eighty-Second Congress, December 31, 1952 (Washington, D.C.: United States Government Printing Office, 1952), 12.

15 *United States v. Paramount Pictures, Inc.*, 334 US 131, 166 (1948).

16 Ibid. 47; emphasis added.

17   "Report of the Select Committee," 18.

18   *Regina v. Hicklin*, 3 Queens Bench 360 (1868); *United States v. One Book Called "Ulysses"*, 5 F. Supp. 182, *confirmed*, 72 F. 2d 705 (1933).

19   *Regina*, ooo.

20   "Report of the Select Committee," 34.

21   *United States*, ooo.

22   "Report of the Select Committee," 125.

23   *United States*, quoted in "Report of the Select Committee," 8.

24   "Report of the Select Committee," 125.

25   There is nothing in the Gathings Committee Report of the specificity regarding readers or their textual interests or uses, which characterize Tania Modleski's or Janice Radway's accounts of popular literature, though Modleski seizes upon the metaphor of the cover in her introduction to *Loving with a Vengeance: Mass-Produced Fantasies for Women* (New York: Methuen, 1984): "It is an important part of my project to show that the so-called masochism which pervades these texts [Harlequin romances, gothic novels, and soap operas] is a 'cover' for anxieties, desires and wishes which if openly expressed would challenge the psychological and social order of things. For that very reason, of course, they must be kept hidden; the texts, after arousing them, must, in Jameson's formula, work to neutralize them" (30). Modleski, following Jameson, seems here to invoke only the metaphor and not its actuality, and it is for this reason, as it is for Radway, that psychological and psychoanalytic modes of analysis of the novels as texts and as function become enticing. Troubling these modes is the instability we have charted at both ends of the subject-object relation of the categories that underpin them: namely, the categories of normative and pathologized sexual practices and gender.

26   "Report of the Select Committee," 45.

27   Angela Weir and Elizabeth Wilson, "The Greyhound Bus Station in the Evolution of Lesbian Popular Culture," in *New Lesbian Criticism: Literary and Cultural Readings,* ed. Sally Munt (New York: Columbia University Press, 1992), 97.

28   B. Ruby Rich, "Homo Pomo: the New Queer Cinema," and Pratibha Parmar, "Queer Questions: A Response to B. Ruby Rich," both in *Women and Film: A Sight and Sound Reader,* ed. Pam Cook (Philadelphia: Temple University Press, 1993), 164–73, 174–75.

29   John D'Emilio and Estelle B. Freedman, *Intimate Matters: A History of Sexuality in America* (New York: Harper and Row, 1988), 288.

30   Ibid.

31   Ibid., 289.

32   Ibid.

33   Ibid.

34   John D'Emilio, *Sexual Politics, Sexual Communities: The Making of a Homo-sexual Minority in the United States, 1940–1970* (Chicago: University of Chicago Press, 1983), 135.

35   Ibid., 137.

36   Barbara Grier (also known as Gene Damon), *Lesbiana: Book Reviews from The Ladder* (Tallahassee, Fla.: The Naiad Press, 1975), 8. Grier is the founder and editor in chief of Naiad, which has republished a number of "golden oldie" lesbian pulps, including *Chris*, though with a strikingly banal, floral cover. Naiad has almost single-handedly kept this literature alive and is the major publisher of lesbian literature in the United States. As the book reviewer (publisher, founder) of *The Ladder*, Grier had an enormous impact on the reception of the books published during "the golden age of the the lesbian paperback" (as noted on the copyright of the republished *Chris* by Naiad in 1988). Lillian Faderman, whose award-winning social history of lesbianism was deemed popular enough to be converted from Columbia's hardcover edition and published by Penguin, adjudicates similarly between positive and negative visions of lesbians in pulp novels in a brief discussion in *Odd Girls and Twilight Lovers: A History of Lesbian Life in Twentieth-Century America* (New York: Penguin Books, 1992), 146–48.

37   The phrase is Marcia Landy's, from her book *The Cinematic Uses of the Past* (Minneapolis: University of Minnesota Press, 1996). Its Nietzschean debt is realized in her understanding of his "critique of historical excess as an over-valuation of past experience to the detriment of the present" (4), a critique that Landy extends in trenchant analyses particularly through Gramsci's con-ception of common sense as folklore.

38   Axel Madsen's recent pulp history of Hollywood lesbians ("HOLLYWOOD'S GREATEST SECRET/FEMALE STARS WHO LOVED OTHER WOMEN") capitalizes on the biographical dimensions of pulp history in the service of this continu-ist project. Its title in paperback, changed from the domestic registers of the hardcover title *The Sewing Circle*, reverberates with my previous discussion of pulp translation and recoding and nicely anticipates *Forbidden Lovers* (Secau-cus, N.J.: Carol Publishing Group, 1996). A parallel history of Hollywood scandal, gossip, and exposés around gay and lesbian life is beyond the scope of this essay, but would provide a supplementary understanding of the regula-tory apparatuses consolidated in the 1930s and their intensifications through discourses of morality in the 1950s.

39   Weir and Wilson, "The Greyhound Bus Station," 95.

40   Eve Kosofsky Sedgwick, "Queer Performativity: Henry James's *Art of the Novel*," *GLQ* 1 (1993): 14.

41   Or perhaps Ellen Degeneres is or wants to be: in her interview with Diane

Sawyer on *20/20,* April 25, 1997, Degeneres invoked Parks, in much the same spirit as does Keeley Moll.

42   I would advance a similar argument concerning the popularity of mystery or detective novels among lesbians (novels that feature female detectives and some lesbian detectives): that as a middle-class lesbian presence within a certain public sphere takes hold, we translate the unease associated with the status quo (sometimes coded as privilege) to fantasmatic encounters with the streets and the law. The terrain of such an encounter is expanding to lesbian detective films, such as the low-budget pulp video *Lesbionage* (1988), which takes the blackmail of an African American lesbian congresswoman as its premise. Thirty-five years measures the distance between *Lesbionage* and its precursor, *Victim* (1961, dir. Basil Dearden). Pulp can thus be understood as taking the pulse of the movement of lesbian publicity and its consumption.

BIBLIOGRAPHY

Abraham, Karl. *Selected Papers on Psycho-Analysis*. Translated by Douglas Bryan and Alix Strachey. New York: Brunner/Mazel, 1927.

Anderson, Robert. *Tea and Sympathy*. In *Famous American Plays of the 1950s*, edited by Lee Strasberg (New York: Dell, 1988).

Anger, Kenneth. *Hollywood Babylon*. New York: Bell Publishing, 1975.

————. *Hollywood Babylone*. Paris: J. J. Pauvert, 1959.

Auerbach, Nina. *Our Vampires, Ourselves*. Chicago: University of Chicago Press, 1995.

————. *Woman and the Demon: The Life of a Victorian Myth*. Cambridge: Harvard University Press, 1982.

Auty, Martyn, and Nick Roddeck. *British Cinema Now*. London: BFI, 1985.

Babington, Bruce, and Peter William Evans. *Affairs to Remember: The Hollywood Comedy of the Sexes*. Manchester: Manchester University Press, 1989.

Backstein, Karen. "A Second Look: *The Red Shoes*." *Cineaste* 2, no. 4 (1994): 42–43.

Barnett, Stephen, and Richard Wolfe. *New Zealand! New Zealand!: In Praise of Kiwiana*. Auckland, New Zealand: Hodder and Stoughton, 1989.

Barthes, Roland. *Camera Lucida: Reflections on Photography*. Translated by Richard Howard. New York: Farrar, Straus and Giroux, 1981.

Bell-Metereau, Rebecca. *Hollywood Androgyny*. 2d ed. New York: Columbia University Press, 1993.

Benjamin, Walter. *Illuminations*. Edited by Hannah Arendt. Translated by Harry Zohn. New York: Schocken Books, 1969.

Berenstein, Rhona J. *Attack of the Leading Ladies: Gender, Sexuality, and Spectatorship in Classic Horror Cinema*. New York: Columbia University Press, 1996.

Berger, John. *Ways of Seeing*. London: British Broadcasting Corporation and Penguin Books, 1977.

Bersani, Leo. *Homos*. Cambridge: Harvard University Press, 1995.

Bérubé, Alan. *Coming Out under Fire: The History of Gay Men and Women in World War Two*. New York: Plume, 1990.

Boehmer, Elleke. *Colonial and Postcolonial Literature: Migrant Metaphors*. New York: Oxford University Press, 1995.

Bonn, Thomas L. *Under Cover: An Illustrated History of American Mass Market Paperbacks.* New York: Penguin Books, 1982.

Braidotti, Rosi. "Revisiting Male Thanatica." *Differences* 6, nos. 2/3 (1994): 199–207.

Bryant, Wayne. *Bisexual Characters in Film: From Anaïs Nin to Zee.* Binghamton, New York: Haworth, 1997.

Burns, Bonnie. "*Dracula's Daughter:* Cinema, Hypnosis, and the Erotics of Lesbianism." In *Lesbian Erotics,* edited by Karla Jay, 196–211. New York: New York University Press, 1995.

Butler, Judith. *Bodies That Matter: On the Discursive Limits of "Sex."* New York: Routledge, 1993.

———. "Lana's 'Imitation': Melodramatic Repetition and the Gender Performative." *Genders* 9 (1990): 1–14.

Carson, Diana, et al., eds. *Multiple Voices in Feminist Criticism.* Minneapolis: University of Minnesota Press, 1994.

Caruth, Cathy, ed. *Trauma: Explorations in Memory.* Baltimore: The Johns Hopkins University Press, 1995.

Case, Sue-Ellen. "Tracking the Vampire." *Differences* 3, no. 2 (1991): 1–20.

Castle, Terry. *The Apparitional Lesbian: Female Homosexuality and Modern Culture.* New York: Columbia University Press, 1993.

Chauncey, George. *Gay New York: Gender, Urban Culture, and the Making of the Gay Male World, 1890–1940.* New York: Basic, 1994.

Chedgzoy, Kate. *Shakespeare's Queer Children: Sexual Politics and Contemporary Culture.* Manchester: Manchester University Press, 1995.

Christie, Ian. *Arrows of Desire: The Films of Michael Powell and Emeric Pressburger.* London: Faber and Faber, 1994.

Clarke, Jane, and Diana Simmonds, eds. *Move Over Misconceptions: Doris Day Reappraised.* London: BFI, 1980.

Clover, Carol J. *Men, Women, and Chain Saws: Gender in the Modern Horror Film.* Princeton: Princeton University Press, 1992.

Clulee, Nicholas. *John Dee's Natural Philosophy: Between Science and Religion.* London: Routledge, 1988.

Cohan, Steven. *Masked Men: Masculinity and the Movies in the Fifties.* Bloomington: Indiana University Press, 1997.

Collick, John. *Shakespeare, Cinema and Society.* Manchester: Manchester University Press, 1989.

Cook, Pam, ed. *Women and Film: A Sight and Sound Reader.* Philadelphia: Temple University Press, 1993.

Corber, Robert J. *Homosexuality in Cold War America: Resistance and the Crisis of Masculinity.* Durham: Duke University Press, 1997.

Corner, John, and Sylvia Harvey, eds. *Enterprise and Heritage: Crosscurrents of National Culture.* London: Routledge, 1991.

Creed, Barbara. *The Monstrous-Feminine: Film, Feminism, Psychoanalysis*. New York: Routledge, 1993.

Cvetkovich, Ann. "Sexual Trauma/Queer Memory: Incest, Lesbianism, and Therapeutic Culture." *GLQ: A Journal of Lesbian and Gay Studies* 2, no. 4 (1995): 351–77.

De Lauretis, Teresa. *The Practice of Love: Lesbian Sexuality and Perverse Desire*. Bloomington: Indiana University Press, 1994.

De Man, Paul. *Blindness and Insight: Essays in the Rhetoric of Contemporary Criticism*. Minneapolis: University of Minnesota Press, 1983.

D'Emilio, John. *Sexual Politics, Sexual Communities: The Making of a Homosexual Minority in the United States, 1940–1970*. Chicago: University of Chicago Press, 1983.

D'Emilio, John, and Estelle B. Freedman. *Intimate Matters: A History of Sexuality in America*. New York: Harper and Row, 1988.

Dennis, Jonathan, and Jan Bieringa, eds. *Film in Aotearoa New Zealand*. Wellington, New Zealand: Victoria University Press, 1992.

Derrida, Jacques. *Memoirs of the Blind: The Self-Portrait and Other Ruins*. Chicago: University of Chicago Press, 1993.

Dijkstra, Bram. *Idols of Perversity: Fantasies of Feminine Evil in Fin-de-Siècle Culture*. Oxford: Oxford University Press, 1986.

Doane, Mary Ann. *The Desire to Desire: The Woman's Film of the 1940s*. Bloomington: University of Indiana Press, 1987.

[Doolittle, Hilda] H.D. *Tribute to Freud*. Boston: D. R. Godine, 1974.

Doty, Alexander. *Making Things Perfectly Queer: Interpreting Mass Culture*. Minneapolis: University of Minnesota Press, 1993.

Dowd, E. Thomas, and James M. Healy, eds. *Case Studies in Hypnotherapy*. New York: Guilford Press, 1986.

Duberman, Martin, Martha Vicinus, and George Chauncey Jr., eds. *Hidden From History: Reclaiming the Gay and Lesbian Past*. New York: New American Library, 1989.

Du Maurier, George. *Trilby*. London: Penguin, 1994.

Dyer, Richard. *Heavenly Bodies: Film Stars and Society*. New York: St. Martin's Press, 1986.

———. *Now You See It: Studies on Lesbian and Gay Film*. London and New York: Routledge, 1990.

Edelman, Lee. *Homographesis: Essays in Gay Literary and Cultural Theory*. New York: Routledge, 1994.

———. "Piss Elegant: Freud, Hitchcock, and the Micturating Penis." *GLQ: A Journal of Lesbian and Gay Studies* 2, nos. 1–2 (1995): 149–77.

Erens, Patricia. "A Childhood at the Cinema: Latency Fantasies, the Family Romance, and Juvenile Spectatorship." *Wide Angle* 16, no. 4 (October 1994): 33.

Faderman, Lillian. *Odd Girls and Twilight Lovers: A History of Lesbian Life in Twentieth-Century America.* New York: Penguin, 1991.

Feuer, Jane. *Seeing Through the Eighties: Television and Reaganism.* Durham: Duke University Press, 1995.

Fineman, Joel. *Shakespeare's Perjured Eye: The Invention of Poetic Subjectivity in the Sonnets.* Berkeley: University of California Press, 1985.

———. *The Subjectivity Effect in Western Literary Tradition.* Cambridge: MIT Press, 1991.

Fletcher, John. "Versions of Masquerade." *Screen* 29, no. 3 (summer 1988).

Freud, Sigmund. *The Standard Edition of the Complete Psychological Works of Sigmund Freud.* Edited and translated by James Strachey. London: Hogarth Press, 1953–1974.

Friedberg, Anne. "On H.D., Woman, History, Recognition." *Wide Angle* 5, no. 2 (1982): 26–31.

Friedman, Lester, ed. *Fires Were Started: British Cinema and Thatcherism.* Minneapolis: University of Minnesota Press, 1993.

Friedman, Susan Stanford. *Penelope's Web: Gender, Modernity, H.D.'s Fiction.* New York: Cambridge, 1990.

Friedman, Susan Stanford, and Rachel Blau DuPlessis, eds. *Signets: Reading H.D.* Madison: University of Wisconsin Press, 1990.

Fuss, Diana. *Identification Papers.* New York: Routledge, 1995.

———, ed. *Inside/Out: Lesbian Theories, Gay Theories.* New York: Routledge, 1991.

Gaines, Steven, and Sharon Churcher. *Obsession: The Lives and Times of Calvin Klein.* New York: Birch Lane Press, 1994.

Gamman, Lorraine, and Merja Makinen. *Female Fetishism.* New York: New York University Press, 1995.

Garber, Marjorie. "Fetish Envy." *October* 54 (1990): 45–56.

———. *Vice Versa: Bisexuality and the Eroticism of Everyday Life.* New York: Simon and Schuster, 1995.

Genne, Beth. "The Red Shoes: Choices Between Life and Art." *The Thousand Eyes Magazine* 7 (February 1976): 8–9.

Gever, Martha, Pratibha Parmar, and John Greyson, eds. *Queer Looks: Perspectives on Lesbian and Gay Film and Video.* New York: Routledge, 1993.

Glamuzina, Julie, and Alison Laurie. *Parker & Hulme: A Lesbian View.* Auckland, New Zealand: New Women's Press, 1991.

Goldberg, Jonathan, ed. *Queering the Renaissance.* Durham: Duke University Press, 1994.

Gramsci, Antonio. *Selections from the Cultural Writings.* Edited by David Forgacs and Geoffrey Nowell-Smith. Translated by William Boelhower. Cambridge: Harvard University Press, 1985.

————. *Selections from the Prison Notebooks.* Edited and translated by Quintin Hoare and Geoffrey Nowell-Smith. New York: International Publishers, 1971.

Grant, Barry Keith, ed. *Planks of Reason.* Metuchen: Scarecrow Press, 1984.

Grier, Barbara. *Lesbiana: Book Reviews from* The Ladder. Tallahassee, Fla.: Naiad Press, 1975.

Gubar, Susan, and Jonathan Kamholtz, eds. *English Inside and Out: The Places of Literary Criticism.* New York: Routledge, 1993.

Hadleigh, Boze. *Hollywood Babble-On: Stars Gossip about Other Stars.* New York: Birch Lane Press, 1994.

Hall, Stuart. *The Hard Road to Renewal: Thatcherism and the Crisis of the Left.* London: Verso, 1988.

Hansen, Miriam. *Babel and Babylon: Cinema and Spectatorship.* London: Routledge, 1993.

Hart, Lynda. *Fatal Women: Lesbian Sexuality and the Mark of Aggression.* Princeton: Princeton University Press, 1994.

Hoberman, J. *Vulgar Modernism: Writing on Movies and Other Media.* Philadelphia: Temple University Press, 1991.

Holderness, Graham. "'What ish my nation?': Shakespeare and National Identities." *Textual Practice* 5, no. 1 (1991): 74–93.

Hutson, Lorna. *The Usurer's Daughter: Male Friendship and Fictions of Women in Sixteenth-Century England.* New York: Routledge, 1994.

Jarman, Derek. *At Your Own Risk: A Saint's Testament.* London: Hutchinson, 1992.

————. *Chroma: A Book of Colour—June '93.* London: Century, 1994.

————. *Dancing Ledge.* Edited by Shaun Allen. London: Quartet Books, 1984.

————. *Derek Jarman's Caravaggio.* London: Thames and Hudson, 1986.

————. *The Last of England.* Edited by David L. Hirst. London: Constable, 1987.

————. *Modern Nature: The Journals of Derek Jarman.* London: Century, 1991.

————. *Queer Edward II.* London: BFI, 1991.

Jarman, Derek, with Simon Field and Michael O'Pray. "Imaging October, Dr. Dee and Other Matters: An Interview with Derek Jarman." *After-Image* 12 (1985): 55–62.

Jay, Karla, ed. *Lesbian Erotics.* New York: New York University Press, 1995.

Jenkins, Henry. *Textual Poachers: Television Fans and Participatory Culture.* New York: Routledge, 1994.

Jensen, Kai. "Holes, Wholeness and Holiness in Frank Sargeson's Writing." *Landfall* 44, no. 1 (March 1990): 32–44.

————. "'A Poet Quite as Large as Life': Literary Masculinity in New Zealand 1932–1960." *Landfall* 45, no. 2 (June 1991): 206–24.

Johns, Captain W. E. *Biggles in the South Seas.* London: Oxford University Press, 1940.

Jones, Ernest. *Papers on Psycho-Analysis*. Boston: Beacon Press, 1967.

Kael, Pauline. *I Lost It at the Movies*. Boston: Little Brown, 1965.

King, Michael, ed. *H.D.: Woman and Poet*. Orono, Maine: National Poetry Foundation, 1986.

Kleinberg, Seymour. *Alienated Affections: Being Gay in America*. New York: St. Martin's Press, 1980.

Koestenbaum, Wayne. *Double Talk: The Erotics of Male Literary Collaboration*. New York: Routledge, 1989.

———. *The Queen's Throat: Opera, Homosexuality, and the Mystery of Desire*. New York: Vintage, 1993.

Kroll, Gerry. "Master Harold." *Advocate*, 22 Aug. 1995, 42–43.

Krutnik, Frank. "The Clown-Prints of Comedy." *Screen* 25, nos. 4–5 (1984): 50–59.

Lacan, Jacques. *The Seminar of Jacques Lacan, Book II: The Ego in Freud's Theory and in the Technique of Psychoanalysis, 1954–55*. Edited by Jacques-Alain Miller. Translated by Sylvana Tomaselli. New York: Norton, 1991.

———. *The Seminar of Jacques Lacan, Book III: The Psychoses, 1955–56*. Edited by Jacques-Alain Miller. Translated by Russell Grigg. New York: Norton, 1993.

Lamb, Jonathan. "Problems of Originality: Or, Beware of Pakeha Baring Guilts." *Landfall* 40, no. 3 (September 1986): 352–58.

Landy, Marcia. *The Cinematic Uses of the Past*. Minneapolis: University of Minnesota Press, 1996.

———. *Film, Politics, and Gramsci*. Minneapolis: University of Minnesota Press, 1994.

Lane, Robert. " 'When Blood Is Their Argument': Class, Character and History-making in Shakespeare's and Branagh's Henry V." *ELH* 61 (1994): 27–52.

LaValley, Albert. *Focus on Hitchcock*. Englewood Cliffs, N.J.: Prentice-Hall, 1972.

Macdonald, Kevin. *Emeric Pressburger: The Life and Death of a Screenwriter*. London: Faber and Faber, 1994.

Madsen, Alex. *Forbidden Lovers*. Secaucus: Carol Publishing Group, 1996.

Marling, Karal Ann. *As Seen on TV: The Visual Culture of Everyday Life in the 1950s*. Cambridge: Harvard University Press, 1994.

Marx, Arthur. *The Secret Life of Bob Hope*. New York: Barricade, 1993.

Marx, Karl. *Capital: A Critique of Political Economy*. Translated by David Fernbach. New York: Penguin Books, 1978.

Mayne, Judith. *Cinema and Spectatorship*. London: Routledge, 1993.

Mellencamp, Patricia. *High Anxiety: Catastrophe, Scandal, Age and Comedy*. Bloomington: Indiana University Press, 1990.

Meyer, Moe, ed. *The Politics and Poetics of Camp*. New York: Routledge, 1994.

Miller, Frank. *Censored Hollywood*. Atlanta: Turner, 1994.

Modleski, Tania. *Loving with a Vengeance: Mass-Produced Fantasies for Women*. New York: Methuen, 1984.

————. *The Women Who Knew Too Much*. New York: Methuen, 1988.

Morris, Desmond. *The Naked Ape*. New York: McGraw-Hill, 1967.

Mulvey, Laura. *Visual and Other Pleasures*. Bloomington: Indiana University Press, 1989.

Nelmes, Jill, ed. *An Introduction to Film Studies*. London: Routledge, 1996.

Nestle, Joan, ed. *The Persistent Desire: A Femme-Butch Reader*. Boston: Alyson Publications, 1992.

O'Brien, Geoffrey. *Hardboiled America: The Lurid Years of Paperbacks*. New York: Van Nostrand Reinhold Company, 1981.

Orgel, Stephen, ed. *The Renaissance Imagination*. Berkeley: University of California Press, 1975.

————. *The Jonsonian Masque*. Cambridge: Harvard University Press, 1965.

Park, James. *British Cinema: The Lights That Failed*. London: B. T. Batsford, 1990.

Peary, Danny. *Alternate Oscars*. New York: Delta, 1993.

————. *Cult Movies*. New York: Dell, 1981.

Petrie, Duncan, ed. *Screening Europe: Image and Identity in Contemporary European Cinema*. London: BFI, 1992.

Powell, Michael. *A Life in the Movies: An Autobiography*. New York: Alfred A. Knopf, 1987.

Radway, Janice. *Reading the Romance: Women, Patriarchy and Popular Literature*. Chapel Hill: University of North Carolina Press, 1984.

Raubicheck, Walter, and Walter Srebnick, eds. *Hitchcock's Rereleased Films: From Rope to Vertigo*. Detroit: Wayne State University Press, 1991.

Rayns, Tony. "Submitting to Sodomy: Propositions and Rhetorical Questions about an English Film-maker." *After-Image* 12 (1985): 63–64.

Renov, Michael. "Topos Noir: The Spacialization and Recuperation of Disorder. *After-Image* 15, no. 3 (October 1987):

Robertson, Pamela. *Guilty Pleasures: Feminist Camp from Mae West to Madonna*. Durham: Duke University Press, 1996.

Rodowick, D. N. *The Difficulty of Difference: Psychoanalysis, Sexual Difference, and Film Theory*. New York: Routledge, 1990.

Rosenberg, Edgar. *From Shylock to Svengali: Jewish Stereotypes in English Fiction*. Stanford: Stanford University Press, 1960.

Rosenstone, Robert A., ed. *Revisioning History: Film and the Construction of a New Past*. Princeton: Princeton University Press, 1995.

Ross, Andrew. *No Respect: Intellectuals and Popular Culture*. New York: Routledge, 1989.

Russo, Vito. *The Celluloid Closet*. New York: Harper and Row, 1981.

Sargeson, Frank. *Conversation in a Train and Other Critical Writing*. Edited by Kevin Cunningham. Auckland, New Zealand: Auckland University Press and Oxford University Press, 1983.

————. *The Stories of Frank Sargeson.* Auckland, New Zealand: Penguin, 1982.

Scott, Bonnie Kime, ed. *The Gender of Modernism: A Critical Anthology.* Bloomington: Indiana University Press, 1990.

Screen, ed. *The Sexual Subject: A Screen Reader in Sexuality.* New York: Routledge, 1992.

Sedgwick, Eve Kosofsky. *Between Men: English Literature and Male Homosocial Desire.* New York: Columbia University Press, 1985.

————. *Epistemology of the Closet.* Berkeley: University of California Press, 1990.

————. "Queer Performativity: Henry James's *The Art of the Novel.*" *GLQ: A Journal of Lesbian and Gay Studies* 1, no. 1 (1993): 1–16.

————. *Tendencies.* Durham: Duke University Press, 1993.

Sedgwick, Eve Kosofsky, and Adam Frank, eds. *Shame and Its Sisters: A Silvan Tomkins Reader.* Durham: Duke University Press, 1995.

Server, Lee. *Over My Dead Body: The Sensational Age of the American Paperback, 1945-1955.* San Francisco: Chronicle Books, 1994.

Sherman, William H. *John Dee: The Politics of Reading and Writing in the English Renaissance.* Amherst: University of Massachusetts Press, 1995.

Shumaker, Wayne, ed. *John Dee on Astronomy.* Berkeley: University of California Press, 1978.

Silverman, Kaja. *Male Subjectivity at the Margins.* New York: Routledge, 1992.

————. *The Threshold of the Visible World.* New York: Routledge, 1996.

Smalls, James. "Public Face, Private Thoughts: Fetish, Interracialism, and the Homoerotic Photography by Carl Van Vechten." *Genders* 25 (spring 1997): 144–94.

Smith, Bruce R. *Homosexual Desire in Shakespeare's England.* Chicago: University of Chicago Press, 1991.

Smith, Stevie. *Collected Poems.* Edited by James MacGibbon. New York: New Directions, 1983.

Sontag, Susan. *Against Interpretation.* New York: Farrar, Straus and Giroux, 1964.

Spacks, Patricia Meyer. *Gossip.* Chicago: University of Chicago Press, 1985.

Stabile, Carol. "Resistance, Recuperation, and Reflexivity: The Limits of a Paradigm." *Critical Studies in Mass Communication* 12 (1995): 403–22.

Stacey, Jackie. *Star Gazing: Hollywood Cinema and Female Spectatorship.* London: Routledge, 1994.

Stewart, Susan. *On Longing: Narratives of the Miniature, the Gigantic, the Souvenir, the Collection.* Durham: Duke University Press, 1983.

Suleiman, Susan Rubin, ed. *The Female Body in Western Culture.* Cambridge: Harvard University Press, 19486.

Taylor, John Russell. "Michael Powell: Myths and Superman." *Sight and Sound* 47, no. 4 (autumn 1978): 226–29.

Thomas, Nicholas. "Kiss the Baby Goodbye: *Kowhaiwhai* and Aesthetics in Aotearoa New Zealand." *Critical Inquiry* 22 (autumn 1995): 90–121.

Thomson, David. "The Films of Michael Powell: A Romantic Sensibility." *American Film* 6, no. 2 (November 1980): 48–52.

———. "The Pilgrim's Progress." *The Movie* 27 (1980): 532.

Tompkins, Jane. *West of Everything: The Inner Life of Westerns.* New York: Oxford University Press, 1992.

Truffaut, François. *Hitchcock.* Rev. ed. New York: Simon and Schuster, 1985.

Turim, Maureen. "Fictive Psyches: The Psychological Melodrama in 40s Film." *boundary 2* 12, no. 3/13, no. 1 (spring/fall 1984).

Tyler, Parker. *Screening the Sexes: Homosexuality in the Movies.* New York: Holt, Rinehart and Winston, 1972.

Van der Kolk, Bessel A., and Onno van der Hart. "The Intrusive Past: The Flexibility of Memory and the Engraving of Trauma." In Caruth, *Trauma: Explorations in Memory,* 158–82.

Walker, Alexander. *National Heroes: British Cinema in the Seventies and Eighties.* London: Harrap, 1985.

Walton, Jean. " 'Nightmare of the Uncoordinated White-folk': Race, Psychoanalysis, and *Borderline.*" *Discourse* 19, no. 2 (winter 1997): 88–109.

Warner, Michael. Introduction to *Fear of a Queer Planet: Queer Politics and Social Theory,* edited by Michael Warner, vii–xxxi. Minneapolis: University of Minnesota Press, 1993.

Weinberg, Thomas S., ed. *S&M: Studies in Dominance and Submission.* New York: Prometheus Books, 1995.

Weir, Angela, and Elizabeth Wilson, "The Greyhound Bus Station in the Evolution of Lesbian Popular Culture." In *New Lesbian Criticism: Literary and Cultural Readings,* edited by Sally Munt, 95–113. New York: Columbia University Press, 1992.

Weiss, Andrea. *Vampires and Violets: Lesbians in the Cinema.* New York: Penguin, 1992.

Whitby, C. L. "John Dee and Renaissance Scrying." *Bulletin of the Society for Renaissance Study* 3 (1985): 3–29.

Yates, Frances A. *The Art of Memory.* Chicago: University of Chicago Press, 1966.

———. *Giordano Bruno and the Hermetic Tradition.* London: Routledge and Kegan Paul, 1964.

———. *Ideas and Ideals in the North European Renaissance.* London: Routledge and Kegan Paul, 1984.

———. *Theatre of the World.* London: Routledge and Kegan Paul, 1969.

Žižek, Slavoj, ed. *Everything You Always Wanted to Know about Lacan (But Were Afraid to Ask Hitchcock).* New York: Verso, 1992.

INDEX

CONTRIBUTORS

BONNIE BURNS received her doctorate in English from Tufts University and is Director of Writing for The Charles Hamilton Houston Enrichment Program at New England School of Law.

STEVEN COHAN is Professor of English at Syracuse University, where he teaches film, gender studies, and narrative theory. His most recent books are *The Road Movie Book* (1997), which he coedited with Ina Rae Hark, and *Masked Men: Masculinity and the Movies in the Fifties* (1997).

ALEXANDER DOTY teaches film and popular culture at Lehigh University. He has written *Making Things Perfectly Queer: Interpreting Mass Culture* (1993) and coedited *Out in Culture: Lesbian, Gay and Queer Essays on Popular Culture* (also published by Duke University Press, 1995). He is currently tackling some cherished film warhorses in the forthcoming book *Flaming Classics*.

LEE EDELMAN is Professor of English at Tufts University. He is the author of *Transmemberment of Song: Hart Crane's Anatomies of Rhetoric and Desire* (1987) and *Homographesis: Essays in Gay Literary and Cultural Theory* (1994). He is currently completing work on two books: *Hollywood's Anal Compulsion* (which will include the essay in this volume) and *No Future: Queer Theory and the Death Drive.*

JIM ELLIS teaches film and English literature at the University of Calgary. An essay on Derek Jarman's *The War Requiem* appears in *The Work of Opera,* edited by Richard Dellamora and Daniel Fischlin.

MICHELLE ELLERAY is a doctoral candidate in the English department at Cornell University. She is working on gender, sexuality, and settler identity in Australia and New Zealand.

ELLIS HANSON teaches in the English department at Cornell University. He is the author of *Decadence and Catholicism* (1997), and his book, *Cruising the Screen*, on queer theory and film, is forthcoming from Duke University Press.

D. A. MILLER teaches English and comparative literature at Columbia University.

ERIC SAVOY is Associate Professor of American Literature at the University of Calgary. He has published, with Robert K. Martin, *American Gothic: New Interventions in a National Narrative* (1997). His recent articles—on queer Henry James, Hawthorne's necrophilia, Bugs Bunny's drag, and the foreclosures of queer theory—appear in *Novel, The Henry James Review, Studies in the Novel, English Studies in Canada,* and *Narrative.*

MATTHEW TINKCOM is Assistant Professor in the English Department and in the Graduate Program in Communication, Culture, and Technology at Georgetown University. He is the author of articles on the Hollywood musical, Andy Warhol, and thrift shopping. He is currently working on a book on gay male camp and postwar cinema and coediting with Amy Villarejo an anthology of new work in film and cultural studies.

AMY VILLAREJO is Assistant Professor in the Departments of Women's Studies and Theatre, Film, and Dance at Cornell University.

JEAN WALTON is Associate Professor of English and Women's Studies at the University of Rhode Island. She has published in *Contemporary Literature, The Lesbian Postmodern, Critical Inquiry,* and *Discourse.* She also coedited the *Queer Utilities* issue of *College Literature* in 1997. The present article forms part of a forthcoming book titled *Further into the Race Dream: White Women, Psychoanalysis, Sexual Difference.*

Library of Congress Cataloging-in-Publication Data

Out takes : essays on queer theory and film / edited by
Ellis Hanson.

p.   cm. — (Series Q)

Includes bibliographical references and index.

ISBN 0-8223-2309-5 (cloth : alk. paper). — ISBN 0-8223-2342-7
(pbk. : alk. paper)

1. Homosexuality in motion pictures.   2. Homosexuality and
motion pictures.   3. Gay motion picture producers and directors.
I. Hanson, Ellis.   II. Series.

PN1995.9.H55O88   1999

791.43′653—dc21   98-37161   CIP